Icon Dresden

Social History, Popular Culture, and Politics in Germany
Kathleen Canning, Series Editor

Recent Titles

The Photographic Fix: Memory, Ideology, and the First World War in the Weimar Republic
Justin Court

Icon Dresden: Baroque City, Air War Symbol, Political Token
Susanne Vees-Gulani

Socialist Subjectivities: Queering East Germany under Honecker
Scott Harrison, Jeff Hayton, and Katharine White, Editors

Interrogating Integration: Sport, Celebrity, and Scandal in the Making of New Germany
Kate Zambon

German Empires and Decolonial Fantasies, 1492–1942
Patricia Anne Simpson

Women in German Expressionism: Gender, Sexuality, Activism
Anke Finger and Julie Shoults, Editors

Queer Livability: German Sexual Sciences and Life Writing
Ina Linge

Moderate Modernity: The Newspaper Tempo *and the Transformation of Weimar Democracy*
Jochen Hung

African Students in East Germany, 1949–1975
Sara Pugach

The Arts of Democratization: Styling Political Sensibilities in Postwar West Germany
Jennifer M. Kapczynski and Caroline A. Kita, Editors

Decolonizing German and European History at the Museum
Katrin Sieg

Spaces of Honor: Making German Civil Society, 1700–1914
Heikki Lempa

Bankruptcy and Debt Collection in Liberal Capitalism: Switzerland, 1800–1900
Mischa Suter

Marking Modern Movement: Dance and Gender in the Visual Imagery of the Weimar Republic
Susan Funkenstein

Anti-Heimat Cinema: The Jewish Invention of the German Landscape
Ofer Ashkenazi

Dispossession: Plundering German Jewry, 1933–1953
Christoph Kreutzmüller and Jonathan R. Zatlin, Editors

Sex between Body and Mind: Psychoanalysis and Sexology in the German-speaking World, 1890s–1930s
Katie Sutton

Imperial Fictions: German Literature Before and Beyond the Nation-State
Todd Kontje

For a complete list of titles, please see www.press.umich.edu

Icon Dresden

Baroque City, Air War Symbol, Political Token

SUSANNE VEES-GULANI

University of Michigan Press *Ann Arbor*

Published in the United States of America by the
University of Michigan Press
First published February 2026

A CIP catalog record for this book is available from the British Library.

Library of Congress Control Number: 2025033259
LC record available at https://lccn.loc.gov/2025033259

ISBN 978-0-472-07790-8 (hardcover : alk. paper)
ISBN 978-0-472-05790-0 (paper : alk. paper)
ISBN 978-0-472-90566-9 (open access ebook)

DOI: https://doi.org/10.3998/mpub.14503024

The University of Michigan Press's broader open access publishing program is made possible thanks to additional funding from the University of Michigan Office of the Provost and the generous support of contributing libraries.

Cover: The installation "Blicke auf Dresden" (2008), highlighting the panoramic Canaletto View of Dresden along the right bank of the Elbe. Photograph by the author (2012).

The authorized representative in the EU for product safety and compliance is Easy Access System Europe, Mustamäe tee 50, 10621 Tallinn, Estonia, gpsr.requests@easproject.com

To my daughters Maya and Annika

Contents

List of Illustrations ix
Acknowledgments xiii

Introduction 1

Chapter 1
Framing the Dresden Bombing Narrative 15

Chapter 2
Staging Dresden before 1945: Court City, Travel Destination, Visual Icon 49

Chapter 3
Dresden after 1945: Past, Present, and Future in Image and Imagination 95

Chapter 4
Constructing the Memory of the Nazi Past: Jewish Life, Persecution, and Postwar Commemoration 139

Chapter 5
The Multiple Pasts in Dresden's Post-Reunification Cityscape: From the Frauenkirche to the New Synagogue 185

Chapter 6
Dresden Memory Culture and the Success of the Far Right 221

Chapter 7
Conclusions: Performing Counterprotest 243

Notes 277
Bibliography 337
Index 363

Digital materials related to this title can be found on the Fulcrum platform via the following citable URL: https://doi.org/10.3998/mpub.14503024

Illustrations

1 Bernardo Bellotto (Canaletto), *Dresden from the Right Bank of the Elbe below the Augustus Bridge* (1748) 3
2 Richard Peter, *View from the Rathausturm toward the South* (1945) 16
3 Ludwig Meidner, *Burning City* (1913) 31
4 Walter Hahn, *View from the Rathausturm* (1945) 36
5 Max Seydewitz, *Die unbesiegbare Stadt* (1961) 38
6 Hilmar Pabel, *View from the Rathausturm onto the Inner City Cleared from Rubble* (1955) 43
7 Bernardo Bellotto (Canaletto), *The Ruins of the Old Kreuzkirche* (1765) 59
8 City Panorama in Klemm's *Vollständiger illustrirter Führer* (1858) 68
9 Illustration in Dietrich's *Der treue Führer* of Bastei viewing platform (1839) 69
10 Postcard, Weisser Hirsch: Dr. Lahmann's Sanatorium (1899) 75
11 Otto Richter, *Dresden sonst und jetzt* (1905) 79
12 English Advertisement for Dresden in British and American newspapers (1906–7) 82
13 Postcard, Augustus Bridge, sent to friends back home by an American Traveler (1899) 84
14 English-language postcard, general view of Dresden (ca. 1912) 84
15 National Socialist brochure and map, "Dresden: Germany's Wonderful City of Culture" (1935) 86
16 Book and document burning at the Dresden Volkszeitung and bookstore (March 8, 1933) 88
17 *Dresden, Deutschland. Zeitschrift für Industrie, Handel, Schiffahrt* (1940) 92

18 Schaarschuch, *Bilddokument Dresden* (1945), Frauenkirche 1933–1945 98
19 Schaarschuch, *Bilddokument Dresden* (1945), Dresden's Painters 102
20 "This Book for Every German" (1950) 104
21 Richard Peter, *Dresden: Eine Kamera klagt an* (1950) 106
22 Child with Richard Peter's *Dresden* (1954) 107
23 *You and Your City: Five Years of Reconstruction* (1950) 109
24 Dresden celebrates its 750th anniversary with a parade (1956) 112
25 Saxony's exuberant August the Strong and his court jester Joseph Fröhlich (1956) 113
26 Rebuilding of the Semper Galleries at the Zwinger (1956) 114
27 *Dresden*, monument to the dead of the bombing and the destroyed cityscape (1956) 117
28 Foldout of multilingual Dresden guide, young pioneers and the destroyed cityscape (1961) 118
29 Dresden brochure with city model on book jacket (ca. 1960) 120
30 *Kleine Städtereihe Dresden* with castle, Katholische Hofkirche, art academy (1965) 121
31 *Brockhaus-Stadtführer Dresden*, Zwinger and Restaurant "Am Zwinger" (1968) 122
32 SED secretary Walter Ulbricht discusses Dresden rebuilding plans (1961) 124
33 Commemorations of February 13 in front of the reconstructed Semper Opera (1985) 126
34 Cover of *Merian Dresden* 1949 with a rendition of the Zwinger 130
35 Damaged Mozart Fountain with bronze statues after the bombing (*Merian Dresden*, 1949) 131
36 Tourists looking at the rebuilt Prager Straße from the Rathausturm (*Merian Dresden*, 1967) 134
37 Engraving of the synagogue designed by Gottfried Semper (1847) 142
38 Otto Dix, *Prager Straße* (1920) 145
39 Public humiliation of synagogue employees in front of the Jewish community center (November 10, 1938) 153
40 Dresden Synagogue (November 10, 1938) 154
41 Large crowds of onlookers at the Dresden Synagogue (November 10, 1938) 155
42 Still image from "Die Zusammenlegung der letzten Dresdner Juden in das Lager am Hellerberg" (1942) 158
43 Burning of bodies on the Altmarkt in Dresden (1945) 164

44 February 13 commemoration with large banner "Never again!" (1955) 166
45 Commemoration event for November 9 in the Hygiene Museum, "Never again Kristallnacht" (1968) 167
46 Commemoration of Victims of Fascism at the Heidefriedhof Memorial Park (1968) 170
47 Dedication of postwar synagogue (1950) 172
48 Hebrew and German inscriptions remembering the Jewish victims of the Holocaust 173
49 Opening of the Rudolf-Friedrichs-Brücke (Carolabrücke) (1971) 175
50 Prager Straße ensemble designed in socialist modernism (1974) 176
51 Mayor Schill speaks at the memorial for the destroyed synagogue (November 9, 1978) 177
52 Young pioneers at the dedication of the commemorative plaque in front of the Frauenkirche memorial (1982) 190
53 Young pioneers marvel at the architectural model of the Prager Straße in socialist modernism (1982) 192
54 Helmut Kohl speaks in front of the ruins of the Frauenkirche (December 19, 1989) 196
55 Consecration of the rebuilt Frauenkirche (2005) 203
56 Two firemen remove one of the Stars of David from the synagogue in Dresden (November 10, 1938) 211
57 New Synagogue in Dresden (completed in 2001) 218
58 White roses at the Dresden train station Leipziger Bahnhof in remembrance of the Jewish victims of the Holocaust (February 13, 2015) 233
59 Large banners erected on the Altmarkt by the AfD (February 13, 2020) 238
60 The memorial of the cremation site on the Altmarkt (February 13, 2022) 240
61 English-language flags on the Theaterplatz for multiculturalism and acceptance (2024) 247
62 Sculpture by Heinz Schmöller at rebuilt Frauenkirche during "Angsthasenprozession" (2015) 249
63 The installation *Monument* near the rebuilt Frauenkirche, by Syrian-German artist Manaf Halbouni (2017) 251
64 Andreas Rosenthal, . . . *angesichts der Güte*, exhibition in Aachen, Germany (2009) 274

Acknowledgments

The research for this book was made possible by several fellowships and grants. I would like to thank the National Endowment for the Humanities and the Baker-Nord Institute for the Humanities at Case Western Reserve University for granting me fellowships. Case Western Reserve University also funded my work with ACES+ Opportunity Research Grants, the Expanding Horizon Initiative, the Freedman Fellowship for Digital Humanities, and the Moody-Bolster Endowment for German Studies.

I received much support, encouragement, and expert advice from friends and colleagues, archivists, librarians, and curators. Without them this book would not exist. The anonymous readers of the manuscript offered superb comments and made the book so much better. I would also like to thank the entire team at the University of Michigan Press for their excellent work and great communication.

I dedicate *Icon Dresden* to my daughters who, as they frequently remind me, think of this book as another sibling they grew up with. But I also want to acknowledge previous generations, my parents Margot and Edelbert Vees and my grandfather Alfred Vees. In the late 1950s, my grandfather, a stone mason and sculptor, came to Stuttgart to help reconstruct the almost entirely destroyed Baroque New Palace after years of wrangling between the state government, preservationists, and the Stuttgart residents about the fate of the bombed-out ruin. When looking at the completed palace as a child, it was hard for me to grasp how an eighteenth-century building could display sculptures on its roof that had been carved by my grandfather. My parents always encouraged me to explore what's behind the façades we see. The result is this book.

Introduction

The Dresden firestorm has remained a touchstone of war remembrance despite the ever-growing temporal distance to the event. Starting in the night of February 13, 1945, the Royal Air Force, and later the US Army Air Force, repeatedly bombed the eastern German city, which resulted in up to 25,000 casualties and the almost complete destruction of Dresden's world-famous Baroque cityscape in the enchanting valley of the river Elbe. While the bombing of the city and its population caused much suffering, it was not unique; all major German cities were facing similar destruction since large-area bombing had become an instrumental tactic in the fight against Hitler's Germany. Overall, about 380,000 Germans were killed in raids and 50 to 60 percent of the urban areas of Germany were obliterated.[1] Nonetheless, an exclusive public narrative arose specifically for Dresden, which depicted Dresden and its population, unlike other cities, as innocent victims and the bombing as a crime. Although this narrative originated in Nazi propaganda, it also defined the remembrance of Dresden's destruction in the socialist East Germany (GDR), in West Germany, and abroad, despite the differences in political context.

Most academic studies of the air war as well as the popular Dresden histories focus on issues of strategy and its effectiveness in winning or shortening the war, the way the population experienced the bombardments, and the question of the legitimacy and ethics of Dresden's destruction.[2] These matters are not the main subject of this book, but it recognizes that Dresden was indeed a justifiable target according to the patterns that governed which cities were chosen in the air war against Germany. It also acknowledges that large-area bombings caused much destruction, anguish, and death on the ground and were unquestionably dangerous missions for the bomber crews above.

Other publications have looked at memory and commemoration practices in Dresden and the way artists and authors have responded to and shaped the memory of the Dresden bombing and its aftermath.[3] Such studies have in common that they define February 13, 1945, as a hard caesura from which Dresden's special position in postwar memory arose. This approach, however, cannot fully explain the origins of the discourse and why and how it was possible that a Nazi narrative of Dresden's innocence and victimhood grew into a long-lasting story, embraced locally, nationally, and internationally as well as across political systems and major social changes. Even today, this narrative not only influences the way Dresden is viewed, but plays an active part in political, social, and cultural developments.

To understand the power of the Dresden bombing narrative, this book relativizes the idea of February 13 as a total discursive rupture. It argues that the paths of remembrance in Dresden from 1945 to today, as well as its rebuilding, can only be fully understood in the context of Dresden's past urban developments and the stories created for the city before 1945. During the seventeenth and eighteenth centuries, Dresden was deliberately designed to raise the image of Saxony's court in Europe. Ever since, Dresden has been embraced and keeps marketing itself as a cultural masterpiece, particularly with images of its architectural ensembles. For the increasing stream of travelers to the Saxon seat and for its residents, these visual representations encapsulated Dresden's essence and defined their interactions with the city. Even though Dresden expanded dramatically in the nineteenth century and developed into a major military and industrial center, these changes have rarely been acknowledged and have not entered the collective mindscape.

The images that have defined how Dresden has been envisioned stem from the eighteenth century. In particular, the *vedute* from the Italian artist Bernardo Bellotto, who called himself Canaletto in Germany, have remained an important reference point for Dresden's identity as a Baroque city of art and culture. Canaletto, who worked in Dresden for Friedrich August II, captured the city panorama on the river in his *veduta* "Dresden from the Right Bank of the Elbe Below the Augustus Bridge." The view of the cityscape from this standpoint is now referred to as the "Canaletto View," and is, along with the Dresden nomers of "Elb-Florence" and "Florence on the Elbe," ever present as a label for the identity of the city. The picture is also widely used in marketing; there are, for example, the upscale Canaletto Restaurant, the Italian Bistro Kahnaletto, a German wordplay as it is located on a barge (German: "Kahn") that is anchored on the river, a panorama painting and light and sound show by the artist Yadegar Assisi, which depicts the Baroque

Fig. 1. Bernardo Bellotto (Canaletto), *Dresden from the Right Bank of the Elbe below the Augustus Bridge* (1748). (Courtesy of Gemäldegalerie Alte Meister, Staatliche Kunstsammlungen Dresden.)

Dresden and includes many elements from Bellotto's veduta, or the expansive Canaletto art and music festival held, with a nod to Bellotto's princely employer, in August.

The Canaletto View is also showcased as a photo and visitor point for locals and tourists. The installation near the bike and walking trail along the Elbe, across from the Old Town, is pictured on the cover of this book. The red metal structure in the shape of an easel frames the exact view Bellotto painted in his famous Dresden city panorama. When angling the lens correctly within the red borders, one can replicate the celebrated painting in a photograph. But this reproduction has little in common with what the artist looked at in 1748. Several buildings in the original painting located between the Frauenkirche (Church of our Lady) on the left and the Katholische Hofkirche (Catholic Church of the Royal Court of Saxony) on the right were demolished and replaced with other structures in the nineteenth century. Other buildings surrounding the two famous Baroque landmarks were added in the nineteenth and early twentieth centuries. The 1945 bombing almost entirely destroyed the striking city panorama, and it took decades to rebuild the historic structures visible today. The Katholische Hofkirche and some of the nineteenth-century buildings, such as the art academy, were already reconstructed during the time of the GDR, while others, such as the castle and the Frauenkirche were only rebuilt after German reunification. So rather than recreating Bellotto's painting, the frame installation captures the lasting attachment and dedication of Dresdners to the idea and ideal of their city as a unique and timeless cultural masterpiece and their perseverance in trying to preserve this image.

Urbanist Ali Cheshmehzangi refers to urban identity as defined on several scales, going from a global level, which reflects the way the city is generally perceived, to a micro, or personal level.[4] As the example of the Canaletto View illustrates, the frame for the city's dominant identity, the way it is understood as special, meaningful, and distinct, was already fully established and communicated early on and remained in place despite the changes and developments of the urban topography over time. Even on the micro level, this framing has remained an important factor. As sociologist René König has pointed out, members of a city's population have "an aesthetic image of their city community in their head, to which they feel more or less connected. This is why certain central buildings in the city have such exceptional symbolic significance."[5] In Dresden, the Baroque cityscape serves as a defining element of this mental image. Yet the city also grows its own dynamics. A sense of place for a location is conveyed "through a unique combination of natural, constructed, and cultural elements" and these become part of the habitus of the city.[6] Urban sociologist Martina Löw asserts that a city itself over time develops what one might call a personality: "as socially constructed phenomena, places develop their own intrinsic logic, which affects the patterns of experience of those who live in them."[7] Cities allow their resident community to distinguish themselves from others by providing specific structures that the population can connect to affectively. Without question, Dresden has developed a high degree of city character and distinction. Its identity is linked to many desirable features such as the beauty of its natural and built environment, its perceived singularity, and its definition as a unique place of culture. It thus offers its residents a strong "locus of meaning."[8] By interacting with the city and affirming its personality, residents have the option to include themselves as part of what constitutes Dresden's strong and positive sense of place, both as individuals and as a group. So, while cities by definition contain many heterogeneous elements—in its cityscape, its people, and its politics, among others—there also exists a communal sense of the city among residents and visitors, a city culture that they both share in and share with others.

While not all members of a city society will fully embrace an established aesthetic image of their place of living, it is a construct that influences the public and private identity of most. Studies show that the longer people live in a community, perhaps even over generations, the closer their self-understanding is tied up with their environment.[9] We can also assume that the more desirable a city identity is perceived by society, the more the city's various bodies will amplify and market this positive image and the more incentive exists for its residents to reflect and embrace it as well. The association of Dresden with beautiful architecture, high culture, and a learned environment also corresponded to norms and values of the nineteenth century burgher class, which no doubt helped with the emergence of a relatively homogeneous city identity. A generally embraced positive image of a city offers an attractive avenue for defining and binding together a resident community and creates lasting stability for the way the city is framed.

It is thus not surprising that for many Dresdners, place identity is an important part of how they define themselves as individuals and as a distinct local collective. From 1998 to 2001, sociologist Gabriela B. Christmann conducted interviews and analyzed text samples about the way Dresden residents see themselves in relation to their home city.[10] She found that certain themes were repeatedly mentioned by the interviewees, which comprised several generations of Dresden-born residents as well as some residents who had lived in Dresden for at least ten years. The results reveal that the subjects define the city via its architectural landmarks, its museums and collections, its natural environment, and its cultural offerings. They describe themselves as friendly, helpful, welcoming, conservative, and strongly connected to Dresden. Many express a desire to stay in Dresden and proclaim a high interest in its development. They articulate a deep-seated relationship to culture and a yearning for the old, pre-bombing Dresden (at the time of the interviews, post-reunification rebuilding efforts had started but were not completed). Christmann notes that the interviewees rarely elaborated on details, but rather relied on catchphrases. As we will see, such findings correspond to important elements of the Dresden bombing narrative, which depends heavily on the story of Dresden as a purely cultural, internationally admired haven of art before its destruction. While the destruction of Dresden might have strengthened the communal bonds by experiencing the bombing as a loss both on a personal and collective level, many Dresden residents were already connected with each other through a long-established shared city identity, which they expressed through determined sets of phrases and tropes.

More recent surveys, even though not as focused or in detail as Christmann's interviews, nevertheless still confirm many of her findings. Representative municipal city surveys also probe the participants on what describes and sets apart their city.[11] In 2022 and 2024, almost 80 percent picked "traditional" to describe Dresden's mentality, an assessment that has not changed since the question was first posed in 2010.[12] A large majority also rated the inner city as attractive. In 2022, the survey asked participants to write down Dresden's characteristics. The answers were overwhelmingly related to the cityscape, its cultural institutions, and the natural environment: Dresden is cultural, beautiful, picturesque, historic, and green. Also mentioned specifically were the Elbe valley and Elbe-Florence, architectural landmarks, the arts, and an attractive Old Town. This assessment is true even for those who are concerned about some of the political developments in Dresden. The terms conservative and welcoming, already strongly emphasized in Christmann's study, are still mentioned as typical city characteristics. In a 2023 survey regarding the "happiness" of the twelve largest German city populations conducted by the University of Freiburg, Dresden's residents indicated that while they were not necessarily content with their personal situation, they were extremely content with their city, in comparison to other large cities, in fact "far above average." Sixty-three percent would recommend an acquaintance to move to Dresden, a higher percentage than for any other of the twelve largest cities in Germany. The popular "happiness atlas" that published the data concludes that the population in Dresden is "in love with their city."[13]

The results of the interviews and surveys imply that the architectural environment plays a key role in the way Dresdners relate to the city. An architecture survey in 2018 asked residents to judge their emotional connection to Dresden.[14] It also measured the residents' attitudes toward a number of buildings in the city and its vicinity and collected sociodemographic data of the participants. The results showed that the more positively the participants rated historic buildings, even if only reconstructed in historical form, the stronger they felt connected to Dresden. While the length of residence and, to a lesser degree, the age of the participants had some impact on their assessment, the appreciation of the historic cityscape was a much stronger predictor. The survey also showed that the stronger residents felt linked to Dresden, the more they participated in public debates, citizen initiatives, and forums that concerned city planning. Consequently, Dresden is not "Dresden" without its architectural splendor. It was designed by Saxony's rulers to enhance the city's reputation among the European courts; after the decline of their power, protecting this legacy has been an important part for generations of Dresdner burghers.

When the Nazi propaganda story of Dresden as an innocent victim of a barbaric crime was circulated after the bombing, it exploited an already imaginary but unquestioned narrative of Dresden's singular function as a cultural haven. It allowed propagandistic exaggerations about the severity of the bombardment and distortions of Dresden's economic, military, and social-political relevance to take hold. The idea of Dresden and its urban identity, rather than reality, served as validation for the bombing narrative at home and abroad and lay the foundation for Dresden's privileged position in Second World War memory.

This book is about how the narrative of Dresden's singular significance as a center of high culture and architecture for almost four centuries, paired with the bombing story and its far-reaching acceptance, became the dominant discourse surrounding the city. In particular, it investigates how this narrative is related to Dresden's identity, which is formed and performed via building projects and urban planning discussions, through public spectacles, art installations, demonstrations, and public commemoration practices within the Dresden space, as well as in widely distributed media such as photographs and paintings, magazines, newspapers, and touristic marketing brochures. It shows how the image of Dresden was publicly controlled and communicated and in which ways such structures kept reinforcing already established communicative patterns regarding Dresden's past and present.

Visual representations of the city have been serving as fundamental vehicles in establishing the way Dresden's identity has been collectively perceived and communicated for centuries. Photographs of the undestroyed and the destroyed Dresden and city paintings such as Canaletto's vedute are experienced by most as an unmodulated, authentic access to the conditions of the past, which are then used to make meaning. As humans, we are receptive to taking in and preserving images, and we tap into collective visual representations for understanding and defining the world as a shared experience.[15] Images can become icons when their meaning is widely agreed upon. Their use instantly activates certain shared narratives within a community.[16] Visuals are also often embedded into a context both to illustrate and to authenticate messages, be it in travel brochures praising Dresden's beauty, posters, books, postcards, souvenirs, or histories. Out of these images, we build visual archives that both support and communicate our communal stories.[17] They thus form a fundamental building block of the narratives surrounding Dresden, its destruction, and rebuilding.

Yet this is also a book about the stories that were not and are not told about Dresden. East Germany discouraged research and debate on antisemitism, the Hitler era, and the Holocaust. The effects of these restrictions are still felt today, as much research remains to be undertaken on how National Socialism rose and played out in the areas that were to become the GDR. Particularly in Saxony, public remembrance since reunification has not focused on increasing the awareness about the National Socialist era as much as it could or should have.[18] Remembrance in Saxony emphasizes the memory of the illegitimacy of the GDR and the Saxon origins of the Peaceful Revolution that ultimately caused East Germany's fall.[19] The history of Jewish life in Dresden before and during Nazi Germany had also been largely ignored in the GDR.[20] This book contributes to shedding light on Jewish life in Dresden, the city's role in National Socialism, and the relationship of the GDR to the Nazi past. *Icon Dresden* introduces the key role of space and place within the material cityscape in understanding them. While Jewish suffering was not denied, the Dresden victim narrative was used to subsume Jewish persecution in the Holocaust to a propagandistic discourse about Western fascist aggression that had caused the destruction of Dresden. Even today, the Dresden remembrance of the Nazi era conflicts not only with the GDR history, but also with the remembrance of February 13. The elements of the bombing story and the way it reimagines Dresden's social, political, and cultural past outside of the National Socialist state remain central tenets and are powerful arguments in political discourses, paradoxically both in support of Dresden's assertion to be a symbol for peace and reconciliation and in justifying the backing of nativist and far-right movements.

By exploring Dresden as a city in the German Democratic Republic, the book also adds new findings to urban space studies in postwar Europe. Even decades after reunification, scholarship in urban history regarding the GDR has almost exclusively focused on East Berlin and, to some extent, Leipzig, while Dresden has not yet been studied comprehensively.[21] Apart from adding a unique local case study, this work helps widen the understanding of GDR urban history. It also contributes to recent explorations of new approaches in urban studies that go beyond architecture and urban planning to include space, place, and representation in comprehending urban development more clearly. Finally, it highlights tourism and marketing concerns as a lasting force for both stasis and change in Dresden's cityscape and identity. Consequently, the book contributes new perspectives on the connection of urban space, memory, identity, and politics after a violent event, while at the same time showing how local differences need to be accounted for.[22]

To preserve a manageable length and a tight focus, this study necessarily cannot discuss all areas in which Dresden and its history and memory are addressed. Its main concern lies with the negotiation of Dresden's identity via shared visual images of the cityscape, building decisions, media, events, and spectacles that aim to speak to a wide audience and often market or are used to market a certain political or cultural view in connection with the cityscape. During events and spectacles and through monuments in Dresden's streets, the material city itself is activated as a shared participant that anchors collective attitude and action. Dresden, and particularly its destruction, has also been the setting and theme of literature as well as films, both within Germany and internationally. In these works, however, the established Dresden narrative, which itself has mythical elements, is transposed to function on a second fictionalized plane as part of an author's fictional construct. This book will thus only occasionally allude to them when they manifest as part of wider social and cultural public discussions. A number of these works have also already been analyzed and contextualized by scholars within the context of the debate about the cultural portrayal of German guilt, trauma, and wartime suffering that arose after reunification.[23]

While publicly accessible, both museums and literary works offer spaces for individual encounters and experiences that lie outside of daily life. The Military History Museum of the German Armed Forces in Dresden references the bombing of Dresden and the destruction it caused in the design of its building and as part of the permanent exhibition. Museums, in common with literary works on real events, contain curated stories; a museum, and the specific group that runs it, composes a narrative out of artifacts and textual descriptions and explanations. In this case, even though the museum is located in Dresden, it is under the control of the German Armed Forces without any local involvement of the city government or its residents. Due to these circumstances, the museum is not included in this study.[24]

Icon Dresden tells its story in seven chapters. Chapter 1 introduces the Dresden destruction narrative and its staying power both nationally and internationally up until today despite its origins in Nazi propaganda. This narrative has been used to perpetuate claims of unwarranted and singular brutality against an innocent and unprepared city of culture without military import, even though historical evidence supports the opposite. Tracing the use of an iconic photograph of the destroyed Dresden in postwar publications reveals that visual city representations play a key role in the Dresden discourse. While perceived as memory aids, these images often function instead as memory makers.

Chapter 2 takes the reader into Dresden's past. It reveals how the bombing narrative does not respond to the loss of the city as it was in 1945, but to a long-established specifically framed image of Dresden as a purely cultural work of art which started as early as the sixteenth century. Four interconnected elements of the past emerge as having determined Dresden's image: the conscious construction of Dresden as a city with high imageability and symbolic and performative function, the large pictorial archive of distinct city views and their distribution, Dresden's rise to an international travel destination, and the wish to preserve established landmarks in the city that perform as sites and sights of attachment for Dresden's residents and visitors alike. An analysis of Dresden's "urban image bank" up to 1945, such as travel guides, paintings, and postcards, as well as descriptions of famous international visitors elucidate Dresden's image formation.[25]

After 1945, the long-established narrative of Dresden as architectural icon and attractive tourist destination was split into two pathways of memory and meaning: on the one hand a discourse of rupture and loss was evoked, which became the foundation of Dresden's victim status, and on the other hand East German officials presented Dresden's socialist rebuilding as a natural progression from Dresden's past as touristic and cultural icon. Chapters 3 and 4 explore these two pathways. Immediately after the war, before-and-after photobooks of heritage sites and their destruction served as rhetorical devices to emphasize the magnitude of loss. At the same time, they made invisible the actual cause for the rupture, in this case erasing the entire period of 1933–1945. This approach soon became limited to political anti-Western rallies during the bombing anniversaries, while otherwise officials presented the socialist future city as a natural continuation of Dresden's past as an attractive tourist site. To this end, new socialist buildings were marketed as tourist attractions. Residents, however, wanted to rebuild Dresden in its historic form, circling back to the past. The socialist party instead implemented a triptych structure in which Dresden's story moves from the undestroyed city to a site of devastation and then to a modern socialist city. As postwar West German travel magazines reveal, the rhetoric about the attractive modern socialist city failed both within the GDR and outside of it. The Dresden population's image rather echoed Western representations that highlighted Dresden as a Baroque icon.

The chapters expose how the GDR promoted the destruction of Dresden as an open wound beyond partisan politics and the way this approach suppressed the realities of Nazism and the Holocaust. Dresden residents defined their city as a global symbol for the need for peace. Such a generalized call for peace erases differences between the suffering under the bombs and the Holocaust. By establishing this relationship, Jewish suffering was not denied, but the Holocaust memorial events did not reflect on the population's guilt and responsibility. Chapter 4 focuses on how the Holocaust and its Jewish victims were discussed and instrumentalized in the GDR and, based on original sources, fills in omissions in the socialist discourse about Jewish history and antisemitism in Dresden. It argues that in Dresden a unique way of remembering Jewish persecution arose, which was particularly successful in avoiding questions about local responsibility. Speeches, newspaper articles, and memorial events demonstrate how in Dresden Jewish persecution and the bombing of Dresden were associated discursively and structurally. Not only were the bombing and the Holocaust evoked together, but the bombing narrative with its focus on architectural destruction and February 13 served as a template for narrating Jewish persecution via the November pogroms.

The lasting importance of the built environment, in particular the Frauenkirche (Church of Our Lady), for navigating history and identity in Dresden and for determining the handling of the Nazi past is the topic of chapter 5. The Frauenkirche's ruins had been preserved in the GDR as a bombing memorial and symbol for peace in the city center. Neither fully removed nor rebuilt, the site became a place where the futures of Dresden and of the GDR were negotiated in performances and counterperformances of the state and the population respectively. The demise of the East German state and German reunification were also navigated through the city's structure. The immediate rebuilding of the Frauenkirche, supported by national and international donations, was understood by many as the long-awaited first step in returning to the iconic Dresden of the past. The rebuilding was characterized as a sacred act, and Dresden's meaning as a peace symbol was expanded to include reconciliation, even though this further cemented the idea of past victimhood. In this vein, the Frauenkirche was also a welcome national symbol that could signal the future of a new, reunified Germany that had left the past behind. A comparison of the support for the rebuilding of the Frauenkirche with the lackluster response to the construction of the New Synagogue in Dresden lays open the continued disconnect between the city's destruction and the Nazi period.

Since 2014, less flattering photos of the Dresden cityscape have gone around the world when it became the backdrop for xenophobic and nativist demonstrations. Chapter 6 reveals how the Dresden narratives have created a fertile atmosphere for the rise of these far-right organizations, such as the homegrown Pegida (Patriotic Europeans against the Islamization of the West) or the national AfD (Alternative for Germany) party. Since the regional and state elections in 2024, the AfD is the strongest party in Dresden's city parliament, and statewide the AfD received 30.6 percent of the votes, just slightly behind the right-center CDU (Christian Democratic Union of Germany). The decontextualized destruction story, the unchallenged claim of innocence and victimhood, and the mourning of the loss of German high culture remain powerful tools to reshape the discourse about the past and recontextualize it in nationalist terms. The chapter establishes how the population's identity as self-proclaimed guardians of culture and a bulwark against governmental intrusion easily dovetails with far-right claims about threats against a German identity by a "political elite" and their decisions on refugees, multiculturalism, and inclusion. During the Covid-19 pandemic, Saxony and Dresden were also home to protests opposing government health measures. The chapter argues that the entanglement of these right-leaning political discourses with the perception that the bombing was an unwarranted attack on an innocent city has largely muted decisive public counterprotests to such groups.

The book ends with shifting the focus to instances that challenge the vocal and dominating voices that claim to define Dresden's identity and counter the radicalization of the political climate in the city since 2015. Dresden's cultural institutions and some political and community groups (often consisting of young members) have started to contest the very meaning and mission of culture many residents embrace and instead champion a more dynamic and inclusive model in their programming. Banners and art installations, challenges to iconic visual views, the production of protest plays, and artistic activities within the cityscape are used to try to interrupt far-right movements and their co-opting of culture and heritage. I suggest that such re-evaluation of what represents culture, coupled with a more comprehensive contextualization of Dresden's history, constitutes a possible way forward in the conflicts that would honor Dresden's cultural significance and remember the detriment of the bombing without the need to distort the past. At this point, however, in a climate where political discourses and social views have hardened all over Europe, it is easy not to engage with challenges to one's own or one's community identity. Currently, the city remains the scene of polarizations fueled by contested ideas of culture and memory.

CHAPTER 1

Framing the Dresden Bombing Narrative

It strikes the viewer as the horrid consequence of a catastrophe beyond human comprehension: a hunched over yet beautiful figure, a look of suffering and pain, a hand pointing downwards to a landscape of devastation seemingly stretching far beyond the borders of the image, and devoid of life. This picture by the Dresden photographer Richard Peter is the iconic image of the bombing war of the Second World War against Germany in German and international memory (see fig. 2, following page).[1] Peter took the photograph when he returned to Dresden in September 1945 and climbed up on the town hall's tower, which was, although heavily damaged, one of the last still accessible in the area. Surrounded by what was left of the balustrade and the sixteen stone figures representing the virtues of good city governance, he looked down upon kilometers of rubble.[2] These were the remnants of Dresden, the Baroque Saxon city so famous for its art collections and architectural treasures and widely known as the German "Florence on the Elbe." The nationally and internationally instantly recognizable cityscape that featured such landmarks as the Dresden Castle, the Hofkirche (The Catholic Church of the Royal Court of Saxony), the Frauenkirche (Church of Our Lady), Brühl's Terrace, the Semper Opera, and the Augustus Bridge, all grouped around the Elbe's gentle serpentines in the wide river valley, was destroyed by several severe air raids and the ensuing firestorm on February 13–15, 1945. Not only was the city center completely leveled, but up to twenty-five thousand people were killed in the attacks.[3] The Dresden firestorm has become a national and international public symbol for the use of excessive and unjust forces in war, causing irreparable losses by victimizing a unique architectural masterpiece and the citizens who called it their home. Yet even though the air raids on Dresden were extremely powerful and caused much suffering on the ground, they were neither the worst nor

Fig. 2. Richard Peter, *View from the Rathausturm toward the South* (1945). (Photograph by Richard Peter, sen. Reprinted by permission of SLUB/Deutsche Fotothek.)

the last bombings of the war, nor was Dresden a militarily insignificant target. While known for its architecture, its art galleries, and its idyllic location in the Elbe valley, Dresden was also one of the last centers of the German war effort that was still almost fully intact in the beginning of 1945.

Despite experts increasingly pointing to Dresden's war significance, these results do not figure heavily into the general perception of Dresden and its war fate. In fact, ever since the Dresden bombing, no other city's destruction in the air war against Germany has been remembered both nationally and internationally to the same extent or has been as widely embraced as a symbol for the brutality of modern warfare. The Dresden bombing has been broadly associated with victimhood, singular suffering, and unequaled losses among both its residents and its historical architecture. Dresden's destruction has, without much opposition, repeatedly been called unjustified, frequently likened to Hiroshima, and connected to casualty numbers far surpassing the actual death toll. Richard Peter's iconic shot from the town hall tower is time and again linked to such descriptions since its first publication in 1950, both as a visualization of the unimaginable and as photographic documentation of the validity of these claims. Together they have formed a visual and verbal narrative whose basic components have consistently remained unchanged despite the various political and societal developments from the Nazi time to today. The Dresden bombing narrative has become an essential element of the identity of the particularly tight-knit community of residents who define themselves strongly through their connection to Dresden but has also dominated the conception of Dresden outside of the city. The mostly homogeneous collective memory around Dresden's cultural significance and loss has made the city a highly determined, almost mythical place built on communal symbols.

This chapter brings to light the foundation of the lasting narrative of destruction that has arisen since February 1945 and lays open the motives and techniques of its construction. They lie hidden under a widely shared and sanctioned story that communicates through highly affective, symbolic means on both textual and visual levels. In the narrative, Dresden, the bombing, and their consequences have been codified with the themes of Dresden's supposed military insignificance, its unmatched iconic cultural heritage, the natural purity and innocence of a haven of creativity and art, the victimization of innocent civilians, and the unmatched and willful brutality and excesses of the bombardments. These elements of the narrative have established themselves as heuristics to understanding and memorializing Dresden's past, which are employed instead of processing the realities of the actual events. I apply concepts of framing theory, as originally introduced by Erving Goffman and developed further in political and communication sciences, to identify the ways in which the narrative has been set up, to analyze its content and its exclusions, and to reveal the resilience of this framing despite the changing political systems and social situations in Dresden.[4]

The chapter asserts that the strength of the communicative frame of Dresden and the bombing, which has proven to be extremely robust to challenges, arises from the deeply symbolic and widespread understanding of the city, which had been viewed as an icon not only after, but already before the bombing. Since the bombing narrative builds on Dresden's predestruction aura, it was widely accepted. I demonstrate how this symbolism was shared not only through verbal means, but also through visual means. Both the narrative of the bombing and its visual counterparts, in particular Peter's "View from the Town Hall Tower," were quickly decontextualized from the original intent of their creations. Instead, I propose that they frame each other in a circle of validation that also strengthened their claim for authenticity. Broadly believed and severed from a specific context of creation, the narrative has been integrated into differing environments such as politics and ideologies, memory cultures, city planning and rebuilding, and touristic marketing to activate specific perceptions and definitions of reality.

I trace the importance of Peter's photograph in the bombing narrative by analyzing its inclusion in publications on Dresden. It has taken on particularly strong communicative powers and has come to represent the Dresden bombing in memory. Drawing on W. J. T. Mitchell and Roland Barthes, I demonstrate how the image and its specific composition connect to already existing symbolic and affective patterns of the viewers but also guide their interpretation of the bombing through various appropriations. The widespread reproduction has turned Peter's photograph into an icon and familiar marker that conveys the established narrative of February 13, 1945, and has the power to lend credence to the framings of discourses and contexts it is placed into.

Dresden's Military Significance

The established narrative about the bombing of Dresden highlights Dresden's cultural significance and military irrelevance. Yet this framing excludes the reality of Dresden's importance for the German war effort. Historians have been debating for decades whether the bombings of German cities toward the end of the war were necessary in securing Germany's swift defeat. Setting this discussion about strategy aside, however, there were legitimate military reasons for targeting Dresden, just like other German cities, for its military and economic significance and its central role in transportation. These realities have never become part of the dominant destruction narrative and are still excluded from the general perception of Dresden and its history in collective memory. Dresden has in fact a long tradition as a garrison town. From early on, after it became the seat of the Dukes and then Electors of Saxony, Saxon troops were present in Dresden, the number largely depending on political circumstances.[5] In 1727 the Dresden garrison included 3,650 men. By 1830, half of the Saxon army, 6,500 men, was stationed there. Starting in 1867, after Prussia had won the war against Austria, in which Saxony had aligned itself with the losing party, the Saxon troops became subordinate to the Prussian military.

Prussia decided to increase the military presence in Dresden and by German unification in 1871 the number of men stationed in Dresden had risen to 10,000. The city had a difficult time with the growing number of military personnel in its dated and fairly small facilities. This situation led to the building of the largest and most modern connected military complex of the German Reich, the Albertstadt.[6] While geographically located on the northern periphery of Dresden, Albertstadt was an independent district under the command of the war minister. Living quarters and administrative buildings, training spaces, shooting ranges, workshops, manufacturing sites for basic goods such as clothing, medical facilities, a Protestant and Catholic church, and a power station and water works were integrated into the Albertstadt and ensured its self-sufficiency. With its location next to a stop on the Saxon-Silesian railway, convenient access and exit routes to the complex were also guaranteed. By 1914, troop strengths had increased to 15,000 soldiers, which rose to 45,000 men during the course of the First World War. The military relied heavily on the practical integrated setup of the Albertstadt to care for its men.[7] After the war, the Albertstadt was significantly downsized, but was still one of the biggest garrisons by the time Hitler came to power. Its facilities made it an ideal place for the expansion of military stationing and training in the Nazi era, and during the war the Albertstadt grew to about 20,000 men.[8] Since there was a constant flow of new recruits replacing those who were called to the fronts as well as troops returning to be regrouped and restructured, this number remained steady during the entire Second World War.[9]

Given the prevalence of military activity in the city, it is not surprising that Dresden had also evolved into an important war production site; at the time of the bombing almost all peacetime manufacturing in this eighth largest industrial city of the Reich, home to 630,216 residents, had been adapted to support the war effort.[10] It was not the first time that Dresden was an active participant in military manufacturing. Already during the First World War, the city was a central site for military production within an industrial complex surrounding the garrison arsenal. The factories produced munitions, weapons, and military equipment.[11] After the lost war, the Treaty of Versailles stipulated that Dresden, as the rest of Germany, had to restructure its sites to engage in the manufacturing of civilian goods instead.[12] Several buildings were to be demolished. But the facilities were never destroyed, so the factories could easily be changed back to the production of military materials when the Nazi leadership openly called for rearmament in 1935.[13] Dresden became increasingly involved in the production of poison gas, anti-aircraft and field guns, small arms, aircraft parts, motors, tanks, and torpedo parts. The city was also home to a subgroup of the famous Zeiss Company, the camera manufacturer Zeiss Ikon, which also produced various optical instruments for the military.[14]

When Dresden was bombed in February 1945, the air attacks were part of a larger bombing strategy that had begun in January 1945 and that targeted Middle Germany. Chemnitz, Leipzig, and Dresden, among others, were coming into focus at this point of the war for their closeness to the Russian front and their economic importance.[15] So Dresden was a major target not just because of its still highly productive industry but also because of its geographical location. With its closeness to the capital city of Berlin, the excellent rail system, the autobahn, and finally the airport, the city had been a central transportation hub from the very beginning of the war, connecting the north and south as well as the east and west of the Reich. It was a key junction for shifting troops and supplies from one area to another. With the Russian troops approaching from the east, it now could serve as flank protection for the capital and as a point of defense at the strategically significant river Elbe,[16] and it was more than ever functioning as a redistribution point to the various fronts. The strategic importance of Dresden was recognized both by the Allies and by the Germans. In fact, in December 1944, Dresden had been declared a "fortress" by the Wehrmacht's army chief of staff General Heinz Guderian as part of an Elbe line of defense.[17] An attack on Dresden, including its work force, could help the Red Army to advance and at the same time generally cut supply chains of both soldiers and war materials.[18]

Dresden was, of course, among many cities that were devastated by bombing raids. Even its destruction in the final months of the war was far from a singular event. Dresden's bombing was part of several bombardments during this time. Particularly, places that played a role in the transportation and shifting of troops and military goods, as well as in the weapons industry, suffered similar fates: Just ten days later, for example, two thirds of Pforzheim was destroyed, between 80 and 100 percent of the city center. In the raids on the city whose jewelry manufacturing had long been changed to the production of detonators and other military needs, 17,600, approximately one-fifth of Pforzheim residents, lost their lives.[19] The historic town of Würzburg in Franconia, an important transportation hub, was bombed a month after the Dresden raids and two weeks before the U.S. Army took control of the city. While the number of victims was smaller in this case, the damage in the culturally significant historic town center was enormous. When widening the scope and looking at the entire air war, other cities, like Berlin and Hamburg, also experienced extreme destruction and suffered overall from large losses of lives. The bombing of Hamburg in 1943 resulted in 40,000 victims, substantially higher numbers of casualties.[20] As historian Sönke Neitzel put it: "The destruction of Dresden was a tragedy; but it was one tragedy among many."[21]

The Rise and Politics of the Dresden Bombing Narrative

The dominant public discourse regarding Dresden's destruction has not integrated Dresden's military import or how it shared a fate with other historically significant cities. In fact, the narrative about the bombing was carefully constructed immediately after the series of attacks from February 13 to 15, 1945, and then activated within the political framework of National Socialist war propaganda. Despite this intentional political framing, the narrative of the illegitimate bombing of Dresden and the detriment it caused became a sanctioned codified interpretation, which was widely distributed, repeated, and accepted as true. It has been inseparably attached to the iconicity of Dresden, defining Dresden's significance both before and after its destruction.[22]

The Dresden raids were understood as a possibility to entice Germans to hold up their morale for a final war effort and to cast the enemies as entirely ruthless.[23] Since Dresden enjoyed significant international fame, Nazi propagandists also saw a chance to reduce support abroad for the bombing of German cities. By concentrating on Dresden as a center of art and culture and denying its military and economic role, they presented the destruction of the well-known city as a barbaric and unparalleled crime not only against innocent civilians, but also against German and European culture. In this framing of the story, Dresden was nothing but a virtuous beautiful and innocent body that deserved the utmost protection and respect from everyone. After the air raids this body lay ruined, a violation, this discourse suggests, of nature itself.

The Nazi propaganda ministry usually preferred to keep the number of casualties and the extent of the destruction by bombs under wraps, both to withhold information from the Allies and to try to secure support for the war among the citizens, but here the potential for a successful international campaign called for claiming maximum destruction. The ministry began to spread rumors about the catastrophic effects of the bombing, coupling this grand cultural loss with claims of an extreme death toll among innocent civilians, not only among the residents of Dresden, but also because the city allegedly sheltered a high number of refugees from the east at the time.[24] A look at international newspapers allows to trace the effects of the efforts to establish a politically advantageous frame around Dresden. In fact, part of their success lay in confirming and amplifying individual international assessments of the bombing that already operated on the idea that Dresden was an exception, both as a cultural treasure and now as a bombing target. The neutral Swedish press, with reference to an eyewitness account, disseminated a report that suggested up to 200,000 casualties instead of the actual 25,000.[25] Follow-up publications proposed even higher numbers.[26] An unexpected "gift" for the German propaganda effort came in the form of an article by an American news correspondent that proposed that with the bombing of Dresden, Great Britain and the United States had at this point actually begun to engage in the strategy of "terror bombing," the very point the Nazi government had charged from the beginning of the air campaigns.

The German reports received a large echo in the international press.[27] Many news publications reacted by extensively repeating German assertions about Dresden's destruction, if at first guardedly. For example, on February 14, the *New York Times* talked about the bombing as being carried out against "the great city of Dresden" and as "jeopardizing the architectural if not artistic treasures that made it 'The German Florence.'" Yet the article was cautious of the news coming out of Germany and tried to fact-check the German "sympathy propaganda." It correctly stated that while Germans claimed that art treasures in the galleries had been lost, many of the important pieces had been removed to safety vaults.[28]

But the discussion did not end there. In part due to the large international reaction, German propaganda did not let go of the topic of Dresden. One of the longest and most influential German articles appeared on March 4, 1945, three weeks after the bombing, in the widely read weekly *Das Reich*. Even though it regularly featured editorials by Goebbels,[29] the paper overall presented a different kind of journalism from the average party newspaper. In looks, style, and tone it strove to imitate the British *Observer*, and many well-known German journalists wrote for the weekly.[30] While by no means critical, independent, or free of propaganda, *Das Reich* managed to sound more solid, genuine, and intellectual in comparison to the shrill tone adopted by many of Nazi Germany's news publications.[31]

In "The Death of Dresden, a Beacon of Resistance," chief editor Rudolf Sparing precisely relies on this calmer and sincere tone when trying to create an air of unquestionable truth about his report.[32] In uncharacteristic detail, the alumnus from the traditional Dresden Kreuzschule boarding school with its famous boys' choir paints a picture of the suffering that the raids caused among the people.[33] The major emphasis lies with the suggestion of a singular cultural loss and that the "Dresden catastrophe is unprecedented."[34] He chastises the Western Allies that with the bombing of Dresden they had "in a self-destructive manner committed the annihilation of occidental culture."[35] Sparing thus charges the Allies with barbarism for having "erased a city silhouette of perfectly harmonious composition from the European skies,"[36] but he also tries to build a commonality based on Western culture. While the two sides were enemies in war, Sparing suggests, cultural heritage still lies beyond politics and ideology, which would make bombing the iconic city of Dresden a barbaric act against Western civilization's heritage. To drive his point home, Sparing repeatedly recalls the individual buildings associated with Dresden. His text resembles an obituary for the culture of the Occident when he recreates the cityscape and its cultural meaning for the readers:

> When will the world understand what it will also mean for them, that that which the idea of Dresden entails can now only be spoken of in the past tense? That there will never again be the sounds of classical music in the courtyard of the Zwinger Palace, that the house at the Altmarkt, in which Weber composed *The Marksman* (*Der Freischütz*), and the Kreuzschule, which was attended by Theodor Körner, no longer stand, that the cupola of George Bähr's Frauenkirche, which, before it was built, opinionated structural analysts had prophesized would never stand, will not outlast future centuries, that Brühl's Terrace with its collections and galleries is now a bomb crater? Dresden functioned as a trustee for all of that. It was property shared by the western world, which was guarded by this city.[37]

Through his description of each individual building and its cultural meaning, Sparing multiplies the horror and seriousness of the bombing. The destruction of each is in itself seen as a crime, and at the same time the details enhance the suggestion of innocence of the victimized city-body that has "died" in the raids. By implying the inherent innocence of high culture, he can strongly disclaim that Dresden had any military significance: "Anyone who saw these ruins must have found it senseless to even try to argue with England or America about what military targets they were seeking in

Brühl's Terrace, the Zwinger, in the vaults of the Frauenkirche, the stage and audience spaces of the State Theaters, the book collections of the Japanese Palace."[38]

Sparing also claims the incomparable seriousness of the attacks and their consequences. The loss of architectural treasures is mirrored by the losses among its residents. He states that Dresden suffered the war's most casualties with reference to its size and alleges that it is impossible to recover or identify the bodies, assertions that open up much room for speculation about the number of dead and suggest yet again conditions that are simply unimaginable. In addition, Sparing implies the use of strafe planes and the cruel tactic of the distinct killing of individual survivors of the firestorm via the machine guns of these low-flying planes (a technique that in fact was never used in Dresden).[39] By repeatedly emphasizing the exceptionality of the city itself, Sparing creates the perfect foundation for an unquestioning acceptance of the assertions that the destruction was singular and unjust.

To ensure the widest possible audience for Sparing's article, both within and outside of Germany, it was also disseminated via radio broadcasts. Sparing's strategy of representation was indeed successful, and the radio broadcast and article were extensively cited in the international press. Already the next day, the *New York Times* quoted Sparing's radio transmission, and, in contrast to the *Times's* earlier article, this time critical commentary was kept to a minimum.[40] The report repeats most of Sparing's claims—Dresden's unique cultural value, the implication of an enormous death toll that did not allow the identification of the individual bodies, the assumption that because of German refugees from the east at least one million people resided in the city—even though there were no reliable sources confirming the report. Neither did the *New York Times* question the singularity of the destruction caused by the raid.

Among other newspapers, the *Chicago Daily Tribune* also repeated Sparing's assertions without commentary in "Dresden Leveled, Nazi says," published on page 1.[41] The *Washington Post* gave the Sparing radio address a positive American spin, suggesting that Germany is finally fessing up to its impending defeat. The article, which almost exclusively quotes from Sparing, is headlined with "Total Annihilation of Dresden from Air Admitted by Nazis."[42] Canadian newspapers also covered the address. The *Gazette* in Montréal, while emphasizing more carefully the German source and the possibility of a propagandistic purpose of the information in its article, nevertheless quotes all the significant points and has the most apocalyptic headline: "Dresden Blasted from Europe; Not a Soul Left, Berlin Claims."[43] The *London*

Times and other British newspapers did not react in any detail to Sparing's radio address and instead repeatedly pointed to the validity of Dresden as a target and the importance of its destruction to disrupt the German troops and assist the advancement of the Soviet forces. At this point, however, the press in Britain was censored regarding its reporting on the war. Still, in debates about the legitimacy of the air war strategy among politicians in Great Britain, the Dresden bombing did lead to addressing the Bomber Command's actions with more urgency. Critics expressed similar sentiments to Sparing's in support of renouncing the practice.[44]

The propaganda did not end with trying to engage the international press; articles in the *Chicago Daily Tribune* and the *Washington Post* indicate that Sparing's text on Dresden was even distributed to British prisoners of war who were in Germany at the time of the bombing and then had contact with American troops near Dresden on their way back home in May 1945.[45] The pieces report that the prisoners had spoken to the Americans about a newspaper that had been distributed to them by the Germans that included a report on "the 'death of Dresden.'" They further narrated that Dresden police had related that 300,000 persons were killed in the fourteen-hour Allied air raid, which leads the *Post* to conclude that the bombardment of Dresden "probably was the most destructive series of raids in history in terms of human life."[46]

As the reports show, the communication of the narrative was carefully framed. Dresden historian Matthias Neutzner identifies a number of premises that define the content of this widespread story.[47] His points can be condensed into three fundamental elements of the narrative that were included in the way the destruction of the city was conceptualized: unrivaled cultural significance, the idea of innocence stemming from the portrayal of Dresden as of no military import and unprepared for attacks, and lastly the singularity of the catastrophe. The organizing principle for this framing is thus the idea of a universality of loss, a loss beyond the German context: Dresden's beauty arises from a fundamental internal harmony, an essence that lies outside of the realm of what can be used, politicized, or influenced by an individual party. This overarching frame speaks to the cultural commonalities and builds on the idea of Dresden as a shared European cultural icon, a reputation Dresden had already enjoyed before National Socialism and the war. It spoke in symbolic and affective ways to beliefs that the international audience already held, and it successfully disconnected Dresden from the political realm. Since Dresden's special cultural position remained unquestioned, this framing could connote the other components of the narrative. These elements could be carefully chosen to tell a specific story about innocence, loss, and responsibility, while other elements of the realities of the bombing were relegated outside of the communicative frame. Dresden's economic and structural city-wide developments since the eighteenth-century Baroque era, its import for defense, transportation, and war production, its strategic location at this time of the war, German responsibility in both starting the war and refusing to accept defeat, the citizens' involvement in the Holocaust, and the very identification of the propagandistic aspect of the framing of this narrative of beauty and innocence are severed from the narrative.

A national and international collective story of the destruction of Dresden thus began to form almost immediately after the February bombardment and found wide distribution. Dresden was increasingly turning into a cipher of loss,[48] and the exclusions in the framing of the discourse surrounding the city have since then remained largely constant in public discussion. Roland Barthes's thoughts about the processes of creating contemporary mythologies can help explain how this propagandistic framing of Dresden and its destruction could both become so widely disseminated and so uncritically accepted even though it had its immediate roots in National Socialist propaganda.

Barthes associates the creation of a modern myth with a process of "naturalization"; an artificially constructed narrative then becomes a contemporary myth when it is accepted as simply given, even if the applied causalities of the story are false. He likens these processes to linguistic systems, but inductive ones—when a name for an object is seen as naturally and logically attached to the object itself—which is how in a myth an event can also be naturally related to certain implications and interpretations without raising any doubts of such relationship.[49] Mythical speech, according to Barthes, "is not read as a motive, but as a reason."[50] He particularly points to propaganda as creating and using these new, seemingly natural and factual associations. It is precisely how propaganda can become effective, namely when its assertions about an association of two distinct entities become inseparable and are not questioned. According to Barthes, "this is why myth is experienced as innocent speech: not because its intentions are hidden—if they were hidden, they could not be efficacious—but because they are naturalized."[51]

Combining the idea of mythmaking and the findings of the framing analysis reveals the Dresden destruction narrative as a striking example of framed communication and constructed relationships that are taken as a "factual system."[52] These characteristics are the quintessential components of the Dresden bombing narrative. They form exactly the kind of story that

Barthes had in mind, one of "blissful clarity" in which "things appear to mean something by themselves."[53] The processes of mythmaking can explain why the city's suggested victim status and its supposed timeless and nonpolitical significance have been so widely accepted. Since everyone agrees on the basic premises of the narrative, it can function across political and temporal lines and develop a strong framing effect or influence.[54] The basic narrative is understood as one anchored within the Baroque Dresden turned rubblescape from which it directly arises. It is thus considered as absolute truth, and by highlighting it as the most foundational element it becomes the primary frame of communication.[55] The other elements of the narrative arise within this overarching frame that connotes these other subframings also as true. Had they not been absorbed into this larger structure, they would have perhaps been seen with more suspicion. The framing effect can also come to play when contextualizing the narrative. Since the narrative is considered independently real, the context in which it performs determines the (political) implications of the tale.

This political framing continued in both East and West. Gilad Margalit has shown how the National Socialist Dresden narrative after the war was incorporated into the rhetoric of the bombings in the German Democratic Republic (GDR), when Dresden was evoked to support the East German campaign against the West and particularly the United States (even though the United States was not responsible for most of Dresden's destruction).[56] Throughout the decades associated with East Germany (1949–1989) and beyond, it was also consistently employed as a narrative that eclipsed questions of German guilt.[57] In accordance with the core narrative of Dresden, while the notion of responsibility of the Western Allies propagated by the East was often challenged by the Western powers, the idea of unfair suffering and undeserved harm, as outlined early on in the National Socialist propaganda and then taken up also in the East German discourse, was not.

The American *Life* magazine's special issue on Germany from 1954 is a good example to demonstrate this attitude. While highlighting economic progress and touristic sites in West Germany, it also contains a section on "The Other Germany."[58] Here, the *Life* correspondent Will Lang shares his impressions about an official tour organized by the East German government for him. GDR officials clearly chose Dresden for the visit because of its international reputation as a city of art and famous architecture and its history of destruction. The city was a showcase for East Germany's interest in culture, but it also gave the GDR the opportunity to criticize the Western Allies. As Lang describes, tour guides emphasized repeatedly the immense losses of cultural treasures (not just German, but universal icons) caused by Great Britain and the United States. While Lang objects to negatively implicating Great Britain and the United States in the destruction, he does not condone the destruction itself, which he still observes around him. He never actually challenges the idea of Dresden's bombing as a crime and the view that it led to an international cultural loss, nor does he question the inflated number of dead, listed in his article as 100,000 civilian casualties. Instead, he uses the very same arguments about the horror of the destruction and its consequences to introduce counterpropaganda against the Eastern Bloc. As Lang emphasizes, "the bombing of Dresden was requested by the Red Army. [. . .]. [T]he bombing took place because the Soviets wanted to prevent Wehrmacht reinforcements from passing through Dresden."[59] The idea of the Dresden bombing as having been exceptional and as resembling a war crime is thus not challenged, but rather reinforced.

The trend of accentuating civilian anguish and cultural loss caused by the bombings of German cities during the war was consequently not only found in the East, but also in the West. In the West, however, commemoration rituals were usually more locally organized and certainly did not display the critical stance toward the Western Allies. Yet even in the West, the destruction of Dresden remained the central reference point for the bombings and overlay all local and individual experiences. For instance, despite the political differences, as Gilad Margalit concludes after comparing the discourse surrounding the air attacks in Hamburg and Dresden from 1945 onwards, Hamburg, even before the Cold War had ended, incorporated more and more elements of the commemorations of the air strikes implemented in Dresden."[60] Given Dresden's symbolic significance even during the Cold War, it is not surprising that since reunification, Dresden's destruction is even more strongly anchored in collective memory as an all-German loss that can be mourned openly.

With the help of framing analysis applied to the immediate post-bombing reporting in the national and international press, it was possible to identify both the basic content structure of the Dresden bombing narrative and the information that was excluded from the communicative framing. The Nazi reporting about Dresden was governed by clear intentions to miscredit their enemies further at home and by trying to create opposition to the actions by the Western Allies in the forces' own home countries. The framing effect was successful because the basic premise of the narrative, namely that Dresden was a shared European cultural treasure innocent of any partisanship, was already ingrained in the cultural memory of many.

The creation of the Dresden bombing narrative can thus be understood as an instance of mythmaking that transposes the narrative onto a symbolic and affective communicative level that in turn is perceived heuristically rather than accepted after rational inquiries into its origins. Consequently, the entire narrative frame is transferred into collective memory and people's belief systems.

In other words, to use the approach by memory scholars Jan and Aleida Assmann,[61] the bombing story as a communicative memory has been so successful because it is anchored in a deeply ingrained cultural memory that was constructed centuries ago and established itself as a key part of Dresden's identity. The idea of Dresden as a unique cultural treasure was transmitted from generation to generation, in public and within family units, and since 1945 the story of its destruction and the subsequent loss have expanded the shared narrative that is being communicated forward. Within Dresden, the cultural memory has established its most powerful influence. The public commemoration rituals and the repeated retelling of the story in public and private discourse that have emerged after the Second World War have strengthened the community and intergenerational connections. Directly anchored in the key identity-forming cultural memory of Dresden's iconic beauty, it withstood change or forgetting even if outer political and social circumstances were changing. At the same time, since the framings are communicated mainly on a symbolic level, the bombing narrative can also be appropriated more easily into a variety of political and cultural contexts without revealing their intentional construction. In the Assmanns' theory of memory, various forms of symbolic codes such as rituals, written and oral narratives, or special places serve as ways of remembering within the cultural memory. In Barthes's approach to mythmaking, he points in particular to the important role of visual images as means of communication in propaganda. We will thus return to Richard Peter's famous Dresden rubble photograph, which plays an integral role in the Dresden destruction narrative and functions within all these categories.

Picturing Destruction

In *No Captions Needed*, communication scholars Robert Hariman and John Louis Lucaites define an iconic photograph as a public image that circulates widely, is reproduced across a range of media, is understood as a representation of a historically significant event for which it has become a familiar marker, and activates a strong emotional response in viewers.[62] Peter's photograph from the townhall tower has emerged as the photograph that has illustrated and complemented the Dresden bombing narrative since it was first published in 1950, not only in Germany, but also in international memory. Since the firestorm in Dresden has been coded as the worst bombardment in Germany during the Second World War, Peter's image has also come to represent and criticize the effects of air war in general. It has developed into a familiar marker that speaks to a collective audience.

As an icon, Peter's photograph contains a strong rhetorical power and evokes a shared sense of meaning in viewers. It conveys an idea of documentary access by offering the audience insight into the center of the physical and emotional devastation caused by the bombing, and it seemingly presents the possibility of grasping, without mediation, the authentic experience on a visceral level. When paired with the established Dresden bombing narrative, each function in the viewer as proof of the other's authenticity. The viewer readily accepts a narrative of exception for Dresden and the singular meaning it must occupy in the collective history of the German past.

The immediacy of the effect of Peter's photograph is often projected onto the image itself by perceiving it as a snapshot of an instance of overwhelming pain, an objective moment of shocked witnessing. Similar to the propagandistic framing of the bombing narrative put forward by the Nazis, but as part of the efforts to reorient Germany toward socialism, the image was meticulously staged and makes conscious use of symbols, beliefs, and conventions already ingrained in cultural memory. It is in fact this conscious construction of the picture that forms the foundation of its powerful message. It took Peter one week and repeated trips up the dangerous tower to set up the shot. Unable to achieve the desired effects with his Leica, he had to track down and borrow a different camera to take the photograph, a Rolleiflex that was shooting in a square format. With much effort, Peter also dragged a five-meter-long wooden double ladder he had found inside the tower up to the top.[63] Standing on its final steps, he could capture the rubble from an angle behind one of the stone figures, an allegorical representation of the virtue of Kindness (Güte; Greek: *chrēstotēs*), designed by the sculptor August Schreitmüller (1871–1958). It worked for Peter that the figure was largely undamaged and that its companion piece, the allegory of Wisdom, had been entirely destroyed. While the actual stone figure from the town hall's tower opens both arms in a receiving gesture, Peter chose a perspective for his motif in which the sculpture appears to have raised only a single arm. Within the context of the destroyed city in the immediate postwar time, a gesture of mercy is thus changed to one of accusation and lamentation about

Fig. 3. Ludwig Meidner, *Burning City* (1913). (Courtesy of Saint Louis Art Museum, https://www.slam.org/collection/objects/13506/)

the desolation below and the cost of war. It is also interpreted by many as an act of expressing a rising nostalgia for Dresden's cultural losses.

Peter's city motif as captured from above has been linked to some of the expressionistic catastrophic urban views from earlier in the century. Indeed, photographs that respond to collectively familiar patterns of artistic designs can be more easily integrated into the viewers' set of cultural codes.[64] Paintings such as the Berlin artist Ludwig Meidner's well-known *Apocalyptic Landscapes* (mostly 1912–1913) have been seen as artistic precursors to the Dresden photograph.[65] In his "Anleitung zum Malen von Großstadtbildern" (Instructions to the Painting of a Metropolis), a text Meidner coincidentally composed during a stay in Dresden and shortly before the First World War, the artist calls for the depiction of cities with streets that are "a bombardment of whizzing rows of windows, dashing beams of light amid vehicles of all kinds and thousands of bouncing bullets, human shreds."[66]

His pictures thus depict catastrophes filled with action and movement, featuring explosions, people in flight and the rule of utter chaos. In contrast, Peter's post–Second World War answer to such apocalyptic fantasies presents a city not during but after its destruction. It is not the urban battlefield or the horror of the attacks that features dominantly in the picture, but the catastrophe's seemingly eternal consequence: it left behind a landscape that is thoroughly annihilated, an urban cemetery, a city that lies lifeless and dead. The true doom of the apocalypse, the picture suggests, is its aftermath.

A gash of sunlight, which pours into the picture from the left, supports this image of complete desolation. The light causes long shadows of the exposed building walls with their empty window holes, shadows so long that they cover and thus hide some of the areas that had already been cleared from the rubble or were sites of renewed vegetation by the time Peter took the photograph. Its original form of publication confirms that showing any progress in removing the rubble in the picture was purposely avoided: parts of the picture that revealed a cleared street were cropped to make it less visible.[67] The angle of the light greatly foregrounds the stone figure's perspective from above by illuminating its downcast eyes. It also offers a crisp outline of its outstretched hand, which guides the onlooker's attention, with seeming authority, to the landscape of ruins below.

While the perspective from above and the space between the stone figure and the rubble landscape suggests an emotional distance by a photographer that sees himself as an objective chronicler of a historic moment, this effect is also carefully developed. To enhance this perception, Peter's agency as the composer of the picture is twice removed from his subject. For one, it is translated onto the Schreitmüller sculpture, which becomes Peter's "proxy pointer."[68] Then again, the camera controls the physical space between Peter and the figure and functions to deflect agency. At the same time, by setting up the figure as though it were a *repoussoir*, bracketing the shot and framing it with the stone figure and its pointing hand, Peter entices the observer to become an active participant in the picture by sharing the figure's gaze at the destruction below. The viewers are left to resolve the tension arising between the marks of a carefully crafted photograph that encourages and guides their participation, and the simultaneous concealment of the deliberate composition and the refusal to prescribe a ready interpretation of the shot. The photograph thus becomes a performance both in itself and in interplay with the viewer, a process that Hariman and Lucaites have likened to "coproduc[ing]."[69]

Peter achieves this effect by falling back on various past artistic approaches and established symbols. The use of a repoussoir for bracketing a painting became a popular stylistic device in late Renaissance and Baroque art for adding spatial depth and for guiding the observer's viewpoint. Peter's inclusion of a repoussoir figure, a figure whose form itself is reminiscent of Baroque style, is a nod to the lost Baroque Dresden and a reminder to the viewer of what has been, the beautiful cityscape of Dresden that has etched itself into their memory and which now has to be overlaid by a landscape of ruins. With the repoussoir figure, the photograph receives a set frame, which seems to suggest the possibility for the viewer to contain and understand the image in its entirety and with it the pictured situation when he or she only looks close enough.

This feeling is supported by the gesture of pointing that is highlighted in the photograph. The gesture is reminiscent of Christian iconography, with a figure usually pointing toward heaven. In Peter's picture, however, there is no authority above; instead, the destruction came about from the sky, and one can only point out its consequences below. The sculpture, with its placement in the photograph between the destruction and the viewer that looks onto it from behind, is symbolically linked to that of an *angelus interpres*, a translator of incomprehensible happenings for the mystified human via its appearance and gesture. This role is repeatedly fulfilled in the Bible by the archangel Gabriel. It is also Gabriel who traditionally with his long horn blows what Milton has termed "the trump of doom" for Judgment Day.[70] The shape and position of a trumpet can also be likened to the semi-raised arm of the sculpture.

The audience was perceptive to such Christian iconography at the time; it was consistently employed in the immediate postwar years to frame the widespread destruction and desolate urban landscapes and the sense of complete defeat and loss among the population. Hermann Claasen's book on the destruction of Cologne, *Gesang im Feuerofen* (The Song in the Fire) (1947),[71] for example, concentrates on photographs of churches and religious motifs. The title itself refers to "The Song of the Three Holy Children" in the Book of Daniel, comparing the bombing to a biblical trial on the way to redemption.[72] Also in other media, for example in Hans Erich Nossack's literary text *Der Untergang* (The End), religious symbolism is central to describing the air war and its consequences.[73] It is this context that seems to explain the repeated—though false—description of the allegory in the reception as an angel, as well as the association of the photograph with Walter Benjamin's "Angel of History."

Yet this unifying, almost hopeful proposition, namely that the pictured site can somehow be fully grasped and understood when looking carefully enough through the figure's eyes, is simultaneously revoked by the way the ruins burst beyond the frame of the picture and dissolve the idea of strict borders of the photograph. This diffusion of limits already arises in Baroque paintings that feature atectonic compositions that continuously strive for an open instead of a closed form: "compositions [that] always give the impression of being more or less incomplete and disconnected; [that] seem to point beyond themselves, to be capable of continuation."[74] To take this a step further, the combination of the pointing hand with such an open composition can be linked to the idea of the "Fingerzeig" ("pointing finger," a sign) in Romantic thought. Just like Baroque, the Romantic movement itself is of course strongly linked to Dresden's past cultural makeup. Brad Prager has shown the Romantic notion of "pointing" as a common path to represent the ruined urban scape after the Second World War.[75] What made this Romantic iconography so attractive that it found its way into so many postwar representations of the ruined Germany? According to art historian Joseph Leo Koerner, "pointing" in Romantic art "stands for the endless deferment of sense, the sheer movement 'beyond,' that uncovers at its destination only another indication of transcendence."[76] The meaning of the landscape or subject pointed to arises thus only in allegorical terms. The war ruins do not contain their own significance, their own history or their future; rather these visions need to be constructed anew, out of the rubble, by the onlooker.

So, while suggesting the availability of an interpretation, when one follows the pointer, the "Fingerzeig" keeps reaching beyond that what is pictured. Expanding philosopher Roland Barthes' understanding of photographs in *The Rhetoric of an Image*, translation theorist Scott Clive argues that the image hovers in a space between the uncoded and coded, and the indexical and iconic.[77] It makes the pictured destruction of Dresden a catastrophe that transcends any one meaning in itself, but still performs across them by evoking shared emotions. The universal catastrophe expressed in the photograph, as it is picturing an unrecognizable landscape of rubble void of the well-known unique architectural markers of Dresden, can accommodate a wide range of reactions—feelings of estrangement and identification, objective distance and emotional closeness, questions of loss, sorrow, responsibility, and directions in designing the future—while at the same time communicating a shared sense of prolonged shock and trauma. This shared sense, together with the suggestion of a documentary rather than an artistic rendering of Dresden's destruction, claims a high degree of authenticity for what the viewer encounters in the photograph, even though such authenticity can be linked to familiarity in symbols and themes rather than immediate experience.[78]

Peter's photograph does not stand alone, however. The Dresden bombing narrative that claims innocence, military insignificance, and a barbaric destruction and victimization of Western civilization in Dresden almost immediately blended with the image, forming what visual theorist W. J. T. Mitchell has termed the "imagetext."[79] The endless ruins in the center of the photograph provide for the viewer the opportunity to anchor the established story of the Dresden destruction within it without having to shift into a different narrative frame. By piercing each other in this manner, by creating a feedback loop between verbal and visual narrative, each frames, codes, and decodes the other. The photograph becomes the canvas through which the imaginary picture arising from the narrative can be framed and authenticated. At the same time, the narrative offers the interpretation for the composition of the photograph and can thus tame the endless destruction in Peter's image. To name just one example, the narrative provides a location, time, and manner, and the photograph elicits the accompanying emotional reactions. Each injects the iconicity into the other and makes them available to perform as signposts in the collective memory of Dresden and its destruction. Yet since they reference each other rather than an external reality, both are highly subject to the political and ideological realm that surrounds them, in which the aspects of the visual and verbal narrative that suit specific political agendas are activated. Institutions, ideologies and groups who try to dominate the public discourse contextualize the visual and verbal narrative so that both photograph and narrative start performing within the collective societal consciousness they hope to influence.[80] Not surprisingly, Peter's photograph has been widely reproduced, imitated, manipulated, and referenced for these goals.

Views from the Town Hall Tower

The elements of the narrative about the Dresden bombing were first introduced by National Socialist propaganda. In contrast, Peter's photograph, which was part of a series of images he took in early fall 1945, was published as an enticement to embrace socialism and engage in rebuilding, while also

Fig. 4. Walter Hahn, *View from the Rathausturm* (1945). (Photograph by Walter Hahn. Reprinted by permission of SLUB/Deutsche Fotothek.)

accusing the Western capitalist system. It appeared in the photobook *Dresden: Eine Kamera klagt an* (Dresden: A Camera Accuses), put together by Peter and published by the Dresden City Government in 1950, a volume that was to document the extensive damage the city had sustained but also highlight the rebuilding efforts undertaken since 1945 (see chapter 3 for a more detailed discussion of the photobook). Yet it was not the entire book that became an all-German icon, but the photograph with the allegorical figure from the town hall tower.

As we have seen, for historical photographs to become iconic, a process of mutual amplification needs to set in. On the one hand the pictures need to possess the visual rhetoric which in its immediacy, symbolism, affect, and theme communicates with the images and narratives already established in the collective memory of a society. On the other hand, they have to be widely reproduced, distributed, and referenced until they become what historian Robert Dale has called "visual commonplaces" and offer "a shared sense of a community's past."[81] In the case of Peter's 1945 photograph, the reproduction of the view from the town hall tower began even before the photograph was published, since a variety of photographers realized that shooting Dresden's destruction from this vantage point offered the potential to express and communicate the feelings in German society after the war.[82]

The town hall tower did not only allow a bird's-eye view of the ruined Dresden, but it also offered deeply symbolic artistic elements for framing the shot. Walter Hahn, an established Dresden photographer who specialized in landscapes, architecture, and aerial views, had already photographed the city several times from the tower before its destruction.[83] He took a picture similar to Peter's famous view; it features the Schreitmüller sculpture and has a comparable composition. The photographs differ in format, and the positioning of the stone figure, which in Hahn's image de-emphasizes the pointing hand. On Hahn's photograph it is more apparent that some of the areas below, particularly the streets, have been cleared of rubble.[84] Peter's picture is the more famous and more widely reproduced of the two, but they are nevertheless so similar that Hahn's photograph is frequently used as a stand-in for Peter's picture in publications, and sometimes even misidentified as Peter's. Hahn's photograph has thus not taken away but rather reinforced the iconic standing of the motif and its deep significance as a collective representation.[85]

After the war, Dresden's destruction was continuously present as a historical, cultural, and visual reference point, and the ideas of innocence, victimization, and cultural loss allowed identification with German suffering and a way of processing the air war and its consequences without having to face questions of guilt. Pictures of the destroyed city, particularly the photograph from the town hall tower, became a central part of a growing body of popular literature on Dresden's destruction both in East and West Germany, as well as internationally.[86] The various occasions in which the bombings were evoked are both an indication of the strong emotional bond to the events among the population, as well as of the successes with framing the story of the Dresden bombing for political, social, or cultural goals.

The following examples demonstrate how Peter's photograph and the Dresden destruction narrative could be framed together to perform as powerful vehicles for societal messaging, while at the same time deepening the collective belief in the narrative's authenticity and thus its iconic staying power. In East Germany, Max Seydewitz, minister-president of Saxony from 1947 to 1952 and then director of the Dresden State Art Collections, participated in mobilizing political viewpoints through use of the photograph, at this point in the interest of 1950s and 1960s East German revisionism. Seydewitz published *Zerstörung und Wiederaufbau von Dresden* (The Destruc-

Fig. 5. Max Seydewitz, *Die unbesiegbare Stadt* (1961). (Kongress Verlag Dresden, Heinz Unzer.)

tion and Rebuilding of Dresden) in 1955 (the title was later changed to *Die unbesiegbare Stadt* [The Invincible City]). The book had reached seven editions by 1983.[87] Seydewitz mainly focuses on emotional witness accounts and fully engages the trope of the unfair loss of the beautiful and innocent city by the bombing through the fascist West.

Not all of the dust jackets for editions of *Die unbesiegbare Stadt* are still available, but at least one, from 1962, features the iconic town hall photograph. While the elements of the image stay the same, the publication uses various visual effects to contextualize the famous picture with a political message. The photograph is mirrored; the stone figure is positioned on the left, pointing toward the right. The black and white image has been colored red to symbolize the firestorm. The change in direction in pointing seems to indicate that the figure is now drawing attention to the future rather than to a desolate present and past. In accordance with the political message of the time in East Germany, which emphasized construction instead of destruction, the hand of the sculpture does not actually point to the rubble landscape, but instead reaches inside an overlaid area that blocks out part of the original photograph and instead fills the ruined space with an image of a heritage site, the famous entrance gate of the Zwinger by the Baroque architect Matthäus Daniel Pöppelmann. There is no obvious connection to the geographical area pictured below the photograph since the damaged Zwinger was not part of the landscape of rubble in Peter's shot. The Zwinger landmark, however, was one of the few that had been rebuilt at the time of the release of the volume, and the readers were acutely aware of this reality.

Yet the view from the town hall tower does not only feature prominently on the cover. In fact, Seydewitz frames his entire book and argument with this image to communicate his revisionist political message via Dresden's fate. The first chapter opens with the author gazing out onto the prewar panorama visible from the tower's viewing platform.[88] He introduces Dresden as it would have been seen through the eyes of a visitor by pointing out the various architectural landmarks in "the magnificent silhouette of the city on the river."[89] He narrates their history and emphasizes Dresden's cultural role. Seydewitz evokes Dresden as a work of art and architecture in perfect harmony with its natural environment: the river Elbe with its wide meadows and the sandstone mountain range in the background. He claims his visit to have taken place in January 1933, so that Hitler's Germany is established as the starting point for Dresden's downfall:

> A splendor lay over the beauty of this city, which human labor and the highest art had created over centuries. Dresden, glorious city on the river . . . A group of SA men marched past the town hall, roaring. Their shouts of "Heil" penetrated the peaceful silence and carried up to the town hall tower. [. . .] [T]he marching SA men reminded us all too grimly that the dark shadow of the swastika was falling ominously on the brightly shining beauty of the cultural and artistic city of Dresden on this clear January day.[90]

This rhetorical move, however, does not change the Dresden bombing narrative, as it does not reflect on the role of Nazism in Dresden, but instead insinuates the city as a victim of fascist rule, a basic premise of East German propaganda.

In the final chapter the author describes himself as returning to the town hall tower in the 1950s in high anticipation for a new view that will arise shortly. Seydewitz adjusts this description to the progressing rebuilding that was occurring over time throughout the numerous editions. In 1955, Seydewitz emphasizes that Dresden "begins to bloom again."[91] He outlines how the panorama of rubble as presented by Richard Peter's photograph is being replaced with a new city rising from the ashes. He invites the readers to imagine the plans that, Seydewitz claims, will feature an ideal mix of past and present: The city will contain restored historical buildings giving credit to its past, but it will also live up to the demands of its inhabitants and appropriately represent the new socialist political system by creating architectural symbols that stand for workers and farmers, not Saxon nobles. For Seydewitz, what is arising is thus a city that will be "more beautiful [. . .] than it ever was."[92] In later editions, Seydewitz describes "beautiful new buildings [. . .] on wide streets; they are surrounded by pretty green spaces so that air, light and sun can penetrate the modern apartments," as well as historical rebuildings, such as the Zwinger, the Hofkirche, and the Semper gallery.[93] Seydewitz takes pains to present the stone figure in Peter's picture not only as pointing to a terrible crime against an innocent city, but now also at a brighter future built on the values of socialism. By activating sentiments of victimhood and loss but also perseverance and an awareness of the importance of Dresden as a historical city, he aims to create support for East Germany's city planning.

Walter Weidauer, mayor of Dresden from 1946 to 1958, offers a different perspective on the Dresden raids in his 1965 publication *Inferno Dresden*.[94] But the core narrative surrounding Dresden remains untouched, and he also faithfully supports the East German political position concerning the bombing. The book was still in print as late as 1990, then in its eighth edition. While at first not featuring Peter's iconic town hall picture, the cover was nevertheless illustrated with another of Peter's aerial photographs taken from the town hall tower in 1945, yet in this case toward the Elbe, which actually would have included the famous cultural sites before their destruction. It does not, however, offer the same emotional accessibility as Peter's photograph with the pointing figure. By its sixth edition in 1987, Peter's more iconic and by then ubiquitous signature photograph, underlain with a fire red background, had replaced the title picture. Weidauer is less exuberant in describing the architectural and human losses in Dresden but assumes his readers to be intimately familiar with this narrative. The book is written from the premise that the bombing was a crime committed against an innocent city of culture that was destroyed in a uniquely atrocious way.

Weidauer describes Dresden's citizens as double victims, first of the Nazis and then of the bombs. He repeatedly claims objectivity, yet he frames the destruction of Dresden within Eastern Cold War rhetoric:

> The destruction of Dresden was to be, as Churchill put it, "a thunderclap" and was intended to terrify the Soviet Union. All the evidence shows that by destroying Dresden, the British and American governments did not actually want to target the Hitler fascists, but first and foremost their Soviet allies.
>
> The action was obviously not aimed at the military defeat of Hitler's Germany, but rather the imperialists were pursuing much more ambitious goals.[95]

Dresden is here presented as the first victim of the Cold War: The destruction was committed by the Western Allies not to end the Second World War, but to hamper the advancement and successes of the Soviet Army and to weaken the Soviet Union's power.[96] The bombing of Dresden is seen as a precursor of the atomic threat. Again, the deep connections established between the Dresden verbal and visual destruction narrative is used to authenticate what are in reality historical inaccuracies so as to support ideology and to redirect societal memory.

In the West, publications about Dresden could also count on numerous editions, and Peter's photograph of the ruined and deserted cityscape and the Dresden bombing narrative were important elements of these representations. The framings here also aimed at changes in collective memory, but the widely unchallenged claim of Dresden's innocence is not used to assign blame for the bombing, but rather to offer a communal platform for Germans to unite in decrying, mourning, and remembering German losses and to regain confidence by building on past cultural achievements. Connecting the Dresden bombing to the atomic bomb gives the feeling of victimization seemingly worldwide support. In addition, since Dresden was controlled by the GDR, a second victimization of Germans could be claimed in support of the Cold War rhetoric, as Germans could be said to be denied the opportunity to rebuild and access their cultural heritage by the socialist regime's repression.

One of the first book-length West German treatments of the Dresden raids was Axel Rodenberger's *Der Tod von Dresden* (The Death of Dresden; the same title as Sparing's national socialist propaganda article) in 1951.[97] His book proved popular: by 1963 Rodenberger's work was already in its eighth edition, and it was republished as recently as 1995. The author had been in Dresden during the raids, and he makes claims of authenticity predicated on his own experiences as well as firsthand testimony from other survivors. Rodenberger left Dresden after the war and resettled in the West. Again, the premises of the Dresden attack that were established immediately after the bombardment are not questioned and they are expressed with the deep pathos so often used to connect with the audience on an affective and symbolic level: "Dresden! Florence on the Elbe! City of museums and the arts. Dresden, city of countless world-famous buildings. Dresden, the city that like no other was the destination for travelers from near and far, is no more. Dresden died, it melted in the blaze of the flames, it burst under the explosions of the bombs. . . . [Its citizens and refugees] were unprotected when facing devastation."[98]

In addition, like Weidauer, he draws connections and comparisons to the dropping of the atomic bomb, but in Rodenberger's case to emphasize even more strongly the important meaning of Dresden as both universal human and cultural catastrophe, since Dresden belonged to all: "It was a trusteeship that Dresden exercised, an occidental common property guarded by this city."[99] Dresden was to be a lasting peace symbol: "The death of Dresden shall remain an eternal memorial. A warning to the people to do everything in their power to avoid a repetition of war and such catastrophes."[100] This idea still strongly resonates today (see chapter 5 for Dresden's role as a symbol for peace and reconciliation after reunification). Rodenberger frames his message in symbolic religious terms, which avoids questions about responsibilities: the bombing "catastrophe" is repeatedly likened to "hell," "Lucifer," and "the work of the devil";[101] the "heavens are crying"[102] but the people are "deserted by God and the world."[103] In his preface, Rodenberger thanks the Dresden residents who not only helped him out with their stories but also sent him photographic materials to "complete and round out his report."[104] The author also includes Peter's iconic image in his publication. In keeping with his allegorical approach to the bombing, Rodenberger suggests a religious link with Peter's picture featuring the sculpture. The photograph shows, according to the author, "a desolate scene without comfort," which leaves the survivors in a world devoid of the guidance and consolation of a higher power.[105] Rodenberger describes his book as a report that is "entirely free of political leanings and tendencies."[106] But he never questions

Fig. 6. Hilmar Pabel, *View from the Rathausturm onto the Inner City Cleared from Rubble* (1955). (© bpk Bildagentur / Stiftung Preußischer Kulturbesitz. Reprinted by permission of Hilmar Pabel / Art Resource, NY.)

the premises of the Dresden bombing narrative as established early on by Nazi propaganda.

A few years after Rodenberger's first edition of *Der Tod von Dresden,* West German photojournalist Hilmar Pabel, during a trip to East Germany, took a picture of Dresden (fig. 6) that references Peter's photograph. The following year, Pabel was awarded a prize for his photograph at the *photokina* exhibit in Cologne.[107] The picture and its reception speaks to how widely the original town hall photograph had already inscribed itself into the memory culture of both Germanys. Yet instead of a landscape of rubble, Pabel shows another world that is nevertheless void of life: While the foreground has remained the same as in Peter's image, the background has shifted by this time. The Schreitmüller sculpture now points to an entirely empty and flat landscape solely interrupted by deserted streets that seem to lead nowhere. The ruins of the original photograph still included the possible promise of rebuilding; this picture now suggests the loss of the famous city to lie with East Germany's policies that make the country uninhabitable. Pabel reframes Peter's image and the bombing into antisocialist commentary within the Cold War dynamics. Both East and West Germany thus rely on the elements of the Dresden narrative of innocence and victimhood and the strong symbolic features of Peter's photograph in their Cold War political discourse. Counting on the deeply felt connection to Dresden and its destiny among its populations, such rhetoric could become a powerful message in the ideological war.

The Dresden narrative coupled with its visual representation proved to be a universally and continuously renewable postwar memory discourse not only in Germany. In 1963, the now infamous British history writer David Irving drew large international attention to the Dresden bombing with the publication of *The Destruction of Dresden*, which quickly became a bestseller.[108] Again, photographs play an important role in the description of the bombing, and the text is complemented by several picture pages. As can be expected, Peter's photograph with the stone figure is included in Irving's work. It is featured prominently in the very beginning, covering the left part of the double page that presents the title.[109] Irving will be, the picture's placement suggests, the reader's *angelus interpres*, explaining and translating the events in a way that would let the audience understand, emotionally and intellectually, the inexplicable singular horror of what has occurred.

It is unclear whether Irving's representation of the Dresden bombing was already informed by his later quest to belittle the gravity of the Holocaust and ultimately to deny it entirely. Yet he is responsible for holding Churchill directly liable for the air strikes. Irving insists that Churchill chose the target despite having received opposing advice.[110] He also further bolsters the exaggerated number of civilian casualties often associated with the Dresden raids, which, according to Irving, amounted to at least 135,000, conclusions based upon false assumptions and forged documents. Irving sets up a direct comparison between Dresden and Hiroshima to strengthen his claim of the singularity of the attacks. He concludes in his book that the atomic bomb on Hiroshima was significantly less severe in terms of the loss of life (he assumes an official death toll of 71,379 in Hiroshima)[111] and proceeds to describe the destruction of Dresden as "the biggest single massacre in European history."[112] Yet despite the unreliability of many of his sources, Irving characterizes his book as an objective historical study based on meticulous research. In addition, Irving claims to give authoritative proof of the minor role Dresden played in the German war effort, thus implying that Dresden was unfit as a target. After a winding discussion, he infers: "By the beginning of February 1945, the capital of Saxony was therefore virtually an undefended city. [. . .] In addition the city was, as we have seen, devoid of first-order industrial, strategic, or military targets-in-being."[113] While most other writings on the bombing simply relied on the symbolic-emotional rhetoric to authenticate their assertions of Dresden's lack of military significance, Irving claims he can back up this notion with historical proof. This claim helped cement the Dresden bombing narrative even more solidly in international memory, since Irving was a British citizen.

Popular texts such as Kurt Vonnegut's *Slaughterhouse-Five* disseminated Irving's message further by retelling the Dresden destruction narrative, whose beginning had already been woven together by the National Socialist propaganda. Vonnegut, who had survived the bombing as a prisoner of war and worked through his experience in this 1969 antiwar novel,[114] mentions Irving's book directly. He incorporates into the text Irving's assumptions about the number of dead and the idea that it was "much worse [. . .] than Hiroshima,"[115] thus spreading the Dresden narrative of the innocent and victimized city further. At another point he repeats Irving's term "massacre" for the Dresden raids.[116] The story Irving tells in his role as *angelus interpres* corresponded to the established bombing narrative projected onto the city and claimed accuracy based on historical evidence. His conclusions were not questioned by Vonnegut (or many others) at the time.

Vonnegut was particularly receptive to Irving's claims, as they seemed to validate his own experience as a survivor of the Dresden bombing and the information he had received after the raids. In a letter to his parents dated May 29, 1945, Vonnegut reports, "On about February 14th the Americans came over, followed by the R.A.F. Their combined labors killed 250,000 people in twenty-four hours and destroyed all of Dresden—possibly the world's most beautiful city."[117] Apart from confusing the order of involvement of the American and British forces, Vonnegut almost precisely repeats the numbers and key ideas about the representation of Dresden as the innocent city of culture that had been disseminated by the propaganda early on. A story published posthumously in 2008 and titled with a Bible verse by the prophet Amos about judgment day, "Wailing Shall Be in All Streets," sheds further light on Vonnegut's interpretation of the raid. The narrative, probably written before *Slaughterhouse-Five* but after Vonnegut had read Irving's book, as it quotes fatality numbers closer to Irving's, illustrates the deep-seated idea of exceptionalism that is applied to the city of art before its destruction as well as to the bombing and its magnitude:

> Dresden was surely among the World's most lovely cities. [. . .] She had marvelous old churches, libraries, museums, theaters, art galleries, beer gardens, a zoo, and a renowned university. It was at one time a tourist's paradise . . . the impression I have is that in Dresden—in the physical city—were the symbols of the good life; pleasant, honest, intelligent. In the Swastika's shadow those symbols of the dignity and hope of mankind stood waiting, monuments to truth. The accumulated treasure of hundreds of years, Dresden spoke eloquently of those things excellent in European civilization wherein our debt lies deep. I was a prisoner, hungry, dirty, and full of hate for our captors, but I loved that city and saw the blessed wonder of her past and the rich promise of her future.[118]

According to Vonnegut, the true Dresden was never actually part of Nazi Germany; rather it was a treasure of Western civilization, an important cultural center existing beyond the restrictions of national borders and the political realm. Dresden is personified as a beautiful, cultivated, admirable woman, a muse, who needs to be protected by all. Vonnegut's story shows again how Sparing's arguments and formulations in "The Death of Dresden" had fallen on fertile ground and had been thoroughly included into the Dresden discourse. Like other depictions, Vonnegut's description emphasizes the visual appeal of Dresden, which he understands as naturally symbolic and infused with such positive values as "honesty" and "intelligence." With the narrative's title, he also falls back on religious symbolism to describe the bombing, which at this point appears to be the only way to capture the severity and unimaginable effects of the experience.

While many of Irving's claims about the exceptionality of Dresden as a target and the attacks themselves have in the meantime been disputed through a steadily growing body of more nuanced and academic historical scholarship, the widely disseminated propaganda early on, the oral and written witness reports, photo books picturing the ruined cityscape, as well as popular publications such as those by Irving, Rodenberger, Seydewitz, and Weidauer had already cemented the Dresden victim narrative surrounding both the city's glory and its destruction. The disjuncture between available evidence and public remembrance lays bare the diverging functionality between history and memory discourse in this case. The memory discourse operates on the level of the symbolic and metaphoric, which defies correction and change. It is one reason why these established perceptions, which so strongly inform the public and cultural reception of the bombing of Dresden, proved and prove largely resistant to the results of academic historical study.[119] The powerful association of certain photographs with a set of the often emotionally charged tropes connected with the bombing help thoroughly cement the unquestioned acceptance of the Dresden narrative with much of the public both within and outside of Germany. The confidence in the absolute reliability of these photographic records, including the impressions and underlying beliefs connected to the pictures, is so strong that historical facts that seem to counter such meanings associated with the images are often mistrusted or dismissed. Peter's iconic photograph from the town hall tower is not seen as an interpretation of the event, but as its authentic depiction. It is understood as an aide-mémoire, which helps experience, comprehend, and memorialize the firestorm and its devastating effects. But with its careful composition based on symbols and emotions, the immediate association with a destruction narrative that was deliberately constructed as part of a Nazi propaganda campaign, and the various political framings within which the photograph has been contextualized, Peter's iconic image of Dresden in ruins and its derivatives are in fact engaged in memory making.

As we have seen, Peter's photograph and its use reveal much about the iconicity in remembering and understanding Dresden and the driving forces behind them: the universalization of the war events and the symbolic interpretations of the destruction, the power of designing and defining views and perspectives about the past, and the role of such narratives regarding questions of responsibility and political framing. Dresden's universally accepted story of suffering and Peter's allegorical presentation of such anguish is thus the perfect foundation for various interpretations of German history and the bombing experience. Yet the question remains why there existed and continues to exist such an extensive and powerful emotional investment in Dresden's destiny and its verbal and visual depictions. As the next chapter will demonstrate, the answer lies in Dresden's past, beginning with the deliberate development of the city into an architectural and cultural center to showcase the sophistication and power of Saxony, and the rise of the verbal and visual narrative to support this image.

CHAPTER 2

Staging Dresden before 1945
Court City, Travel Destination, Visual Icon

There exists a large archive of Second World War rubble images from cities all over Germany. Yet as we have seen in the previous chapter, when it comes to illustrating the severe effects of the air war, Richard Peter's photograph from the town hall tower and the narrative of Dresden's destruction are most prominently represented. At first carefully constructed for two different political purposes, image and narrative have become untethered from their initial political framings and form an interconnected unit. They provide for each other the stage to perform their meaning and at the same time appear to vouch for each other's authenticity. These visual and textual narratives successfully activate Dresden as the *locus classicus* of the remembrance of the horror of the bombing war in collective memory after 1945, in Germany and abroad. Even though the actual bombing of Dresden was, contrary to its perception, not exceptional, the widespread postwar memorialization of February 13, with its emphasis on the suffering, victimhood, and innocence of Germans, has been unique.

This chapter explores the precursors that made it possible that the pictorial and verbal narrative has barely shifted since its creation, despite a variety of political framings and activations for differing goals. The Dresden bombing narrative, which represents Dresden as the victim of an unfair and unimaginable attack on a cultural icon, is not only erected on Dresden's ruins, but also on the lasting imprint of the memory of the widely admired, harmonious silhouette of the city before its destruction. I will show that it is this pairing that planted the mythical elements of Dresden's destruction story deeply into the collective postwar memory. Such anchoring, I argue, was possible because Dresden had been already perceived within a framework that included mythical components. In fact, what was to become the "Icon Dresden" had been deliberately constructed since the sixteenth century. Dresden was designed, built, cultivated, branded, and marketed to align with a desired image the Saxon rulers felt would give Dresden a premier reputation as a cultural haven, a standing they hoped would also increase the political power of their court. I will demonstrate the development of Dresden as a cultural icon from the sixteenth century to 1945, as well as the meaning that arises from this codification. Even though by the twentieth century Dresden had developed extensively in population size and demographics, architectural makeup, industry and trade, political situation, and military significance, the city remained framed as a cultural masterpiece, unchanged since its peak representative phase in the eighteenth century.

I have identified four interconnected elements that brought about these developments: the conscious construction of Dresden as a city with high imageability and symbolic and performative function, the large pictorial archive of distinct city views and their distribution, Dresden's rise to an international travel destination and the influence it had on the city and its residents, and the established landmarks that perform as sites and sights of special attachment for Dresden's population and visitors alike. The analysis will reveal that the discourse on the bombing of Dresden can evade questions about the military validity of the bombing, the city's responsibilities, and questions of guilt regarding the Nazi times because it does not respond to the loss of the actual city from 1945, but rather to a long-established specifically framed image of Dresden as a purely cultural haven with similarly cultured residents.

The Making of the "Florence on the Elbe"

The American urban planner Kevin Lynch claimed he came up with the main ideas for his groundbreaking book *The Image of the City* (1960) on a travel fellowship in Europe when gazing at the cityscape of Florence from the left side of the river Arno.[1] He was surprised how, despite the industrial activity he observed close to his location, his perception still foregrounded Florence's landmarks, the Dome's large cupola and the Campanile, which rose from the city center. These landmarks characterized Florence's reputation and made it distinct. They also served as reference points in navigating the city. Inspired by this experience, Lynch came to believe that the visual quality of a city is a decisive part of how a built space would be perceived both in terms of aesthetics and livability by its residents and visitors. To describe this process,

Lynch developed the concept of imageability as a measure for the quality, enjoyment, and beauty of an urban environment. According to Lynch, every person in a city will form mental images and maps of their environment. He identifies three important principles in the city that will be reflected in these images: identity (what makes the city distinct), structure (its patterns, interrelations, and maneuverability), and meaning (the perceived reality, the cultural dimension associated with the city). The higher the city's imageability, or the stronger and the more vivid images it could provoke, the higher was the quality of the built environment. The more these individual mental images overlap collectively, the richer, more beautiful, and more harmonious the city is experienced, and the more it becomes an important part of a collective identity.[2]

It is not hard to imagine that Lynch, at another time, could have also been inspired by contemplating the prewar city panorama of Dresden from the bank of the river Elbe. In fact, Dresden is not only an example of a city that had been widely perceived as beautiful, but one in which the concept of imageability was a guiding principle in the city's development. Dresden is the result of careful and intense urban planning and design, starting in the first half of the sixteenth century and reaching its high point in the eighteenth century. In 1547, Dresden became the court residence and capital for Saxony under Duke Moritz. The duke had expanded Saxony and had won the right to elect the German king, which in turn also enhanced the status of the new capital. From then on, Dresden's development and growth was increasingly determined by the Saxon rulers and their desire for power and representation instead of by the city's own government and council. With careful planning, the Saxon court tried to create and control the emerging identity for Dresden, since it was understood as reflective of their own.

In this spirit, Moritz, and then his successor, embarked on building an extensive and modern fortification system for Dresden that would stand out among other cities in northern Europe. To find models for their defense system, they looked to Italy and its novel designs, which had been developed to satisfy the need to protect against new weaponry.[3] Under the Italian architect Rocco di Linar, Dresden became the site of a fortification system in both Old and New-Italian style.[4] While Moritz no doubt wanted to be well-protected, he also hoped to send a clear signal about Saxony's power. With its expansive and modern defense system, Dresden was distinct among the northern European court cities.

Dresden developed increasingly from a rural community into a trade and artisan town that attracted new residents. With this expansion also came the building of additional living quarters, churches, and other communal institutions, as well as an effort to introduce cobblestone streets and better hygienic conditions. Particular emphasis was placed on expanding and developing court buildings, constructing entertainment venues for music and art, and creating representative architectural ensembles. Again, many involved important Italian builders and artists.[5] As early as under Duke Moritz, for example, the Dresden castle was completely redesigned, resulting in the first Renaissance four-winged castle in Germany. Italian artists and architects, among them the brothers Gabriel and Benedikt da Tola and Francesco Ricchino, decorated the walls widely with *sgraffiti*, a technique of scratching pictures into plaster that had gained popularity during the Renaissance and provided impressive artistic elements.

Italy's cities thus served from early on as inspiration for the design and urban development of Dresden. Art historian Barbara Marx even traces the oft repeated nomer "Elbflorenz," or "Florence on the Elbe," as a descriptor for Dresden back to the sixteenth century.[6] The city of Florence did not provide the exact blueprint for Dresden's redesign, however. Rather, Florence was embraced as the cradle of the Renaissance whose cityscape modeled an ideal urban structure characterized by the laws of aesthetics and composition. The term "Elbflorenz" captures this relationship. Referring to Dresden as Florence suggested that the structuring of Dresden, its ensembles and flow, paired with its cultural atmosphere, deserved as much a positive response as the already famous Italian city. By adding the local river to the expression and thus clearly marking the city's location, the term also emphasized Dresden's unique identity. The significant resources and the effort employed by the Saxon rulers in Italianizing Dresden, while at the same time keeping it distinct, signal their belief that such a development would elevate their reputation within Europe. The dukes hoped that turning Dresden into a vessel for exceptional artistic accomplishments and an urban work of art would communicate the power and sophistication of the Saxon leaders and their citizens.[7]

According to urban anthropologist Peter J. M. Nas, such generally embraced patterns mold "the city into a vivacious piece of art" and create a city's widely shared association with a distinctive character and atmosphere.[8] Meaning arises through the interaction of various stakeholders. In the case of Dresden, the city was constructed to communicate Saxony's significance to the rest of Europe via different symbols and their performance. Some urban linguists have termed this communicative aspect of the city "declarative": the understanding and view of the city is shaped by what it is declared to mean, but also by how well such meanings can be anchored in the actual cityscape and in how far people embrace and validate these declarations and their representations collectively.[9]

With the building policies and cultural developments instigated under Friedrich August I (later also King August II), who is better known as August the Strong, and his son Friedrich August II (also King August III), in the eighteenth century, the representative and declarative function of Dresden for the Saxon court reached its high point and cemented Dresden's lasting identity as the unrivaled German (Saxon) cultural masterpiece. Dresden was built as the stage on which the cultural importance the Saxon court claimed for itself could be successfully performed. To grasp the processes that led to this effective creation of Dresden's prestige, it is helpful to break down which type of signs and symbols were integral in producing the image. According to Nas, four types of symbolism are at work in the creation of a city's structure of meaning: material (the architecture or interaction between cityscape and landscape), discursive (narratives, visual representations, and myths), iconic (famous people associated with the city), and behavioral (rituals, structured behaviors, and celebrations) symbol bearers.[10] As we will see, these various signifiers, which created lasting core meanings, became the foundation for the way Dresden is reflected in collective memory.

Already in 1718, when the Enlightenment writer Johann Michael von Loen visited the city on one of his many travels, he was overwhelmed by the plenitude of architectural treasures from the past and present that were brought together in the city: "On the one hand, the city of Dresden appears to be a mere folly, in which all architectural styles pleasantly mingle, on the other hand they can still be enjoyed individually as well."[11] Dresden was succeeding in pleasing both on the macro and the micro level, as a place in which the mere visit to the city became part of what one could describe as a theatrical experience. The Dresden Zwinger, designed by the architect and builder Daniel Pöppelmann in collaboration with the sculptor Balthasar Permoser, is a key example of the power of material symbolism in evoking meaning. It was named after the part of the former fortification system that had been located where the new building went up. The Zwinger in a fortification system is an enclosure made up of two defensive walls that could slow down the enemy by trapping it. Now this kill zone was to have a very different purpose. The Baroque Zwinger was originally conceived as an orangery, but it was then designated as gallery space and a backdrop for festivities. Indeed, the Italian-inspired ensemble, with its ornate playful façades and decorations and its open areas, resembled a stage set rather than a collection of functional buildings.[12] Pöppelmann's Baroque design, that references many symbols in its structure, is thus performative; it is both a backdrop for spectacles and a spectacle in itself.

This performative function of the material environment became increasingly important to August the Strong's vision. Dresden was to shine as a unified whole in which moving around became an event. He added other buildings, such as the new Baroque Frauenkirche, whose impressive cupola was soon to rise above the Renaissance and Baroque burgher houses surrounding it. To overcome the city's physical division caused by the river, August dramatically changed the architectural landscape on the right side of the Elbe by adding an array of Baroque buildings and palaces.[13] To tie the city parts together, August changed the main bridge starting in 1728. The Pöppelmann design of the "splendidly adorned bridge" afforded beautiful views onto the Dresden cityscape, an urban tableau that now also included the Elbe and its wide meadows.[14] For this purpose, Pöppelmann added areas on top of each pier on which pedestrians could step out to rest and enjoy the surroundings. Friedrich August II continued his father's projects and plans and added the Katholische Hofkirche (The Catholic Church of the Royal Court) to the Dresden panorama. The Italian architect Gaetano Chiaveri made full use of the church's location near the Elbe and supported the theatrical arrangements already implemented in the city. Instead of facing inwards, the Hofkirche was positioned in such a way that it would unfold its biggest effect on the viewer when arriving via the redesigned Augustus Bridge.[15]

August the Strong and his son Friedrich August II strove to reflect Saxon's cultural sophistication not only by building a city to resemble an artistic masterpiece, but also by choreographing and staging new customs and rituals. They were tapping into what Nas describes as behavioral symbolism to encourage the reception of Dresden as on par with the well-known southern European cultural centers. Friedrich August II was a declared enthusiast of Italy, expanding on the relationship fostered under his father. During August the Strong's time, not only were Italians called to build in Saxony, but Saxon representatives also traveled to Italy for cultural exchange. The art museums and galleries in Florence were an important influence on Dresden, but despite the frequent comparisons between Florence and the Saxon residence, there was in fact more direct cultural contact with Venice than with the city on the river Arno.[16] Venice had become a favorite travel destination for various noblemen or wealthy bourgeois in the eighteenth century. Paintings, drawings, and engravings picturing sights of Venice were extremely popular in Europe, letting those not privileged enough to travel there bring the city panorama into their living rooms.[17] The Saxon rulers admired this widespread veneration for the Italian city and eagerly imitated and emulated Venice's customs, culture, and atmosphere, striving to achieve a similar status for Dresden.

When Friedrich August II married his Austrian bride Maria Josepha in 1719, many guests from all over Europe journeyed to Dresden. It was an ideal occasion to stage the city as a German Venice, and August the Strong provided an opulent Venetian spectacle. After getting officially married in Vienna, the couple arrived in Dresden on the waters of the river Elbe in a galley designed by Alessandro Mauro that was inspired by the luxuriously decorated Venetian state galley, the Bucintoro.[18] For the next weeks, Italian-themed events were held all over the city,[19] and Venetian artists provided paintings, illuminations, and other decorations.[20] During a Diana festival, for instance, animals were driven into the waters of the Elbe and then shot by hunters in gondolas of various sizes. "Diana" herself arrived on a highly decorated boat topped by a large shell.[21] Such festivities were not just entertainment.[22] Rather, they created spectacles in which the city featured as a stage with lavishly designed sets. Immersed in this setup, the participants turned into performers actively participating in creating Dresden's city-identity through discursive, iconic, and behavioral symbolism as a place of sophistication, art, entertainment, and culture. With the city and people interacting with each other, they formed a series of *tableaux vivants*, a live exhibit of the best and newest the arts—and Saxony—had to offer.

Yet such performances alone were not enough to create a reputation for Dresden as an exceptional cultural haven. Art could not just be created via architectural splendor and spectacles, but it also had to be owned. To this purpose, August the Strong sent out his court staff to purchase important pieces, particularly from Italy. Venice at that time had become a central location for the international art market, and court representatives from Dresden bought there "as much as possible as fast as possible."[23] When Friedrich August II took over, he eagerly continued collecting. Under his leadership, purchases were undertaken more carefully to guarantee an organized and homogeneous whole, not just a collection of valuables. The public display of a selection of the artistic treasures became now an important concern; the gallery (then still located at the Jüdenhof) was redesigned, the collection was limited to Italian art, paintings were hung in themes and pairs to encourage comparisons, and a number and catalogue system helped with locating the art pieces.[24] As fine arts curator Gregor J. M. Weber asserts, selecting, ordering, and organizing the paintings became a work of art in itself, resembling the creation on a canvas, thus reaching far beyond mere decorative goals to a true concern with content.[25] Friedrich August II was interested in building a harmonious ensemble, mirroring the aesthetic appeal of the cityscape and allowing opportunities for visitors and residents to immerse themselves and bond with the displays.

These processes at work in Dresden—both on the micro and macro level—led to the careful construction of what could be called a Gesamtkunstwerk, or total work of art.[26] The term originates with the philosopher and writer Karl Friedrich Eusebius Thrandorff, but it became widely known as part of Richard Wagner's conception of the opera.[27] For Wagner, the Gesamtkunstwerk was to combine text, music, and stage (including the opera building) into a synergetic work. Since then, it has been applied within various other contexts to denote the synergy of arts, spatial arts, and architecture. The concept is here employed in this wider sense; yet the Wagnerian conception regarding the opera is also connected to Dresden. Wagner grew up in Dresden and its cultural offerings, particularly Carl Maria von Weber's operas, had a deep formative effect on him. He even sang in the famous boys' choir, the Kreuzchor.[28] He returned to Dresden in 1842 to take the post of royal court kapellmeister and it was here that Wagner developed the theory of the Gesamtkunstwerk. In 1849, he had to flee into exile after taking part in the unsuccessful insurrection during May of that year, like his friend, the architect Gottfried Semper.[29]

The philosopher Odo Marquard, in his influential essay "Gesamtkunstwerk und Identitätssystem" (The Total Work of Art and the Identity System), probes the relationship of reality and art when striving to such totality: When the aesthetic picture itself is raised to reality, when reality is not seen "as reflected in art, but as a total work of art," Marquard sees a push toward an inversion in which "not reality itself is the work of art, but the work of art itself strives to become reality."[30] The separation of art and reality is thus complicated to the point of targeting the erasure of reality in favor of the aesthetic construct.[31] This process can lead to the confusing state that what is perceived as a total reality/work of art is based only on a partial and idealized reproduced reality—termed by Marquard an "indirect extreme Gesamtkunstwerk"—and can finally cause the manifestation of "the mythological" or "a tendency to a new myth" within the Gesamtkunstwerk (a process Marquard views with suspicion).[32] Indeed, more and more, the Saxon rulers strove to transform their residence into a place of mythic proportions through restructuring and rebuilding. They engaged in constructing and performing symbols, not just for fame but for Dresden to embody a cultural and aesthetic utopia.

Dresden thus became a particularly successful version of what urban anthropologists have recently been studying as the hypercity, which emphasizes mediation in comprehending the city and its total idea: "The hypercity encompasses the entirety of urban signifiers or symbol carriers that combine in a dynamic process of signification to represent the city, both to its inhabitants and to the rest of the nation-state, the region and the world."[33] According to this theory, a "symbolically coherent hypercity is one in which production and consumption merge," which means that the total idea of the city is embraced as the city itself.[34] In Dresden, the meaning of the city was both consciously produced and widely accepted as that of a unique cultural masterpiece. The symbolic structure came to represent the city as a whole in the consciousness of both inhabitants and visitors alike; not only was Dresden perceived as a total work of art, but the residents built their own identity firmly onto this idea, themselves becoming representatives and guardians of the city's character. Identity and city, or, as sociologist Richard Sennett has put it in reference to the relationship of residents with their hometown, "flesh and stone," became more and more intertwined, strengthening Dresden's image as a purely cultural haven represented by special architecture, artefacts, atmosphere and population.[35] So even though Dresden was developing more and more into a center for trade and artisan production, and its population kept growing significantly, the way it was framed and the way the city declared itself omitted what did not conform to the aesthetic ideals encoded in its hypercity. By focusing on its cultural and exceptional side, reality became subordinate to the idea of reality.

Since Saxony was concerned with its reputation beyond the borders of the state, the processes that Nas describes as discursive symbolism were particularly important to strengthen Dresden's identity, as it could be most easily shared. Considering the emphasis on Dresden as a work of art, visual reproductions became powerful tools in framing the perception of the city. By establishing timeless, unchanging ideals of Dresden on the canvas, which were perceived as faithful reproductions, they were also formative for the future. We will investigate the long history of visual depictions of Dresden in the next section but will first look at the most significant and famous paintings of the Dresden cityscape by the Venetian artist Bernardo Bellotto. They were closely connected to Friedrich August II and his mission. Bernardo Bellotto's uncle and teacher Canaletto, a name Bellotto adopted in Germany, had become famous for his appealing vedute of the city of Venice. Bernardo Bellotto, as Dresden's court painter, followed his mentor's artistic convictions and painted a series of pictures of Dresden in similar style, including the well-known view of "Dresden from the Right Bank of the Elbe with the Augustus Bridge" from 1748, which is pictured in the introduction. Bellotto's perspective on Dresden in general and his panoramas in particular have deepened Dresden's reputation as a center of art and culture and as a unique example of a successful Baroque city. They have helped define the Dresden cityscape in the memories of both its inhabitants and others around the world up to the present.

Today, Bellotto's views are iconic and are seen as a window that allows one to experience the authentic Dresden before its destruction in 1945. Apart from the many changes in the city panorama since 1748, however, even Bellotto did not depict the mid-eighteenth-century Dresden realistically, but instead inscribed "the silhouette into accepted artistic patterns," putting principles of design above actual dimensions, colors, and arrangements.[36] In other words, Bellotto painted Dresden the way it was supposed to be according to the aesthetic expectations of the time, not the way it was. And yet, even today, building developments in Dresden are measured against the so-called "Canaletto View," the iconic embodiment of what is conceived as the "authentic" Gesamtkunstwerk Dresden.[37]

During this time, the city's reputation as a center of art and culture flourished. But it also drove Saxony into financial ruin, so that it became an easy target during the Seven Years' War (1756–63) and parts of Dresden were damaged and destroyed. This experience had a profound and lasting effect on the citizens of Dresden at the time. The young Dresdner Caroline Lucius reported in a letter about a festival that included a firework display in 1764, four years after the Dresden siege by the Prussians during the war: "The rockets looked beautiful, but they sound horrific to me, they swoosh and hiss like the carcasses during the siege and like the bombs when they flew through the air over our house."[38]

One of the most significant architectural casualties of the siege was the Renaissance Kreuzkirche (Church of the Holy Cross), which partially lay in ruins after it had been bombed with cannons by the Prussian troops. During rebuilding efforts after the war, additional parts of the church collapsed. Bellotto recorded the destruction in a painting in 1765. The well-known picture eerily foreshadows the later series of photographs and drawings of the destroyed Dresden cityscape and its landmarks after 1945. They also reflect Bellotto's own situation. Bellotto had been called to Dresden in 1747 and almost immediately been named a royal painter with a steady and generous salary from the court. He also painted for the royal courts in Vienna and Munich. After the Seven Years' War, he found himself in a very different position. Friedrich August II had died in 1763, and it was not possible to sponsor Bellotto further in the weakened and broke postwar Saxony. To make

Fig. 7. Bernardo Bellotto (Canaletto), *The Ruins of the Old Kreuzkirche* (1765). (Courtesy of Gemäldegalerie Alte Meister, Staatliche Kunstsammlungen Dresden.)

things worse, Bellotto's house had been severely damaged by the war.[39] The artist created some final vedute, among them the painting of the ruins of the Kreuzkirche, which so strikingly contrast with earlier works depicting the beautiful and harmonious cityscapes. Then Bellotto was forced to turn his back on Dresden for good. Yet neither Bellotto's melancholic pictures nor the suffering of the population after the state's financial ruin have left any lasting traces in the way Dresden's Augustan era has been remembered locally or outside of the city. The established symbolism instead anchors Dresden's special meaning in this era and marks it as the most glorious time in the history of Saxony and its capital.

Dresden's Rise as Travel Destination and Its Deepening Urban "Mindscape"

Dresden's reputation as a city of culture had spread widely within and outside of the German-speaking realm. With this rise in significance, Dresden had started to attract some of the earliest tourists: Englishmen and their tutors making a continental "grand tour" of what were considered essential locations to refine the young students both in knowledge and manners. France (particularly Paris) and above all Italy were viewed as the highlights of these educational undertakings, and it was important that a student already knew how to present himself when arriving there. Next to Berlin and the university towns of Heidelberg and Munich, Dresden was one of the favored German destinations, since this "Florence of the North" could serve as a place to cultivate and prepare the traveler. The northern European courts were perceived as valuable training and testing grounds to equip the young men with the skills needed to succeed in Italian society. In the words of Lord Chesterfield in his instructional letters to his son who was touring Europe from 1748 to 1749: the "rough-diamond young Tourist might be 'rubbed at three of the considerable courts of Europe—Berlin, Dresden, and Vienna,' before arriving in Italy 'tolerably smooth and fit for the last polish.'"[40] Indeed, Lord Chesterfield expresses a deep satisfaction with his son's progress in acquiring manners at his first stop, the Dresden Court.[41] Yet as Lord Chesterfield, somewhat disappointed, must observe, while providing good examples in behavior, the Saxon city proved not to be the best place for his son to overcome an "ungraceful and disagreeable manner of speaking" and to excel in proper enunciation of German. It is left unclear in the letter whether this problem was related to the lack of societal experience by the young man or to the Saxon dialect.[42]

Even though Saxony suffered poverty and Dresden was a site of partial destruction after the Seven Years' War, the city still managed to retain and build upon its reputation as an exceptional place of art and culture and remained a popular destination for travelers in the second half of the eighteenth century. The established urban mindscape of Dresden, the shared view of a city which arises "between the physical landscape of a city and the people's visual and cultural perceptions of it," included expectations about emotional and sensual feelings that could only be evoked by the city itself and would forever enrich the traveler's life.[43] Social theorist Dean MacCannell thus compares touristic travel with pilgrimages to holy sites, as they similarly incorporate the idea of special insight and deeper knowledge through the encounter with a specific (holy) place.[44] Indeed, descriptions of Dresden visits by travelers often draw on spiritual language and characterize their visits as highly emotional experiences.

In 1768, for example, Johann Wolfgang Goethe, at that point a young university student in Leipzig, made the day-long journey to pay a visit to the city's art collections. In his memoirs, *Dichtung und Wahrheit* (Truth and

Fiction), Goethe expresses his excitement about the gallery and notes both the excellence of the facilities and the artful display, organization, and quality of the paintings; he felt as if he had stepped into a "sanctuary."[45] Toward the end of his visit, Goethe ventures out to view other parts of Dresden and ends up on top of the cupola of the Frauenkirche. Yet when he looks down upon Dresden and surveys the extent of its war damage, he is shocked by the severe contrast between the harmonious order of the museum and its content and the disorder that has arisen in the city's architectural ensemble:

> These delightful experiences, preparing both mind and sense for true art, were nevertheless interrupted and dampe[ne]d by one of the most melancholy sights,—by the destroyed and desolate condition of so many of the streets of Dresden through which I took my way. The Mohrenstraße in ruins, and the Church of the Cross (/Kreuzkirche/), with its shattered tower, impressed themselves deeply upon me, and still stand like a gloomy spot in my imagination. From the cupola of the Church of Our Lady (/Frauenkirche/) I saw these pitiable ruins scattered about amid the beautiful order of the city.[46]

Goethe clearly perceives the loss of the buildings as a void, a deficit that interrupts a carefully crafted whole that he had come to assume when thinking of Dresden, even though he had never visited before. Goethe's expectations were met by the museum, but not by the cityscape. His shock is thus not only caused by observing the dire consequences of war. Goethe is denied the deeper insight into beauty, harmony, and cultural greatness he expected based on the established mindscape that had developed for Dresden. Goethe does not question the image he had created of his destination when he observes its actual state. Instead, the preconceived image is equated with the authentic Dresden, while his actual observations and feelings are considered as false. Comparable to the situation after the Second World War, the scenes of destruction carry within them the remembrance of the undestroyed Dresden and its awe-inspiring significance and influence, even for those who had never seen the city before the bombing. They remain the dominant image evoked by the idea of Dresden, which is deemed more authentic than the actual city environment.

Other travelers also found their way to Dresden, regardless of the wounds the long conflict had left on the cityscape. While today visitors usually picture Bellotto's famous and much publicized vedute from around 1750 as the historical Dresden, copies of Bellotto's paintings were not yet widely available to these early travelers. This circumstance does not, however, mean that Dresden's city silhouette was unknown. Bellotto's vedute stand in a long tradition of topographic depictions of the city. Pictorial representations of Dresden were already disseminated in the sixteenth and seventeenth centuries when illustrated *Städtebücher* included copper engravings or etchings on Dresden.[47] The artistic techniques as well as the selected perspective became iconographic for future representations.[48] Urban scholar Franco Bianchini calls attention to the key role in creating a communal city mindscape of what he refers to as "image banks." Image banks contain discursive representations that share similar themes and sentiments in such media as paintings, guidebooks, local narratives, or myths.[49] The extensive representations within this image bank not only depicted the present, but also added more impetus to build and arrange Dresden in the fashion of a portrait. The making of pictures and the subject's meaning are intertwined since the pictures "express a set of messages which constitute a more wildly held and conventionalized body of discourse."[50] It explains the lasting repetition of specific pictorial content and compositions that can be detected in Dresden's representations.

Dresden and Its Surroundings as Artistic, Intellectual, and Societal Stage

An ever-increasing number of publications of personal travel reflections, guidebooks, and pictorial representations speak to Dresden's spreading fame and the deepening of its distinctive character and atmosphere. The more mobile citizens became both geographically and in society, the more important a destination Dresden turned out to be and the more travel accounts, guidebooks, and pictures became available. In this feedback loop, Dresden's reputation as a city of art, beauty, and harmony in both its architectural and societal composition was strengthened, and the perception of the city merged with its declared meaning in collective consciousness. Dresden's cultural reputation made it an ideal destination for an educational journey (*Bildungsreise*), which by now the German *Bürgertum* regarded as an important step in developing their own identity, as individuals and as a social group.[51] The travelers believed that by visiting Dresden and exposing themselves to its aesthetic aura, they would gain artistic sensibilities emitted from the cityscape and its collections. Dresden offered a special experience and the promise to become someone special oneself.

It is remarkable that this trend was barely influenced by the European political situation of the time. Despite the repeated conflicts with France in Europe since the start of the revolutionary wars in 1792, travel guides kept being published and visitors still made it to the city on the Elbe. In 1807, for instance, in a guide specifically geared toward foreigners, the anonymous author justifies the publication of another Dresden book with the circumstance that there was a strong demand for such publications.[52] In another guide, *Neuester Dresdner Wegweiser für Fremde und Einheimische* (Newest Dresden Guide for Foreigners and Natives) from 1797,[53] the author Johann Gottlieb August Kläbe responded to increased numbers of short-term travelers with a small, light format that could be easily carried around by the visitors. In contrast to other available Dresden books, it stands out with its concern to offer solely the most important information, highlighting various buildings and the art collection. The guide thus already selected and ranked for the travelers and even the locals the interactions with the city. Through such preselection, the way Dresden was viewed and understood became ever more tightly codified, restricted, and limited, which, however, also simplified communicating and sharing Dresden's meaning universally.

Other accounts about Dresden came from the travelers themselves, many of them writers, artists, and musicians for whom Dresden became a fitting stage on which they could perform their identity, inspire and be inspired, and interact with other intellectuals. They were attracted by its reputation and offerings, and their visits and reflections further established the city's reputation. One of the many visitors to Dresden was the philosopher Johann Gottfried Herder. In 1802, he confirms in a contribution to his serial *Adrastea* the success of the Saxon efforts to make Dresden a capital of art and, in accordance with the ideals of the Enlightenment, a place of cultural education outside of Italy. Praising the efforts of the Friedrich Augusts, he calls Dresden—in view of its excellent art collections comparable to Florence—"German Florence," and one of the "colonies of art which need to be viewed as preparation for guiding the student across the Alps."[54]

For the Romantic writer, Shakespeare translator and theorist August Wilhelm Schlegel, Dresden and its galleries take on a similarly important role, yet he finds inspiration rather than education in the city. He chooses the Dresden art collection and its famous works as a backdrop to discuss fundamental questions about the role of painting and its relationship to reality in the 1798 dialogue "Die Gemälde" (The Paintings) which he coauthored with his wife Caroline.[55] The text features a conversation between the painter Reinhold, his friend Louise, and the writer Waller in the rooms of the gallery. While fictional, "Die Gemälde" is both homage to the city of Dresden with its artistic treasures and to the circle of friends Schlegel and his wife frequently met there. Among them were other important thinkers who contributed to the conceptual formation of the Romantic movement, such as the philosopher and literary critic Friedrich Schlegel, August Wilhelm's brother, the writer Novalis, and the philosopher Friedrich Schelling.[56]

The highly influential text, which is built on the idea of the Geselligkeits-ideal (sociability) of the eighteenth and nineteenth centuries, performs the creation of an artistic moment through a group of friends that populates the story.[57] In its course, it poetically discusses many of the works on display in the Dresden gallery. But when the critical conversation turns to fundamental questions of how to approach art, the three friends leave the exhibition space and stroll outside. Here, the painter Reinhold chooses a spot on the Elbe with a view of the surroundings, which he identifies as a more apt place to continue their discussion:

> We cannot possibly find a more suitable and charming place. In front of us the calm river; beyond us emerge, behind the green riverbank, the soft wavy meadows; down below the city with the cupola of the Frauenkirche is reflected in the water, above rise vineyards which closely follow the bend of the river, sown with cottages and on top covered in pinewoods.[58]

The ensemble of cityscape and landscape Reinhold creates in his account is so intense that it is not only inspirational for their conversation, but if the reader were not aware that the characters had left the gallery, Reinhold's description would be taken as that of one of the exhibited paintings.

Through the naturally artistic setting and the powerful imagination of its viewers, reality and art merge into an idealized setting of absolute beauty; in fact, the landscape of Dresden and its surroundings spurs the friends' imagination in a more artistic way than the works on display. In addition, the paintings in the museum are besieged by "crowds of gawking strangers," which the friends view as a distraction from engaging with the art itself. The paintings are unable to offer them the artistic inspiration they expect from them.[59] The encounter with the actual landscape, however, sparks a moment of creative performance characterized as a true internal, artistic, and creative experience. As Louise assesses when looking across the river onto Dresden and its scenery: "Ever since I busy myself much with such things [art], I perceive a real region more like a painting, and I turn a landscape piece into a true view."[60] Imaginary mindscapes and artistic compositions can thus overpower actual realities and shape the perception of the world.

When Heinrich von Kleist traveled to Dresden in 1801, he was inspired by young artists who were drawing the city and what Kleist describes as its "grandiose, majestic" landscape. Artists themselves became part of the meaning of Dresden as physical presences in the city- and landscape, as creators of discursive symbols, and as part of the ritual of celebrating the beauty of Dresden's ensemble. They confirmed their artistic identity by recreating the city on the canvas. Kleist reports in a letter that he even considers, despite his advanced age of twenty-four, whether he should not change his path, leaving his position in the Ministry of Economics at Berlin and becoming a painter (he settles on writing instead).[61] Throughout his life—albeit short—Kleist was affiliated with Dresden, frequently returning to the city.

He was not alone in his fascination: an anonymous author who identifies himself only as "a traveler [writing] for other travelers," laconically comments in his Dresden guide from 1799: "Whoever has once in his life enjoyed the delightful view from the Dresden Bridge, will not find it unnatural, if someone wants to spend the rest of his days in this city"[62] The peculiar formulation of a positive assessment through a double negation of the emotional response to the Dresden panorama, "will not find it unnatural," appears to point to a tension between the cityscape and the onlooker. The highly constructed and deliberately designed Dresden panorama causes an exceedingly pleasurable but unreflected reaction; the panorama is not perceived in its parts, but has taken on a seemingly natural, timeless aura.

The narrative of Dresden as a work of art became an important trope, even appearing in the titles of books. The travel guide quoted above is tellingly named *Neue Ansicht von Dresden* (A New Picture/View of Dresden); another guide, published in 1817 by W. U. Lindau resorts to *Neues Gemählde von Dresden* (A New Portrait of Dresden).[63] The depictions of Dresden, later complemented also by photographs, were so similar that they did not only reference the material Dresden, but also earlier representations. The carefully composed "picture" of Dresden, so strongly fostered by the Saxon rulers, was being reconstructed over and over again in various narratives and artistically transposed in an already idealized form onto canvases and etching plates. A meta-image of Dresden emerged from this image bank, which informed the collective mindscape of Dresden and thus the perceptions of the travelers. As already evident in Goethe's reaction, since discursive symbols such as images and accounts were widely available, the recognition of Dresden and its meaning frequently took place "in reverse"; before visitors arrived in Dresden they already felt a certain familiarity with the city through its widely available depictions. These images were in turn projected back onto the city by the visitors. The comments by the Danish writer Hans

Christian Andersen, who in 1831 reached Dresden coming from Meißen on his first trip outside of his homeland, are a typical example of this process. Andersen describes his arrival in the city as a déjà-vu:

> The farther we recede from here [Meißen], the higher do the mountains become; and we soon see, as through a bluish veil, the German Florence. Dresden lies before us, with its high towers and cupolas. When I reached Augustus Bridge, which I knew so well from engravings, it appeared to me as if I had, in a dream, been here once before.[64]

As both Schlegel and Andersen's fascination with Dresden indicates, while not a Romantic school like Heidelberg or Jena, Dresden's unique combination of architectural design, the extensive art collections and the art academy (founded in 1764), as well as Dresden's natural setting, made it an attractive place for many of the young proponents of this new artistic direction. Dresden became a meeting point for intellectuals. In fact, since during the Romantic movement, apart from "Bildung" in the traditional sense, experiences in nature became an important second purpose for traveling, the city's surroundings now contributed strongly to this fascination. Dresden profited from its proximity to the so-called Sächsische Schweiz (Saxon Switzerland), an area of sandstone mountains with a multitude of peaks and hollows that inspired many Romantic writers as well as painters. The area was not seen as entirely separate from Dresden; the city and its artistic treasures were strongly connected to the landscape. As the Austrian playwright Franz Grillparzer notes in his diary in 1826 when visiting Dresden: "The area resembles a paradise. [. . .] I am not sure whether it was my habit of the last few days of making the galleries my home, or whether the unique qualities of this landscape inspire such observations, but each scene and view presents itself to me very much like a painting. I have never experienced this phenomenon to such a high degree."[65]

The most famous visual artist of the nineteenth century connected to Dresden is no doubt the Romantic painter Caspar David Friedrich. Friedrich arrived in Dresden as a student at the Art Academy in 1798 and lived there with short interruptions until his death in 1840. Friedrich and fellow artists could be regularly found hiking through the Saxon highlands. The canyons, rough, wild, and fairly untouched, offered the perfect natural and spiritual setting for their artistic visions. In many of Friedrich's paintings, various landmarks from different locations of Saxon Switzerland are combined to create new, idealized landscapes that break with traditional spatial and temporal principles of perspective.[66]

The paintings allow glimpses onto the sublime that Friedrich so strongly senses in the natural world. These artistic modifications of nature, which leave behind the then established principles of landscape depiction, reveal the tension between attempts to replicate the environment and the necessary transformation and change that will accompany any translation onto the canvas by the artist.[67] The idealized landscapes complement the similarly produced artistic cityscapes of Dresden. While these paintings and prints are less obviously straying from faithful reproductions, it is nevertheless helpful to remember their tendency to idealize and highlight certain forms and compositions to satisfy artistic expectations. Landscape and cityscape in their artistic symbiosis are raised to the Romantic idea and ideal of the natural Gesamtkunstwerk in which, as we have seen, not only various different artistic media are represented, but in which the separation between aesthetic concept and reality is overcome.

The changed attitude toward nature and the notion that actual landscapes could offer aesthetic pleasure was not limited to the artistic elite. Tourist guides also reflect these changes in taste. While Dresden does not offer the medieval sites so highly revered during this period, as a publication from 1842 laments, its author Friedrich Gottschalck nevertheless regards Dresden as an essential travel destination because of its artistic treasures, harmonious cityscape, and awe-inspiring natural setting, thus echoing the idea of an all-encompassing experience:

> Where else are art and nature in such splendid union as they are here! Where else would the latter offer such lovely pictures, such charming landscapes, so that one can label them with the beautiful name "Switzerland," while the former's treasures, through the generosity of the rulers of the country, were accumulated here in such masses, that their residence was also called Florence on the Elbe.[68]

Guidebooks reflected this perceived harmonious balance of city and nature with numerous illustrations, which pictured both the city and the landscape. After additional etching and engraving techniques had been developed toward the end of the eighteenth century, markedly the more rapidly and cheaply reproducible wood engraving, such illustrations had become much more affordable. These newer techniques made the spreading of images, copies of well-known paintings as well as drawings specifically designed for these books, even more prevalent.

As we have seen, the Dresden illustrations firmly drew from the already established visual archive. One favored perspective of the city was its pan-

Fig. 8. City panorama in Klemm's *Vollständiger illustrirter Führer* (1858). (Artist unknown, Klemm, courtesy of Sächsische Landesbibliothek—Staats- und Universitätsbibliothek [SLUB].)

orama. The pictures included part of the river and either looked upstream or downstream onto the cityscape. In addition, the view from the north, with the Augustus Bridge leading into the town, gained more and more popularity. In motif, point of view, and scope they strongly resembled the widely circulating individual prints of earlier etchings and paintings, which in turn were based on the illustrations in the *Städtebücher*. The illustration above from Klemm's *Vollständiger illustrirter Führer durch ganz Dresden, seine Umgebung und die Sächsisch-Böhmische Schweiz* (Fully Illustrated Travel Guide for Dresden, Its Surroundings and the Saxon-Bohemian Switzerland) exemplifies the indebtedness of such pictures to earlier versions of the motif.[69] Guidebooks also reused drawings from other, earlier publications on Dresden, thus recirculating already-known images and reinforcing them as representing the totality of the city.[70]

The city portraits in the guides were complemented by nature illustrations, in particular of the Saxon-Bohemian sandstone mountains, which had become fashionable international tourist attractions in their own right.[71] As a travel guide from 1839 on Saxon Switzerland proudly declares, "For over thirty years, the Bohemian-Saxon Switzerland or Bohemian-Saxon Elbe highlands have been admired both within and outside of the country. // To visit them is now, so to speak, a duty for any worldly traveler."[72] To satisfy demands of tourism, locals started to equip particularly nice viewpoints of

Fig. 9. Illustration in Dietrich's *Der treue Führer* of Bastei viewing platform (1839). (Artist unknown; Karl Wilhelm Medau Verlag, courtesy of Sächsische Landesbibliothek—Staats- und Universitätsbibliothek [SLUB].)

the mountain panorama with large platforms and create easier access paths for the less adventurous nature travelers. In addition, state-licensed guides became available for visitors.[73]

One of the famous sites that experienced more and more development with paths and platforms, a restaurant, and night accommodations, was a jagged rock formation named Bastei.[74] It became the most popular visitor spot both for Germans and international travelers in the Saxon sandstone mountains and indeed remains a visitors' magnet today.[75]

Foreign Visitors in Dresden

Dresden and its surroundings were by the mid-nineteenth century firmly established on international travel routes as an iconic stop; it was even referred to as such in fictional works. In William Makepeace Thackeray's novel *The Newcomes* (1854), the protagonist Clive Newcomes, who is traveling through the continent, mentions Dresden as a favorite British spot when he comments in a letter from Rome home to England: "thither, as elsewhere we carry our insular habits with us. We have a little England at Paris, a little England at Munich, Dresden, everywhere."[76] Indeed, Dresden's reputation as a city for education and culture, situated in a beautiful natural environment, not only encouraged international visitors, but also inspired them to stay there for longer periods. Several colonies of foreigners established themselves in Dresden: wealthy Russians, English, and Americans, who came for art, enjoyment, and sometimes out of political reasons, as well as Czechs and Bohemians, who mainly worked as servants or craftsmen.

Henry Adams, who spent considerable time in Dresden during his European travels in the late 1850s, even humorously questions whether German is the primary language in the city. In a letter to his brother Charles, he notes that "the city is full of strangers and occasionally a pretty face. One hears Russian on one side, French on the other, English everywhere, German occasionally and samples of every other tongue at intervals."[77] From 1858, an Anglo-American Club organized the social life of the "English Quarter." An English-language Anglican church was erected in 1869, and in 1883 the American church St. John was finished. A Russian church was consecrated in 1874. English and Russian newspapers were printed, shops had staff capable of speaking English and Russian, and English, American, and Russian food items were provided.[78]

Just like Henry Adams, many American travelers during the nineteenth century favored the city, and many stayed for several months or even years. The clergyman Henry M. Field explains Dresden's unique role in his popular European travel log *Summer Pictures* from 1859: "Of all the German capitals, none unites so many charms to invite the traveler, and especially to attract and detain foreign residents, as Dresden. [. . .] For a man of elegant tastes, what more could be desired than this quiet enjoyment of learning and leisure, surrounded at once by the beauties of nature and immortal works of art?"[79] Adams and Field belonged to a second wave of American journeymen and women to Germany. They had been motivated to venture to Europe by popular accounts and letters of earlier travelers, who were usually part of the East Coast intellectual and financial elite and had sought inspiration in traveling abroad. Some had undertaken their studies in Germany, others came for leisure and cultural travel. A number of Americans also felt a need to undertake their own grand tour, following the long-established British example.

These early American visitors to Dresden include several well-known figures. Among them was Henry Adams's grandfather, John Quincy Adams, who served as ambassador to Berlin from 1797 to 1801. A bit more critical of the world and less playful than his grandson, he was still very much taken by Dresden's surroundings and its "very handsome bridge over the Elbe" when he visited in 1799. While he considered the Zwinger to be "in a bad taste of architecture,"[80] the cultural possibilities and the art collections impressed Adams greatly. As he shares in his memoirs, he received "a little further insight into the principles and history of the art, or rather [the art gallery] has served to convince me how little I knew of them before, and how little in so short a time it is possible to acquire."[81]

Washington Irving traveled from Paris to Dresden in 1822, spending the winter in the city to learn German and to visit the theater and the art galleries. The American was already an established writer both in the United States and Europe, and he recorded in his diaries detailed descriptions of the numerous dinners and balls he was invited to in the Saxon capital. His journals reveal a rich entertainment culture in Dresden, and Irving spends much time "waltzing," being out until three in the morning and going for the "chase."[82] Irving is coveted by all of Dresden society, including the king, and his calendar is so full that he even mixes up appointments, "stop[ping] by mistake" at people's houses on the wrong days.[83] Irving clearly enjoys his special position in Dresden and the beauty of the city, but at the same time keeps a bit of an ironic distance to the world at the Dresden court and his surroundings. Irving is thus both shocked and intrigued by his encounter with the German writer Jean Paul, whose manners defy the world of Dresden and its society, which likes to marvel at its own significance. As Irving comments in his journal:

> Jean Paul—a comic or rather humorous German writer—about fifty years old. The Germans are very fond of his writings—rather coarse in manner and habits—drinks—carries a poodle dog with him wherever he goes—at dinner it lies behind him on his chair—went to see the Dresden Gallery—the attendants told him civilly that his dog could not be admitted—then said John P., "I cannot see the Dresden Gallery," and in fact he went away without seeing it.[84]

While his social calendar takes up most of his time, his diaries reveal how, despite his long stay and his detached outlook, he never loses his admiration for the beauty of the Dresden cityscape, whose "fine effect" impresses him repeatedly, particularly if seen within its setting left and right of the Elbe's serpentines.[85]

In 1830, Irving's contemporary and fellow writer James Fenimore Cooper also visited Dresden. Together with his family he spent several months in an apartment overlooking the Altmarkt, and they enjoyed the cultural offerings, including German lessons for the children. In addition to the nice surroundings, Cooper also praised the mild climate of the Elbe valley, which he credited for lessening his stomach issues, leaving him feeling better than he had in the previous five years.[86] Boston bluebloods George and Anne Ticknor stayed in the city for several months in 1835, after George Ticknor had already visited and admired Dresden in 1816 during his studies at the University of Göttingen. Similar to the impressions of fellow travelers, the Ticknors also thought that Dresden distinguished itself from other places by its outstanding collections, its theater performances, its architectural beauty, the impressive landscape, and "the whole tone of the place [which] is quiet, intellectual and cheerful."[87] This description of Dresden's atmosphere, which resembles rather the mood of a library than that of a city of considerable size, reflects George Ticknor's own interests and educational convictions and his admiration for the Royal Saxon Library. Impressed by the library's collection, but even more by its ready public access and free lending policy for everyone, he saw this system as a path to create a more educated and enlightened population, which he believed he had observed in Dresden. Back in Boston, he became involved in founding the Boston Public Library in 1848 and promptly implemented such lending practices for that institution.

Such travel accounts became immensely popular and inspired other intellectuals, such as Reverend Field, not only to travel in Europe, but also to publish their experiences, often to great success. Dresden is repeatedly described as an attractive destination for writers, artists, and other intellectuals in these works,[88] and it continues to be awarded a unique status among European cities. In line with the earlier accounts, particularly by the Ticknors, Dresden is not viewed as a city of trade and industry, but rather as a place that is through its very nature reserved for the higher pursuits of learning and reflection. American poet Bayard Taylor's excitement in his popular book *Views Afoot* (1846) is another typical expression of this sentiment:

> At last in this "Florence of the Elbe," as the Saxons have christened it. Exclusive of its glorious galleries of art, which are scarcely surpassed by any in Europe, Dresden charms one by the natural beauty of its environs. It stands in a curve of the Elbe, in the midst of green meadows, gardens and fine old woods, with the hills of Saxony sweeping around like an amphitheatre, and the craggy peaks of the Highlands looking at it from afar. The domes and spires at a distance give it a rich Italian look, which is heightened by the white villas, embowered in trees, gleaming on the hills around. In the streets there is no bustle of business—nothing of the din and confusion of traffic which mark most cities; it seems like a place for study and quiet enjoyment.[89]

As in previous accounts, Dresden is again linked to beauty, culture, and a calm, learned preindustrial world, in which business has not distracted from its intrinsic aesthetic value. Even its landscape resembles a cultural icon, a Greek amphitheater, making Dresden a natural successor to this cradle of Western culture.

These widely held views, however, ignored the actual industrial development of the city. The large presence of travelers in Dresden already speaks to the rise of the tourism industry. Yet by 1850, Dresden was also well on its way to becoming an industrial center for the production of fine mechanics, aided by the expansion of the train network as well as the ship traffic. With the industrial progress, the number of residents also increased significantly. Between 1832 (the year of the first census) and 1849 the number of inhabitants increased by almost 50 percent to 94,092; by 1900, 396,146 residents were counted. Yet these developments are rarely reflected in the travelers' accounts, which cling to the established patterns and descriptions associated with Dresden. As Ticknor scholar Thomas Adam observes in the couple's journals, they largely ignored the building of the Leipzig-Dresden railway connection, the most prominent project underway during their stay, "as much as they ignored all other signs of advancing industrialization. For the Ticknors, Saxony was to be a Romantic and premodern heaven for the arts, culture, and education. Nature and society were to be harmonious and untouched by modern destructive life. Traveling to Saxony was, thus, traveling back in time."[90]

The attractive environment paired with the mild climate in the Dresden region, as well as the downplaying of its industrial importance when marketing the city to visitors, were the basis for another favorable label for Dresden, namely that of a healthy city. John Quincy Adams, for example, sent his wife Louise, weakened by two miscarriages, to medicinal baths in a health spa near Dresden for an extended stay. The purely cultural and harmonious city and nature body was thus complemented by the idea of the natural, purely healthy human body. By the second half of the nineteenth century, natural medicine was popular and fashionable, and a number of Dresden's suburbs, most famously the Weiße Hirsch, started to focus on professional and long-term care in private clinics. The district was kept free of factories and carefully landscaped with trees, walking paths, and benches. The private clinics specialized in natural remedies, such as Dr. Lahmann's Sanatorium, which offered opportunities for recuperation and rest and promised to "reform the life" of the patients and to counter the "damage from an unnatural lifestyle." At the same time, the clinics offered all the newest comforts as they became available, from central heat to electricity.[91] Dresden thus appealed to the many tourists who by now had discovered the pleasures of leisure and health travel for themselves.[92]

The combination of cultural and educational opportunities, striking nature, healthy climate, and the established foreign societies encouraged more and more families from abroad to send their children to Dresden for extended stays to study the German language and culture. Soon enough, Dresden became an educational hotspot for young foreign women; young Russian women, who were said by some to come mainly for an education in entertainment, as well as mild-mannered and industrious English Miß' became known features of the city.[93] Sigmund Freud even comments on the presence of the young British women in a letter about his visit to the Dresden art gallery in 1883. Freud facetiously blames their continuous studious attendance at the galleries for hindering him from stealing one of his favorite art works, *The Tribute Money* by Titian: "I would have loved to walk away with it, but there were too many people, Englishwomen who were copying, Englishwomen who had sat down and were quietly conversing, English-

Fig. 10. Postcard, Weisser Hirsch: Dr. Lahmann's Sanatorium (1899). (Kunstverlag Max Köhler, Dresden.)

women who were strolling around and contemplating."[94] Indeed, among the British living in Dresden, there were four to five times as many women as men, with a concentration among girls of fifteen to nineteen years of age.[95]

It might have also been Dresden's outstanding reputation for educational opportunities and its healthy climate that convinced the American Roosevelt family to send their fourteen-year-old son Theodore, who suffered from asthma, and his siblings to board with a family in Dresden in 1873 for five months to learn German.[96] In letters to his father, Theodore emphasizes how he enjoys very much his opportunity to study in Germany and demonstrates his progress by writing his letters in German, even diligently using the difficult Old German, or Kurrent, script. But he also claims (with faulty grammar), that the Dresden climate actually worsens his asthma and gives him headaches. He implies that it might be a good idea with regard to his health to leave Dresden soon: "Ich glaube, dass die Luft Dresdens ist nicht gut für mich" (I believe the Dresden air is not good for me).[97] To make sure that his point truly comes across, he adds a note in English to another German letter in which he describes his predicament in more detail:

> Corinne and I have always on Sundays read the Bible together and Elliott joined us today. I have just recovered from the mumps. If it was not that I would never have such a chance for German again I really think I would have to leave Dresden. During the last month, I have scarcely been entirely free of asthma for one week, and today it is rather worse than usual. Of course, these sicknesses put me back in my studies a good deal, and when I am well, I am almost always working double. And then I can neither box nor swim much—the latter not at all in fact.[98]

Yet letters to his friends suggest that the young Theodore's wish to leave the city might have had other motives. The teen was clearly bored by the bourgeois life in Dresden; to this effect he explains apologetically to his friend Harry Godey that he has not written more often because there is "nothing to tell" as life in the Saxon city is very "monotonous."[99]

This negative endorsement by the future American president, however, could certainly not curb the continued and increasing national and foreign fascination with Dresden. In fact, the number of visitors to Dresden grew from 62,576 in 1853 to 287,219 in 1900, an increase of more than 350 percent.[100] With the rise of mass travel, tourism became an increasingly important economic factor for Dresden. Originally designed to represent a powerful and sophisticated principality among the European nobility, Dresden by this time had reached iconic status as a unique place that promised unrivaled cultural experiences and was foundational for the educated. In Dresden itself, the local residents had bound up their collective identity with the city, thinking of their connection to the Baroque Dresden as the most important characteristic that distinguished them in the world. Yet their narrative about Dresden as the unique, purely cultural and artistic masterpiece was not only based on their emotional link but went hand in hand with the realization that to attract tourists and their money, it was this particular image of Dresden that needed to be propagated most strongly.

The Making and Marketing of Dresden for Leisure Travel

These developments of the tourist sector in Dresden would not have taken place without the proper infrastructure. By 1837, the first steamships ran on the Elbe; by mid-century, they were navigating many passengers up and down the river, bringing in new visitors.[101] But it was Dresden's role in the introduction of train travel to Germany that helped most significantly with the city's expansion of its tourist business and international reputation.

In 1839, the first German long-distance train opened to much excitement between Leipzig and Dresden.[102] Soon other connections followed, making it an important traffic spot both when traveling the east-west and the north-south axis in the rapidly expanding network of train lines.[103] The availability of trains quickly changed travel behavior. Not only was it possible for many more people to arrive much faster at their destinations, but travel also became attractive to new populations since the availability of cheaper tickets for the third and fourth classes suddenly made it more affordable.[104]

Leisure travel guidebooks focusing on the available train connections soon followed. The 1852 *Illustrirter Dresden-Prager-Führer* (Illustrated Dresden-Prague Guide) promises the reader in its subtitle a "Picturesque Description" of Dresden, the Saxon Switzerland, the Dresden-Prague train route, as well as Prague. It fulfills this promise by offering a stunning 144 illustrations, in addition to city and train maps. It also emphasizes—on a grand scale—the international possibilities and power such train connections brought with them: "This train's commercial, strategic and cultural impact is significant in the broadest sense [. . .]. It supports the convergence of both Saxon and Austrian interests and makes particularly Saxony the center of a great connection between North and South, between the Orient and the distant America."[105] The inclusion in the train network from the very beginning strengthened and helped expand the city's national and international touristic appeal manifold.

Surely the train served as an economic tool to transport goods and businessmen faster and more easily, but it also made Dresden part of a touristic network that allowed the traveler to concentrate on important sites of historic and cultural significance without spending days struggling in uncomfortable carriages. While the surroundings were still strategically explored via day trips from the cities visited, the train ride itself offered a speedy overview rather than an intense engagement with the world between the individual destinations. A look out the window from the compartment conveyed at the same time the illusion of a quickly moving, blurred environment, and that of a very gently changing wider landscape in the background. Thus, the traveler's gaze became trained to observe the surroundings more and more as panoramic views instead of a sequence of detailed close-ups.[106] The scenery resembled a slowly changing painting within its (window) frame. The text acknowledges this different mode of seeing and identifies these transformations as requiring guidebooks to direct the gaze of the traveler in an entirely novel way, even by instructing the traveler where best to sit.

The illustrations feature views that would be encountered from the train. They have rounded borders that evoke a window frame and suggest the picture to be a selection of a larger image. Since the traveler's views are now entirely mediated by the train and its course, the speed of travel, and the unchangeable nature of the prescribed stops, whatever does not appear in the compartment window falls to the wayside. A hierarchy of attainable perspectives is thus established, and places are privileged depending on their accessibility via train and their panoramic appearance. These changed perceptions that came with the new transportation options complemented and reinforced the modes of framing already employed in both the way Dresden presented itself and the way the travelers came to see it. Arriving in Dresden by train, visitors were sufficiently schooled to respond to such framings through the new ways of seeing and gazing they practiced on their journeys. They readily ignored parts of the city that did not fit with the idea of Dresden as the city of art and culture and the picturesque images they expected.

Along with the increase in tourism, Dresden had in fact also developed into a key industrial center. Yet while the tourist guides largely ignored these developments, publications geared toward increasing economic investments tried to profit from Dresden's cultural fame to gain attention. In her work on Dresden's identity structures, sociologist Gabriela Christmann has shown how economic publications drew a parallel between the industrial and cultural significance of the city.[107] In a 1903 book enthusiastically reflecting on Dresden's industrial development, for example, Dresden is named a "city of art, industry and tourism." This triad shows the importance that industrial developments had reached by this point, but it also displays how the authors try to elevate Dresden's industrial meaning by claiming for it the same global reputation as for its already well-established artistic and touristic attractiveness. Named first and last, art and tourism are still the defining pillars on which Dresden rests.[108] Yet tourism itself also took on economic importance for the Dresden burghers. The protection of Dresden's reputation of cultural and artistic significance remained a priority. Not only people's identity but also their livelihood was tied to Dresden's historic city and landscape. A law from 1878 thus blocked the building of factories and chimneys within and immediately surrounding the Old Town.[109] Even if the idea of cultural exclusivity was more and more removed from reality, the preformed mindscape of Dresden could remain largely unchallenged.

Very much in this spirit, the librarian and archivist Otto Richter published, already in 1905, the first picture book to concern itself directly with changes in Dresden's cityscape.[110] Worried about the modernization of Dresden, he hoped that *Dresden sonst und jetzt* (Dresden Then and Now) "would

Fig. 11. Otto Richter, *Dresden sonst und jetzt* (1905). (Artist unknown; Baensch, Verein für Geschichte Dresdens, courtesy of Sächsische Landesbibliothek—Staats- und Universitätsbibliothek [SLUB].)

help spread the understanding that it is a thankful task of our generation to guard the creations of our ancestors and to preserve the historical character of our city as much as possible against the onslaught of modern demands."[111] As the passage reveals, Richter associates Dresden's and its citizens' meaningfulness with Dresden's historic cityscape. The book employs a format of before-and-after pictures that juxtaposes on each page drawings that had served as travel mementos and postcards from the previous sixty to eighty years with photographs of Dresden at the turn of the century. Richter matches the perspectives of the pictures to highlight the changes. With this format, Richter authenticates the historical drawings of Dresden as unaltered depictions of a past reality against which the present can be measured. The ideal that Richter puts forward is a static one. Change and progress in the cityscape are coded as inherently negative and destructive, which for Richter is obvious in the comparisons.

It is not surprising that Richter relies on already iconic idealized city depictions to utter his warnings against the potential loss of Dresden's meaning. Again, the Dresden Baroque skyline and the Augustus Bridge leading over the Elbe feature as sites that need to be protected. As figure 11 demonstrates, the liveliness and natural beauty of the river, which invites people to stroll and rest, has disappeared in favor of industry, making the river and its banks objects of exploitation. While the natural scene lovingly framed the Dresden cityscape on the other side of the river, it is now an alienating presence that distorts instead of enhancing the view. The newly built bridge, the Carolabrücke (1895), covers up the skyline and the natural curvature of the Elbe. Otto Richter expresses what was becoming a more and more decisive characteristic of the Dresden city discourse: the strong emphasis on cultural preservation and conservation and a suspicion against new developments in the cultural, natural, and architectural sphere.

Dresden's status as an "exceptional city of art and culture" lured tourists and their money. Table 1 illustrates how the number of visitors to Dresden climbed significantly from the mid-nineteenth century, with some variations during hard economic or war times; international guests were tracked separately only later on.[112] The city responded to the rise in visitors with a deliberately planned commercialization and more intentional branding. In 1876, Dresden businessmen founded the Verein zur Förderung Dresdens und des Fremdenverkehrs (Society for the Promotion of Dresden and Tourism), the first of its kind in Germany, according to the society. It had offices in Dresden (from 1901 on conveniently located in the main train station), where visitors to the city could receive advice on lodgings, the various requirements for

TABLE 1. Dresden Visitor Numbers

Year	Visitors	International
1853	62,576	
1856	74,183	
1859	48,372	
1860	60,317	
1865	73,031	
1866	46,290	
1867	74,228	
1876	125,032	
1880	161,262	
1890	201,111	
1900	287,219	
1901*	284,173	
1902*	300,439	
1903	361,175	
1904*	390,770	
1905*	372,177	
1906*	401,818	
1907*	483,249	
1910	387,911	
1911	535,374	
1913	482,410	7,705
1914	380,790	
1915	257,832	
1916	261,627	
1919	363,433	
1922	478,316	
1924	392,453	26,659
1927	429,207	47,623
1928	428,562	51,185
1930	409,606	61,803

Note: Dresden visitor numbers as published by the Dresden Statistical Office.

* Indicates numbers reported by the Society for the Promotion of Dresden and Tourism.

long-term stays, and other useful information.[113] Starting in 1900, the society organized festivals to enhance Dresden's attractiveness. While the number of travel guides had risen dramatically already, the Dresden travel association also offered its own guides and maps in various languages and began an intense advertising campaign. Soon they distributed Dresden leaflets and posters in public places such as on ships and in trains, and they arranged newspaper ads in England, Russia, and the United States.[114]

Beginning in 1908, the society had permanent offices in both London and New York. Again, it was the Dresden cityscape, through paintings or

Fig. 12. English advertisement for Dresden in British and American newspapers (1906–7). (Courtesy of Stadtarchiv Dresden, Prof. Paul Naumann.)

photographs depicting a view onto the Baroque skyline from across the river, that was most prominently displayed in the association's advertisements. Particularly successful was the idea to lend out slides featuring various city views, buildings, and art works for talks about Dresden all over the world.[115] Later, several films featuring the historic Dresden were successfully distributed worldwide as well.[116] There was even an early form of "product placement": according to the society's documents, international movie companies were provided, free of charge, with footage featuring the city, which they in turn included in their films.[117]

In addition, framing the cityscape via a train compartment window became a widespread phenomenon.[118] On the one hand such illustrations suggest the ease of travel to the city; on the other this approach continues the tradition of introducing Dresden through several set views. While industrial progress can ease the strain of getting to the city, in Dresden itself signs of progress can be easily excluded. They are not shown as part of the city itself, but only facilitate observing its beauty. Indeed, the reader of the advertisement is strongly drawn into the picture by following the gaze of the travelers, a setup that today evokes references to Peter's destruction photograph from the Rathausturm.

Yet distribution of Dresden images also happened without the association's efforts. With the increased number of tourists also came an increased demand for postcards. There were already a variety of goods available with typical representations of Dresden, predominant since the publications of the early *Städtebücher*. Small engravings and etchings with the city panorama could be used as home decor. Plenty of other souvenirs also featured the Dresden panorama, such as porcelain coffee pots, decorative wall plates, or commemorative coins. With the invention of the picture postcard around 1870, the pictorial encoding of the city became ever more dominant and the Dresden cityscape more and more famous.[119] In Dresden, the demand for cards was so large that even printers from other major cities would produce postcards with Dresden illustrations and send them to Dresden to be sold there.[120]

Postcards are mass-produced selections of views and "the most widely disseminated tourist icons."[121] When sent to family and friends, these visual representations are often complemented by short personal anecdotes and refer to favorite touristic activities, which encourages a distinct way of thinking about the city. They also serve to authenticate and commemorate the visit for a traveler. Since the number of postcard images is limited, these illustrations participate in collectively communicating and defining a location's perceived identity.

Dresden's panorama was still changing up to the end of the nineteenth century, with buildings such as architect Gottfried Semper's opera house and synagogue from the first half of the nineteenth century, and Constantin Lipsius's Art Academy from 1894 in neo-Renaissance and neo-Baroque style. But these additions, while celebrated as individual structures, did not influence the encoding of "Dresden" with the already established trope of the Baroque city. By the end of the nineteenth century, Dresden was entirely marketed as a finished masterwork with a firm place identity. The touristic experience in Dresden was thus more and more shaped and guided by the multitude of preconceived images formed from postcards, guides, travel narratives, and souvenirs that predetermined both the expected experiences

Fig. 13. Postcard, Augustus Bridge, sent to friends back home by an American traveler (1899). (Gebrüder Scheizel, Dresden.)

Fig. 14. English-language postcard, general view of Dresden, ca. 1912. (Published by Arthur Capper, Kansas, Made in Germany.)

and their meaning.[122] As sociologist John Urry argues, this circumstance leads to what he has termed "the touristic gaze." The ideal images that the travelers have consumed and internalized before their trip not only shape their expectations and determine their itinerary, but, by staying within the framing of their internal images, also influence the way they perceive and experience the city.[123] Yet the framing gaze is not reserved to the tourist. As we have seen in Otto Richter's publication of then-and-now pictures, many residents in Dresden also defined themselves by connecting to the idealized historic representations, not the actual city they lived and worked in. This circumstance can also explain the stability of Dresden's image. Branding a place involves associating it with stories to reflect a certain picture to the outside, while also reinforcing the local identity. In Dresden, the representation of Dresden to the outside and the city's perceived identity on the local level overlapped considerably; the narratives were able "to create a sense of place 'attachment'" for both groups.[124]

Preserving and Marketing Dresden's Image and Heritage from 1914 to 1945

While during the First World War and then during the Depression the international colonies largely dissolved and international and national travel decreased, Dresden by that point had already so thoroughly established itself as a unique city of art and beauty that even without the exceptionally high prewar visitor numbers its special reputation carried on. Dresden was seen as a true expression of European culture and as an international treasure. It kept this reputation even though, as we have seen at the beginning of chapter 1, it also served as a key military base all the way up to the end of the First World War and had developed increasingly into an important industrial production center in the previous century. In the financially difficult years after the First World War, the Dresden government thus marketed itself via two different routes. It tried to preserve Dresden's reputation as a purely cultural center of exceptional value, emphasizing the city as a European treasure that lay outside of national interests and boundaries, but also engaged in other, specifically targeted campaigns to attract international businesses to pay attention to Dresden as an industrial site. Yet even in these campaigns, the image of the cultural masterpiece dominated.

In the (since 1927) bilingual German-English *Book of the City of Dresden*, published by the city council between 1924 and 1930 and geared toward possible investors and trade partners, the push to increase international interest in Dresden is apparent.[125] In the early numbers of the city book, articles on

Fig. 15. National Socialist brochure and map, "Dresden: Germany's Wonderful City of Culture" (1935). (Verkehrsamt der Stadt Dresden und Dresdner Verkehrsverein, Rüffer, Dresden.)

the cultural Dresden go hand-in-hand with reports on industrial potential. Later on, however, Dresden's cultural meaning and beauty is starting to be mainly suggested via illustrations. So while in 1927 there were still features on the art collections, the climate, and the artistic offerings of Dresden among those reports focused on business, future city planning, and the industriousness of the Saxon work force, by 1930 the articles only address contemporary business concerns such as cigarette and chocolate production, the manufacturing of machines, and beer brewing. Still, the pictures themselves were to serve as a powerful reminder that Dresden, while being attractive for industry, in its heart was and would always be a beautiful place. Despite the city government's targeted outreach to businesses, the overall message of Dresden as a cultural center remained dominant in Dresden's reputation. This message was not challenged by political changes. In fact, the city government kept building and banking on Dresden's solid reputation as a cultural tourist destination and exhibition facility during the prewar Nazi era, both nationally and internationally.

On a national level, and with the economic crisis, numbers of domestic visitors had dropped from 275,351 in 1930 to 161,547 by 1933, but by 1937 that number had risen back to a solid 271,173.[126] While a few posters and leaflets of the time display National Socialist symbols, for instance the picture of the town hall with Nazi flags on a pamphlet that advertised various museums and their exhibits (1935), such political themes were actually kept to a minimum, most likely to avoid the possible backlash with international visitors, but also because the city was not to function as a tourist attraction for the history of National Socialism. Dresden instead was to showcase past and current cultural achievements in Germany.[127]

This circumstance does not mean that the Dresden residents and the city government were immune to the Nazi ideology, including its cultural demands. On the contrary, the institutions and citizens of the capital of the Gau Saxony had quickly and without resistance adapted to the new cultural directives of the Nazi government. Members of the avant-garde, which had been well-represented in Dresden, and Jewish members of the city's cultural institutions were swiftly removed from their posts and Social Democratic institutions and newspapers were forbidden.[128] Dresden was the site of some of the earliest book burnings in Germany on March 7 and 8, 1933.[129] While the book burnings by Dresden university students happened alongside the nationally coordinated actions in May, the SA targeted leftist bookstores and publications already before. On March 7, it burned materials at the Bellmann bookstore, a Social Democrat hangout, but the photograph of the book burning on the Wettiner Platz on March 8 has held an iconic place in illustrating early Nazi book burnings in Germany. While often erroneously mixed up with the university student book burnings and identified as its first iteration, it nevertheless is an important indicator of the steps taken to publicly stage the smothering of unwanted ideas and destroy the organization of the opposition.[130] Two policemen in the front of the building do not interfere in the action, but in fact seem to stand guard for the SA men who are burning a large pile of papers and books. In the background the signage of a bookstore can be seen. The building was the publishing house and bookstore of the Dresdner Volkszeitung, Dresden's Social Democratic daily newspaper, and the SA had destroyed and plundered the offices and then started to burn the

Fig. 16. Book and document burning at the Dresden Volkszeitung and bookstore (March 8, 1933). (Unknown photographer; © SLUB/Deutsche Fotothek, reprinted by permission.)

materials they found.[131] So while this is not a picture of the systematic book burnings of a long list of literary works by authors that the Nazis considered undesirable, it is an effort to control and squelch opposing political thought and take over the sole political power in Saxony. The photograph's negative includes the telling description: "Purge [Säuberung] of the Dresdner 'Volkszeitung.'" Following these activities, modern art was publicly discredited on a large scale via an exhibit in September 1933, which was repeated in 1935. This Dresden exhibit was the first show of this kind titled "entartete Kunst" or "degenerate art," the same title that would later be used for the first centrally organized 1937 Munich show.[132]

Despite the political support of the Nazi ideology in the city, which will be explored in greater detail in chapter 4, touristic advertisement relied on emphasizing the historical nature of Dresden, its characteristic skyline, its artistic treasures from the past, its architecture and landscape, and its unchanged traditionalism. This marketing was not only helping Dresden's tourism economy but was also to serve the Nazi cause: With Dresden, the government could legitimize its cultural approach by presenting it as continuing an artistic tradition within the frame of the historical and cultural icon. National Socialism could thus contextualize itself in the already established Dresden mindscape. In this vein, Dresden hosted many national events, such as the first Reich's Theater Festival in 1934 or the first Reich's Garden Show in 1936. The opening celebrations of such occasions were often attended by high Nazi officials, even Hitler himself at the Reich's Theater Festival. In addition, far-reaching renovations of important architectural and cultural markers for Dresden, such as the Frauenkirche, were undertaken to prevent them from falling in disrepair (see chapter 4 for more detail).

The National Socialist leadership thus encouraged the continuation of Dresden's special standing as a tourist destination and cultural icon. Nationally, Dresden was a popular destination for tours offered by the Kraft durch Freude (Strength through Joy) organizations of various regions. With their affordable group offers these organizations were powerful promoters of domestic travel. For example, the 1938 brochure from the Gau Württemberg-Hohenzollern emphasized that traveling within Germany would give a citizen the chance to "form ties with his fatherland, to get closer to its beauty and its cultural treasures, which will evoke and shape his pride and love for his Homeland."[133] In this Kraft durch Freude brochure, Dresden and its surrounding areas feature frequently as destinations. For 39.60 Reichsmark, participants could take part in an eight-day tour that included hiking through Saxon Switzerland and a visit to Dresden and its attractions.[134] On another trip, the travelers reached Dresden via a folding kayak journey on the Elbe for only 35.60 Reichsmark.[135] All trips included transportation from Stuttgart and back.

Dresden was particularly strongly advertised in historical and cultural terms for international tourism. The city felt a sharp decrease in international visitors after Hitler came to power, with numbers falling from 58,907 in 1931 to 32,140 in 1933. The responsible city agency in Dresden attributed this downturn to what it termed the "heinous propaganda about Germany" but also to currency devaluations.[136] Yet concerns with tourism were quickly taken out of the sole hands of the local organizations. In June 1933, all tourism matters became the final responsibility of the Reich Committee for Tourism, which was part of the Ministry of Propaganda. From then on local organizations had to answer to the committee, which more and more dictated the approach and implementation of tourism matters.[137]

In the case of Dresden, the National Socialist tourism promoters were keenly aware of the international pull of the historic city of art, and it became one of the primary stakes in German propaganda efforts to create a positive image of Germany internationally. For instance, in the English-language monthly *Germany: Periodical for Scenery, Travel, and Touring*, which was published by the Reich Committee for Tourist Traffic in 1934, Dresden was showcased as a must-see historic travel destination in which the modern world is easily forgotten:

> [N]o one can escape the unforgettable and overpowering impression made by the city. The sight of the enchanting silhouette formed by the graceful tower of the palace, the filigree-like parapets of the Court Church and the sturdily German dome of the Frauenkirche is an experience that never grows stale. The city of baroque art and the capital of Augustus the Strong has remained true to its traditions, and its appearance of stately gaiety [. . .]. Even the noise of the traffic seems agreeably muffled here.[138]

Following earlier examples, these descriptions were always illustrated with the iconic views of Dresden's cityscape and famous architectural sites. When Germany hosted the Summer Olympics in nearby Berlin in 1936, international visitors of the Games were specifically targeted with a brochure that pictured a train traveling toward Dresden's cityscape and proclaimed: "Berlin-Dresden in only 1 1/2 hours."[139] Such campaigns were successful. By 1937, international tourism in Dresden had increased to 63,872, which was still less, however, than the 71,241 international visitors that Dresden hosted in 1930.[140]

Shortly before the Summer Olympics in 1936, Germany held the World's Recreation Congress in Hamburg, a meeting that was used to advertise Germany as an international travel destination. Germany was showcasing its Kraft durch Freude program, for which the former American Olympic Committee president and president of the International Board for the Recreation Congress, Gustavus Town Kirby, offered much praise in his opening remarks. The meeting's official guide includes descriptions of the various areas of Germany. The Gau Saxony is, not surprisingly, represented by a photograph of the Dresden old town cityscape with the Augustus Bridge. The description, however, de-emphasizes the Italian artists and architects who had been working in Dresden and instead portrays the city as an expression of "German genius" in building, art, music, literature and thought: "All these ingenious men of Upper-Saxon blood reflect true Germanness; they mirror creations bound to race and folk."[141] Such a reinterpretation of the basis for Dresden's cultural significance was, of course, in accordance with the National Socialist ideology, but its effect went even further. Since Dresden's cultural import was nationally and internationally accepted, reclaiming the city as a purely German achievement but a European treasure, and reading it as a racial success, could both help confirm the National Socialists' claims of superiority and establish them as part of a history of unbroken greatness and cultural achievement within Germany.

Even during the first war years, Dresden was still framed as a touristic attraction, also beyond Germany, albeit by particularly targeting an audience in the sympathizing countries of Italy and Spain. To that end, the magazine *Deutschland—Zeitschrift für Industrie, Handel und Schiffahrt* (Germany—Magazine for Industry, Trade, and Shipping) published a special issue on Dresden in 1940, which appeared in German, English, Italian, and Spanish. The magazine was meant to encourage tourism as well as international trade and economic exchange. The ongoing war is not mentioned. Many pages concentrate on Dresden as a cultural city, featuring traditional images and descriptions. In addition, however, the publication also highlights Dresden's attractiveness as a viable trade partner. The writers repeatedly perform a careful balancing act, trying to leave intact Dresden's cultural and artistic reputation but also pointing to its economic development:

> The city has preserved all those assets which have been responsible for its high international prestige. Neither the charm of its unique cityscape nor the matchless beauty of its surroundings has in any way been affected by its rise to industrial leadership [. . .]. Industry and scientific and artistic achievements [. . .] harmoniously develop to their full potential, each as part of different impulses and abilities of one and the same body."[142]

This balancing act, in which industrial development is interpreted as part of the larger Gesamtkunstwerk Dresden, also extends to politics. While the political system is repeatedly praised for its important innovations and impulses both in culture and industry, the authors also make sure to emphasize the unchanging nature of Dresden and its meaning. In fact, the publication ends on this note of consistency that makes up Dresden's essence. The magazine, with a nod to its Italian audience, concludes by evoking the idea of Dresden as an Italian city of the north with the quotation from an enthusiastic traveler from the nineteenth century:

> The romantic passionate sigh, which at the Elbe searches with its soul that land where the lemon blossoms bloom, is as timeless as it is unspoiled. It is the feeling of fully giving oneself over to absolute beauty, a feeling which sooner or later arises in everyone strolling through Dresden, even today, when a different banner flies above the towers of this wonderful city.[143]

Fig. 17. *Dresden, Deutschland. Zeitschrift für Industrie, Handel, Schiffahrt* (1940). (Verlag Adolf Ernst Schulze und Co., Schnackenburg.)

Similarly, but for a German audience, a *Wochenschau* newsreel from November 1941 employs a touristic gaze with Dresden as part of the series "Bilder aus der Heimat" (Pictures from the Homeland).[144] Even though Germany was by now in its third year of war, the inviting commercial and leisure aspects still characterized the short film. The newsreel contains an "animated postcard" from Dresden, in which characteristic idyllic views of the city are highlighted. It begins with a panning shot from across the river Elbe onto the cityscape of the Old Town, then presents closeups of the Semper opera building, the Katholische Hofkirche, and finally the Frauenkirche. The following shot transports the audience onto the viewing balcony of the town hall tower (the same one featured in the famous 1945 photograph by Richard Peter), where two tourists lean on the balustrade, enjoying the panorama. Then the camera adopts their point of view and slowly pans over the city and its surroundings. These clips were widely shown in German movie theaters as well as to soldiers at the front. They were part of a propaganda effort that was to link soldiers to their home, overcoming any possible disconnect, and at the same time strengthen the civilian audience in their emotional bond to their German nation.[145]

On the surface this clip might be one of the few documents allowing a last glimpse at the undestroyed Dresden with its architectural icons and within its beautiful surroundings. Such a view, however, would be buying into the National Socialist propaganda machine, which here showcases Dresden as part of the idyllic peaceful *Heimat.* In fact, as we will discuss in more detail in chapter 4, the destruction of architectural treasures had already started well before the city was severely bombed in February 1945. There is no reference in the film clip that by then the Dresden Synagogue—a part of the Old Town panorama and designed by master builder Gottfried Semper, the same architect who had constructed the much-praised opera building—had been burned to the ground during the November pogroms in 1938. Its rubble had been quickly cleared and the building had disappeared from the Dresden panorama and from most people's memories as if it had never existed. The clip reveals the possible dark side of a collective mindscape that overpowers actual reality. The city's meaning can stay stagnant instead of reflecting the developments and changes both in the city body and the people who live there. The missing synagogue in Dresden's panorama and the meaning of this circumstance are not recognized since the building had always been located within a blind spot of Dresden's image based on its eighteenth-century appearance.

By applying concepts from urban and tourism studies, this chapter has shown that the reasons the Dresden bombing was universally condemned and could be so easily used by political groups to create propagandistic discourses are found in the construction of the material city and its idealized identity. Dresden's development into a highly symbolic place as an icon of beauty and culture was, starting with its designation as the seat of the elector of Saxony, a carefully planned and deliberately constructed process. Its imageability and symbolic and performative function were built as declarative elements into Dresden's city morphology. The Saxon court developed core values for Dresden's identity based on those they associated with prestigious Italian cities of high culture that were admired throughout Europe. From architecture to art collections to festivities, Dresden served as a performative space to erase its reputation as a provincial court. With the rise in travel among the German and international bourgeoisie, a feedback loop was created that spread Dresden's fame and its core values particularly through visual means, but also through travel narratives, guides, and specific marketing campaigns. It established a collectively shared visual mindscape and meaning of the city.

Much of the local population also internalized and identified with these values, as they allowed them to feel unique and distinct from other Germans and at the same time part of a cosmopolitan community. Furthermore, residents started to profit more and more from the rise of tourism as an economic sector, which deepened their commitment to defining Dresden as a unique cultural haven. The city became an icon through the unreality of its appearance and the collective perception of a specific aura; it was viewed as a beautiful painting of a Baroque cityscape come to life, in harmony with itself and with the surrounding landscape. The hypercity of Dresden with all its symbolic levels thus defined the way the actual city was viewed: Dresden's identity was an idealization, framed in a way that included only elements that complemented its symbolic image, but that excluded others that might challenge or change this identity. Such framing was also continuously reinforced by the preconceived expectations of travelers and by the strong interconnection of the residents' identity with Dresden's cultural significance. Economic, societal, and political developments of the nineteenth and twentieth centuries remained unmarked on the Dresden mindscape. As we have seen in chapter 1, the blind spots that arose through these idealizations and framings made it possible to engage in a selective remembrance culture after the end of the Second World War. Dresden's political embrace of National Socialism and Dresden's significant role in the German war effort could be downplayed and a narrative of destruction marked by victimhood and loss arose. Yet Dresden was not only defined by absence, loss, and destruction after the war, but its prewar reputation remained. As chapter 3 will demonstrate, despite the architectural losses Dresden was nevertheless presented as a beautiful city, an important travel destination, and an international cultural center.

CHAPTER 3

Dresden after 1945
Past, Present, and Future in Image and Imagination

The beginning of Germany's so-called Zero Hour is usually linked to the country's capitulation in May 1945; in Dresden, however, February 13, 1945, is perceived as the consequential turning point in the war experience, and destruction and capitulation are conflated. February 13 has been described as a discursive caesura between celebrating Dresden as the Baroque city and the mourning and nostalgia in response to its loss.[1] I propose, however, that the discourse about Dresden in the postwar era reflects instead a split of the already established narrative of Dresden as a unique cultural icon and attractive travel destination into two pathways of memory and meaning, which reflect the traumatic dichotomy of mourning and denial: On the one hand, a narrative of rupture and loss based on Dresden's destruction during the air war arose, which is the foundation for Dresden's largely accepted victim narrative outlined in chapter 1; on the other hand, the discourse of the city's identity as a unique cultural icon, its exceptional position within Germany and Europe, and its attractiveness for residents and travelers alike, as explored in chapter 2, still continued and came to be connected to reconstruction. The East German socialist government tried to frame each narrative in a way that would most benefit its postwar political positioning in Europe and its vision for the future. As I will demonstrate, these official discourses created variations in meaning about Dresden's destruction and reconstruction that could not be fully reconciled into one coherent story and increasingly diverged from the way many residents interpreted Dresden's future within these two narrative strands.

As we have seen, the narratives about Dresden have a strong symbolic component often expressed and shared via visual representations of certain city views that became part of a collective cultural memory. It is thus not surprising that visuals, such as Richard Peter's famous "View from the Town Hall Tower" played an important role in the postwar representation of what was portrayed as a barbarian crime against an innocent place of culture and a symbol for the devastating consequences of capitalism. In support of this rhetoric, it was of great interest for the Socialist Unity Party of Germany (Sozialistische Einheitspartei Deutschlands, SED) to emphasize the horrors of the bombing and what it had done to the city. To express this loss, particularly in the time immediately after the war, comparative photography of Dresden became an important tool. The pairings of pictures from before and after February 1945 make visible the rupture and loss that many felt regarding the city. The viewer oscillates continuously between the undestroyed and the destroyed, unable to see one without the other. The trauma of the event is inscribed in the visual traces of material destruction, as well as the lingering images of what had been there, but the event itself lies in the unpictured space between the two photographs. It makes it possible to broaden the gap to include the entire period of 1933–1945, so that questions of responsibility and guilt can be suppressed.

Yet while the German Democratic Republic (GDR) used Dresden's architectural and artistic history for its official anti-Western propaganda, the country's socialist philosophy was suspicious of Dresden's past function as a royal seat with its representative architecture. It thus relied strongly on Soviet planning principles in rebuilding. To harmonize the past with the reconstruction, party leaders in Dresden continued to insist on Dresden's significance as a national and international cultural icon and tourist attraction, which was now, however, to be achieved by rebuilding Dresden as an ideal socialist city. At the same time, local communal feelings in Dresden strongly favored historic rebuilding over the approaches of the new politics.[2] The tensions between the local community rooted in the past and the official policies of the SED defined by a vision for the future finally led to a mixed approach. Dresden was to contain several historical reconstructions as markers of its history, yet they were to be contextualized as part of a socialist urban structure. To find acceptance for the socialist rebuilding, it was communicated within the visual traditions of the comparative before-and-after images already established. The government hoped to complete the pairs of photographs with a third image, suggesting a triptych of life, sorrow, and healing of Dresden and its people. They outlined, displayed, and praised the official plans and results of the rebuilding efforts in local brochures and national and international travel guides. To this end, socialist buildings of

Dresden were framed as tourist attractions in their own right and marketed as signs of the continued significance of Dresden as a national and international tourist destination.

The publications by the city government of Dresden and later by the centralized East German tourism publisher, as well as West German travel books such as the popular *Merian* guides, show the developments and shifts over time of the parallel narratives of Dresden as victim and as functional cultural icon. I will demonstrate here and in the following chapters how, despite the efforts by the GDR to build an affinity between the idea of Dresden and socialism, the historic city silhouette from before February 1945 continued to be identified by most as the authentic Dresden. This traditional view could all the more succeed since the propagandistically used narrative of destruction, which idolized the past Dresden as a way to criticize and demonize the West, continuously undercut the official message to view the socialist rebuilt Dresden as the attractive and culturally meaningful successor to the pre-1945 city. In fact, the attempts at socialist rebuilding in Dresden even strengthened this opposition to the official approach: While the rubble pictures still held within them the possibility of re-erecting the historical cityscape in its entirety, the socialist rebuilding defied this indexicality in a way that was perceived as inauthentic. It did not represent the established mindscape of Dresden as a historical architectural ensemble, which was continuously reinforced in remembrance rituals or when trying to prove East Germany's legitimacy to the world by highlighting its care for Germany's heritage sites. Dresden residents also enjoyed some of the comforts brought about by the new rebuilding measures applied in the city, such as modern living spaces. Yet within the dichotomy of the two narratives of Dresden and in their search for a postwar identity, many residents engaged in imagining an alternative to the official view of the third panel for the Dresden rebuilding triptych, namely the city's total resurrection in its historic form.

Early Photo Books of Dresden's Destruction

The first comparative picture book of Dresden after 1945 was put together by photographer Kurt Schaarschuch as *Bilddokument Dresden: 1933–1945* (Picture Document Dresden: 1933–1945). It was published as early as December 1945, several years before Richard Peter's collection with the iconic "View from the Town Hall Tower" discussed in the first chapter.[3] *Bilddokument Dresden* is made up almost entirely of pairs of photographs from before and after the devastating bombing. It privileges panoramic views or

Fig. 18. Schaarschuch, *Bilddokument Dresden* (1945), Frauenkirche 1933–45. (Kurt Schaarschuch, courtesy of Stadtmuseum Dresden.)

famous architectural sites such as the opera building or the Frauenkirche with Luther statue. The pictures showing Dresden in ruins mostly stem from July 1945, earlier than many other photographs from this time. But the pictures' counterparts, the photographs of the undestroyed Dresden, were only programmatically dated as "1933."[4] In fact, Schaarschuch had taken these pictures throughout the 1930s.[5]

National Socialism remains absent in the photographs, and the collection suggests a world in which Nazi rule has been abolished. It indexes instead the destruction caused by the Allies as the most pressing problem faced by society after 1945. The preface of the collection by Kurt Liebermann, the director of the news office of the socialist city council, frames the photographic pairs accordingly. He implores the citizens to rebuild Dresden in the spirit of the new political reality and brushes aside the question of guilt among residents by assigning responsibility solely to a small group of "Nazi war agitators."[6] The ruins themselves take center stage and request action: "the rubble of one of the most beautiful cities in the world calls the forces willing to rebuild to join the new reconstruction."[7] This rally call, which tries to guide the reader in imagining a positive future, is echoed in the last photograph in the collection, overwritten with ". . . Despite It All, Rebuilding 1945."[8] It pictures a worker who attacks the rubble with a pneumatic hammer. The worker's figure in the foreground overpowers the ruined Dresden cityscape arising behind him on the other side of the Elbe. Together, the preface and the last image frame the collection and suggest a direction for the material and social future of Dresden within the confines of a new political self-definition.

Bilddokument Dresden was so successful that 120,000 copies of the book had been printed in several editions by the end of 1946.[9] This high demand and supply is impressive given the lack of paper and the tough economic situation of the immediate postwar months. Furthermore, the buyers of Scharschuch's book lived and worked among the very ruins displayed on the pages, which would seem to make the pictures of the rubble unnecessary. These circumstances suggest that the publication and its comparative structure offered a sense of orientation to its readers after their world had entirely changed. Media historian Tom Allbeson sees such photo books as both providing the idea of a "record for posterity" and "a crucial site, where individual experience and collective memories interacted and the meanings of the bombing war and of the postwar urban environment were negotiated."[10] The before-and-after photographic pairings offer these spaces through their segmented representation. While both pictures together point to a major event, this event itself remains absent. As visual scholars Jordan Bear and Kate Palmer Albers point out, "They depend as much upon the evidentiary aspects of visible temporal bookends as they do upon acknowledging that the more powerful way of articulating the central event is to leave it unseen. The before-and-after pair relies on the imaginative participation of the viewer."[11] The photographic pairs also mirror the experiences of the survivors who have trouble with describing or representing the bombing experience. At the same time, however, by leaving the event itself absent, it is possible to negotiate the causes of the destruction without contextualizing the events historically and politically. They fall outside of time so that uncomfortable truths about the Nazi years, but also the new political situation, can remain hidden in this gap.

So unlike Liebermann's preface to the collection that outlines an interpretation of the events, Schaarschuch performs such negotiations in the presented pairs. They do not include references to the National Socialist past, but they also do not point to any future direction.[12] Instead, with the selection of the images and the contrasts he sets up, Schaarschuch allows additional layers of meaning to arise that break through the political framing within which they are presented by the foreword and the final photograph. Standing in for all, the toppled Luther statue in front of the ruins of the Frauenkirche bemoans the loss of German cultural achievements in an uncultured time. Similarly, while most images from before the destruction show a busy city with cars, bikes, shoppers, visitors, and children, Dresden lies predominantly empty and dead in the photographs from 1945. The many images of passageways, streets, and staircases from before the bombings are almost continuously contrasted with heaps of rubble that do not suggest a clear inner or outer path for Germany's or Dresden's future at this point after the war. Schaarschuch presents a world in which time has stopped: the compilation includes various pictures that feature damaged clocks, such as on church towers and the town hall. Even the Zwinger's famous carillon with its strings of Meissen porcelain bells is reduced to a ruined relic that is barely recognizable.

As we have seen, the heritage sites in Dresden had not only been understood as representations of the city's cultural value but served as a stage set for the forming and performing of the residents' place identity and sense of belonging. This "transactional relationship" between the people and the place made each an active agent of the other's identity.[13] Without such "embodied placemaking" between the population and its environment, life in the ruins was experienced as disorienting, chaotic, and impossible to navigate.[14] The before-and-after images in Schaarschuch's book, however, affixed each pictured ruinscape to the well-known places they had once been. The before images provided a space in which viewers could glimpse a feeling of belonging without being implicated in the unrepresented change that had occurred. By oscillating back and forth between the photographic pairs, the residents were able to reassemble the most important fragments of the former city. The process projected a sense of order onto the inner and outer turmoil they experienced, and it was possible to preserve some spatial continuity. Projecting the old cityscape onto the rubble and nostalgically imagining its resurrection allowed the population to retain a sense of their place-bound identity.[15]

As political references remained mostly absent, residents of Dresden could at this point redefine themselves outside of any political expectations, guilt, or responsibility by retaining a sense of collective local identity based on Dresden's prewar narrative. In fact, with the famous cityscape lost, the comparative approach could support and even heighten Dresden's prewar iconicity. It helped increase the inner emotional attachment to the cityscape that after the war needed to be imagined rather than perceived. Before the destruction, the idea of Dresden as solely culturally significant was dependent on a careful framing of the city's image, which excluded the many visible signs that the city's growth in the nineteenth and twentieth centuries made it into an important industrial location. Yet for those who wanted to peek beyond the predetermined frames, the industrial and modern developments had been there to see. After the destruction, however, Dresden's cityscape was defined only by what had been preserved in dominant images and representations that had helped establish the mindscape of the purely cultural city.

Close to the center of the collection, in a pair of photographs featuring artists, Schaarschuch provides aesthetic commentary on these post-bombing and postwar conditions.[16] Art historian Ludger Dehrenthal sees them as an invitation to mourn the loss of worthy artistic motifs, but Schaarschuch here also speaks to artists' and regular citizens' central role in processing the events.[17] Titled "Dresden's Painters," they suggest that in the past and present, the city only rises fully through creative processing.[18]

In the earlier photograph on the left side of the book, the painter's canvas partially obstructs our view of the actual cityscape, which we observe being crafted on it. In the second photograph, an artist sits amidst a sea of rubble.[19] We see a specific ruin, which lies beyond the frame of the photograph, only as it issues from the painter's brush. Schaarschuch suggests that

Fig. 19. Schaarschuch, *Bilddokument Dresden* (1945), Dresden's Painters. (Kurt Schaarschuch, courtesy of Stadtmuseum Dresden.)

it is through this mediated access to the city, through the selection of certain frames, that the viewer grasps Dresden's true meaning, former splendor, and cultural importance. The photographer points to the loss of cultural heritage, represented in the painting by the ruin of the symbolic Frauenkirche. He inscribes himself in the Dresden tradition of visual encoding and stresses that this approach involves obligatory mediation. At the same time, Schaarschuch emphasizes that he views this approach as authentic, since the core of Dresden's identity can be understood from 1945 onwards only through this very process of mediation. While in the past one could take in the city and its representations from a distance, the second picture, a close-up of the artist, implores viewers to take on a different perspective and use their own mediative powers. The title "Bilddokument" itself implies that objectivity ("Dokument") is achieved here only through the photographic lens, but the comparative structure of the pictorial arrangements captures the affective reaction to the changes.

Richard Peter's famous collection of (Dresden) rubble photography discussed in chapter 1 makes similar claims to objectivity, but with less self-reflection about the mediated nature of the views it presents.[20] Unlike Schaarschuch, it neither dramatizes the various layers of translation from actual cityscape to picture book nor explores the possibilities of place making. Peter encourages the viewer to feel that the situation itself was responsible for any emotional reaction, not the photographer who took, composed, and published them. As a convinced communist, Peter saw the photographs as a vehicle in support of the political mission of the newly founded GDR: to rebuild the country in new terms and with fresh possibilities of emotional attachment. He also translated this approach into the title of his work, which turned the camera into the active agent: *Dresden: Eine Kamera klagt an (Dresden: A Camera Accuses).*

Peter nevertheless steers the reception. In chapter 1 we saw how the iconic image from the Town Hall Tower was carefully and deliberately composed and how the photographer uses symbols to direct the viewer's perception. Allbeson even detects "a sense of anger" in Peter's work, in contrast to Schaarschuch's melancholic mood.[21] The cover design is loud and striking; on a black background, the word "Dresden" appears in large, stretched, flaming-red capital letters which fill almost the entire jacket, emphasizing the shock value of the content and mirroring the blaze of the firestorm. It is overlaid with the rest of the title in white letters, "eine Kamera klagt an." The positioning of the subtitle on top of the word "Dresden" mirrors the camera's role as an intermediary and catalyst that links the reader/viewer with the

Fig. 20. "This Book for Every German" (1950). (Photograph by Richard Peter. © bpk Bildagentur / Deutsches Historisches Museum Berlin / Art Resource, NY.)

realities captured in the photographs. Peter does not clearly identify who or what is being accused. Yet the rhetoric fits into the East German political discourse of the 1950s, which emphasized terror and war as part of the Western agenda, while a wish for peace dominated the East.

In this spirit, when the photo book became available, its publisher started an advertisement campaign, which introduced the book as "Required Reading for Every German." The poster features a replica of the book cover in the middle; it is surrounded by images from Peter's work that blend together through blurred edges. The photographs display Dresden both before and immediately after its destruction. On the right edge of the poster looms the Schreitmüller figure, seemingly recommending and handing the book depicted in the middle to the people looking at the poster. Directly below, a picture features Dresden's rebuilt town hall, which was not only the home of the sculpture, but also the seat of the new socialist city government. By showing images from before and after the destruction, as well as after rebuilding, combined with a slogan that emphasizes all of Germany, Dresden serves as an important symbol for the beginnings (a country in ruins), but also for the future (a community working together, a commitment to the people and their needs) of a new state that was just about to emerge.

Dresden could function as a strong signal beyond the East German context. The emphasis on "every German" implies that the collection is educational for readers within and beyond the borders of what had been the Soviet-controlled zone and by 1949 had become the German Democratic Republic. At this point East Germany still evoked the possibility of a unified Germany that was to be strictly neutral and demilitarized, which went hand-in-hand with public displays of the strong devotion of East Germany to peace. This rhetoric suggested that the West, by not agreeing to this plan, showed a lack of commitment to a peaceful future in Europe and a lack of desire to break with old fascist structures and ideas. On the anniversaries of the bombing of Dresden, this call for a unified Germany in the name of peace was a dominant feature in speeches, on banners and in newspaper reports, underscoring how the destiny of Dresden was serving as a message and lesson to all of Germany.[22]

Indeed, Peter's book was seen as a poignant tool to justify and support the GDR's existence and mission. *Dresden: Eine Kamera klagt an* was published with a print run of fifty thousand in high-end copper print, again remarkable for this time of still scarce resources.[23] Part of the reason for this expensive edition might have been that the city used the book as a prop. It was the custom of the city government to utilize it as an official present for Western visitors and journalists. Accordingly, when the American *Life* journalist Will Lang visited Dresden and the city government in the 1950s, he also went home with a copy of Peter's book in his luggage.[24]

Peter draws heavily on the already established visual archive of the city. While a vast majority of the photographs in the collection were taken after Dresden's destruction and are not paired with earlier photographs, many of these pictures still invite comparisons to famous pre-bombing views. Moreover, the collection begins with three atmospheric prewar night shots of the Hofkirche, the castle, and the Augustus Bridge, a photograph of the Zwinger, and a panoramic shot of the entire cityscape visible along the Elbe. They greatly reinforce this framework of mental comparison. These early photographs that feature the soft light of lanterns create a romantic, beautiful, and calm atmosphere. Such illumination also signals peacetime; starting with the

Fig. 21. Richard Peter, *Dresden: Eine Kamera klagt an* (1950). (Reprinted by permission of SLUB/Deutsche Fotothek, Richard Peter, sen.)

war, cities were put under strict blackout orders so as not to provide easily identifiable targets for enemy planes. When looking at these photographs, the viewers were very much aware that the next time Dresden was lit up, the city was ablaze with the all-consuming firestorm.

In Schaarschuch's publication the destruction and catastrophe are contained within the frame of a positive future, but only barely so. Such an optimistic outlook is relegated to a poem at the beginning and the depiction of a worker at the end, while the pairs of photographs do not indicate opportunities. Peter, however, offers a much stronger element of hope.

In Peter's *Dresden: Eine Kamera klagt an*, a sizable final section under the heading "Rebuilding" concludes the photo book with an upbeat tone: It features pictures of people working at clearing debris, creating order, and reestablishing a functional cityscape.[25] The photographs suggest that men and women, old and young, all take part committedly, communally, and humbly in rebuilding Dresden and their new lives, even if it means burdening themselves with back-breaking work. The book became a way to motivate such volunteerism for their own and their children's future. For example, in a photo series in 1954 on children born in 1945, Peter's photo book became

Fig. 22. Child with Richard Peter's book, pointing to photos picturing reconstruction efforts (1954). (Photograph by Erich Höhne and Erich Pohl. Reprinted by permission of SLUB/ Deutsche Fotothek.)

a key prop when a nine-year-old, wearing the blue neck scarf of the socialist youth organization Young Pioneers, proudly points to the pictures that display the people and state's efforts to clean, repair, and rebuild the city.

The section also includes illustrations of already finished rebuilding projects, such as the town hall and the theater, one the central space for the new government, the other a space for sharing in cultural experiences. The images are thus filled with signs indicating a new political, social, and cultural environment and suggest a positive future under the socialist leadership.[26] With its arrangement, *Dresden: Eine Kamera klagt an* tells a story of destruction and resurrection, a symbolism reflecting its time of production, which coincided with the official founding of the German Democratic Republic.

Rebuilding and Marketing Dresden as Socialist City and Travel Icon

After the founding of the GDR, publication aims focusing on Dresden began to shift more and more from openly mourning the losses or documenting the past and the ruined present to voicing positive rebuilding messages and emphasizing the future city. Increasingly, the theme of the bombing raids and their devastating effect was officially reserved for the anniversaries of the firestorm, when newspapers, commemorations, and other events highlighted the destruction of Dresden as an unmatched cultural loss caused by the fascist capitalist system. "Fascism" was also evoked when defining the future of the city since socialist society was characterized as the antithesis to fascism. The definition of fascism, however, often remained vague without reference to the historical realities of Nazism in Dresden or Germany. Marketing Dresden's rebuilding as a success story of continuing Dresden's cultural significance as an artistic center of world format could help lend legitimacy to the new socialist state, both within and outside of the GDR, could shift the focus onto the future, curb the melancholy about the lost past, and evade questions regarding the Nazi years.

City celebrations, brochures, and booklets in the 1950s and 1960s emphasize such continued national and international appeal of postwar Dresden. With this approach the Socialist Party also tried to provide opportunities for Dresden citizens to reorient their identity. The discourse changed progressively to the present-day Dresden, thus widening the perspective from its historic morphology to include the rebuilding of the city in a socialist style. The heritage sites were defined as individual units, not as an ensemble, and were rhetorically integrated as islands of history within a quintessentially socialist city. This way, the historical cityscape was not an expression of a noble system any longer, and the rebuilding was presented as reflecting the construction of a socialist society. The hope was that the residents' pronounced place identity would merge with the new political order and its urban representation since it also emphasized Dresden's unique character and cultural significance. In the discourse about Dresden, the relationship of the signifier and signified rhetorically remained the same, and even the indexicality, which made the cityscape central, theoretically remained constant. But the city's index itself, in structure and makeup, changed significantly.

The booklet *Du und Deine Stadt: 5 Jahre Aufbauarbeit der Stadtverwaltung Dresden* (You and Your City: 5 Years of Construction by the Dresden City Government), published in the fall of 1950 by the Dresden city council, reflects the tension between these two attitudes toward Dresden, one domi-

Fig. 23. *You and Your City: Five Years of Reconstruction* (1950). (Der Rat der Stadt Dresden.)

nated by the past, the other by the future.[27] The title emphasizes progress as well as the role of each resident in this development. The cover illustration further supports this message. While it utilizes conventional symbols, including the Meißen lion from Dresden's traditional coat of arms, the design makes it clear that a new era has begun. Not the city colors of black and yellow, but red dominates. Additionally, the lion is turning to the right instead of left, as if toward the future of Dresden. Instead of aggressively roaring, the lion is pictured with a trowel, busily putting brick upon brick. The coat of arms and its noble roots are dissolved, suggesting that Dresden is now writing a new history for itself, one of purposeful togetherness, industry, and without class distinctions. The title also consciously uses "Aufbau," (construction) not "Wiederaufbau" (reconstruction/rebuilding), for describing building activities, which implies not a re-emergence of the past, but instead a focus on the future.[28]

Yet when opening the brochure, another layer of the Dresden postwar discourse emerges with a second title page named *Dresden: einst und jetzt* (Dresden: Then and Now).[29] A pre-1945 night photograph of the castle and Hofkirche reflected in the river Elbe and an aerial view of the undestroyed Dresden illustrate this cover: "Dresden in the drama of lights."[30] A series of paired photographs of Dresden's premier heritage sites from before and after 1945 follow.[31] The positive message from the outer title, highlighting progress, is, like the positive foreword in Schaarschuch's photo book, relegated to the background by the brochure's inner title, which emphasizes the comparison between a beautiful past and a desolate present.

The use of two title pages illustrates the predicament Dresden found itself in. Politically, the city government wanted to draw attention to what the rebuilding afforded the Dresden residents, to highlight the wide involvement of the community in these efforts and the possibility of finding new ways of place identity through this progress. Yet most residents still suffered from the loss of their old city environment, which had been an integral part of their identity and had regulated their sense of comfort in the world.[32] Since the heritage sites had offered them a feeling of belonging, their destruction had shattered this security, leaving behind only a nostalgic imprint to restore a sense of well-being.[33]

The structure of this early booklet reflects the attempt by the socialist city government to present ways for citizens to overcome their melancholy. To get to the point of embracing a positive outlook and build affective attachment to the new cityscape, the before-and-after pairings had to be expanded to include pictures representing the future. In this triptych structure, the first two panels offered a possibility to work through the shock of destruction of the bombing night, as well as the everyday environment the population found itself in. They provided a shared experience and allowed readers to mourn the demise of the icon Dresden. The third panel offered the opportunity to embrace the rebuilding efforts in accordance with the political goals of the government. In this sense, the booklet did not only show the results of five years of material rebuilding efforts, but it also tried to model the path to rebuilding a new communal place attachment defined by the future of the socialist city instead of its past. Accordingly, in a later section of the book, photographic before-and-after pairs contrast the ruins with rebuilding successes, while the original first state of the historic Dresden has been dropped.

In 1956, Dresden held the 750-year celebration of its founding. The events included a parade, concerts, plays, and special exhibits. Some were more, some less directly political, yet the planning committee strongly emphasized the educational aspect of the festivities: "the citizens of our city will become familiar with the deep connection of the 750-year-celebration and the national and social fight of the German people."[34] Such an approach, however, necessitated a reinterpretation of the past by retelling developments as part of a socialist future. As the planning guide emphasized, even in its typesetting: *"What the progressive part of our citizens at all times in history hoped and longed for, what they fought and sacrificed for, has become reality in the German Democratic Republic, in the Dresden of the workers and peasants."*[35]

While the festivities celebrated history, they were nevertheless supposed to present an optimistic, forward-looking city, country, and citizenry that was not caught up in an "escape into the past."[36] Companies, schools, and other groups were expected to send their members to participate in the programming.[37] This way not only would there be a large crowd available to create impressive photos and films for marketing Dresden and the event, but the residents would be performing physically a newly provided identity within the material spaces arising around them. These spaces were not only characterized by socialist architecture, but the urban environment was similarly occupied by communist street names, socialist symbols, monuments, and banners.[38] By publicly performing Dresden's cultural significance within its 1956 cityscape, the new direction for Dresden's future taken under socialist leadership was supposed to be communicated as a natural progression from the city's past to a (better) present and future.

Most floats in the parade tried to display the societal progress since 1945, but some also included historical show elements, particularly from the Augustan era. But they often highlighted the suffering of the workers and

Fig. 24. Dresden celebrates its 750th anniversary with a parade (1956). (Photograph by Erich Höhne and Erich Pohl. Reprinted by permission of SLUB/Deutsche Fotothek.)

farmers for the ruling class's gain and glory.[39] Yet many residents felt a sense of pride and ownership concerning the cultural achievements of the period, including a strong affinity to its noble rulers, and negative representations proved unpopular and turnout among locals were not up to expectations.[40] Similarly, a special commission had been formed to attract foreigners, and large banners greeted "visitors from east and west."[41] But the outcome of these efforts was also disappointing. As the unofficial concluding report of the city council notes, "the expected tourist crowds did not come."[42]

Yet one part of the anniversary program was able to gather much attention not only on a local and national level, but even internationally. When the Soviet Union had returned part of the city's famous art collection, which it had confiscated after the war, it was decided to display the works in their traditional home, and the Semper Art Gallery was rebuilt.[43] The exhibit opened to the public in the completed east wing during the 750th anniversary celebrations and the event was widely reported in the national and international press, including in the *New York Times*.[44] The gallery building formed an ensemble with the Zwinger, whose traditional rebuilding had begun immediately after the war with overwhelming support from the popu-

Fig. 25. Saxony's exuberant August the Strong and his court jester Joseph Fröhlich (1956). (Photograph by Erich Höhne and Erich Pohl. Reprinted by permission of SLUB/ Deutsche Fotothek.)

lation, including financially via a lottery.[45] Even when pressures increased to abandon reconstructing heritage sites, the rebuilding of the Zwinger was continued until it was completed in 1963.[46]

Despite the failure to attract many international visitors, the anniversary events still represented the first attempt since 1945 to press ahead in reclaiming the label of a prized tourist spot for Dresden. In the following decades, a string of official publications marketed Dresden and its city development as tied to its previous reputation as a famous travel destination. The past was ultimately presented as a precursor to a projected future. With this approach, the temporal direction of trying to define present experiences was reversed. While Dresden was traditionally identified by its history, in these publications (and the GDR in general) the future was to determine the

Fig. 26. Rebuilding of the Semper Galleries at the Zwinger (1956). (Photograph by Erich Höhne and Erich Pohl. Reprinted by permission of SLUB/Deutsche Fotothek.)

present sense of being, even though such future was "an inherently rhetorical construction." Yet it is often precisely "the idea of the future" that can develop powerful ways of "holding groups together by promising an eventual embodiment of collective values."[47] This way, Dresden's development could be seen as progressively leading to a future instead of judging the present through the lens of the past.

Rhetorical framing took on an important role in this context. The planning of individual rebuilt heritage sites and cultural highlights such as the art galleries were a nod to Dresden's past identity and Germany's cultural achievements, while a vision of communally engaging in socialist construction was to evoke a positive and attractive future environment without noble and bourgeois suppression. Within this discourse, heritage sites and collections are presented as serving the people by having become "real socialistic establishments for the edification of the entire population."[48] The sites' meaning has thus been changed to one expressing socialist cultural achievements, and the socialist city remains a cultural icon in the official discourse: "the new Dresden is one of the most important towns of culture and art in the world."[49] The guides thus try to rhetorically reform the way Dresden was viewed by redefining the place of Dresden's past in the city's character and by linking it to a future local identity. By insisting on Dresden's continuing cultural significance and attraction for tourists, not just based on its history but also its present state and the plans for its future, city leaders hoped to represent socialism as harmony and progress instead of emphasizing a radical caesura. Dresden in ruins was a setback, but according to this interpretation, such setbacks had not stopped the positive progression of Dresden over the past 750 years.

Such rhetoric, however, was a difficult sell to a population that grew up with a collective identity based on achievements of the past, which they also understood as the elements of their identity that differentiated them from others. Furthermore, as shown in chapter 1, on the anniversaries of the bombing, this discourse of a lost past was foundational for the propaganda against the West. During these anniversaries, the past was elevated as the defining force for the present and the bombing was presented as a deep rupture. So while during the 750-year celebrations in 1956, Dresden was officially characterized as moving forward into the future and as a place in which the long-term vision of an equal and just society was being realized, during the tenth anniversary of the bombing in 1955 and all subsequent anniversaries, the city remained defined by its history and the loss of "irreplaceable cultural treasures sacred to the entire world."[50] In the commemoration rhetoric Dresdners are presented as natural leaders in peace activism against the warmongering West because of the losses they endured. This characterization demarcates their purpose and goals through the experience of a lost past.

Such contradictory messaging continued. By 1958, almost ten years into the establishment of an East German state, the Sachsenverlag published a lavish coffee-table book of pictures simply titled *Dresden*, which serves as an excellent example of the attempt to restrict the memory of the bombing to times of commemoration. In the photo book, the focus has clearly shifted away from picturing the destruction to emphasizing Dresden's revived beauty with both historic and modern sites.[51] It contains almost two hundred images of Dresden's cityscape, from heritage sites to pictures of post-1945 apartment houses, shops, factories, and cultural venues. The publication aims at presenting Dresden as an attractive, fully functional city, even if for that purpose it mixes pre-bombing pictures with new ones. The photographs contain sparse captions and no precise dates so that it is unclear whether photographs displaying heritage sites show Dresden at the time of publication or before February 13, 1945.

In stark contrast to earlier picture books, the ruins of Dresden only feature prominently on one page spread.[52] The image is paired with a photograph of a memorial stone at the Heidefriedhof, which had been erected in 1954 to honor the bombing victims.[53] This photograph thus frames the bombing as a historical event. While the city brochure on reconstruction from 1950 suggested a visual path to the readers to work through the bombing and its effects, in this case the process is presented as completed and the experience as overcome. The photo shows how memorialization was at this point taking place at specifically created commemorative sites during specific times. Mourning Dresden's past was not processed individually, but was part of an institutionalized process of remembering through communal rituals and ceremonies such as gatherings and the laying of wreaths.

Similarly, the preface by Dresden writer Ludwig Renn also highlights the continuity of Dresden's cultural meaning despite its destruction. He reintroduces the familiar concept of Dresden as an international tourist destination. Dresden is thus still marketed as a worthy cultural center, but now its innocent beauty has also become a reflection of the GDR's fundamental spirit. Just like Dresden deserves continuous admiration and outshines all other cities, Renn suggests, so does the GDR as the better Germany of the two: "Dresden, you city imbued by nature, in which the art of living was never eclipsed by the daily grind, you will plod on, but you will also enjoy pleasure and offer visitors worthy goods [. . .]. Dear readers of this book, carry its pictures into the world, not only to bear witness to the Germany with the better spirit, but also to delight the visitor with modesty and charm."[54]

By the 1960s, pictures of ruins had almost entirely disappeared. A multilingual Dresden brochure from 1961 also only contains one picture of the destroyed Dresden, and it is hidden inside a foldout at the very beginning of the book.[55] When opened, a black and white photograph by Richard Peter of the destroyed Dresden is countered by another photograph on the opposite page, one of only two pictures printed in color. It does not show either the undestroyed or the rebuilt cityscape, but rather a group of young smiling pioneer girls and boys who descend a modern staircase in their uniforms holding flowers, seemingly to welcome the visitors to the rejuvenated Dresden. The pairing of the photographs suggests that the gray, lifeless, jumbled past is history and that the new socialist Dresden offers a happy, positive path for the new generations.

On par with the rest of the GDR after the building of the wall in 1961, the emphasis on progress and the future became the defining rhetoric for Dresden in the 1960s. It featured Dresden as having developed progressively

Fig. 27. *Dresden*, monument to the dead of the bombing (*left*) and the destroyed cityscape (*right*) (1956). (Photographs by Erich Fritzsch (*left*), Willy Pritsche (*right*), Sachsenverlag Dresden.)

Fig. 28. Foldout of multilingual Dresden guide, young pioneers and the destroyed cityscape (1961). (Rat der Stadt Dresden, Referat Fremdenverkehr.)

from an attractive heritage site to an equally attractive site of mixed historic and contemporary architecture. Similarly, the publications suggest that the city developed from a beautiful place with unfair politics into an equally beautiful city that belonged to and served the people. It also marketed extensively to visitors from the Eastern Bloc to boost international tourist numbers: "Dresden is lovely and rich again," one advertisement brochure proclaims, "it is younger than ever! The town attracts visitors from all over Germany and from abroad in a new way."[56] In 1965, a publication claimed that "the name Dresden has won back its old power of attraction."[57] Even large empty spaces, buildings in ruins, or places under construction receive a positive spin: empty lots are described as "strips of new lawn, trees and flowers."[58] Construction is hailed as a draw for tourists: "the new building activity [. . .] has achieved such an efficiency that these building sites have become places of interest even for visitors."[59] These messages in the travel brochures by Dresden's Tourism Department were to be complemented with related tour offers for the travelers as well as souvenirs and postcards featuring new construction.[60] For example, as the department reports to the Ideological Commission of the SED-city leadership, a program was implemented to educate guides both "ideologically and professionally" in how to present to visitors the large city model of the future Dresden displayed in the townhall. Regarding picture postcards, the department started to control more strongly the way they pictured the city and removed forty cards from circulation. In cooperation with the magazine *Stadt-Rundschau*, they ran a competition for the readers to suggest "good postcard motives" that would mainly picture the new Dresden. To ensure solid circulation of the official brochures, postcards, and other souvenirs, shops in the tourist areas were mandated to stock them.[61]

The reality of Dresden at the time, its living conditions and challenges, were given less and less attention in favor of painting the rebuilding as almost fully completed and Dresden as remaining a cultural center in the world. The booklets boast about the growing numbers of visitors, with "groups of tourists from the Soviet Union, Czechoslovakia, from Poland and Hungary, as well as Danish, Swedish, British and French tourists."[62] Numbers went from 300,000 in 1964 to 1,361,000 in 1967 to "year after year two million tourists [. . .] among them thousands of foreign guests" in the 1970s.[63] While the capacity to host visitors in Dresden was significantly increasing in the 1960s, it was not growing by this rate, and the numbers are most likely highly exaggerated.[64]

The city of Dresden thus communicated a discourse of success aligned with the ideals and goals of the GDR. It significantly deviated from a reality that still showed clear signs of the traumatic past. While suppressed for most of the year, the city's losses rose again to a defining feature of Dresden and its population at every anniversary of the bombing, undercutting the positive discourse in these publications. At the same time, these advertisement brochures for Dresden became more and more multimodal, and in fact images started to dominate them. Beyond the covers, the pictures within the brochures often outsized the text. As Urry has shown, images and the act of seeing, or "sight-seeing," play a key role in experiencing a location as a traveler. Tourist brochures are promotional materials, which engage in creating an affective and cognitive link even before the tourist reaches the destination through "destination image formation."[65] They aim to capture the viewers' attention, introduce the core values of the advertised place, and suggest an atmosphere and environment at the location in which the readers can see themselves. They can also be instrumental in changing some preconceived notions of a place.[66] In a city like Dresden, which was in the process

Fig. 29. Dresden brochure with city model on book jacket (ca. 1960). (Rat der Stadt Dresden.)

of rebuilding, such brochures were not only for travelers but were also used as (propagandistic) instruments in forming the local image. Just the printing of such brochures already suggests that a place is attractive and desirable, even for visitors. They provided interpretations for the already completed construction projects and created an enticing image of the rebuilt and future Dresden. Since building was also seen as re-education of the citizens, the goals of presenting a positive image of place were intertwined with lifting and positively defining socialist values.

The cover designs of official Dresden booklets are representative of the kinds of tools that were used to try to increase the appeal of Dresden, socialism, and the GDR in the 1960s. Early on, these covers did not contain photographs of the actual cityscape. In one guide, for example, the front picture consisted of a bird's-eye perspective of Dresden, but it displays an architectural model of the future city. The plans highlight a socialist vision in which a number of individual heritage sites are included as if exhibited.[67]

By 1965, the printing of tourist guides had moved from the local to the national level (by the state-owned Brockhaus (Leipzig) publisher). While local agencies were still involved in the preparations, the guides became more streamlined and were part of different series that the central publisher established. For example, there was the *Kleine Städtereihe* (Short City Guides) and the *Brockhaus Stadtführer/Atlas* (Brockhaus City Guide/Atlas), which built on the name recognition of the publisher's long tradition of offering

Fig. 30. *Kleine Städtereihe Dresden* with castle, Katholische Hofkirche, art academy (1965). (Rat der Stadt Dresden, Richard Peter, sen.)

such guides and maps.[68] They also served more widely as representations to the international community.

The Dresden guides market the vast socialist rebuilding of the city, but include also historical reconstruction, such as the completed Hofkirche and the Zwinger, to highlight the GDR as a steward of German culture. They exaggerate the progress of rebuilding, however. For example, the volume of the *Kleine Städtereihe* on Dresden features a cover photograph that pictures a seemingly completed cityscape of historic and socialist buildings.[69] Yet the corner tower of the castle pictured existed only as a shell at the time and was not restored until after reunification. The dome of the art academy consisted of the metal frame alone until its restoration in 1968. The historic cityscape is framed with images of socialist progress: The flag of the GDR is blowing in the wind and citizens, tourists, cars, streetcars, and buses move busily about. The cityscape on the Elbe also includes the first high rises of Dresden

Fig. 31. *Brockhaus-Stadtführer Dresden*, Zwinger and restaurant "Am Zwinger" (1968). (Brockhaus Verlag, Werner Wurst.)

erected in socialist slab constructions. Together, the image suggests the city panorama as a socialist achievement.

Later guides continue to picture a symbiosis of old and new on their covers. The *Brockhaus* from 1968 features a photograph that includes a segment of a contemporary façade at the Postplatz square on the right, while showing the reconstructed Zwinger, Dresden's important Baroque landmark, on the other.[70] The modern building out of "formwork panels on a concrete frame," which was completed in 1967, housed the restaurant complex "Am Zwinger." The construction was hailed as an ideal representation of socialist architecture and an achievement of modern comforts made available to everyone. With more than 1,400 seats, the restaurant complex was the largest in East Germany at the time of its opening.[71] Again, the cover photograph takes pains to suggest that Dresden was a city bustling with life, renewed energy, and a content population. Men and women are going to work, others are shopping, and a tourist group listens carefully to a guide; all of them move seamlessly back and forth between the historic environment and the suggested modern conveniences of socialist life.

This cover photograph, however, is a fitting symbol for the discrepancy between the way East Germany officially wanted to portray the city and the way that many residents viewed Dresden. Every Dresdner was aware that the restaurant was built almost exactly on the spot where the Sophienkirche, Dresden's oldest church going back to the fourteenth century and home to the first Gottfried Silbermann Organ in Dresden (1720), had stood. The removal of the salvageable ruins of the church ordered by the leadership of the SED started in 1950 with the blasting of the remaining tower and was finished in 1963 with the removal of the last of the church's remnants.[72] While the Hofkirche and the Kreuzkirche had been rebuilt right after the war, the SED at this point more strongly opposed the rebuilding of churches.[73] The final push to remove the Sophienkirche came from the Socialist Unity Party's chairman Walter Ulbricht himself.[74] As a party member recalls about one of the chairman's visits to the city: "I would like to remind you of the time when Walter Ulbricht was in Dresden and said, 'whenever I drive past the Sophienkirche, I would just love to knock it down with my car.'"[75] During a visit in 1961, Ulbricht sealed the fate of the remaining parts of the Sophienkirche once and for all. He looked at a city model outlining the rebuilding of Dresden and proceeded to remove the Sophienkirche from the ensemble, a clear sign to the city politicians.[76] This incident also exposes how rebuilding could be arbitrary and subject to personal tastes rather than city planning. As historian Paul Stangl has shown, such arbitrary decision making even affected Berlin.[77]

In contrast to the party leadership's excitement, the oversized modern building replacing the Gothic church was largely viewed negatively by the public. In fact, the population termed the restaurant and its postmodern socialist cube design "der Fresswürfel" (The Feeding Cube). The building was seen as a "disgrace and eyesore."[78] It is just one example of how the population's attachment to Dresden remained with the pre-bombing cityscape despite the official rhetoric and the immense efforts invested in redefining the city's identity. The alternative Dresden offered by the party did not provide the connective tissue between the city and its residents that for centuries had been the foundation for their collective local identity and

Fig. 32. SED secretary Walter Ulbricht (*middle*) discusses Dresden rebuilding plans (1961). (Photograph by Erich Höhne and Erich Pohl. Reprinted by permission of SLUB/Deutsche Fotothek.)

for the way Dresden was perceived internationally. The building of apartments, libraries, and other amenities was seen as necessary, and the historical rebuilding was widely supported. Yet regarding the socialist architectural ensembles, to most, "Dresden" did not signify a socialist city with individual historic markers or cultural highlights that served the GDR in showcasing its commitment to art and industry. The rebuilt heritage sites were not understood as educational spaces to study the past, but as part of the citizen's identity.

This attitude explains why the most successful postwar publication on Dresden was Fritz Löffler's *Das alte Dresden: Geschichte seiner Bauten* (The Old Dresden: History of Its Buildings).[79] The art historian was part of the building preservation institute and strongly opposed the radical clearing of ruins, as well as contemporary building projects on historic sites. Based on the belief that appreciating Dresden meant to preserve and document the city's historic significance, the destruction and rebuilding of Dresden are covered in only a few paragraphs in the four-hundred-page book. Löffler did not engage with the political rhetoric of East Germany concerning both the history of Dresden and its current state, but concentrated solely on artistic details of the built environment. Despite hostility toward Löffler's projects by Mayor Walter Weidauer, the preservationist managed to influence rebuilding decisions in the city and was able to publish his book in 1955.[80] These conflicts within the city government and with the SED exemplify how, particularly when concerning local outcomes, the lines of decision making were not always clear, just as the message on Dresden's postwar symbolism kept changing. Neither local dynamics nor centralized political structures remained steady.

Löffler's book was extremely successful, particularly in Dresden, and a second edition already appeared in 1956, the year of the anniversary festivities of the city. Many subsequent editions followed (the seventeenth edition was printed in 2012), which allowed readers an escape into the Baroque Dresden of their memory, the city before its destruction. It offered a steady, unchanging space to which one could retreat without asking questions about the responsibilities for the destiny of the city or socialist city planning initiatives. Dresden poet Michael Wüstefeld describes this attitude as one unique to Dresden residents: they "continuously insist on the history of the city and view new developments [. . .] with skepticism or even rejection."[81] Therefore, Löffler's book was considered the "bible" of the lost city.[82] Thomas Rosenlöcher, another local writer, reports how the book was even useful as currency. Since there was always a shortage of products, bartering flourished in the GDR. According to Rosenlöcher, Löffler's book was so highly prized that in Dresden one could get a hot water tank in exchange for a copy.[83] Most residents accepted some of the amenities offered by a more modernized Dresden, but it was not a basis for developing an identity that could trump their relationship to their lost city. Nothing, not even a hot water tank, could provide as much warmth as immersing oneself in the historic Dresden and its art, culture, and wonder.

In the 1970s and particularly the 1980s, the attitude of government and residents to the historic city started to converge in some points. The significant progress of rebuilding Dresden and a stronger interest in showcasing the GDR positively to an international community led to less opposition to rebuilding in original appearance. In fact, the architectural focal point of the time became the (mostly) historical reconstruction of the Semper Opera Building, which had remained in ruins for several decades. Since the structure was not just a heritage landmark but also had a distinct contemporary cultural function by staging operas and making them available to all, the rebuilding could be more easily integrated into socialist ideology. At the same time, it could bring positive international attention to the GDR. Not

Fig. 33. 1985 commemorations of February 13 in front of the reconstructed Semper Opera. (Photograph by Erich Höhne. Reprinted by permission of SLUB/Deutsche Fotothek.)

surprisingly, the completion and opening of the Semper Opera House was thus extensively celebrated as a huge success not just by Dresdners but also by the GDR government. To maximize the effect, the opening was scheduled for February 13, 1985, the fortieth anniversary of the bombing. Dresden once again was the site of a national and international propaganda effort, but while the suffering of the Dresden residents and the city itself was highlighted, direct accusations against the West remained in the background. Instead, the events emphasized the achievements of the GDR; the rebuilt Semper Opera House was presented as a sign of progress and respect for culture, as well as a symbol to East Germany's and socialism's absolute opposition to conflict. As Gerhard Schill, the mayor of Dresden at the time, put it: the opera constitutes a "Pearl of Reconstruction—Committed to Peace."[84]

To this end, Erich Honecker and many other SED functionaries visited Dresden for the opening of the opera building and the commemoration of the fortieth anniversary of the bombing. This time, the main speech for February 13, given by Erich Honecker personally, was held in front of the opera at the Theaterplatz, utilizing the background of the rebuilt landmark to its fullest effect. While appealing to peace, Honecker also used the occasion to point to the successes of the GDR to overcome adversity and presented the country as a place that does not have to shy away from comparisons with the rest of Europe: "Today, Dresden is a thriving, up-and-coming city. [. . .] Tonight, we will reopen the new Semperoper, one of the most traditional opera houses in Europe. [. . .] It attests to the high status of culture in our country."[85] With this attention by the central government to February 13, the visit also gave renewed energy to the local commemorations of the bombing anniversaries and the acknowledgment of the unfair suffering of the Dresden population. It reconfirmed to the city that Dresden's losses were indeed a singular national and international tragedy of high importance and that its role as a beacon of peace for the world remained central. Internationally, the rebuilt Semper Opera House was lauded. The city government celebrated the rebuilding and its opening as a success for Dresden and the GDR.[86] There were also renewed discussions about rebuilding other famous sites. By this time, however, much of Dresden had already been reconstructed in socialist style, both in the heart of the city and its surrounding areas.

West German Travel Magazines

Even though access to Dresden was severely limited for West Germans, both for tourists and for writers and photographers, travel books on Dresden were printed regularly in West Germany starting in the late 1940s. As we have seen in chapter 1, Dresden was an ever-present historic icon in the West, with numerous publications mourning its destruction, such as photo books, personal accounts, or histories. But Dresden's long-standing reputation as a significant national and international cultural tourist destination also continued to produce books and magazines that introduced the city and its main sites to potential travelers. For many years, however, such guides described an imaginary city. In fact, at this time Western and Eastern representations resembled each other, but in opposite temporal directions. In East Germany, publications described an envisioned socialist future that was not yet realized, while in West Germany the focus lay on the past that at this point existed only in memory. Since most West Germans would not actually be able to travel to the city, the publications opened the door for a visit within the confines of one's own home to an innocent past, which in turn succeeded in preserving the image of the historic city of culture.

The popular *Merian* magazines serve as a good example for postwar Western travel publications on Dresden. The series, which still exists today, was started and designed by Heinrich Leippe in Hamburg in 1948.[87] This early date is surprising considering that Germany was still in ruins, entirely occupied, and had only just received a common currency. The importance afforded Dresden in the series is reflected by the fact that it was already included in the lineup in 1949, even before Berlin. A second volume on Dresden appeared in 1967, and another soon after reunification in 1995.[88] Since then, a *Merian* issue on Dresden has been published every few years. The different editions of the *Merian* magazine can provide an excellent way to compare the ways in which the perception of Dresden progressed.

Travel magazines are read for their enticing photographs and texts, which make one curious, allow one to dream about an attractive and different world, and offer satisfaction for all senses. They promote a location by using discursive strategies of visual and verbal codes that hope to turn readers into visitors.[89] The *Merian* issues are filled with essays on a specific city, region, or landscape, often solicited from known travel writers or local experts. They feature introductions to history, culture, culinary experiences, important sites, and other area highlights. From the beginning, the magazines were also richly illustrated. The drawings and photographs in the *Merian* magazines each tell their own story, but as a series of images, they respond to each other and form a "large narrative" about the pictured location.[90] During the difficult conditions in the postwar era, travel magazines could help escape the harsh reality of everyday life by emerging oneself in a different, conceivably better and more whole world.

We have seen how East German brochures about Dresden tried to engage in destination image formation that highlighted a socialist future for Dresden. It presented new socialist construction as attractive, and historical rebuilding was described as functioning as part of a socialist and educational system rather than as a basis for identity. Given the state of Dresden in 1949, the West German magazine necessarily also needed to depict an enticing future location where readers could see themselves visiting and enjoying their stay. But this possible future was firmly based on the re-establishment of the past, which would confirm the images that had been created over centuries. Despite the destruction, the authentic Dresden was characterized by the beautiful "Florence on the Elbe." Consequently, the 1949 *Merian* magazine begins, without explanation, with an essay in the form of a letter originally written in 1939 that describes the historic city unaware of its later destruction. Martin Raschke's "Einladung an einen Freund" (Invitation to a Friend) feels as if it is directly addressing the readers. Raschke emphasizes that Dresden really needs to be seen in person to appreciate its splendor, but nevertheless attempts to describe the city's unique beauty:

> Dearest friend, I wish you were here to share with me the beauty everywhere! So now I can only ask you, at least in your imagination, to climb one of the towers, to see far and wide. Do you feel the wind blowing? . . . Look around! Look around! [. . .]
>
> Believe me, I knew a man who said that this here is the center of the world. He showed me the city, how at night its lights were reflected in the water, and, inhaling deeply the scent of the summer's brackish water, he said: Does this not remind one of Venice?[91]

In the postwar *Merian* issue, the text thus offers a visit to the pre-1945 Dresden, which is also set up as its only appropriate future.[92] In fact, Dresden does not experience destruction in the magazine, except in occasional allusions, until page 49 of the 96-page magazine.

The *Merian*'s essays are richly illustrated with pre-1945 Dresden photographs. From paintings by Canaletto to romantic scenes of the city to aerial photographs, they highlight Dresden's architecture and artistic meaning. Together with the texts, they induce a strong affective response. As Fritz Diettrich emphasizes in his contribution "Kindheit in Dresden" (Childhood in Dresden):

> What the camera does with torturous realism, we thoughtful humans should not try to imitate, we should neither begin nor finish such action. I do not want to sadden all those who look at these pages, and do not want to disturb them with such superficial depictions, but I would like to try carefully to create a fata morgana out of loosely connected memories, in which the beloved city rises again in its noble silhouette.[93]

The authentic and true Dresden is imprinted in the mind of each person; the *Merian* guide calls up these images in the reader, activating, but also creating memories that define the present and the expectations for the future. These

Fig. 34. Cover of *Merian Dresden* 1949, showing a rendition of the Zwinger. (Hans Hermann Hagedorn, Hamburg.)

thoughts are echoed again and again in the contributions. Dresden writer Gottfried Fischer-Gravelius denies that such destruction is actually possible: "We felt [. . .] sorrow about the losses, but also the certainty that all that was and all that was gone would be preserved in a secret chamber of the soul of the world and would be protected immortally."[94] Such a view necessarily implies that any future rebuilding that does not replicate the past would be considered inauthentic.

Toward the center of the *Merian* issue, the destruction of Dresden is finally fully thematized in "Der Untergang" (The Destruction) by Dresden native Rolf Engert, who describes his own experiences.[95] For Engert, the bombing signaled a complete breakdown of civilization. According to the author, Dresden had united German and European culture so that its destruction equaled a dismemberment of communal cultural ideals, bodies,

Fig. 35. Damaged Mozart Fountain with bronze statues after the bombing in *Merian Dresden* 1949. (Photograph by Walter Hahn. Reprinted by permission of SLUB/Deutsche Fotothek.)

and souls. The accompanying photographs drive his point home. They depict stone statues with missing limbs, ruins of famous Baroque buildings, and two photographs of piles of bodies to be cremated on the Altmarkt square.[96] Dresden, Engert suggests, deserved to remain unchanged and consistent against the fluctuations of politics or war.

Another essay reveals similar feelings regarding the famous art works housed in Dresden.[97] Ludwig Grote laments, "with *The Sistine Madonna* we have not only lost the most famous painting in Dresden, not only one of the most valuable works of art [. . .]—For us Germans it meant much more. It was a miraculous icon [. . .]. We gave it its divine aura, which flowed from the depths of our souls, and from our powerful beliefs and emotions."[98] As such comments show, when talking about Dresden and its losses, it was possible to express safely the frustration about losing the war while still claiming German cultural superiority. It is not surprising that there is an understanding throughout the magazine that any city construction that does not follow historic models leads to another destruction of Germans' cultural essence. In a time of loss, art and culture were to provide a form of German national exceptionalism that otherwise had to come to an end.

In this spirit, the preservationist Fritz Löffler appeals to the readers with urgency to "Save Dresden!"[99] Löffler emphasizes that the situation has reached a crucial and dramatic point that will decide whether Dresden's (and Germany's) cultural significance will continue or end. The *Merian* magazine thus outlines two futures. One in which Dresden will not be worth a visit since it has lost its soul and significance and one that does not only offer cultural wonders but would be a site that could give back an identity to all Germans within a European context. By taking pains to portray Dresden's cultural import as beyond political divisions, which makes the city an innocent victim of war and conflict, saving Dresden would be a legitimate way to preserve German dignity and unity. This symbolic meaning of Dresden as an all-German icon remained a basic premise among many East and West Germans. As we will see, forty years later similar arguments about Dresden's significance for a reunified Germany again ignited rebuilding debates.

When in 1967 the *Merian* publishers returned to Dresden as a theme for another issue, they faced an entirely changed situation. By this time, the GDR had fully established itself, the building of the wall had hardened the borders, and the clearing of rubble and the rebuilding of Dresden had progressed.[100] Indeed, due to the political climate, it became a challenge to put the volume together. Part of the issue had to be prepared "in secret"; the GDR refused to give a *Merian* journalist a visa to conduct research in Dresden, so he had to sneak in two short visits to the city on a fake "transit-trip" to and from Prague.[101] The readers of the 1967 magazine were facing similar issues if they wanted to visit the city. At the time, traveling to Dresden from West Germany was extremely burdensome and severely restricted. While the conditions in both Germanys had radically changed between 1949 and 1967, it remained true that the readers of the West German travel magazine would largely journey to Dresden in their imagination.

Like the earlier issue, the 1967 edition also features a picture of the Zwinger on its cover; now, however, it is a photograph of the restored structure instead of a drawing, as by this time the Zwinger had been rebuilt in its original appearance. Similarly, the magazine again contains many photographs and illustrations and a mix of essays by both East and West German authors. The contributions either return to the past to discuss the historic city before the bombing or look for other aspects of lasting meaning. Dresden is recognized for the unchanging beauty of its location in the Elbe Valley and for its continued importance as a center for music and art.

Concerning Dresden's atmosphere and physical appearance, however, the mood is somber. While some contributions to this *Merian* volume display a resigned acceptance that the GDR is now in charge of shaping the city and its atmosphere and emphasize that Dresden still offers culture, many express an emotional attachment to the way Dresden was before 1945. For example, the art historian Sigfried Asche concludes that Dresden was an "artwork," which "lasted till 1945. Then the lights went out."[102] In an essay on Meissen porcelain, the author Dorothea Stein ends with a telling bon mots by the Dresden-born Romantic author Jean Paul: "Memory is the only paradise from which we cannot be driven."[103] The writer Peter Härtling, who spent part of his childhood in Dresden before its destruction, also illustrates this sentiment in his memory text "Eine eingebildete Landschaft" (An Imagined Landscape), tellingly written in the third person:[104] "It is not a city, but an imaginary landscape. Looking back, music springs from it that fills him with longing for his home." Yet he does not want to give in to these feelings and will not be convinced to do so, not even by "the cousins, who write from Dresden: 'The Zwinger is just as magnificent again as it used to be.'"[105]

Even a contribution that sets out to assess the rebuilding without the prejudice of applying the nostalgic lens of the past ultimately comes to a negative conclusion. In "Für die Menschen von Morgen" (For Those Who Are the Future), Brigitte Jeremias underscores that Dresden has survived a number of catastrophes but had each time recovered and changed into another worthwhile place.[106] She compliments the outer ring projects in Dresden, which include apartment buildings, schools, shops, and small parks, yet she is extremely disappointed with the construction in the city center. The Altmarkt, a square with historicized bourgeois houses, is categorized as a worthwhile attempt, but it is still "not really impressively rebuilt."[107] The Prager Straße, originally a street full of shops and cafes, had been expanded and rebuilt into a contemporary ensemble, which strikes Jeremias as a "cement desert" in which people feel "out of place."[108] She also rejects the Frauenkirche ruins' preservation as a memorial, which she views as incompatible with true German cultural values. Even Luther agrees with her on this point, she facetiously observes: "maybe that is why Luther looks so indignant on his pedestal in front of the heap of rubble [the ruins of the Frauenkirche] at the Neumarkt."[109] On her stroll through the city center, Jeremias only truly appreciates two places, the Zwinger and the Katholische Hofkirche, both rebuilt in their original appearance.

The illustrations complement these assessments. For example, one image by Richard Peter offers almost the same perspective as his 1945 picture of the devastated Dresden, but now tourists are leaning on the balustrade and are looking down onto the Prager Straße, where large hotels, apart-

Fig. 36. Tourists looking at the rebuilt Prager Straße from the Rathausturm in *Merian Dresden* 1967. (Photograph by Richard Peter, sen. Reprinted by permission of SLUB/Deutsche Fotothek.)

ment buildings, and student dorms rise within the still vast empty spaces of the city.[110] For Peter, who was strongly committed to socialist rebuilding, this picture most likely indicated progress and success; West German audiences would instead interpret this photograph through the lens of the past. While the devastation from 1945 at least contained the possibility of historical rebuilding, it now was entirely gone.

The 1967 *Merian* issue on Dresden defies all expectations of its own genre. Instead of promoting a city, enticing its readers to want to travel to the location and offering interactive stories that allow them to picture themselves at the destination, the travel magazine mainly appears to promote staying away. The author Peter Härtling even emphasizes adamantly his refusal to visit. For him, not even the individual historical reconstructions can make travel to Dresden worthwhile. The *Merian* magazine from 1949 had called for help with saving Dresden from communist rebuilding plans. The 1967 magazine, rather than stirring the urge to travel, seems to fulfill the obligation to see whether the fears expressed in the 1949 edition had become a reality. It clearly shows that while the music and art collections still manage to delight, the cityscape does not. Not even when applying the criteria of modern architecture to judge the new Dresden can its rebuilding stand up to scrutiny. The only option is to widen the view to the unchanging beauty of the Elbe Valley. The contributions describing and paying tribute to the fascinating landscape surrounding Dresden with its many castles take on a significant role in the magazine; in contrast, they were entirely absent from the first *Merian* edition even though the castles had not been destroyed. Since in 1967 the hopes for a return to a fully historic cityscape in Dresden had been shattered, such descriptions of the surroundings could help recoup some of the feelings of wonder originally associated with the city itself.

The third *Merian* issue on Dresden was published in 1995 during completely different circumstances. Five years after German reunification, the political, social, and cultural landscape had entirely changed from the second volume. In fact, the magazine is closer in its conception to the first Dresden issue from 1949: in both, the authors try to grapple with new political and cultural realities that were just beginning to take hold, and they were concerned with their effects on the city and its people. The 1995 issue parallels the discourse of the 1949 edition; it focuses on Dresden's historic, prebombing cityscape, its contemporary reconstruction, and the mission to save Dresden. The rebuilding of Dresden in the GDR is portrayed as a continuation of the city's destruction by other means, and at times seen as almost worse than the firestorm: "The reconstruction damages after the war with overly wide streets are almost impossible to reverse."[111] Some buildings are viewed as so abhorrent that only "enemies" of the city could have thought them up: "There have been constructed a few [. . .] buildings, in the face of which every friend of Dresden can only cover his head in shame—that would have the advantage that he would then not have to see how the beautiful view of the Elbe from Brühl's Terrace near the Carola bridge is blocked by two ugly, colossal structures."[112] Dresden conservationist Hans Nadler, who had fought for safeguarding the historic city remnants and pushed for historical rebuilding throughout the GDR times, even talks about an act of "Kulturschande" (a cultural defilement) if such East German additions to the Dresden city ensemble remained standing.[113]

Applying the term "Kulturschande" points to concerns and grievances beyond the actual buildings. The message is clear: after reunification it was time to reconnect with the true Dresden and have the historic prewar city rise again as an ensemble while expunging as much as possible of what was added to the city during the GDR period. This sentiment is expressed with pride in the magazine as a victory of the beautiful old city over its continued destruction: "Dresden was a Baroque gem and a significant European center of culture. And it is in the process—after years on the sideline—to rise again into the first league of cities in Germany."[114] The magazine's assessment is a promise to its readers that they can start envisioning themselves in attractive surroundings and will be able to enjoy what generations of other travelers did before Dresden was destroyed in 1945. The apparent oxymoron of the *Merian* issue's subtitle, "The New Old Elbflorenz," would thus imply a return to harmony both in the cityscape as well as in the interpersonal sphere. In a unified Germany, the articles propose, a unified attitude to Dresden's destiny is possible again. While the East German government hindered the *Merian* journalists from officially traveling to Dresden and controlled East German contributions to the 1967 volume, this edition "was instead created in harmonious eastern/western German cooperation of authors and photographers," including also members of different generations.[115] As the editors proclaim, "most Dresden residents are emotionally involved and are happy that their city, which had been divided into a small, artificial heritage district and a residential zone, became again what it once was: a harmonious united body. For them, the city represents an organism with its own life and soul."[116]

The magazine does contain one critical voice of such selective approaches to Dresden. The contribution by poet Durs Grünbein, "Zaubertrick" (Magic Trick), diagnoses a confused attitude toward the passage of time in Dresden (which ironically manifests itself in the very publication that includes his reflections):

> The old-Saxon burgher houses in their new splendor let one forget the prefabricated high rises from yesterday. Whether Brühl's Terrasse or the Italienische Dörfchen [Italian Village]—on the left bank of the Elbe the old vedute will soon be revived in all their details as urban dreamscapes. At first, imperceptibly, temporal forms will become unhinged. Past perfect and future tense will mix in opposite ways, the present time will slip off the

> restored façades just like the present tense. Quickly, quickly, as if an entire war film were playing backwards, the stones find their old places, walls rise to construct the old buildings, the newest museum pieces.[117]

Yet Grünbein's concerns find no echo; instead, the reversals of time in the "New Old Dresden" are celebrated. The message of the post-reunification *Merian* magazine is clear: Dresden is not just a memory, a place that can only live on in the imagination, but it is rising again as a tangible presence that can be toured, enjoyed, and admired. Through the consistent messaging which emphasizes the past as Dresden's future, the city is recovering its iconic cityscape and with it its true identity. Such a revival has since been presented as much as an architectural and cultural revival as an emotional one. Historical reconstructions were also a substantial factor in developing the tourism industry, which in turn was recognized in Dresden as a key financial pillar for the city. The economic aspect of the rebuilding and its impact on recreating the old cityscape, however, has been successfully excluded from the established official discourse about recreating the heritage sites.

As we have seen, the GDR's marketing of Dresden's renewed touristic attraction—declaring socialist architecture in Dresden to be appealing to tourists and restoring individual historic buildings as educational islands within a socialist city—was not successful. In the last decade of the GDR, even the socialist party embraced historical rebuilding in Dresden more broadly. The completion of the Semper Opera in 1985 was extensively celebrated and brought some of the positive foreign press the GDR sought. There were also discussions about rebuilding other famous sites. But much of Dresden had already been reconstructed in socialist style by this time, both in the heart of the city and its surrounding areas. In addition, the East German government's attempts to separate the discourse of Dresden's destruction from the discourse about its rebuilding could never take hold in the population. The tension between the two main arguments connected to the Dresden cityscape remained unresolved: On the one hand, the destruction narrative that highlighted the immense cultural loss was used to paint the West as fascist and barbarian; on the other hand, the city leaders insisted that in the GDR the destroyed Dresden rose again in a style that was as attractive as the Old Dresden, but more livable, healthier, and more equal.

In the West, Dresden's reputation stayed connected to the image of the Baroque city and the memory of its 1945 destruction. The difficult travel provisions made trips to the city almost impossible and the actual form and feel of postwar Dresden remained vague. After reunification, the discourse of destruction and cultural continuation could thus fully take hold not only in Dresden, but also in the rest of Germany, and internationally. In fact, the rhetoric of before-and-after destruction stories and images regarding the Dresden bombing became stronger than it had ever been, except that it was now stripped of socialist political implications. Photo books on Dresden, featuring the effects of the bombings, were reprinted and sold with great success. Richard Peter's *Dresden: Eine Kamera klagt an* appeared in new editions, but without the voluminous section of post-1945 GDR construction that had been added to the second edition. Also, numerous newer picture books and guidebooks on Dresden were structured around before-and-after images. Since historical rebuilding has been underway, some of these publications have been expanded to include yet again three-way comparisons, but these picture triptychs now celebrate the re-emergence of the historic city and not socialist rebuilding projects.

Since Dresden's role as victim of the war had been successfully established and never truly questioned, and the imagined mindscape of Dresden was already firmly established as reality, the site was the ideal place to rework German wartime experiences in a reunified Germany and provide aspects of a new founding myth encompassing all Germans with an emphasis on reconstruction, peace, and reconciliation. This discourse, however, excluded an acknowledgment of Dresden's history of antisemitism as well as the entanglement of Dresden society in Jewish persecution in Nazi Germany. In the emotional discourse about Dresden, its loss and its anticipated final recovery, the role of Dresden and its residents during Nazism could remain mainly absent from popular memory. The reprinting of picture books of Dresden from before and after the bombing, as well as the broad discussion on German suffering that sprung up around them reinforced the already established exclusions of questions about responsibilities. The next two chapters will thus emphasize the ways in which antisemitism and Jewish persecution have become blind spots in Dresden memory culture. Together they show how in the GDR and the reunified Germany the emphasis on February 13 as a unique singular loss has severed the Dresden destruction from its historical context of Nazi Germany. At the same time, the emphasis on the universal meaning of the suffering of the city and its population makes it possible to ignore the Jewish experience of perpetration and suffering as a distinct and singular experience by including it in a general discourse of victimhood.

CHAPTER 4

Constructing the Memory of the Nazi Past *Jewish Life, Persecution, and Postwar Commemoration*

In the decades after the war, history and memory discourses in East Germany regarding the National Socialist past were to align fully with the socialist worldview propagated first in the Soviet Zone and subsequently in the German Democratic Republic (GDR). In this approach, imperialist capitalism was identified as the decisive structure underlying Nazism. By equating capitalism with fascism and persecution, Jewish suffering was not denied, but it was minimized, sidelined, or subsumed. The role of antisemitism was downplayed, and instead Jewish persecution was wrapped up in a story of communist resistance.[1] Yet I assert that in Dresden, due to its specific memory culture, the contextualization of the Holocaust after the war, while incorporating these elements, also developed a unique orientation. Communist resistance was similarly highlighted, but the Jewish persecution during Nazi Germany was encoded by associating the events with the bombing of Dresden. Both are described as fascist acts, and stories of the bombing and of Jewish persecution shared a narrative structure. By impressing the elements of the already established bombing narrative onto the discourse of Jewish persecution, questions about the responsibilities of the Dresden residents regarding the fate of Jews and the war events could be deflected.

As we have seen, the Dresden bombing narrative is told as one of continuity even though it is expressed through the idea of a "before," which denotes the revered and unique ensemble of heritage sites, and an "after," which is characterized by the ruins of this cityscape. When telling the story of the destruction of Dresden through this binary, the full extent of the rupture that caused this ruination, namely the Nazi years from 1933 to 1945, can be suppressed and condensed into one, decontextualized event, February 13, 1945. By identifying solely February 13, 1945, as the caesura, the destruction appears as an unjustified, nonsensical catastrophe and a crime against an innocent city. I will demonstrate how this structure is also employed when discussing Jewish persecution. In Dresden, Jewish persecution is similarly coupled to an event of material destruction, the burning down of the Dresden Synagogue on November 9, 1938, even though Jewish persecution defined the entire Nazi era and grew out of a long history of antisemitism in Saxony. The persecution was also discursively integrated into the history of destruction: the November pogroms from 1938 and the bombing of Dresden in 1945 were often evoked together to illustrate the continued assault of fascism on humanity. Through this association, a community of sufferers of both events was conjured up, which found its strongest expression in the physical destruction of the city and implied a common understanding of the tragedy of losing irreplaceable cultural sites as acts of perpetration.

Given the GDR's restrictive memory politics and the control of sources and historical research, scholarly attention to the Holocaust and the history of Jewish life and antisemitism in Saxony could only begin in earnest after reunification. Few studies have explored the history of antisemitism and nativism in nineteenth-century Dresden and its influence on the developments in the 1930s.[2] The GDR's relationship to Jewish communities and East Germany's remembrance regarding Jewish persecution in Nazi Germany has also become an area of inquiry after reunification, but at this point, such research focuses almost exclusively on Berlin, particularly in English-language studies.[3] Regarding Dresden, mainly local scholars and enthusiasts have worked on interrupting the established GDR storyline with historical realities both about National Socialism in Dresden and the interpretations of the Nazi past put forward during the GDR. There is also an effort to investigate the treatment of the Jewish community under socialism. Much of this work has been undertaken as part of initiatives within Dresden and Saxon Jewish organizations and has not yet reached the wide audience it deserves. When looking at Dresden, nationally and internationally, the bombing garners the most extensive attention in scholarly and popular writing, so that other areas of inquiry are easily overshadowed.

Consequently, this chapter has three goals. First, it sheds light on Jewish life, antisemitism, and Nazism in Dresden before and during Hitler's Germany. When removing the lens of Dresden's destruction for analyzing Dresden society, it emerges how the experiences of the Jewish population in the city were distinct from those of other groups of Dresden residents, which helps to disentangle the postwar idea of a combined community of suffering. It also gives voice to the period 1933–1945 in Dresden's history and demonstrates that Dresden residents were in no way less engaged than other places with Nazism, its ideology, and crimes. The chapter reveals how Dresden's cityscape and cultural heritage became closely linked to National Socialism and functioned as an expression of Nazi cultural ideals both symbolically and in material form. It introduces and analyzes the unusually rich archive reflecting Jewish persecution, containing rare films and photographs, which were largely ignored, suppressed, or used for propaganda during the GDR. Second, it demonstrates how the rhetoric about Jewish persecution in Dresden was unique by associating it with the bombing narrative and portraying both as fascist acts, even if this representation included misinterpretations and exclusions. Third, it highlights how the concentration on November 9, 1938, and the destruction of the Semper-designed synagogue when discussing the Holocaust supports the idea of presenting the loss of architectural heritage as an act of perpetration, which aligns with the view of all Dresdners as a community of suffering. The chapter argues that this association explains why even today the National Socialist period in Dresden and the involvement of its residents in persecution has not played a larger role when talking about Dresden's history.

Jewish Life in Dresden Before 1933

When George Bähr built Dresden's most idolized landmark, the Frauenkirche, from 1726 to 1743 during Dresden's architectural high point, there was no Jewish community to speak of in Dresden. In 1727, Dresden had 46,472 inhabitants. A census in 1734 concluded that only 109 Jews lived in the city.[4] Other sources even speak of only half that number.[5] Trade, living, and religious restrictions, as well as extreme financial burdens such as particularly high taxes, made it almost impossible for Jews to settle in Dresden.[6] These rules set by individual associations and districts became stringent laws over the course of the eighteenth century. When more Jews hoped to make their home in Saxony's capital, they were countered with complicated and costly rules.[7] Still, they did lay the groundwork for some form of legitimization for Jewish life in Dresden, even if, in comparison to other German areas, all of Saxony only advanced slowly in improving the situation for Jews.[8]

It took until the 1830s before laws allowed Jews a fuller integration into the community and the state.[9] After years of private and secret initiatives to come together in several small makeshift prayer rooms, it became at last

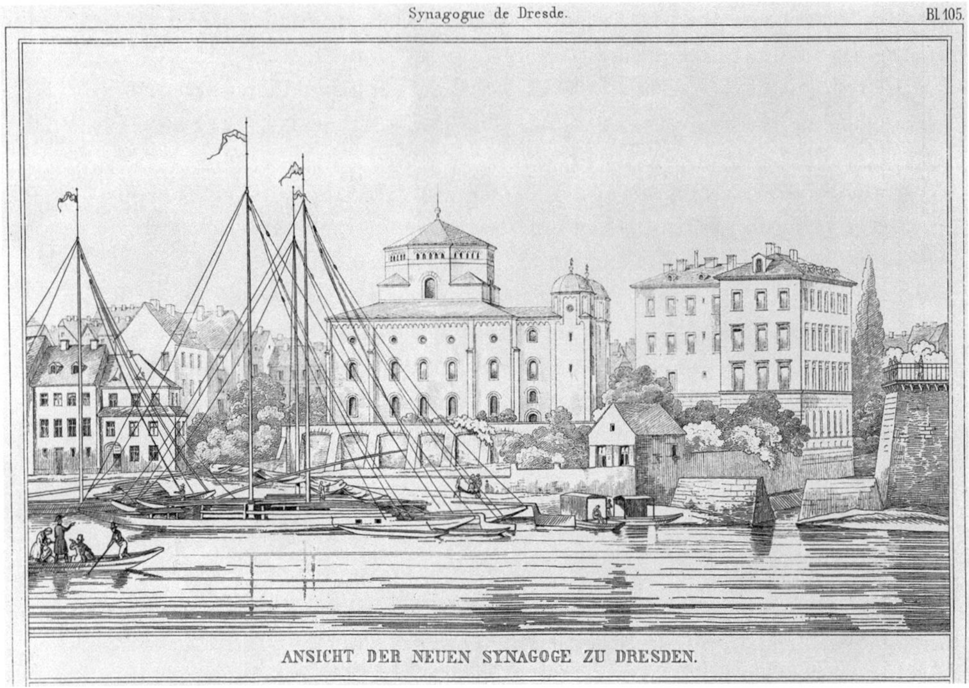

Fig. 37. Engraving of the synagogue designed by Gottfried Semper from 1847. (Artist unknown; reprinted by permission of SLUB/Deutsche Fotothek.)

possible for Dresden's Jews to form a legally registered congregation, to get together in public, own community ground, and start constructing their own house of worship.[10] Yet between these new laws and their successful realization lay numerous hurdles erected by the city government.[11] In particular, the city refused to provide a plot for the construction, which for the small, relatively poor Jewish community (at this point fewer than one thousand members) meant an almost complete stop of their plans.

Finally, the congregation managed to purchase land on the Elbe, near the Brühl's Terrasse in the northeastern part of the historic city center. They hired Gottfried Semper, who had become a professor of architecture in Dresden in 1834. In parallel to the synagogue, Semper also worked on the Dresden opera and theater building, which would become the foundation for his international fame.[12] The synagogue design combined an imposing neo-Romanesque exterior with a lavishly appointed interior influenced by Islamic styles and stood out by the seamless interplay between these two spaces. Notwithstanding constant money woes, the building was completed in 1840, shortly before Semper's theater project.[13]

Yet despite registering this notable milestone and the expansion of rights for Jews in Germany, the Jewish community continued to be viewed with suspicion by many Saxons. By the end of the nineteenth century, Saxony had become a stronghold of antisemitic political agitation, even though the number of Jews in the state was actually very small.[14] In 1871, at the time of the founding of the Reich, only 3,357 of the 2.5 million Saxon residents were Jewish (in Dresden 1,246 of ca. 200,000 residents). By 1900, the number of Dresden residents had grown to 396,146 and only 3,029, less than 1 percent, were Jewish. In Saxony overall the number of residents had reached 4.2 million, of which 12,416 were Jewish.[15] In addition, there were hardly any Jewish representatives who had found access to politics, government, or the law. In 1892, Emil Lehmann, who was one of the only Jews who held a political position within Dresden and Saxony, expressed his frustration with the success of antisemitic claims of a "destructive Jewish influence on the state": "Their political influence comes down to zero. Neither in the chambers, nor in the county or district committees, neither in the city council nor in the city councilor assembly, nor in the chamber of commerce, not as legal assessors, not as jurors, not as judges in the commercial court does one find believers in the Jewish faith in Saxony. [. . .] Where is the Jew in Saxony?"[16]

Dresden was a center for nativism coupled with antisemitism. In 1879, the businessman Alexander Pinkert published several antisemitic pamphlets and brochures to great success. His booklet, *Die Judenfrage gegenüber Handel und Gewerbe* (The Jewish Question Regarding Trade and Commerce), which linked the economic downturn to Jews, appeared in four editions within two months of its publication.[17] While seen critically by the liberal part of the bourgeoisie, which was also at home in Dresden and welcomed Jewish integration, Pinkert and his supporters could nevertheless expand their reach and form a long-lasting antisemitic movement in the city and the state. It was centered on the founding of their political club, the Reformverein (reform society), which later spun off societies beyond Dresden and Saxony.[18] To ensure the distribution of the club's beliefs, they also published their own newspaper, the *Deutsche Reform* (German Reform), which, under various different titles, became the only antisemitic newspaper in the Reich that was continuously published for decades, during certain periods even as a daily.[19]

In the 1880s, the Reformverein succeeded in placing representatives onto the Dresden city council during local elections, and in cooperation with two other local political clubs, the antisemitic group gained the council majority.[20] It was the beginning of a twenty-year era of dominance of antisemitic groups in local politics in Dresden. Dresden also sent repeatedly antisemitic representatives to the Reichstag.[21] Even when the Reformpartei's influence ceased by the end of the 1890s, the fundamental anti-Jewish prejudice within Dresden and Saxony did not.[22] By that time, antisemitic sentiments and arguments had been firmly absorbed into conservative-nationalist circles.

At the beginning of the twentieth century and throughout the Weimar Republic, Dresden was thus a politically complex city. On the one hand a liberal bourgeoisie that supported contemporary art and progressive movements had established itself, on the other a conservative, nationalist, antidemocratic, and often antisemitic bourgeoisie was strongly represented.[23] In addition, as a heavily industrialized state, Saxony was a stronghold of the Social Democratic Party of Germany (SPD) among its working-class population, which was also reflected in Dresden.[24] The city structure changed as well. While Dresden's identity and image was determined by its Baroque architecture, it also grew throughout the nineteenth century to accommodate more residents and create amenities. For example, the city built a new street, the Prager Straße, to connect the train station with the city center, which developed into a lively district widely known as a premier shopping destination with expensive stores, boutiques, and entertainment options. Within this varied climate of politics, culture, and city development, there was also room for a distinctly modern intellectual life to develop, particularly regarding the visual arts. Ludwig Meidner, for example, whose expressive paintings of envisioned catastrophes we discussed in chapter 1, spent time in Dresden before the First World War, and in the 1920s such well-known artists as Hans Ludwig Kirchner, Emil Nolde, and Otto Dix lived, worked, and exhibited in the city.

Otto Dix is known for working through his experiences of the First World War in harrowing war depictions and paintings of traumatized and broken veterans. Dix was a keen observer of Weimar society and its ruptured social and political situation. For Dix, as he stated in a letter in 1947, the "what" determined the "how" in his paintings.[25] He also frequently expressed his social criticism by linking it to an actual locale. So, while Dix uses the paintings to criticize the sociopolitical situation in Germany, they also give insight into the local situation.[26]

His 1920 work *Prager Straße*, painted while he was a master student at Dresden's art academy, depicts a busy street scene along the well-known shopping area. It is a place to see and be seen, but Dix looks at what is made

Fig. 38. Otto Dix, *Prager Straße* (1920). (Courtesy of Kunstmuseum Stuttgart.)

invisible in this postwar culture of consumption by focusing on a begging war invalid huddling on the ground. The clash between the horrific legacy of the First World War, the political turmoil of the time, and the attempt to re-establish a conservative normative bourgeois society that ignores the lessons of the recent past create a dynamic and unsettling scene of a fractured world.

Regarding the politics of the time, *Prager Straße* is framed by two events. The painting was completed after the March 1920 Kapp-Putsch in Berlin had been thwarted. In this coup, national reactionary groups tried to topple German democracy. One of the instigators was General Erich Ludendorff, a proponent of the so-called "Dolchstoßlegende" (the Stab-In-the-Back Myth), which blamed the loss of the First World War on treason by leftist groups and Jews (in 1923, Ludendorff would work with Hitler to try to carry out another coup in Munich). At the same time, the Weimar Republic geared up for its second election. The problematic political situation and the election campaign find expression in Dix's work.

Dix shows the underbelly of postwar life in Germany.[27] Between the rushing feet of passersby, two crippled war veterans are pictured in their daily struggle for survival. One, who appears with hollow eyes and fallen-in cheeks to be barely alive, has been reduced to begging, with his right hand being his only human limb. The other veteran is better dressed but misses the entire lower half of his body. While he can move, he can only do so with the help of a small wooden cart and two sticks. Yet despite this handicap, he keeps his torso upright; he moves through the crowd, his "stride" swift and his gaze forward as would be expected from a military man in Germany. The wooden cart functions as a "workaround" to blend into society and ignore the war and its lasting horrific legacy. Dix unmasks this attitude as entirely preposterous by creating this grotesque scene.[28]

The shop windows in the background increase the unease that the crippled men create in the viewer. One shop displays artificial body parts, another features accessories—hats, wigs and gloves—displayed on partial fashion dolls, such as busts and hands. Besides the two veterans in the center of the painting, the only other fully visible figure is a girl in the background who is drawing with chalk. This representation of the future generation of the country, however, also appears distorted; her legs look as if badly glued onto a paper doll with her feet turned in another direction than her body. The composition acutely suggests to the viewer that the new Weimar society is founded on fractured ground.

Yet Dix gets even more specific about the questionable political climate in Dresden and the Reich. In the middle of the painting, Dix collaged a part of a newspaper or poster into the painting with the noticeable headline: "Juden raus!" (Jews Out!). While actually taken from a pamphlet opposing antisemitism, when cutting away this context Dix calls out front and center the strong antisemitic movements of the time in Dresden and beyond and also expresses the fruitlessness of opposition.[29] The phrase appears to grow out of the mouth of a dog, which is walking into the picture right ahead of its bourgeois owner on the left side of the painting. Dix only shows us the man's hands and his cane. One finger of the right hand is extended, thus seemingly pointing to the heading "Juden raus!" It suggests a close relationship between parts of the bourgeois class and antisemitic attitudes.

Another political advertisement is also visible, placed as if further back in the street. It is tethered on all sides and upside down. While barely readable, it is recognizable as a Social Democrat pamphlet, since it calls for a vote for "Liste 1 Buck" to combat a possible "Dictatorship from the Right." Wilhelm Buck was a Dresden and Saxon politician who did in fact get elected and served as the governor (Ministerpräsident) of Saxony until 1923, even though the Social Democrats lost many votes in the 1920 election compared to the previous year's results. But, by centering the almost unharmed pamphlet with its antisemitic headline in the painting while the SPD's poster is crumbled, tethered, and in the background, Dix cautions the viewer about the dangerous path the country is on. His inscription on the back of the canvas, "Dedicated to my contemporaries," confirms that the painting is a warning not to ignore the political and societal situation of the time, which he sees centrally expressed by the unwillingness to acknowledge the horror of the war and the openly growing antisemitic sentiment in the population.[30]

Since Dresden was usually pictured as a paradisiacal Baroque cityscape, a silhouette of world renown, Dix could set up particularly strong contrasts by situating his work here. Not only could he highlight those left behind by the busy consumerism of the famous shopping mile Prager Straße, but he could offer a close-up of society that revealed a much different picture from the idyllic Dresden panorama the city was known for. The artist depicts a city made ugly by the social-political attitudes of its population, which displays the biggest dangers to the fragile Weimar Republic. Indeed, in Saxony the demise of democracy ultimately already started three years after the picture was finished, in 1923. At this point, the Reichswehr forcefully removed the Saxon government led by a Social Democratic and Communist alliance. While the danger of communist unrest was stopped with this action, in the process it also strengthened the ultimately antidemocratic, nationalist bourgeoisie.

Dresden and National Socialism

Saxony and its capital Dresden, with their long-developed and well-established antisemitic and nationalist-conservative base, were early supporters of National Socialism. A number of Saxon districts, particularly in southwest Saxony (such as Zwickau and Plauen) became some of the earliest Nazi Party (Nationalsozialistische Deutsche Arbeiterpartei, NSDAP) strongholds outside of Bavaria.[31] Dresden was the capital of the party's administrative region ("Gau") of East Saxony. While at first the Nazi Party here suffered from power struggles in their own ranks, by the time the economic crisis hit with full force in 1929–30, these conflicts were settled and the party was ready to make full use of the unstable situation.[32] The party won many new members and managed to be voted into the city parliament. By January 1933, with the votes of the Dresden bourgeoisie, it had captured the majority of the seats, beating out the SPD, even though some of the blue-collar districts had remained committed to the Socialist and the Communist Party.[33] The NSDAP was led by Martin Mutschmann, a zealous National Socialist, long-standing antisemite, and enthusiast of Saxon folk art and culture.[34] He emerged as the most powerful Nazi figure in Saxony after Hitler came to power.[35]

Mutschmann hoped to make Saxony, the most populous state and of significant economic import, the model region of National Socialist Germany, with Dresden as the crown jewel. The rigorous implementations of party directives, particularly also against Jewish residents, were part of this plan.[36] For example, in Dresden, in an act of prophylactic obedience, all Jewish city employees were already dismissed even before it became an official policy.[37] While Dresden still attracted national and international tourists to its Baroque cityscape, the lives for Jews in the city became more and more restricted, and Jewish residents in Dresden, like in other German cities, were excluded from public life.[38] Living arrangements were also regulated. Mutschmann established thirty-two so-called "Jew houses,"[39] and, starting in fall 1939 and progressing very swiftly, Dresden Jews had to move into the cramped quarters. Ilse Frischmann, one of the few Dresden Holocaust survivors, recalls that her family was already moved as early as the end of 1938, as the very first Jewish family in Dresden.[40] Dresden thus led the way in curbing the rights and movements of Jewish residents, as most other German cities only established such concentrated living quarters a bit later.[41] As part of the trope of the exemplar region and the importance of deep regional ties, Mutschmann continuously encouraged the general population to engage more directly with the persecution of Jews.[42]

Dresden's famous cityscape was physically and symbolically intertwined with National Socialism, not just with banners, flags, and the renaming of streets and squares, but also with characterizing the city as an appropriate place through which to communicate National Socialist values. In chapter 2, we saw how Dresden was still advertised as an attractive international travel destination and marketed as a symbol for how National Socialism was intimately related to Germany's history of high culture. This cultural connection was also signaled when it hosted the first Theater and Culture Week of the Reich (Reichstheaterwoche) in 1934. When Hitler came to the city in honor of the events, the "German Florence," with its Baroque architecture and the Semper opera building, became the imposing backdrop for his rally. In his opening speech, Goebbels had already confirmed that Dresden had been specifically chosen for the festival because it was a "singular place in Germany for creativity, music, and art," and because of its connection to Richard Wagner. Dresden was seen as the fitting place to represent what National Socialism considered "German art."[43] The Old Town could consequently serve to present Hitler as the legitimate German ruler, since it was adequately embodying Germany's history of cultural achievements. The presence of Hitler and National Socialism was considered a two-way street. Through the heritage sites, Hitler received the backdrop he deserved, while Hitler made sure to bring Dresden back to "true" culture.

In this vein, Dresden had also cleared its art collections of those pieces that did not conform to the propagated values. It was presented as particularly shocking that the world-famous collection in Dresden, full of masterworks, would also contain so much contemporary art, even art that had been bought with public funds.[44] Some of these works were the ones exhibited in the Dresden townhall in 1933 in the "Entartete Kunst" (Degenerate Art) show previously mentioned.[45] The newspaper *Dresdner Neueste Nachrichten* outlines in its review how the exhibition "offers indeed a repulsive example" and succeeds in showing why "the natural sensibilities of the people [turn them away] in disgust" from such art, which only expresses "the debased, the common, the wretched."[46] The exhibit was understood as an important way to educate the young about the chaos of the recent past, now "overcome," and the mayor personally requested to make the exhibit accessible to visitors age fifteen and up.[47] The collection also toured several other cities in the nation. It was the precursor for the infamous 1937 Munich exhibit by the same name.[48]

Dresden was also subject to city planning and renewal in accordance with Nazi ideas of urban architecture and design. As Saxon's Gau capital, Dresden had been designated by Hitler as one of a number of cities in Germany that would be redesigned on a larger scale to represent National Socialism, the so-called Neugestaltungsstädte.[49] In Dresden, with its architectural reputation, the impact of combining the old with the new would be particularly powerful. The Old Town's landmarks, as iconic travel destinations and symbols of Germany's grand past and cultural superiority, were to remain relatively unaltered. In fact, to preserve the famous artifacts, extensive restoration work, which had started in the 1920s, continued throughout the 1930s and even still during the first war years. The Frauenkirche, for example, needed broad remedial work to ensure its safety. The interior was designed in new colors and frescos were being restored. These works went on until the end of 1942, despite the bombings of Germany becoming more and more frequent.[50]

Other parts of Dresden were to be redesigned to reflect renewal and National Socialist ideas and values. Between 1933 and 1939, many buildings and parks were built, and infrastructure projects such as the expansion of the streetcar network and the connection to the Autobahn were undertaken.[51] Paul Wolf from the Planning and Building Department also emphasized that the Old Town had to become airier and healthier by breaking up the built environment while keeping its historic core. This approach was part of a National Socialist strategy to modernize the city.[52] It was based on "the idea that Germany's cities, towns, and countryside were becoming 'sick' and needed to be restored to health," a process called *Altstadtgesundung* (literally: "old town recuperation").[53] These aesthetic concepts were in fact not new, but, as Andrew Demshuk convincingly shows, had already been propagated as part of Weimar modernism, even though Nazi ideology officially objected to modernist ideas.[54] Wolf outlines in a report plans for changes to Dresden's Old Town and to other parts of the inner city, such as the area around the Prager Straße and the large city park, the Große Garten:

> In Dresden, the area of the restoration of the Old Town presents particularly difficult tasks. [. . .] Here, questions about the architectural design of the regeneration districts are all the more prominent.
>
> Of the greatest importance, however, is the plan for the redevelopment of Dresden's city center, which provides for a series of street openings and breakthroughs in connection with promenades and which opens up significant future possibilities by building on the historical conditions and, using them as a foundation, developing them further.[55]

The most changes promised the planned redesign of areas around the Große Garten, which is about one mile east of the Old Town. It included the building of an area of monumental structures that were to symbolize and help perform the collective National Socialist worldview and its superiority. The Dresden architecture professor Wilhelm Kreis designed a Gau Forum in a bombastic neoclassical style, which was to feature expansive administrative buildings, a large space for rallies, a seventy-meter-tall bell tower, and an oversized event hall with ceilings up to forty meters high.[56] A tree-lined avenue was to connect the Forum with the Old Town. When Mutschmann celebrated the first cut of the spade of the Forum in March 1939, he emphasized his goal to create "great architectural landmarks in a new monumental building style," which represented the new political and social time and which were "to shape the Saxon capital's cityscape for generations to come."[57] Consequently, the often conjured up Baroque Dresden was supposed to be framed not just politically, but also architecturally with National Socialism. But, while Mutschmann declared that the "plans are ready," the war put an early stop to most of these projects.[58] The Gau Forum was never built, but today's Dresden still contains structural witnesses to Nazism, yet their origins have been all but forgotten. Among the completed National Socialist projects was the design of the park along the river Elbe on the Neustadt side, with an open-air arena for rallies. It is now a popular spot for public movie viewings and rock concerts during the summer months.[59]

It was in this arena in 1944, when, following the assassination attempt on Hitler, many Dresdners came together for an emotional rally and to pledge their unending support.[60] The crowds echoed the masses that had assembled ten years earlier when Hitler visited Dresden for Theater Week in early Nazi Germany and who Goebbels, very pleased with the visit, had described as "in ecstasy."[61] Even though the destruction narrative often overshadows Dresden's role in National Socialism, it does not mean that Dresden was exceptionally less enthusiastic for the regime. Just like in other cities, many Dresden residents manifested lasting support for National Socialism and its cultural, social, and political goals throughout the entire Third Reich. Its cultural and historical significance and reputation did not render it immune to or locate it above politics. Rather, with its well-established antisemitic and nativist base and its cultural history, it was a fertile ground for the party and its ideas.

The November Pogroms in Dresden

In October 1938, after Germany had annexed Austria, a new chapter of persecution was opened when Polish Jews were deported from Germany. In this phase, Dresden expelled 724 individuals to Poland, 90 percent of the Polish Jewish population of the city.[62] Shortly after, during the November Pogroms, the Dresden SA and other Nazi groups went on a rampage through Jewish businesses. The Gestapo and the SD (Sicherheitsdienst—the SS's intelligence service) arrested and mistreated Jewish residents, and set several buildings, such as two Jewish-owned shopping centers, on fire.[63] They also plundered the synagogue and burned it down. There, members of the Jewish community were publicly humiliated in front of the smoking ruins, and the entire council and some of the temple's staff were arrested. Many of them were transported to the concentration camp at Buchenwald the next day.

The destruction of the synagogue and other activities against Jews are documented surprisingly well in the case of Dresden, with witness accounts, photographs, and even film materials. In the GDR, however, such documents were not easily accessible and rarely shown, and then only when they aligned with propagandistic goals or were mislabeled, since the state tried to de-emphasize the role of ordinary Germans in Jewish persecution. While socialism and its official discourse surrounding Jewish persecution and antisemitism have disappeared, the discourse of innocence and the avoidance of the Holocaust still dominates the public perception in Dresden. From the documents, large parts of the events can be reconstructed, and they stand in stark contrast to the idea of the innocent city. They again reveal the complicity of the Dresden population in the Holocaust, defying any idea that the situation in Dresden differed in a positive manner from other urban areas in Germany. As we will see, Dresden is not an exceptional case for the way its leaders and residents engaged with National Socialism, but rather for the unique structures of remembrance that have been prioritized in the city.

The synagogue was already torched in the evening of November 9. News of the events and the burning synagogue spread quickly. The soldier Hans Schneider, for example, had heard about the fire from comrades who were returning from the city center to the barracks. When he went to the scene, he encountered "25 to 30 people" who "stared at the flames."[64] Schneider asked the bystanders why the fire department was not there extinguishing the fire, and a young man, with a smirk on his face, told him, "yes, the firemen were here, but they just did a little something and were otherwise mainly busy with making a big breach in the wall."[65]

Other witnesses also reported that the fire department had deployed many firemen and vehicles to the scene. As a subsection of the local police force, however, they received orders not to extinguish the fire and intervene only if there was a danger that it would spread to the surrounding areas. If Schneider's recollection is accurate, the breach was possibly one way the firefighters could contain the blaze to the synagogue building. It is not clear who gave those orders or how the firefighters felt about them, but there is also no known attempt to disregard the directives. The synagogue fire appears to remain a taboo in the organization to this day. The Dresden Fire Department published a carefully detailed chronology for its 150th anniversary, yet this large fire, which almost entirely destroyed the synagogue, remains unmentioned. In the section on "Deployments that Made History," the chronology outlines a church fire in December 1930 and then jumps to the winter of 1944–45 when the first air raids occurred in Dresden, followed by descriptions of the 1945 firestorm.[66]

The report by the Jewish congregation's head clerk and bookkeeper, Leo Jehuda Schornstein, offers particular insight into the horrific events playing out at the synagogue the day after the fire.[67] Schornstein reports how he was

Fig. 39. Public humiliation of synagogue employees on November 10, 1938. (Photographer unknown. Courtesy of the Archiv der Jüdischen Gemeinde Dresden.)

forced to hand over all the congregation's cash stored in the administration building, as well as all the priceless objects for worship that had not already been destroyed or plundered. They were placed into a laundry basket to take away from the site. The surviving Torah scrolls were also removed from the buildings, and Schornstein and other staff members had to carry them across to the unharmed community building. Schornstein estimates that there were about two thousand people watching them, and he remembers many shouting threats. The Gestapo made sure to offer a cruel spectacle. As Schornstein narrates, "Before taking us outside, they put Torah covers over our heads, tied children-sized aprons from the building's preschool around our necks, and put the synagogue leaders' top hats on our heads by collapsing them, which created a macabre, strange and demeaning impression."[68]

Several photographs available in the archive of the Dresden Jewish Congregation portray the suffering inflicted on the Jewish population during the pogrom in Dresden and corroborate Schornstein's account. One of them pictures Schornstein and two other staff members of the congregation carrying the religious objects in the humiliating get-up Schornstein describes. It is likely that the photo had been taken by a Nazi sympathizer, potentially

Fig. 40. Dresden Synagogue, November 10, 1938. (Photograph by Helmut Hoffmann. Niedersächsisches Archiv / Abt. Oldenburg / NLA OL Erw 84 Akz. 2008/052 Nr. 169, reprinted by permission.)

even by a participant: SD leader Johannes Clemens is shown standing next to the men and appears to smile and pose for the camera. Decades after the events, these photographs were anonymously sent to the Jewish community from abroad.[69]

Another set of pictures from November 10 (first published in 1995) were taken by the young soldier Helmut Hoffmann, who, like Schneider, had heard the news about the synagogue fire at his barracks.[70] Together with a group of other curious fellow soldiers, Hoffmann went to the site around noon and brought his camera along. Private photography of the occurrence was generally immediately stopped and the film confiscated, but Hoffmann managed to photograph the ruin of the synagogue from a distance, as well as the spectators. The picture confirms Schornstein's description of a large crowd of onlookers that had gathered to see the ruins and to watch the humiliating spectacle put on by the Nazi perpetrators.[71]

Fig. 41. November 10, 1938, large crowds of onlookers, humiliations of synagogue employees take place in front of the community center. (Photograph by Helmut Hoffmann. Niedersächsisches Archiv / Abt. Oldenburg / NLA OL Erw 84 Akz. 2008/052 Nr. 169, reprinted by permission.)

Other post-reunification documents describe the shock of discovering the destruction resulting from the events of November 9–10. In her memoir from 2001, *Das Lied ist aus* (The Song Is Over), Henny Brenner (b. Wolf) talks about witnessing the results of the attacks against Jewish institutions and residents while growing up in Dresden.[72] Henny was the child of a Jewish mother, and her family only survived persecution due to the chaos following the firestorm in 1945. When the fourteen-year-old was riding the streetcar in the morning of November 10 to reach her Jewish School, she saw the destruction of the Synagogue firsthand: "When the street car passed the Zeughausplatz, one could already see from a large distance a crowd of people and smoke rising: 'The synagogue is burning,' was said at once." This shocking experience repeated itself for Henny on this day; Nazis had wreaked havoc in her school, she saw broken shop windows and ordinary people plundering the businesses. By the end of the day, the horror of the events was now permanently inscribed for her in the Dresden cityscape through the very absence of the Semper Synagogue: "In a few hours the Nazis did not only manage to destroy the center of the Dresden Jewish community with its rich history, but also to deprive the city of one of its most impressive buildings."[73]

A directive from the Saxon minister of the interior required the demolition and removal of the remaining ruins of the synagogue by the Technische Nothilfe, a technical emergency response and civil defense agency under Nazi control.[74] The rubble was eventually used as landfill and for road construction.[75] Already at the time of the GDR, a film detailing the removal of the ruins of the synagogue was discovered, which constitutes a rare document of such clearings that were going on all over Germany.[76] In 1988, excerpts from the film were used in the GDR TV documentary "Als die Synagogen brannten–Pogromnacht 1938" (When the Synagogues Were Burning—Pogrom Night 1938) by Günter Wittenbecher, which was shown on November 8, 1988, at 8 p.m., the most prominent time slot on television.[77] This documentary, while interpreting the antisemitic acts through a communist lens focused on capitalist motivations among the perpetrators, nevertheless offers details through film materials and witness reports rarely publicized before in the GDR. It was part of the increased attention to the November Pogroms in the GDR during the fiftieth anniversary of the events, which we will explore in more detail later in this chapter. The East German *Berliner Zeitung* hailed the Dresden film excerpts as a recent discovery by the documentary filmmaker in the State Film Archive.[78] Parts of the footage, however, had already appeared in the West German documentary by Dieter Hildebrandt, "Der gelbe Stern" (The Yellow Star), from 1981.[79] One can assume that the existence of the film was known before 1988, but that there was little desire by the East German state to make it available. The film, or slides taken from the film, were also part of a Dresden exhibition commemorating the fiftieth anniversary of the pogroms. The exhibition was privately organized and took place in the Kreuzkirche.[80] Scenes in the beginning display the synagogue still with the two Stars of David on its towers and with its rubble smoking. Later sequences show the controlled blasting of the partially destroyed structure.[81] The November Pogroms were another step in forcing out Jews more thoroughly from society and from the city's spaces. Even though the synagogue was a historically significant building designed by Gottfried Semper, the same architect responsible for the opera building, the removal of the synagogue from the Dresden ensemble did not cause outrage among citizens, and its architect remained unmentioned. Public memory of Dresden's destruction often overpowers the remembrance of this first willful destruction of significant architecture in the cityscape.

In January 1942 the situation intensified when the first organized deportations of German Jewish residents from Dresden took place (as mentioned above, Polish Jews had been deported to the Polish border in 1938). In the earlier transports, the victims were taken to Riga, in later transports to Theresienstadt, and they were eventually murdered in Auschwitz. Those performing forced labor for the armament industry, mainly for the company Zeiss-Ikon in the Goehle factory in Dresden, were at this point still excluded from deportation. Yet they were not to remain in the city; instead, the Zeiss-Ikon company, the Dresden Gestapo, and the Dresden local chapter of the Nazi Party worked out a plan to establish a camp in close proximity to Zeiss-Ikon's production site, but outside of the city limits, the so-called "Judenlager Hellerberg." The Zeiss-Ikon company provided the place and all the necessary provisions. On November 23, 1942, the Jewish forced laborers and their families were moved from the "Jew houses" to the camp.

Again, there is exceptional film material documenting the actions in Dresden against Jews. The Zeiss-Ikon management meticulously recorded the rehousing of the Jewish forced laborers and their families to Hellerberg. They sent one of their employees, Erich Höhne, a photographer and technician at Zeiss who would become a well-known GDR press photographer after the war, to film the entire process. Höhne ended up capturing a long and cruel journey. In 1945, Höhne removed the film, titled "Deportation of the last Dresden Jews to the camp at Hellerberg on 23rd/24th November 1942," from the Zeiss archives and took it home with him.[82] We can only speculate about his intentions for taking the two reels, but fifty years later, when Höhne dissolved his own archive, he passed them on to the camera man Ernst Hirsch, who was known for his large collection of film and photo materials on Dresden. Hirsch was able to restore the film and make it public. It was only then, in 1995, that the world learned about its existence.[83]

The almost thirty-minute-long film gives unique insight into the cruelty and depravity shown by all involved in the transfer, which directly included the management of Zeiss-Ikon, and is consequently an invaluable source in understanding the seamless relationship and close collaboration between the regime and industry during the Hitler years. The film had been partially edited and there are some propagandistic subtitles, but it was never completed and does not seem to have ever been used for such purposes.[84] It shows the entire process of moving the Jewish forced laborers and their families out of the city and into the camp through several episodes, titled with their locations. In the beginning, we see the loading of trucks with furniture and personal possessions at "Jew houses." Men wearing the star carry

Fig. 42. Still image from "Die Zusammenlegung der letzten Dresdner Juden" (1942). (Courtesy Bundesarchiv-Film.)

chairs and bookshelves, bundles and suitcases, while guarded by officers in civilian clothing. It is obvious that these actions did not take place secretly or unnoticed; it is broad daylight and the camera captures several pedestrians walking by when the trucks are loaded.[85] In these and subsequent scenes, the camera focuses time and again on the luggage, which has been labeled with the owners' information.

The second episode is the most dreadful of the film, and the camera does not spare the details when it shows the Jewish forced laborers and their families at the public decontamination agency. Clothing and shoes had to be removed to be disinfected, and the film spends much time showing how the women had to put on big wooden slippers that make them slide around helplessly on the wet ground. One woman starts to gaze down, embarrassed, when she realizes that the camera is focusing on her while her hair is roughly searched for lice. Old and young men are waiting naked to be examined by a Jewish physician, and again the camera captures the humiliating procedures in detail. At various points, higher Gestapo/SS officers, among them Henry Schmidt, who was heading the transfer, are seen chatting and laughing, also with representatives from the Zeiss-Ikon company.[86]

The film concludes with the arrival in the camp at Hellerberg and shows both the outside areas and the inside of the cramped barracks. Again, the camera zooms in on intimate details, such as a pile of undergarments a woman unpacks from her suitcase. While clearly recorded from the perspective of the perpetrator, the film nevertheless bears witness to the events and the conditions of the Jewish forced laborers and their families. Whatever was the original goal of the film—the attempt to ridicule and demonize the Jewish laborers, as the interspersed propagandistic subtitles that were edited in later suggest, or to represent the great efficiency and working together of industry and party, even, perhaps, to try to orchestrate the appearance of order, adequacy, and good sanitary conditions outside and within the camp (for example, in a scene in the camp, the film focuses extensively on boys intently washing their hands, then captures two women with towels strolling toward the bathhouse)—it also ends up showing the deep embarrassment, the suffering, and the pain on the faces of the victims as they endure the humiliating procedures.[87] The experiences of the Jews in Hellerberg are also confirmed by other sources. In his secret diaries on his survival as a Jew during the Dresden Nazi years, Victor Klemperer also comments on Hellerberg. He knew a number of people who had been deported to the camp, and he received reports about the conditions. In his entry from November 26, 1942, Klemperer notes how the forced inmates try to survive by reframing their condition as one of privilege:

> [H]e was in good spirits. "It's not so bad—if nothing worse happens to us, then we can bear it." But I soon noticed how abject his satisfaction was. He had imagined it would be even more dreadful; he was happy simply because no one beat him. The room shared by nine married couples—"one gets used to it." The latrines: "only open at the front—but with dividing walls and lids, no urinals—no toilets, of course." The washroom—"across the yard and very cold, but there are big washbowls there." The food—"it wasn't right yet yesterday, but it will be sorted out." Pitiful![88]

After these actions, only a small number of Jewish residents remained in Dresden: those, like Klemperer, who were married to an "Arian" spouse, or children with only one Jewish parent, like Henny Brenner. Dresden had effectively erased its Jewish history and culture; most Jewish residents had fled or were deported, houses, businesses, and any other possessions had been taken away, and the synagogue, their most prominent symbol and material marker of their presence and belonging, had disappeared. While a few of the remaining Jewish residents were able to avoid deportation when Dresden was intensely bombed in February 1945, most Dresden Jews who had not been able to emigrate early on had already been killed in Auschwitz.[89]

The Memory of Jewish Persecution in Socialist Dresden, 1945–90

Particularly in the first two decades, the Soviet Zone/GDR discouraged paying close attention to the Nazi years and the Holocaust outside of the parameters that aligned with the state's goals. As part of this approach, Nazi persecution and the Holocaust were not denied, but the element of antisemitism in Jewish persecution was downplayed in favor of an emphasis on market theories. National Socialist fascism was explained as a necessary outcome of capitalism, since the "leaders of the Nazi party and of other extreme reactionary" groups stood in the service of "monopoly capital."[90] While the capitalist West Germany was described as the heir to the fascist structures established under Hitler, East Germany was presented as being erected on the principles of the heroic communist resistance. The responsibility for crimes committed from 1933 to 1945 was predominantly assigned to a fascist capitalist elite, a "Hitler clique," not the general population.[91]

The definition of who constituted a Nazi victim was thus both widened and narrowed in the early decades of the East German state. On the one hand, GDR citizens were portrayed as welcoming the Soviet forces who finally freed them from Nazi tyranny. On the other, political (communist) resistance was soon elevated to have been the main target for Nazi persecution, while the persecution based on racial, religious, sexual, ethnic, or intellectual traits was de-emphasized or subsumed. For example, officially, the Day of Remembrance for Victims of Fascism, which was celebrated every year starting as early as September 1945, was dedicated to all victims. In the beginning, this approach led to a diverse makeup of the organizing committees.[92] Yet soon, with Cold War rhetoric and a stronger grip of centrally organized politics on the sector, the tenor of the commemorations started to be prescribed by the political needs of the central government, which foregrounded active political resistance against (capitalist) fascism.[93] Already in 1947, for instance, a large banner proclaimed that a "Battle against Fascism—Battle for Peace."[94] The messaging foregrounds active resistance in the past and the need to keep fighting, since fascism, according to the official discourse, continued to rule in the West. While Jews were not excluded from the commemorations, this largest victim group was not of central concern.

In other instances, however, it was seen as politically advantageous to foreground Jewish suffering, such as when trying to gain respect for the GDR internationally. The GDR's approach to Jews and their plight was thus contradictory. On these occasions, Jewish persecution was emphasized more strongly as part of the antifascist founding myth the GDR put forward to gain acceptance. The GDR was the "better" Germany, where Jewish citizens did not need to fear continuing persecution since antisemitism and racism had been eradicated.[95] The re-establishment of Jewish religious communities after the war was indeed encouraged and supported.[96] The majority of returning Jews, however, were secular, and many of them were left-wing intellectuals.[97] Such Jewish background remained often publicly unacknowledged, and, as nonreligious Jews, they were not official members of the Jewish congregations.[98] Holocaust survivors and their families received generous pensions from the government and other privileges, such as a place at the university or minimized waiting time for an apartment.[99] The proclamations about the better, antifascist Germany were also continued even when political and antisemitic Stalinist politics in 1952–53 led to arrests and subsequently to the emigration of many Jews to the West.

The official remembrance of Jewish persecution became more nuanced and more diverse in the 1970s and 1980s, yet it also remained complicated and depended on the relationship to Israel, as well as on international patterns of Holocaust remembrance. West Germany had increased memorial events and expanded on a discourse about Jewish suffering and German responsibility.[100] With the new political climate initiated by West German chancellor Willy Brandt's *Ostpolitik* (1969–74) of normalizing the relationship of the two Germanys, the GDR did not want to appear less committed. In addition, the GDR at this point was more established and stable as a country. Citizens who grew up after Nazism and within the GDR system were interested in the past. Finally, commemorations of Jewish suffering could serve as a way of countering critics who claimed that East Germany's anti-Israel politics were antisemitic.[101]

The anniversaries of the November Pogroms with their high international recognition were thus chosen as an additional day of remembrance.[102] November 9, 1938, had already been regularly commemorated within the local Jewish congregations and without much media attention. The larger commemorations then started to serve as state-governed signaling events that were to display the GDR's participation in the value system of the world community.[103] In addition, the collaborations with the congregations could be used to indicate unity between official and Jewish remembrance. At the same time, focusing on November 9 also allowed Jewish suffering to be concentrated into one event, again de-emphasizing the long-term, large-scale involvement of the population in Jewish persecution and murder. The increased attention also politicized and controlled the remembrance more strongly. It became another occasion to celebrate socialism's lasting antifascism that was proclaimed to stand in contrast to the fascist, capitalist West, Nazi Germany's heir.

The official GDR parameters of Holocaust remembrance and their development over the course of the postwar decades also informed commemorations in Dresden. Dresden's remembrance of Jewish persecution, however, brought together these statewide parameters with a unique discourse. In response to the bombing experience, the past, present, and future in Dresden was viewed through the lens of February 13, 1945, and Dresden consequently had established a distinct victim narrative regarding the city and its residents very early on, a discourse that also borrowed some symbols of Holocaust suffering from the time right after the war. Since the bombing narrative and the commemoration culture of February 13 were already structured around an individual date that emphasized imperialist, fascist victimization of the civilian population and the physical destruction of iconic buildings, the basic building blocks of the bombing discourse could be transferred onto the remembrance of November 9 and the destruction of the synagogue. By paralleling its narrative structure to that of February 13 and adjusting the symbolic meaning of November 9 as standing in for the Holocaust and all Jewish suffering, the idea of all of Dresden as a community of suffering was strengthened. Even after the ideological lens of GDR society was removed in 1989–90, this understanding could be carried forward beyond reunification.

The traces of this special discourse in Dresden are found in the ways the bombing and Jewish persecution were discursively approached in texts, in remembrance rituals, and in the monuments and buildings that were integrated into the city as markers of victimization. Accordingly, this section will explore the linguistic structure and discursive function of the vocabulary of remembrance, as well as specific spaces in the city: commemoration events, the socialist rebuilding plans, memorials at cemeteries, the synagogue erected at the New Jewish Cemetery, and the monument in remembrance of the destroyed synagogue. But it will also demonstrate how this official take on the events was challenged from below by private and Christian groups who sought contact with Jewish communities and tried to open a dialogue about the past.

Immediately after the war, the provisional local government in Dresden actually responded positively to requests by the Jewish community to commemorate the local Jewish persecution independently from other groups within the city space.[104] Discussions in the city council were underway as early as 1946 about developing a park and erecting a monument at the city's expense commemorating the destruction of the synagogue at its former location at the Zeughausplatz. The Socialist Unity Party (Sozialistische Einheitspartei Deutschlands [SED]) itself suggested that such a memorial was a moral duty, as the SED leader explained: "My group considers it its duty of honor to contribute to the reparation of a crime and a cultural disgrace with this motion."[105] Yet, the green space was not developed for decades and such local initiatives were often sidelined by a centralized approach that preferred an emphasis on antifascist (communist) resistance, the idea of a Nazi minority as perpetrators, and the power of capital and imperialism instead of antisemitism as the driving force behind their actions when discussing the Nazi past. In particular, the focus lay on celebrating the present GDR as a society that had successfully eradicated fascism. These claims were paired with calls for action against countries the GDR officially considered to be imperialist, warmongering, and fascist nations, such as the United States, Great Britain, and West Germany. Formulaic, parallel linguistic and visual elements and structures thus enveloped the bombing of Dresden and Jewish persecution throughout the postwar period.

Tropes to remember the Dresden bombing remained steady over time, and in the first decade, as well as later during significant anniversaries, they were also reported on nationally. They display a fluidity in images and symbols between the bombing and Nazi persecution. For example, on February 13, 1949, the national newspaper *Neues Deutschland* illustrated articles on Dresden's destruction with a photograph that showed a pile of dead bodies being cremated on the Altmarkt in the city center, part of a series of authentic pictures that are, however, also reminiscent of the well-known photographs from the Nazi killing camps.

The caption strengthens this association when naming the Gestapo as responsible for these cremations, as if the dead had been victims of Nazi perpetration: "The Gestapo had the piles of corpses cremated on the market square."[106] These cremations of several thousand fatalities in Dresden, however, had been a desperate measure taken more than a week after the attack to avoid the spread of disease since the bodies could not be buried fast enough, as not enough graves had been prepared.[107] The ashes were later interred at the Heidefriedhof cemetery in a marked area alongside other casualties of the bombing.

Similarly, the consequences of the war and of persecution are not clearly distinguished linguistically or in commemorative acts. In 1950, the president of the GDR, Wilhelm Piek, ordered the laying of wreaths in remembrance of the "victims of the Hitler-war," which included persecuted groups, at a Dresden memorial of the bombing during the commemoration events of February

Fig. 43. Burning of bodies on the Altmarkt in Dresden, illustration for article on February 13, 1949, in *Neues Deutschland.* (Photograph by Walter Hahn. Reprinted by permission of SLUB/Deutsche Fotothek.)

13, implying persecution and innocence of the Dresden population.[108] Thirty years later, in a speech in Dresden for the fortieth anniversary of the bombing, party chairman Erich Honecker still did not distinguish between battlefields, concentration camps, or bombed cities, or between actions by Nazis or Western Allies: "Coventry and Dresden, Leningrad and Stalingrad, Oradour and Lidice, Warsaw and Rotterdam, Majdanek and Auschwitz, Buchenwald and Dachau, Bergen-Belsen and Ravensbrück, Hiroshima and Nagasaki—all these places—and one would have to name many more, today signify a program for peace in the world."[109]

During commemorations of the Dresden firestorm, representatives from the Dresden Jewish congregation and, before their dissolution in 1953, from the Dresden branch of the Vereinigung der Verfolgten des Naziregimes (Association of Victims of the Nazi Regime/Federation of Antifascists, VVN) were among the participants, suggesting an acceptance of the comparability of Nazi persecution and the bombing of Dresden.[110] The local newspaper strengthened this impression by publishing messages from other VVN groups on the occasion of the anniversaries that similarly expressed solidarity and shared victimhood with the population: "We stand with the people of Dresden" and will fight with the "severely tested inhabitants of the city of Dresden for a free and beautiful Germany."[111]

The vocabulary employed in the bombing discourse resembles the language of the observances on the Days of the Victims of Fascism, as well as the expressions used to refer to the November Pogroms when they started to be more frequently commemorated in the 1970s. The discourse of suffering that formed around the bombing, which was from early on presented as "one of the most heinous crimes of the past war," was translated onto the remembrance of November 9.[112] In both discourses, the bombing and the November Pogroms/Holocaust, the descriptions emphasize the cruelty of the events and use the term annihilation: In 1951, for example, February 13 was titled a "monstrous act of inhumanity" and "barbaric," which led to the "bestial murder" of civilians and was a "criminal work of annihilation."[113] Such formulations lasted into the 1980s. On February 13, 1985, Walter Weidauer, the former mayor of Dresden, wrote in his newspaper contribution "So That Life Has a Future: Never again Inferno Dresden," that "there was no limit to the brutality." He also called the bombing "barbaric" and a "crime."[114] Once November 9 received more attention, similar terms were used to describe the burning down of the synagogues and the Holocaust. It was "one of the greatest crimes," and people were "bestially murdered" with "barbaric cruelty." It was an "annihilation."[115]

Both the Frauenkirche site and the site of the synagogue built in 1950 are associated with the idea of serving as a warning and a material symbol for peace. The rubbled Frauenkirche "urges the living to fight for peace and happiness of mankind," as an article in 1985 proclaims. The Frauenkirche's symbolism is extended over generations: "On sandstone blocks lie small pictures—painted by students of a third grade [. . .]. They picture them 'playing in the new Dresden.' 'We want to live in peace' they wrote on them."[116] Similarly, the synagogue erected after the war to replace the Semper Synagogue serves as a "place of warning and admonition"[117] and is to be seen as an "appeal" to fight against war and uphold peace.[118]

Both the Holocaust and the bombing of Dresden are said to have been caused by fascist imperialism.[119] Newspaper articles that remembered the Dresden bombing and those on Jewish persecution, particularly those referring to November 9, repeatedly coded their meaning with the same formula: the maxim of "Never again February 13" or "Never again Inferno Dresden" was regularly intoned and put on signs and banners, just like November 9 was commemorated under the slogan "Never Again Kristallnacht."[120] Even

Fig. 44. February 13 commemoration with large banner "Never again!" (1955). (Photograph by Erich Höhne and Erich Pohl. Reprinted by permission of SLUB/ Deutsche Fotothek.)

when November 9 and February 13 are not explicitly compared, the rhetoric surrounding both events implies that they are similar moral transgressions and criminal actions.

With this approach, the violence of war and of persecution were equated. The German war of aggression, the Dresden bombing, and Jewish persecution were all described as the results of the destructive forces of fascism, imperialism, and the capitalist system. Particularly in the first few decades of the GDR, monetary gain, greed, and the hunger for murder and plundering are identified as the root causes for the war, but also as those for the Holocaust, an argumentation regularly intoned by Walter Weidauer during and after his Dresden mayorship in newspaper contributions about February 13.[121] Remembrance of both February 13 and the Holocaust (in the

Fig. 45. Commemoration event for November 9 in the Hygiene Museum, "Never again Kristallnacht" (1968). (Photograph by Erich Höhne and Erich Pohl. Reprinted by permission of SLUB/Deutsche Fotothek.)

November 9 commemorations) convey the same message for the future, namely a call to fight fascism and imperialism to achieve peace, and praise for the GDR in having entirely erased them. This is also expressed by associating the West with antisemitism, Nazi perpetrators, large cooperations only out for profit, and the pursuit of a future nuclear war. For example, on November 9, 1968, the *Sächsische Zeitung*, in one of the first articles on the pogrom, titled the text with: "Kristallnacht. Thirty Years Later: Jewish Persecution in West Germany." The article points to the capitalist monopoly as a continued driving force in antisemitism in contrast to the antifascist GDR.[122]

In Dresden, both these calls are not only tied to the experience of war and death, but also to the violent destruction of significant landmarks. The loss of architectural masterpieces such as the Frauenkirche, the Zwinger, and the Semper Opera have always remained at the core of the Dresden mourning rituals. When the Holocaust was officially remembered in Dresden, in particular when it became tied to the representative date of November 9, the expressions of commemoration are similarly linked to the loss of the city panorama by emphasizing the "great" Gottfried Semper's important role in

Dresden's architecture and praising the unique design of the synagogue. In November 1978, the *Sächsische Zeitung* illustrated such praise with a historic drawing of the synagogue that pictures it from the perspective of the river (see fig. 37).

The accompanying text pairs the destruction of the synagogue and the Holocaust with the bombing of Dresden and its deadly force as two forms of annihilation: "the Kristallnacht was also the beginning of the annihilation of Dresden."[123] This connection is made in almost every article on the November pogroms, year after year. The burning down of the synagogue is presented as Dresden's first experience of the destructive force of the capitalist Hitler-fascism, for which the bombing of Dresden, a similarly fascist act by the capitalist British and Americans, served as the finale. It thus links November 9 and February 13 not in order to appeal to the readers to take responsibility as a people for supporting persecution or starting a war, but the pairing instead suggests a shared unique victimizing gravity caused by the "exploitative society" that only few were part of.[124] A postcard first printed in the 1970s by VEB-Foto-Verlag Erlbach in the Vogtland, and still available in the 1980s, similarly illustrates the overpowering effect of these conflations. It displays a picture of the Semper Synagogue from before its destruction in 1938. The caption identifies the building as "Dresden Synagogue, 1838–40, Gottfried Semper. Before its destruction by Anglo-American bombing units on February 13, 1945."[125]

This rhetoric also shaped the memorials in the city. The most prominent and pronounced example is the Ehrenhain (Grove of Honor), a memorial park located at Dresden's largest cemetery, Heidefriedhof, where most of the casualties of the Dresden bombing are buried in mass graves.[126] The Memorial for the Victims of Fascism was first established in 1948 and then expanded several times until it was completed in 1965.[127] Behind an obelisk with the sign of the International Federation of Resistance Fighters (FIR) is the start of a 450-meter-long path that ends at a monumental wall memorial for the victims of the Dresden raids. The memorial path leads first along rows of stones marked with the names of antifascist fighters, and then reaches fourteen pillars standing in a large circle around a fire bowl for an eternal flame, each listing a place name. Six columns are inscribed with the locations of concentration and death camps, seven list places that were sites of atrocities committed by Germans during the Second World War, or that were bombed by the German Luftwaffe. One pillar is inscribed with the name "Dresden."

Since they are arranged in a circle, no place or situation takes precedence over another. The Dresden bombing, the Luftwaffe's air raids, and the

Holocaust are equated. This inherent problem of the memorial takes on an even larger dimension when one reaches the commemorative wall for the Dresden bombing victims at the end of the grove; there is explicitly no difference made among the almost eighteen thousand dead buried here. As a poem by the German Jewish communist poet and Dresden city council member Max Zimmering on the sandstone wall states:

> How many died? Who knows the number?
> Your wounds show the agony
> Of the nameless, who burned to death here
> *In this hellfire ignited by human hands*[128]

The victims remain "nameless" and are a diffuse group but are now unified in death. Deeds and affiliations in life are avoided as are any other specifics in the entire memorial park. There is no distinction drawn between National Socialist perpetrators and supporters who are surely among the dead honored at the cemetery or the Jewish victims who died in Auschwitz.[129]

Art historian Christiane Hertel likens the setup and rhetoric of the Grove of Honor to a dance of death motif, which she sees underlying the memorial as an endless circle of victimhood.[130] Since 2010 the opposite side of the memorial park is marked by the bronze "Grieving Girl in a Sea of Tears," a private donation by a patron who survived the bombing of Dresden as a nine-year-old and wanted the sculpture to memorialize the traumatic experience of her childhood. The city of Dresden installed it "as a visualization of the eyewitness generation."[131] It has since been incorporated into remembrance rituals by various groups, including the far right. It has also become a site of counterprotests against the memorial rituals as well as vandalism from the far left.[132] With this addition, the Grove of Honor is now framed by memorials to the bombing victims.

Already starting in 1950, a wreath-laying ceremony at the memorial wall for the bombing victims became an integral part of the official Dresden remembrance rituals on February 13. After the circle of columns surrounding the eternal flame was finished, it was also included in the commemorations. According to public proclamations, thousands of Dresden residents and guests participated in the commemorations every year. Come each September, the Ehrenhain was again the site of a wreath-laying ceremony with thousands of Dresden residents and guests, yet this time for the yearly commemoration events on the Day of Remembrance for the Victims of Fascism. In both cases, the mass demonstrations were characterized as protest ral-

Fig. 46. Commemoration of Victims of Fascism at the Heidefriedhof Memorial Park (1968). (Photograph by Erich Höhne and Erich Pohl. Reprinted by permission of SLUB/Deutsche Fotothek.)

lies (*Kampfkundgebung*) for peace with a particular emphasis on opposing the Western policies regarding atomic weaponry. The *Sächsische Zeitung* would publish the call to participate in mass demonstrations in the days before and on the day of the event. For example, on February 13, 1965, the newspaper announced, "Dresden Calls: National Resistance against Bonn's Plans for Nuclear War." Similarly, on September 11, 1965, it publicized a "Protest Rally against West Germany's Nuclear War Policies." In 1985, the *Sächsische Zeitung* on February 13 called for participation in the commemorations with "Dresden—a Reminder and an Obligation: Unite All Forces for the Fight for Peace," while in September 1985 the announcements declared, "Anti-Fascist Legacy Lives in Our Deeds for Socialism and Peace," "Day of Remembrance—a Day of Obligation," and "Preservation of Peace Is the Most Important Task."[133] Kurt Hager, who was responsible for educational and cultural policies in the GDR, was the main speaker at the 1985 remembrance events for the victims of fascism. In his speech, he does not only include the victims of National Socialist perpetration, but he also reminds the audience of the fortieth anniversary of the "destruction of Hiroshima and Nagasaki, Dresden and Magdeburg."[134] From the beginning, persecution and the destruction of Dresden were thus conceptually, linguistically, ritually, and spatially associated with each other.

Apart from the Ehrenhain at the Heidefriedhof, other cemeteries also contain memorials for the casualties of the bombing and the victims of the National Socialist state. In some cases, these memorials are spatially separated, in others they are combined. For example, at the cemetery Neuer Annenfriedhof, a large wooden cross and five metal slabs memorialize more than six hundred casualties of the bombing. The victims are identified as "young men forced into the city during the war and Dresden residents," which equalizes their experience and standing. Similarly, at the Alte Annenfriedhof, a memorial stone at a free-standing grave area blurs boundaries in its dedication to the "victims of National Socialism and [. . .] victims of the air attacks on Dresden."[135]

While there was no specific memorial for the destroyed synagogue in Dresden before the 1970s, the city as well as the state financially supported rebuilding the bombed-out mourning hall at the New Jewish Cemetery into a small synagogue, a strong commitment given the severe needs in all areas faced by the city. Even though the synagogue was a few kilometers away from the original location and outside the immediate city center, it offered the Jewish community again a meeting space for worship. The new synagogue was dedicated on June 18, 1950, in an elaborate ceremony that included not only representatives of Jewish congregations, but also city and state officials, the Free German Youth, and musical contributions by the famous Dresden boys' choir, the Kreuzchor.[136]

Among the speakers was Mayor Otto Wagner, who emphasized the socialist future as the way to peace but also found clear words regarding the crimes against Jews during National Socialism and the guilt not only of Hitler but of the German people.[137] Already at this time, such utterances had become rare. In fact, despite the relatively large celebration, the newspaper article on the opening of the synagogue is short. It also changes the content of Mayor Wagner's speech to align more readily with de-emphasizing the role of the Nazi past and the guilt of ordinary Germans. According to the manuscript available in the archives of the Dresden Jewish Congregation, Wagner ends with the request that all Dresdners remember the past and put their energy into preventing such actions from repeating themselves and that each Dresdner offers their hand to the Soviet friend. The newspaper article, however, claims instead that Wagner told the citizens of Dresden to take the hand of friendship offered to them by the Jewish people.[138] Other speeches, such as by Julius Meyer, the president of the organization of the

Fig. 47. Dedication of postwar synagogue (1950). (Photograph by Erich Höhne and Erich Pohl. Reprinted by permission of SLUB/Deutsche Fotothek.)

Jewish communities, much more strongly express what was establishing itself as the official discourse: the emphasis on the capitalist system and the engagement of large companies, the responsibility of a smaller group of National Socialists that controlled the people, and the continuation of fascism in the West, which has to be fought at all costs.[139] In particular, he emphasizes the need to fight for peace and against the threat of the atomic bomb, repeating the very same talking points that characterize the discourse regarding the bombing and destruction of Dresden in February 1945.

A surviving artifact from the previous synagogue, the Semper-designed Star of David, had been placed on the tholobate of the new synagogue.[140] Through the relic, the community retained a tangible symbol that signaled a continuation of the former Jewish congregation and reconfirmed its roots in Dresden.[141] This symbolism was not, however, visible to the outside. By installing it on the new synagogue and integrating it without explanation into the design, the artifact's power to symbolize the loss of the members of the congregation, the Semper Synagogue, and the ground it had stood on, became limited. Before the 1970s, the remembrance of the horrors of the Nazi period for Jews in Dresden was thus mainly delegated to the congregation's

Fig. 48. Hebrew and German inscriptions remembering the Jewish victims of the Holocaust. (Photograph by Erich Höhne and Erich Pohl. Reprinted by permission of SLUB/Deutsche Fotothek.)

own circle. Inside the synagogue, a marble plaque next to the Torah shrine remembered the persecution of Jews during the Nazi era more explicitly:

> In remembrance of the dead
> and as a reminder for the living
> the Jewish community of Dresden has
> dedicated this plaque in 1950
> to the numerous brothers and sisters
> who from 1933–1945
> fell victim to murderous fascism.[142]

Even within their own sphere, the Jewish community stuck with the official GDR approach and subsumed the perpetrators under the wider term "fascism."

In fact, only a short time after state and religious officials opened the synagogue at the cemetery, the SED pressured and even imprisoned leaders of the Jewish communities with charges of imperial spying and other made-up claims. The head of the Dresden Jewish community, Leon Löwenkopf, finally found himself in prison for several months as a supposed Zionist secret agent.[143] There were also preparations for anti-Jewish show trials modeled after those in the Soviet Union. Many Jews, particularly community leaders, decided to flee to the West.[144] During this time, the Jewish congregation in Dresden shrank from 160 registered members in 1951 to 114 in 1953.[145] While these overt antisemitic actions stopped shortly after Stalin's death in 1953, it is undeniable that the relationship of the GDR to Judaism and its Jewish citizens remained complicated, as did the relationship of Jews to the state. Officially, the GDR supported the religious freedom of the Jewish communities and portrayed itself as beyond prejudice, yet the GDR refused to pay Israel reparations for the Holocaust (claiming that its state was Nazi-free) and vehemently opposed Israel's statehood. Even though East Germany took pains to describe its stance as solely "anti-Zionist" and not "antisemitic," the distinction was mainly theoretical.[146] Some of the leading Jewish community members were also active SED party members and officially supported the myth of the postracist society. Yet there was also discontent with the lack of acknowledgment of the specific Jewish plight under National Socialism.

The location of the original synagogue in the city center was not only unmarked, but it was also subjected to socialist land policies, rebuilding, and modernization efforts, essentially continuing the National Socialist policies that had seized the space.[147] The entire area's layout was changed significantly, with a new bridge, a new design of the Carolabrücke that had been partially blown up at the end of the war by SS soldiers, the widening of roads and streetcar tracks, and the enlargement of the Rathenauplatz, as well as new buildings on the other side of the square.[148] The new bridge, completed in 1971, was celebrated as an example of the GDR's engineering skills and modern achievements, as it was one of the longest and widest GDR bridges to be built using prestressed concrete. Most likely due to corrosion, part of the bridge collapsed in September 2024. There were immediate petitions to rebuild the bridge in its historic form from 1895.[149] Ironically, as we have seen in chapter 2, the archivist Otto Richter in 1905 showcased the Carolabrücke from 1895 as an example of the negative city developments that he felt took away from Dresden's beauty.

Chapter 3 demonstrated how such changes were part of a larger reimagining of Dresden as a representative socialist city in which only a small number of iconic architectural treasures were rebuilt in their original form as islands of history. The emphasis was instead placed on the enlargement of central city squares and the creation of wide marching avenues, which did not correspond to Dresden's historical proportions. Similar goals had also

Fig. 49. Opening of the Rudolf-Friedrichs-Brücke (Carolabrücke), view toward the former location of the synagogue (1971). (Photograph by Ulrich Häßler. Courtesy of Bundesarchiv / 183-K0704-0001-013, reprinted by permission.)

fueled the developments of the rebuilding plans in Dresden during National Socialism, as discussed earlier in the chapter. In fact, in Dresden the city planners found some assistance with designing the socialist city in drafts created during National Socialism for the "Redevelopment of Dresden's City Center." The idea of the "healthy city" propagated by the GDR and the need for massive marching paths and places for assemblies were remarkedly similar to the National Socialist prewar plans for Dresden's Altstadtgesundung, the concept of "bringing the Old Town back to health."[150]

Apart from the area around the synagogue, the Altmarkt was increased threefold into an immense demonstration square, and the streets connecting the city's east and west sides were widened up to three and a half times, sixty-five to seventy meters, to form a major throughway in accordance with Soviet examples.[151] Again, the Prager Straße can serve as a good example for how the socialist city was supposed to keep some of its character while also becoming distinctly socialist. While in the early twentieth century, the Prager Straße served upscale commerce, the socialist government tried to

Fig. 50. Prager Straße ensemble designed in socialist modernism (1974). (Photograph by Peter Sniegon. Reprinted by permission of SLUB/Deutsche Fotothek.)

provide not only a pedestrian promenade, but also an alternative to what the Old Town had been before the bombing by creating a harmonious architectural ensemble. It was, however, to be made in a distinctly socialist modernism. This north-south axis, previously some fourteen to eighteen meters wide, was expanded to sixty-eight to eighty-five meters, but was to remain a lively place for Dresdners and tourists to stroll leisurely through the city. It was turned into a pedestrian zone with large hotels and apartment buildings, but also art installations, a round cinema, restaurants, a department store, and, at the far end as part of the Old Town, an expansive cultural center, the Kulturpalast, as a new focal point.[152] The Frauenkirche in the heart of the Old Town at the Neumarkt, which will be the main topic in the next chapter, was left in ruins and declared a memorial. It became a second official space for remembrance events in addition to the grove at the cemetery.

In 1975, the site of the Semper synagogue finally received its own memorial. It is designed in the shape of a menorah with six branches (to represent the six million Jews killed in the Holocaust) and carries the inscription: "As a constant reminder of the victims of fascism: Here stood the Synagogue of

Fig. 51. Mayor Schill speaks at the memorial for the destroyed synagogue (November 9, 1978). (Photograph by Erich Höhne and Erich Pohl. Reprinted by permission of SLUB/ Deutsche Fotothek.)

the Israelite religious community of Dresden, built 1838–1840 by Gottfried Semper, consecrated by chief rabbi Dr. Zacharias Frankel and destroyed on 9 November 1938 by the fascists."[153] The inscription itself only speaks of "victims of fascism," so that Jewish victims are solely symbolically referenced in the branches of the menorah and the mention of the rabbi and synagogue. Yet at the same time, the menorah is an incomplete religious symbol, since it is missing its middle branch. So on the one hand Jewish persecution is implied to have been limited to religious persecution, even though it was not based on religious practice, while on the other hand, by changing a key part of the religious symbol and by referring only to "victims of fascism," the specifics of the antisemitic persecution are downplayed by subsuming Jewish victims. In contrast to the characteristically vague identification of the perpetrators as "fascists," the monument's inscription is specific on the description of the lost building itself. Gottfried Semper and the construction period are mentioned to emphasize the architectural and cultural loss that Dresden suffered on November 9.

When the pogroms received wider attention beginning in the 1970s and November 9 started to serve as a public day of commemoration, Dresden played an important national role in the events since it was the seat of the GDR Association of People of Jewish Faith. The ceremonies, however, were now more nationally controlled and had to follow central guidelines. They included the laying of wreaths at memorials and Jewish cemeteries, as well as speeches by high-ranking officials. For the fortieth anniversary of the November Pogroms in 1978, there was also a book publication, *Gedenke! Vergiss nie!* (Remember! Never Forget!), which bundled the most important addresses and writings about the events and added some educational articles.[154] Similar to the inscription on the Dresden Synagogue memorial, the commemorations mostly referred to the specific event of November 9 as highlighting the persecution of Jews by Nazi groups, instead of the long period of persecution that took place. The speeches also distanced such persecution from the ordinary citizens and from the pre-1933 past. In fact, ordinary citizens in Dresden are portrayed as having welcomed Jewish integration for a century, which only ended through external fascist-capitalist hostility. As then Dresden Major Gerhard Schill stated at the synagogue memorial in 1978 in his speech "Racial Hatred as a Component of Imperialist Policy": "140 years ago, in 1838, the residents of Dresden gathered here to take part in the groundbreaking ceremony for the building of a synagogue. [. . .] Exactly 100 years later, during the night from the 9th to the 10th of November, the building, as part of an organized, criminal act by Hitler-fascists, was razed to the ground."[155]

While by this time commemoration events about November 9 happened all over the GDR, the Dresden bombing largely ceased to be a centrally organized national propaganda event and received much less attention in the national press. The GDR tried to make overtures to the West and thus toned down its anti-Western rhetoric.[156] In Dresden, however, the commemorations remained the most important occasion for the citizens to gather, and the bombing continued to be contextualized as a perpetrator event, so that the association of February 13 and November 9 did not cease. Still, the discussion of November 9 became more varied. In addition to the official remembrance by the central administration, there were also conversations initiated by individuals and private groups. Yet they did not include a broader rethinking of the Dresden bombing and its remembrance practices.

Among the differing views that arose about the Nazi past within the GDR during this time, the peace movement was the most significant counternarrative to state-wide positions. The peace activists were mainly active within churches, which had preserved a certain level of independence and provided a place that offered a moderate level of free expression in many communities in the GDR. In Dresden, however, an official peace discourse had already been developed in regard to the bombing, with the Frauenkirche memorial and February 13 as central pillars. The peace movement in Dresden, when challenging party approaches, thus engaged both with the Dresden raids in 1945 as well as with the November Pogroms, the Holocaust, and Judaism as part of their mission to achieve peace and unity.

Regarding the Holocaust, the group "Aktion Sühnezeichen" (Action Reconciliation), which focused on signaling an awareness of responsibility, privately organized a yearly get-together to take care of and clean the Jewish cemetery.[157] Another autonomous group, the Dresdner Arbeitskreis Begegnung mit dem Judentum (Dresden Working Group Encountering Judaism) was founded by Catholic and Protestant faith leaders to teach about the Jewish religion, facilitate contact between Jews and Christians, and to try to take a closer look at the years 1933 to 1945 beyond the state-prescribed framework. Throughout the 1980s, the working group organized events that gave people the chance to become more aware of Jewish life in Dresden in the past and present. They also touched on the plight of Dresden's Jews during the Nazi era.[158]

The state saw such initiatives as challenging the GDR's official narrative of the past, both within the country and internationally. Governmental institutions thus tried to redirect the focus back onto individual Nazi criminals to undermine questions about the involvement of "regular" people or about the situation in the GDR. In 1987, the Gestapo man Henry Schmidt was put on trial in Dresden for the crimes he had committed against the city's Jewish residents. Schmidt's case was well-situated to gain high publicity. He had been the head of the Gestapo's department responsible for Jews ("Judenreferat") and had been organizing and leading most of the deportations of Jewish residents from Dresden. He was also integral in the establishment of the working camp Hellerberg for the Zeiss-Ikon company (and features several times in the Hellerberg film discussed earlier in the chapter. During the time of the trial, however, the existence of the film had not been revealed). His guilt was undeniable. The trial became a publicity spectacle. The media took a large interest, and Schmidt was nicknamed "The Eichmann of Dresden" in the socialist press.[159] In addition to news reports, a documentary was produced, and the trial was detailed in a book publication.[160] Western papers also showed significant interest, and their journalists were openly welcomed. In contrast to the ordinarily complicated procedures for traveling to and reporting from the GDR, in this case visas were easy to acquire. On September 29, 1987, Schmidt was sentenced to life in prison.

Before the 1980s, Schmidt had not been investigated even though he lived with his family in an East German town under his own name and worked in a state-owned business. For his exemplary work in the company and support of the GDR, he had been awarded several honors. It is not clear whether Schmidt's real identity was only discovered in the 1980s or whether it had been known all along.[161] It was and would have been exceedingly easy, however, to find and identify Schmidt. In fact, as historian Beate Meyer has noted, the research documents to Schmidt's case mention about a dozen other Gestapo men living in the GDR. Even though their identities and locations were known, none of them were confronted about their crimes.[162] It shows that the trial of Henry Schmidt in Dresden was not motivated only by a wish to capture former Nazi criminals and bring them to justice, but that it held an immense political component.

Since Dresden and its residents had been accepted internationally as innocent victims of the air war, questions about the responsibility of other Dresden residents were easy to ignore. Many witnesses, including a number from abroad, described Schmidt's crimes in great detail. The trial shows both the progress and the continued difficulty the GDR grappled with regarding the Holocaust. Henry Schmidt was a ruthless Nazi criminal who had caused tremendous suffering and was an integral part in the systematic killing of the Jewish population. Putting Schmidt on trial was, while long overdue, an important step in acknowledging Nazi-era crimes specifically targeting Jews. Since witnesses of Schmidt's atrocities were heard, it gave the surviving Jewish victims the chance to tell their stories of suffering in public without their narrative being subsumed under the larger trope of the antifascist resistance fighter. At the same time, however, the GDR misused the trial and the witness reports for their own agenda of polishing their image as the only antifascist German state. Jewish victims were thus victimized again, as their stories were abused for propaganda instead of leading to the long-neglected self-reflection in East Germany regarding the Nazi past.

There was also mistrust rising to the surface among the Jewish population about the government's motives for their increased attention to the Jewish plight. In Dresden, some members of the Jewish community felt that a sudden memory boom about the Holocaust could not make up for the severe lack of interest in Jewish culture and religion over the previous decades. There was also doubt that it would have any influence on the overpowering dominance of the discourse of suffering associated with the bombing in Dresden.[163] In the December 1987 edition of the *Nachrichtenblatt des Verbandes der Jüdischen Gemeinden in der Deutschen Demokratischen Republik*, the internal newsletter distributed among all the Jewish congregations in the GDR and put together by the leadership of the Association of Jewish Communities in East Germany, the report on the trial includes a reflection on commemorations of victims in Dresden: "Tens of thousands of Dresdners publicly commemorate the destruction of their city. Where are the public references to the persecution of their fellow citizens? And who commemorates the brave non-Jewish spouses who dared to do all they could to save their Jewish relatives?"[164]

Even though the trial partially failed in easing concerns about the sincerity of the state's acknowledgment of Jewish suffering, it proved a successful strategy to regain control over a discourse regarding perpetrators. The trial seemed to reaffirm the GDR's claim to its status as an antifascist state. While the party knew of other former National Socialist criminals that should have been prosecuted, doing so would have undermined their repeated declarations that East Germany was already Nazi-free and that Schmidt had been an exception. With its guilty verdict, the trial foreclosed any questions about other perpetrators.

Yet the trial did not deter the autonomous groups interested in understanding the Jewish plight during the Nazi era from continuing their own work and preparations for the upcoming fiftieth anniversary of the November Pogroms. One of the actions taken by the working group Begegnung mit dem Judentum for the fiftieth anniversary of the November Pogroms was particularly progressive considering GDR memory politics, and exceptional considering the Dresden memory culture and its focus on February 1945. The members installed a plaque at the Kreuzkirche that acknowledges specifically Jewish victims without including references to communist resistance fighters or the Dresden bombing or entirely generalizing the perpetrators as "fascists." Instead, the inscription touches on the question of guilt and responsibility for the Holocaust among German Christians:

> With shame and grief Christians remember the Jewish residents of this city. [...] We kept silent when their places of worship were burned down, when Jews were deprived of their rights, were driven out and murdered. We did not recognize them as our brothers and sisters. We ask for forgiveness and shalom.[165]

While the plaque speaks specifically for Christians, and the use of the passive voice describes them collectively as solely bystanders, the inscription nevertheless emphasizes responsibility instead of fellow victimhood.

Similarly, since churches in the GDR were given more freedom to express themselves in their own congregations and buildings, it was possible for the working group to put together a unique exhibition for the fiftieth anniversary of the November Pogroms, titled "Juden in Sachsen: Ihr Leben und Leiden" (Jews in Saxony: Their Life and Suffering).[166] The exhibition was the first to provide a single focus on Jewish history in Saxony and included much information that had been previously inaccessible to the public. It was here that slides of the film that featured the blasting and demolition of the synagogue were shown.[167] The plaque and exhibition formed a surprisingly strong counterpoint to the official ceremonies at the synagogue memorial and the various other party-led events put on for the anniversary.

While private initiatives within the Jewish congregations and other faith organizations had always followed some of their own paths in remembering Jewish history and the Holocaust, by 1988 Dresden's politically streamlined memory discourse surrounding November 9 started to crack, which had the potential to profoundly affect the remembrance culture surrounding February 13 and to open up questions about the exceptional role awarded to Dresden. As we have seen, Dresden's engagement in antisemitism and persecution during the Nazi era was by no means less pronounced, but was in full accordance with the rest of Germany. In fact, Saxon National Socialism could build on a long-standing history of antisemitism in the state. In addition, there exists an archive of documents that detail persecution in Dresden, and the city itself contains several examples of National Socialist city planning in its midst, even today. Dresden readily became an important center to represent National Socialist German artistic tastes and cultural ideology, be it by cleansing its collections of art that did not conform to Nazi aesthetic principles, by creating a Degenerate Art exhibition and book burnings, by having its architectural treasures serve as a backdrop for leading Nazi personalities, or by convincing international travelers to visit Nazi Germany.

After the war was over, the rhetoric surrounding the bombing on February 13, 1945, was used to deflect responsibility of the city and its inhabitants. It was aided by the GDR's standpoint, which blamed the Nazi horrors on a small clique of fascists, which in turn were readily equated with the Western states in Cold War politics. In Dresden, the narrative of February 13 became the template for discussing the Holocaust, which was mainly represented by

November 9, 1938. In rhetorical terms, in commemoration rituals, on memorials, and by an emphasis on the destruction of architecturally significant landmarks, the Holocaust was not denied, but residents and Jews were presented as a community of suffering. In this role, they were imbued with the task to warn the world about the necessity for peace. Ironically, while these associations built on GDR propaganda finally started to crack in the 1980s, reunification and its new perpetrator definitions and rebuilding decisions actually restrengthened the concentration on February 13 and the idea of shared victimhood.

Again, it is the built environment that illustrates most convincingly the city's priorities and attitudes toward the past. The next chapter will thus look at post-reunification Dresden rebuilding projects, in particular the Frauenkirche and the New Synagogue, and the differing echoes they received locally, nationally, and internationally. The discussion reveals that the disconnect with the Nazi past continued in Dresden even after reunification. At the same time, the rebuilding of the Frauenkirche, while freed from socialist messaging, remained not only tied to the already established peace discourse, but its symbolic meaning was extended to include reconciliation.

CHAPTER 5

The Multiple Pasts in Dresden's Post-Reunification Cityscape
From the Frauenkirche to the New Synagogue

The previous chapters have shown how with the destruction of the historic center in 1945 and with the subsequent socialist policies for removal and rebuilding, many of Dresden's traditional *lieux de mémoire* (Nora) or *loci* (Rossi) became spaces relegated to memory without a material anchor.[1] Consequently, the intangible features of the locus, such as feelings, meanings, and symbolic perceptions, were severed from their physical references in the city.[2] Even though the mapping of Dresden's memory and identity via imagined spaces was able to accommodate the traditional Dresden narrative of the "German Florence," which was the necessary frame for the destruction story, there was a need to supplement the photographic representations of the city in ruins with material sites. At these places residents could come together to perform their past and present through mourning and commemoration rituals and could ground their identity.

In postwar Dresden, the ruins of the Frauenkirche emerged as the key material fix point for identity. In contrast to the highly politically charged memorial park at the Heidefriedhof cemetery, the Frauenkirche offered spaces for diverging remembrance during socialism. The site, neither rebuilt nor cleared, was able to serve as a sacred shrine in which the contained incomplete icon worked as a place of signification that was able to accommodate various stakeholders—be they public or private, individual or collective, local or foreign—by including the different narratives about the city's past and present, the sorrow about its loss, and the wishes and hopes for Dresden's future.[3]

After the end of socialism and its ideological control over official memory, many yearned for a stable and homogeneous symbolic message and value system outside of socialist ideology. In Dresden, such a message also entailed building decisions.[4] The Frauenkirche site unites the architectural past of Dresden as well as its loss; it has housed a pluralism of interpretations within what Rossi has termed its "repository of history,"[5] but, in its fragmented state, it has also featured an open future. During and after reunification, the Frauenkirche was consequently a suitable site and symbol to negotiate further this period of political and societal change and emotional upheaval. As a foundation, the basic underlying premise of Dresden's unique cultural significance and its unwarranted destruction remained unchallenged as providing the fundamental morphological system on which to erect a post-reunification identity for the city and its people. The question became which other aspects within the repository would be activated and which would be cast aside. This process was negotiated both rhetorically as well as in material terms, but it ultimately led to the call to rebuild the Frauenkirche in its original form and as a symbol for peace after the successful revolution against the German Democratic Republic (GDR).

I argue, however, that by calling for the rebuilding of the landmark in its historic "authentic" form, as if correcting its loss caused by outside forces, its post-reunification symbolism did not only allow the continuance of a peace discourse, but the church's meaning could be expanded to be a symbol of reconciliation. Since the rebuilt Frauenkirche was perceived as legitimate authentic heritage, representative of Dresden's unique past and its cultural value, it was elevated to a symbolic superstructure and powerful vector overarching Dresden's future identity, memory culture, and its relationship to building practices. By raising the Frauenkirche to a meta-symbol in its role as a beacon for "peace and reconciliation" and as standing in for the true Dresden, the rebuilding could function as a driving force in neutralizing all concerns about the less glorious parts of Dresden's past. It not only allowed the continuation of the concept of a Dresden community of suffering, but it also introduced the residents as a community of peacemaking, who led by the example of accepting reconciliation despite the anguish caused by both the war and the GDR. The worldwide support for the project and for Dresden speaks to the perception of this symbolism as legitimate. In terms of Dresden's past, this approach allowed that an evaluation of the responsibilities for Jewish suffering during the Nazi years could be effectively omitted from the dominant discourse.

This chapter will illustrate the ways in which rebuilding decisions and the discourse surrounding them are related to the memory politics regarding Dresden's past, and in particular the National Socialist entanglements, by exploring the interplay between the highly symbolic Frauenkirche destroyed in February 1945 by Allied bombing, the rise of a narrative about the rescue of the Star of David from the Semper synagogue by a Dresden fireman, and the building of a new synagogue at the location of the Semper synagogue before it was burned down during the November Pogroms in 1938. The discourses surrounding the two building projects show that despite the political changes, the consistent patterns of remembrance in Dresden regarding the National Socialist past carry beyond 1989–90, even though they are contextualized differently. A clearer picture emerges about Dresden's post-reunification framing of its memory politics and the exclusions and generalizations it entails, framings that have been setting the course for the city's present and future role within Germany and the world.

The Frauenkirche Memorial in the 1980s and the Framing of Past and Future

While immediately after the war, plans were made to rebuild the Frauenkirche, the idea was soon abandoned. The site was to be cleared, similar to the Sophienkirche. In this case, though, pressure from the Dresden preservation office coupled with protests from the population, which yearned for a full rebuilding of their icon, convinced the city government to halt its plans of a complete clearing. While not rebuilt, the Frauenkirche was kept in its ruinous state and designated as an antiwar memorial in 1966. A modest commemorative plaque was installed stating that the Frauenkirche had been destroyed by Anglo-American bombers.[6] Apart from the memorial grove at the Heidefriedhof, the Frauenkirche ruins in the Old Town functioned as an important space for public commemoration events, in particular during the 1970s and 1980s.[7]

In the 1980s, Dresden, and later Leipzig, became the sites in which the basic beliefs and ideas of the socialist state were challenged by parts of the population who wished for political and societal change. In Dresden, these overarching concepts were contextualized mainly through the locus of the Frauenkirche. In its broken materiality, the Frauenkirche provided a mediated symbolic frame that allowed it to be claimed as physical proof for a variety of concepts and political futures. The official discourse and its challenger both focused on a story of mourning for the past, emphasized loss and victimhood, and presented the Dresden bombing as a catastrophe that was so horrific that it could inspire the wish for peace in the world. Yet as the following examples show, the vision of the future for the country diverged: The GDR desired to gain political stability, support, and unity by pointing to the destruction as well as the positive ways the GDR had overcome it, whereas a growing number of protesters saw the Frauenkirche in its perpetual ruins as a reflection of the oppressive, inflexible system of the GDR and the Eastern Bloc and viewed the socialist countries as sources for instability in the world.

Not surprisingly, it was an anniversary of the bombing that became the first occasion in which the official discourse and rituals surrounding the Dresden destruction were openly challenged, with each group staking claims on representing the most desirable path to peace. In the early 1980s, the pastor and GDR antiwar activist Christoph Wonneberger had started to hold regular prayers for peace in the Dresden Kreuzkirche, attracting scores of mainly young people worried about the consequences of the escalating arms race.[8] He later continued leading these prayers in the Nikolaikirche in Leipzig. Churches in the GDR were spaces that were officially independent from the government. While they were heavily infiltrated by the East German secret police, the Staatssicherheit (Stasi), the state did not openly interfere. Both the Nikolaikirche in Leipzig and the Kreuzkirche in Dresden were instrumental to the final undertaking of the Peaceful Revolution. In Dresden, on the bombing anniversary in 1982, a group of people began walking from the Kreuzkirche to the ruins after peace prayers, leaving the protection of the semiautonomous space of the church.[9] They wanted to take part more directly in the political arena, even though, in the months before, Stasi agents had tried to undermine this plan.[10] By gathering at the Frauenkirche memorial, the protesters were undercutting with their own peace discourse the official commemoration rituals for February 13 at the location, which had included a political peace rally and guards of honor in front of the ruins during the day. Each group identified through their presence the Frauenkirche as a *lieu de mémoire* that justified their beliefs and activities. The party's rituals at the Frauenkirche were marked by speeches and slogans; in contrast, the protesters expressed their criticism through silence and burning candles. It is unclear how many gathered at the site of the Frauenkirche. Estimates for the numbers of attendees of the peace prayers at the Kreuzkirche speak of four to five thousand, but not all of them went to the Frauenkirche.[11] The police were deployed to the area, but, most likely due to the presence of Western media, the demonstrators were allowed to carry on.[12] Members of the Stasi put together a detailed report about their surveillance of the peace forum, which, however, downplayed the demonstration at the Frauenkirche, most likely because the Stasi officers did not want to admit that they had been unable to prevent the event as they had been instructed to. They instead painted it as small and unimportant due to their "timely initiation of appropriate security measures":

> At around 9.45 p.m., a smaller number of participants went to the ruins of the Frauenkirche, where a total of around 400–500 young people [. . .] had gathered. They lit candles (about 50 of them), sang songs [. . .] and laid flowers. A group of six people erected a cross (0.70 m high) made of crate boards with the inscription "35,000 dead—why?" at the ruins. At around 11 p.m., the gathering dispersed in a calm and disciplined manner.[13]

Over time, these gatherings at the Frauenkirche morphed into the large Monday protests against the GDR government in 1989 under the slogan "Wir sind das Volk" ("we are the people"). Both the state and its challengers were thus concerned with how to define the concept of peace, not with questioning the proclamation of its necessity. Both tapped into the ruins of the Frauenkirche as representing the suffering during the Nazi and war period. Consequently, despite the conflicts, the notion of a fellowship of victims of fascism, established early on in the GDR—between communists, Jews, "ordinary" German citizens, the bombing victims, and the city of Dresden as a unique cultural center—remained largely unchallenged.

With the threat of continued public demonstrations against the GDR and its official programs in the 1980s, the Socialist Unity Party (SED) reacted both on the local and national level in more public ways to reinforce their exclusive access to Dresden's symbolic cityscape, in particular the highly contested Frauenkirche. The party stepped up visible gestures of "owning" the cityscape with its old and new architecture by reclaiming it as a backdrop for large spectacles that affirmed the official ideology of the GDR and its vision of the future.[14]

One example is the meeting of the Young/Thälmann Pioneers, the East German political organization for children and youth, held in Dresden in August 1982. It emphatically drove home the official message that peace and socialism were synonymous, while the capitalist West was described as warmongering due to their increased armaments and nuclear weapons. Out came a curious mixture of military language, patriotism, criticism of the West, and appeals to peace in speeches and on banners.[15] At a massive demonstration in the city center with, according to official claims, more than 150,000 participants, Erich Honecker, the SED's general secretary (the political leader of the GDR) who had traveled to Dresden for the event, describes

Fig. 52. Young pioneers at the dedication of the commemorative plaque in front of the Frauenkirche memorial (1982). (Photograph by Erich Höhne and Erich Pohl. Reprinted by permission of SLUB/Deutsche Fotothek.)

"the beautiful Dresden" as "a city full of joyful and happy children" for whose peaceful future the party fights.[16] The GDR thus mobilized to the fullest its founding myth as a restorer and staunch defender of peace against the (fascist) threats from the West. Staging the demonstration in Dresden, the SED did not only aim to spread propaganda, but also to signal that the Dresden narrative was firmly tied to the official peace discourse and that its symbols were unavailable for competing world views.

To drive this point home, the pioneers' gathering also included a ceremony involving the Frauenkirche memorial. With much fanfare, a large commemoration plaque was installed close to the ruins.[17] The plaque itself served as a material marker indicating ownership of the cityscape and the

Frauenkirche, and the inscription was to cement the GDR's propagandistic rhetoric about the bombing as the only valid view: "The Frauenkirche Dresden—destroyed by Anglo-American bombers in February 1945. Its ruins commemorate tens of thousands of dead and remind the living to fight against imperialist barbarism for the peace and happiness of humankind."[18]

While not mentioning directly the inner-GDR conflicts carried out in the cityscape, then Dresden mayor Gerhard Schill underlined in his speech the exclusive right of the GDR government and SED to the monument and city center. To this end, Schill acknowledged the Frauenkirche memorial as a specifically apt site of criticizing the stationing of US missiles in West Germany, whose "warheads are then aimed at us."[19] With this assertion, the private peace protesters could be viewed as obsolete since the state was already representing their concerns and their wish for peace in their stead. Schill also emphasized Dresden's postwar existence as having been entirely depended on socialist rebuilding: "What imperialism has destroyed, socialism has brought to new bloom."[20] This view echoes the rhetoric described in chapter 3 regarding Dresden, which tried to erase the contrast between the architectural history of the city and its socialist rebuilding by declaring the surviving or rebuilt historic structures on the same footing as socialist additions to the Old Town. The most important goal was "to preserve what has been created, to add more and more beautiful designs, and to make sure that we never allow war to destroy [Dresden] again."[21] By declaring Dresden was no longer destroyed, Schill suggests that its spaces have also ceased to be available as symbols for alternative political ideas. Finally, by filling the Neumarkt with thousands of young pioneers, the space becomes entirely occupied, symbolically cutting off the predominantly late high school and college-age peace protesters from physically grounding and demonstrating their beliefs. They are denied the opportunity to impact the future outside of the established political norms.

The staging of socialist control over the future of the city and its meaning did not stop with the memorial event. The children were similarly part of photo ops that highlighted the successful rebuilding of Dresden as a socialist city. The young pioneers not only marched through the socialist ensembles at the Prager Straße but were also filmed spending time in the city museum marveling at the original architectural model of its socialist design. Yet just as the people's yearning for the traditional cityscape remained, such rhetoric and events could also not quench the private peace movement and its mission. The competition for the meaning and contextualization of Dresden's destruction narrative continued.

Fig. 53. Young pioneers marvel at the architectural model of the Prager Straße in socialist modernism (1982). (Photograph by Ulrich Häßler. Reprinted by permission of Ullstein Bild.)

While the Socialist Unity Party still concentrated on their long-standing opposition to the West as responsible for suffering and injustice, the peace and civil rights activists turned their attention to the postwar situation and criticized the GDR and its oppression of the population. They also implied that the socialist regime was a continuation of the Nazism of the previous period, which, according to many Dresdners, had victimized Dresden and its citizens. So even though the private residents engaged in the peace movement were often also involved in a reassessment of the Nazi past, as both sprang from the semiautonomous spaces offered by the church and both undermined official policies, the fundamental viewpoint that dominated the remembrance of the 1945 raids on Dresden did not change. When the peace movement became a wider revolutionary movement asking for freedom and democracy, the interest in the specifically Jewish experience during the Nazi era and Dresden's role in it was further diluted, since the GDR regime was added to the pool of perpetrators. This expansion also opened up a direct path for younger generations to join the collectively shared victim identity, cementing the discourse even further into a shared cultural memory. While the bombing experiences were only affecting them indirectly via the stories of those who had lived through the bombing and the rituals they participated in, they could claim direct personal and collective suffering under the dictatorship of the socialist state. It was this mindset with which many Dresdners started into the German reunification process.

The Frauenkirche's Reconstruction as Sacred Journey

Rebuilt from its ruins during the first fifteen years of the unified Germany, the Frauenkirche and its perceived meaning became an active participant in the process of the reconstitution of a collective identity and narrative for the city and its residents. The post-reunification discourse about the rebuilding of the Frauenkirche is carefully structured and tightly woven together with the actual re-erection of the building. The narrative and the construction of the historic site each provide a normative frame for the other, within which Dresden's post-reunification identity arises. It resonates deeply not only with many residents, but also on a national and international level. While the demise of the GDR and the reunification with the Federal Republic fundamentally changed the lives of all the citizens of the new states, from economics and politics to culture and even language use, Dresden stands out in the way that memory, the discourse about the past and future, and the built environment were redefined, reorganized, and developed.

To make visible these complex post-reunification processes at work in Dresden, elements of the concept of societal language planning, as originally identified by linguist Einar Haugen, can assist in capturing such practices and their intentionality.[22] Usually, language planning is a public or policy effort to reshape norms and values by changing the use of language. For example, when postcolonial societies implement a shift from the language of the colonizers to local languages while establishing an independent society, this development includes language planning. Language planning works on two planes: corpus planning (the selection and codification of the vocabulary) and status planning (the enhancement of the prestige and usage of the selected vocabulary).

While there was no official public body regulating language in the new German states after reunification, the necessity arose to reorient the language tied up within the political and social system of the GDR. Some specialty terms became obsolete with the transformed political situation, and others in the corpus needed to be recoded to reflect the changed social, cultural, and political landscape. Since East Germany was integrated into the Federal Republic's systems and politics, the pressure was immense to adopt West German vocabulary and meanings. This change in language, however, also reflected an identity crisis among many citizens and their regions.[23] Yet since Dresden had remained coded as exceptional and iconic even in the GDR and its meaning had been defined by a narrative that was widely embraced, the fundamental building blocks for a post-reunification identity and story were already available in this instance. The Frauenkirche's rebuilding served as the material anchor in constructing this identity based on the city as a morphological space; the processes of expanding and reorienting the Dresden narrative that arose with the reconstruction served to contextualize this self-understanding within the new societal structures. In the process, it also effectively limited the symbolism of the site to a distinct meaning.[24]

The post-reunification modifications in the public rhetoric regarding the Frauenkirche can be likened to both conscious and unconscious language-planning processes. Dresden could be publicly rebranded by reforming the corpus away from the GDR's definitions, vocabulary, and context. After the fall of the wall, the official meaning the Frauenkirche had occupied in Cold War politics in the previous decades, as a site of anti-West propaganda, was delegitimized and had to be contextualized differently.[25] Of particular relevance is the recoding of the trope of "peace" so frequently evoked in the context of the Frauenkirche ruins. It is exemplary of the discursive shift regarding Dresden after the demise of the GDR.

As we have seen in the previous section, the underlying meaning and the associations conjured up when using the word "peace" were strongly defined by GDR politics, which from the start claimed a monopoly on its definition and instrumentalized its connotations to support its own societal vision. The GDR described itself as a "peace state" in contrast to the Western capitalist ("fascist") countries hungry for war.[26] At the same time, the state increasingly militarized the GDR society, particularly via the education in the Free German Youth (FDJ, the East German political youth organization for those over the age of fourteen) and other organizations. The SED tried to conceal the inherent conflicts between the two ideas with such slogans as "armed peace."[27] Yet with the official SED's claim on defining "peace" removed, its meaning and its associated lexical field within the Dresden discourse shifted.[28]

If we think in terms of corpus and status planning about the language with which Dresden, and in particular the Frauenkirche, was and is encoded after reunification, the reasons for the success of this shift in representation stand out more clearly. As the examples will show, the language corpus employed to redefine the discourse surrounding the Frauenkirche drew on already deeply ingrained cultural traditions by indexing the common linguistic expressions of the Christian foundational narrative of the life, death, and resurrection of Christ.[29] Dresden was seen as being restored into its rightful place again by reintegrating it into the culture of the Occidental West, which socialism had rejected. The support for the rebuilding became a sacred act carried by the power of faith. This corpus was easily included into the established ideas about the meaning of the city, which had been encoded as exceptional and its loss as catastrophic. The discourse about the rebuilding of the Frauenkirche is thus written forward by merging a mythological (Christian) frame with another, already established, mythical system, namely the story of Dresden's Baroque cityscape. With this double framing through some of the most fundamental and broadly understood symbols in the Western world, the rebuilding was poised to be a moral and cultural obligation rather than a decision.

Consequently, the Frauenkirche did not serve any longer as a symbol for peace in the form of a denunciation of the West, which had been based on the state of its ruined body. Instead, the process of the rebuilding and the church's completion in its original form were at this point characterized as active peacemaking. Culturally, the rebuilding project was represented as the return of essential heritage in the form of an authentic nationally and internationally revered work of architecture that symbolized Germany's tradition of high culture. Between the Frauenkirche being inherently a Christian landmark, the significance it had been awarded as a concept and material expression of culture, and a rebuilding movement that was seen as having grown from "below," the Christian discourse of the reconstruction was not understood as an analogy to illustrate the importance of rebuilding, but as a genuine ethical act.[30] The Christian symbolism and rhetoric thus implied a humanitarian aspect: not only was the rebuilding an expression of the opportunity for peace, but through the coupling with Christianity and in particular the passion of Christ, "suffering," "peace," and "reconciliation" became the trinity on which post-reunification Dresden re-erected its Old Town and its identity. Two important events worked as catalysts for the successful shift in contextualization and rhetoric concerning the Frauenkirche memorial. On a national level, the speech by the chancellor of the Federal Republic at the time, Helmut Kohl, in front of the Frauenkirche in December 1989, and locally, the founding of a citizen initiative that called for the rebuilding of the Frauenkirche already as early as October 1989, even before the fall of the GDR regime.

In an effort to achieve his political goal of German reunification instead of the alternative of two independent states, Helmut Kohl tapped into the

Fig. 54. Helmut Kohl speaks in front of the ruins of the Frauenkirche (December 19, 1989). (Photograph by Rainer Mittelstädt. Courtesy of Bundesarchiv / 183-1989-1219-034, reprinted by permission.)

Dresden narrative and described the Frauenkirche ruins as a symbol of a humanitarian and cultural violation. When Kohl addressed East Germans directly in December 1989, he did so in Dresden, on a day of a Monday demonstration, thus linking his appearance to the Peaceful Revolution and Dresden's cultural significance and loss. Ironically, part of the shift away from the Frauenkirche's role as an official political propaganda tool for the GDR was in fact initiated by a highly staged political act that was strategically made to appear apolitical. "Dresden" could anchor the West German chancellor's words within the ideas of freedom, unity, and peace, as well as in the Dresden destruction narrative of past innocence and victimhood. Consequently, one of the central actions of Kohl was to lay down a wreath to honor the dead of the Dresden raids. With this act, he also shifted the rhetoric of the GDR remembrance, which concentrated on the guilt of the fascist West, to one that emphasized German victims and culture, without assigning specific responsibility to anyone.[31]

By coming to "a place so rich in traditions" to gain support for reunification, Kohl established the city as a site that synthesized the past's traumatic experiences for all Germans, making it the emotional and cultural heart of both Germanys.[32] Speaking in front of the Frauenkirche memorial about unifying the German states, Kohl presented the site as a central symbol for the need of such unity. The Frauenkirche was thus marked as the sacred space for Germany's rebirth. The wreath ceremony and the destroyed Frauenkirche backdrop were only problematized through a veiled reference to Germany's responsibility for the Holocaust. Within the symbolic matrix set up to understand the fall of the GDR regime and the future of a reunified German nation via Dresden, there was little room for a re-evaluation of the past.

Instead, Kohl presents Germany as fully integrated into a European discourse about the Second World War, implying that Germany shares the experience of wartime suffering with other European nations. Dresden, with its widely unchallenged position as both a European treasure and innocent war victim, could serve as the perfect place to stage and establish such a shift in memorialization. Within this structure, German reunification, according to Kohl, would consequently not endanger but would strengthen European unity. In this sense, reunification is portrayed as the final step in building reconciliation among former enemies. Not surprisingly, Kohl uses structural metaphors to drive his point home:

> The "House of Germany"—our common home—has to be built under a European roof. That must be our political goal.
>
> In a few days [. . .] the last decade of this century begins. A century which has seen much hardship, much destitute, many deaths, much suffering, especially in Europe and also here in Germany—a century, that has also imposed a special responsibility on us Germans—in view of the terrible things that have happened.
>
> Here, in front of the ruins of the Frauenkirche in Dresden, at the memorial to those who died in Dresden, I have just laid down a wreath—also in memory of the suffering and the dead of this beautiful old German city.[33]

In his speech, Kohl directly connects Dresden's story of innocence and loss to the national project of abolishing the separation of East and West Germany, which had remained one of the major and most visible political consequences following the Second World War. Tapping into the highly symbolic Dresden narrative, Kohl staged a meticulously planned, but seemingly "spontaneous" emotional performance.[34] Within this process, not only was the Frauenkirche treated as an all-German and European symbol of unity, but with this idea Kohl also expanded the church's role as a beacon for peace and reconciliation to serve as a guarantor for the nonthreatening unified Germany: "In the future, only peace can unfold from Germany—that is the goal of our unity!"[35] By tying in this mission with the impending Christmas holidays, which Kohl refers to as "the celebration of peace," he also connects this new beginning as a unified, peace-loving Germany with Christian mythology.[36]

The crowds responded strongly to the atmosphere and enthusiastically waved the German flags that had been distributed before the event, so that the press was offered emotionally and visually powerful motifs.[37] The scene suggested a chancellor overcome by both the large crowd's calls for reunification and the highly symbolic significance of the Frauenkirche backdrop. With this staging, the Christian Democratic government hoped to control in advance the kind of memories and interpretations that would emerge in regard to Kohl's visit, thus trying to put together a positive foundational narrative for the reunified Germany.[38] Indeed, the press responded with enthusiasm, and images of the event found distribution around the globe. The accompanying writeups declared reunification a fait accompli after Kohl's speech. In fact, as political scientist Markus Driftmann has noted, the retelling of Kohl's visit in the press at the time, and in the collective memory of today, matches the archetype of the literary genre of the heroic epic, including its mythic and religious undertones.[39]

On the local level, the events and their reception confirmed the widely held belief among the population that Dresden possessed singular significance, both because of its cultural meaning and the horrific destruction it had endured first in 1945 and then by the GDR's attitude to city building. The members of the initiative formed in 1989 to rebuild the Frauenkirche published an "Appeal [Call] from Dresden" (Ruf aus Dresden) on February 13, 1990, the forty-fifth anniversary of the bombing.[40] The title clearly references the "call" to rescue Dresden's architecture from the GDR plans that had been published in the 1949 *Merian* magazine discussed in chapter 3. They hoped to start a "worldwide campaign" to rebuild the Frauenkirche as a "Christian world peace center in the new Europe," which would give back to world culture "an architectural work of art of unique significance" and be the beginning of restoring "one of the most beautiful cityscapes in the heart of Dresden."[41] The rebuilding of the Frauenkirche is described as a sacred act of deep ethical significance. By asking the entire world for financial support, in particular also the "victorious powers" of the Second World War, such help is implied to be an expression of the commitment to a positive peaceful future.[42]

Christian symbolism remained a key frame for the appeals for restoration and distinctly characterized the rebuilding as a response to the GDR's view of the Frauenkirche ruins as a statement against the West. In his Dresden speech in December 1989, Kohl had already linked German reunification wishes to Christmas and thus to a holy birth. In the "Call from Dresden" the authors call upon the Christian symbolism surrounding Easter to strengthen the absolute necessity of their cause. Comparable to the narrative of the passion and salvation of Jesus, the Frauenkirche is understood as an innocent victim of senseless violence, becoming a symbol for suffering and loss.

According to Christian mythology, Jesus' suffering was transformed by his rise from the dead, which served as a signal for change and the chance for new, positive beginnings. After the resurrection, he wears instead of the diminishing crown of thorns a crown of peace and overcomes humiliation. To take part in the kingdom of peace and achieve salvation, the story goes, one needs to acknowledge Jesus' sacrifice and the miracle of his resurrection and spread the word about his message of peace.[43] The representation of the rebuilding of the original Frauenkirche parallels this narrative: the appeal for donations describes how the rebuilt structure would serve as "a stone witness [. . .] that proclaims the gospel of peace" and restores the "crown of Europe." Such narrative stirs up deeply ingrained beliefs of Western culture. It is suggested that it is up to the people during this transformative time to create a future for the unified Germany by restoring values based on Western cultural traditions, traditions that had been interrupted by war and socialism.[44] The rebuilding of what is presented as the cultural crown jewel would create a site that could anchor a unifying identity based on the supposed innocence of the historic Baroque artifact. Like for those that were said to believe in Jesus as the Messiah and embrace Christianity, believing in the utmost importance of the project of rebuilding and support it with passion as well as donations would bring salvation. Being part of rebuilding the "authentic" Frauenkirche was a profession of one's faith in the idea that the future would be good if it reconnected with the German cultural achievements of the past. These achievements are coded as cultural and as politically innocent.

The implications of embedding the Frauenkirche in this fundamental religious story of passion and salvation go even further, of course. The vital tenet of the Christian religion rests on the idea that the innocent Jesus' suffering and death on the cross and subsequent resurrection absolves from their sins all those who believe in him.[45] Through his death, forgiveness and peace on earth are possible. Since the destruction of Dresden and the Frauenkirche by bombs is described within such a Christian framework, the narrative proposes the Frauenkirche's violent and undeserved destruction as the ultimate sacrifice, which at this point turned into an offer of redemption.[46] Rebuilding the Frauenkirche in its authentic form is thus a gift of reconciliation to a world that had violently taken it away. Accordingly, the rebuilt Frauenkirche has been frequently referred to as "the miracle of Dresden."[47]

The Frauenkirche site thus took on the role of what one could call a local and national *meta-lieu de mémoire*, a site in which the various narratives about Dresden's past intersected and from which the story for Dresden's post-reunification future was emerging. As a *meta-lieu de mémoire*, the church functioned and functions as a powerful attractor inviting emotional identification with Dresden and its history. By such rituals as placing candles in front of the Frauenkirche and adhering to collective "silent remembrance," the site is reconfirmed year after year as an "object of worship."[48] At the same time, it acts as a beacon to the world that signals the importance of re-establishing and protecting Dresden and its heritage, and warns of the possible cost of war, violence, or untrustworthy political systems.

Through this highly publicized historical rebuilding project, a memory loop emerged that allowed the idea of the old Dresden to bridge with the contemporary rebuilding. By calling both the old, lost structure and the rebuilt one "authentic," any contests over meaning disappeared in favor of a re-won stable and harmonious identity without the need for significant changes or for testing established remembrance patterns for their validity. In the mind of many locals, the re-won stability instead held responsibilities for the future: the duty to carry on with recreating Dresden's old glory, to guard and protect the city from any future attempts to damage it, and to continue mourning rituals to remember the losses as a warning of the necessity for peace in the world. Through the recreation of the city morphology of the past under the general banner of peace and reconciliation, questions about past responsibilities were neutralized and pushed aside.[49]

By expanding the view of Dresden beyond the local and understanding it as showcasing the national, even the European identity of the new world order, it became an important unifying component among the residents in their post-reunification lives. The mission to be custodians of their unique and significant surroundings, and to warn the world of possible other catastrophic scenarios gets passed on from generation to generation through the physical presence of the rebuilt historic cityscape, the established language with which it is encoded, and the duties it is deemed to demand from its inhabitants.

The Rebuilt Frauenkirche as Attractor and Amplifier in the Peace and Reconciliation Discourse

The incredible number of donations from around the (Western) world that financed the Frauenkirche's reconstruction, and the far-reaching interest taken in the process, suggests the high importance that was attached to the rebuilding of the Frauenkirche both as a symbolic and material act, but it also indicates the success of the rhetorical framework within which the project was presented. The Christian symbolism also dovetailed well with the long-established and widely accepted view of Dresden as a worthy urban travel destination, which served as a second inspiration for the strong support of the reconstruction. The models from tourism studies describing the relationship between sites, sights, and tourists, which we explored in chapters 2 and 3, prove helpful in explaining how both aspects could fuel such an effective rebuilding campaign.

The idea of reconstructing the sacred icon, the marker that has been idolized as the symbol for Dresden's significance, reignited the long-established "sacralization" of the city and its architecture in people's minds.[50] The destruction and lack of rebuilding of the Frauenkirche had left Dresden without this dominant material marker, or, as MacCannell calls it, "The Real Thing."[51] It complicated the relationship between visitors and the site. Tourists usually form their expectations for their experience from narratives as well as the "mechanical reproduction of the sacred object" such as pictures and photographs before they even see the object in person.[52] With this gaze, the travelers transpose their created experience onto the attraction during their actual visit. Even though already preconceived, the presence of the marker authenticates this experience for them, thus supporting in the traveler's mind the expected exceptionality of the site/sight. Urry takes this a step further and claims that a landmark does not contain any special intrinsic value or meaning at all, but its perception and value depend solely on the frames within which visitors use their gaze.[53]

Urry has been criticized for his claim that there is no inherent value in a visitor site.[54] Other researchers believe that urban cultural heritage sites over time "acquire certain character and functions that often become part of the local identity."[55] This intrinsic character is not entirely closed off to visitors, so that travelers and locals do not completely deviate in the way they perceive landmarks. In fact, in the case of rebuilding, such as the Frauenkirche, the framings applied by visitors and locals strongly overlap. After forty-five years of living with ruins, the tourists' and locals' understanding of Dresden and their need for authentic experiences had fully converged. In each case they had only the established narrative framings and reproductions such as photographs or paintings to draw on, making tourists and locals visitors in an idea of a sacred past of the city that lacked material anchors. Tourists use images of the location they will visit because of their geographical distance from the desired site. In the case of Dresden, this geographical distance can be compared to the residents' distance in time from the undestroyed historic Dresden. So instead of creating expectations of an authentic experience at home and then transposing them onto the material object at the destination, the Frauenkirche was in fact rebuilt with its repository of history and symbolism included so as to be able to "authenticate" the imagined expectations for visitors and locals alike.[56] By the very process of declaring the structure a unique original historic site, and viewing its function in sacred terms, it was authenticated as "The Real Thing."

Consequently, historical reconstructions of lost landmarks complicate the idea that a landmark functions without intrinsic value, as Urry had asserted. On the one hand, such rebuilt landmarks should be the perfect examples of Urry's assertions, since the buildings were not actually original buildings erected in the past that took on distinct meanings over time but would appear to acquire such meaning only through projection. On the other hand, when rebuilding the object, its sacralization and interpretation is already woven into its structure, since rebuildings are usually only undertaken when there is a wide consensus among residents and others about the structure's significance as a special marker and sign. During reconstruction its meaning is codified within normative rules. Variants, such as the more fluid understandings of the (symbolic) value and meaning of the Frauenkirche, which had developed when it lay in ruins, are more and more excluded. At this point, since some of the original stones, which have a darker color, have been used in the church's rebuilding, they can serve as a reminder of the original's destruction and that the current Frauenkirche is a replacement. But the historical material authentication through several original stones is only temporary. Over time they will be indistinguishable as the rest of the façade takes on the same weathered look.

For its consecration alone, on October 30, 2005, more than sixty thousand people came to the Dresden Neumarkt.[57] The resurrected Frauenkirche fulfills the role it was built for: it offers the most important symbol through which Dresdners and others can reconnect to a prewar and pre-GDR past and can exclude the years 1933 through 1990. Such nostalgic idealization, or

Fig. 55. Consecration of the rebuilt Frauenkirche in 2005. (Photograph by Siegfried Bregulla. Reprinted by permission of SLUB/Deutsche Fotothek.)

as geographer David Lowenthal calls it, such "domesticating" of heritage could serve the needs of the former GDR citizens in the 1990s who were looking for ways to redefine themselves under the new political and social circumstances.[58]

Yet it was also a powerful attractor for West Germans. As implied early on in Kohl's speech about Dresden, the city could serve as a symbol for overcoming the past. The rebuilt Frauenkirche was the ideal answer to this desire. The public discourse and its highly symbolic connotations suggested that National Socialism, the war, and the socialist regime in the years in between were forced, unwanted, and unwarranted interruptions of the natural order in the cultural city of Dresden. With the rebuilding, Dresden, and indeed the entire area of the GDR, could join back into its rightful place among the culture of the Christian Occident. A rhetorical bridge between pre-1933 and post-1989 was built out of the overarching ideas of peace and reconciliation that dominated the discourse and could overlay a more intense exploration of the Nazi engagement in Dresden, as well as the policies toward this history in East Germany. At the consecration, then German president Horst Köhler confirmed such focus on the future: "The reconstruction of the Frauenkirche is a unique expression of the good that lies within a civil society and its citizens and is waiting to be awakened. [. . .]. Peace is a gift, but you have to work for it again and again, and sometimes what reconciliation can achieve is nothing short of a miracle. The Dresden Frauenkirche can give us the strength to work even harder for peace and reconciliation together and without boundaries."[59]

In material terms, the reconstructions of historic landmarks and their surroundings, as well as the destruction of GDR buildings, could cover what many understood as the physical wounds that had been inflicted on the city. Psychologically, the rebuilding was seen as a calling and helped to reinstall the confidence of the Dresden residents in their city and in themselves by returning a sacred object that for them signifies their (idealized) past. As a booklet about the rebuilding of the Frauenkirche states, "We are allowed, yes we must heal wounds, if we can. The reconstruction of the Frauenkirche is not a way of avoiding history. The new Frauenkirche will be again a monument to history: not only for the Baroque Dresden, but also for the courage to rebuild out of destruction, for the moral will of the present to heal, to start anew and to devise the future."[60]

The strong commitment to the rebuilding of the Frauenkirche in the population in and outside of Dresden stood in stark contrast to the general attitudes among preservation experts and architects as well as many culture critics. For them, the Frauenkirche constitutes "a new building of Dresden's landmark, which follows the forms of the original."[61] In the weekly *Die Zeit*, Dresden-born historian Achatz von Müller even described such rebuildings as "monumental knicknacks."[62] Yet such judgment ignores the power of the symbolic meaning of the built environment. After the fall of the wall, rebuilding the Frauenkirche was not only presented as a return to a world of sacred signs and values, but also a symbol of steadfastness against further destruction. While one political system had wanted to rebuild Dresden in a socialist style, the new capitalist approach made the city vulnerable to the visions of investors and architects, which would destroy Dresden's unique character and, by extension, that of its people. The initiators of the rebuilding campaign decidedly presented their project as a natural continuation of the Peaceful Revolution, which had already employed the symbolism of the destruction. Fighting for Dresden's past cityscape was seen as a courageous and moral obligation comparable to the revolution against a dictatorial regime. Art historian Hans Joachim Neidhardt, a strong supporter of the historical rebuilding, insists, "the residents of this city now have, after a long time of suppression ended when we succeeded in our fight for democracy in 1989, the right and duty to engage in the discussions and decisions regarding the planning of their city center."[63] Such statements imply that "true Dresdners" are those who value and protect the sacred city and its spiritual and historical significance against the continued outside threat to its essence. According to this approach, protecting the city from destruction is a struggle for heightened morality and peace. By rebuilding Dresden in its historic form, the city and its people offer an opportunity for reconciliation.

In fact, for many residents, the rebuilding of the Frauenkirche was a watershed moment. It exemplified the opportunity and amplified their wish to have back a part of the city they viewed as the sacred well from which they could feed their identity and redefine their commonality. Like a chain reaction that is fueled by positive feedback, the wide acceptance of the rebuilding project of the Frauenkirche, despite the experts' opposition, set in motion a movement to expand the Baroque reconstruction to the surrounding buildings on the Neumarkt and to most of the Old Town, in contrast to the plans of the city officials and the Dresden planning office, which were eager to modernize their city and attract capital.[64] They had found Western investors ready to erect contemporary buildings at the marketplace despite the reconstruction of the Frauenkirche in its center. The city council was worried about too many building restrictions. Given the economic circumstances after reunification and that the Neumarkt had not been close to its eighteenth-century form for almost fifty years, such a plan did not seem too far-fetched. But for many residents these plans fostered deep mistrust of the West and its investors, as well as of local politicians who, they feared, might be causing a "third destruction" of the city.[65]

In reaction to the investors' plans and to some of the already completed contemporary façades that had quickly gone up in the Old Town, a citizen's initiative to "Save the Neumarkt" was formed to lobby for historical reconstruction or, in their words, "the recovery of [Dresden's] delightful city panorama."[66] The Neumarkt, which consisted of an ensemble of burgher houses and the Frauenkirche before 1945, had witnessed no major new construction aside from the modern annex to the eighteenth-century police headquarters. The large, seven-story annex was erected in close proximity to the Frauenkirche ruins in 1979 and constructed with prefabricated slabs. It was finally torn down in 2005.[67] The Society Historic Neumarkt, consisting of about seven hundred members, countered theoretical concerns among experts about such reconstructions with the deeply intertwined spiritual identity between the city and its residents. They declared the Neumarkt the essence, or the "heart and soul," of Dresden and referred to the "artistic sensibilities" of the people who actually live in the city as clearly favoring buildings in their historic forms.[68] Numbers backed up their claims: In 2002, the society collected more than eighty thousand signatures (with more than sixty-three thousand from Dresden residents) for a public petition to hold a referendum for the rebuilding of the Neumarkt in historical style.[69] Dresden's historical reconstruction also resonated positively with Germans outside of the city, and the Frauenkirche project served as a model for other communities in Germany to initiate similar plans.[70]

While the referendum was denied on the city level, the society organized numerous events, installed a permanent information booth, and garnered much press in the process. Finally, the Neumarkt was rebuilt to mimic the original layout, heights, roofs, and most façades, and it now houses predominantly commercial spaces and hotels. In 2023, the negotiations for filling the last open space on the marketplace were completed and a historical reconstruction of the Hotel Stadt Rom in its original shape from 1740 will be erected (it had been damaged and renovated several times before it was destroyed by the firestorm in 1945). The society has expanded its efforts beyond the Neumarkt and is still actively and successfully lobbying for historical rebuilding. A series of surveys conducted by the society over the years show that Dresdners beyond a doubt favor such historical reconstructions over modern architecture.[71] Independent surveys also confirm such findings. In fact, since the 1990s the attitude of Dresdners to rebuilding has, with one period of exception in 2002, barely changed.[72] Through the initiative taken by the residents, it became possible to assemble in the Old Town a coherent stage set to perform again the Dresden narrative of singular cultural significance that showcases the city, its environment, and its residents as an innocent, intricate, and spiritual Gesamtkunstwerk.

These preferences held true if it meant the destruction or change of buildings or ensembles erected during East German times. In fact, even contemporary buildings were preferred to much of the East German architecture. If historical reconstruction was not deemed possible, the minimum goal was to try to get back to the dimensions of streets and areas the way they were before the raids. The Prager Straße, for instance, which in its GDR form many viewed as a key example for one of the "most spectacular and successful" architectural ensembles in the socialist style, was soon scaled down at several spots by buildings placed onto the wide pedestrian zone.[73] While contemporary architecture was employed, the city also tried to recreate the Prager Straße's historical purpose of an upscale shopping area. Significant examples of socialist 1970s architecture, such as the Centrum Warenhaus Dresden or the Restaurant International, were blasted to make room for a contemporary but generic shopping mall. When the GDR structures along the street were not torn down, their renovations were aimed at covering up the socialist roots as much as possible.[74]

Since then, Dresden residents, represented through various groups as well as strong personal engagement, have repeatedly demonstrated their unwillingness to compromise with building concepts, particularly within their city center. Now, however, the goals of the city council and residents have started to converge. After all, it became clear that the rebuilding returned Dresden to its primary place as an attractive tourist attraction with all its economic benefits. The number of guests has almost continuously risen since 1990 (in 2015 and 2016 Dresden's numbers dipped due to the political climate in the city, which will be explored in more detail in the following chapter). In 2019, before the Covid-19 pandemic depressed travel worldwide, Dresden had hosted more than 2.3 million visitors (4.7 million overnight stays), of which more than 20 percent were international travelers.[75] By 2022, the tourism market in Dresden had already recovered from the lockdowns by more than 80 percent, and by 2024 by 99 percent.[76] Tourism has become a 1.3-billion-Euro industry for Dresden.[77]

The rebuildings can satisfy many desires among the city population in terms of their view of history, their idea of authenticity and prestige, and their function both for the residents themselves and the visitors they can attract. Consequently, tourism also gives the rebuildings economic significance. Like the language-planning processes after reunification, the material processes are able to shift the memory of the past and the expectations for the future and inscribe them into the city structures. In fact, the rebuilding itself has become part of Dresden's appeal to tourists. In Dresden, the use of "the past as heritage [that] transmits exclusive myths of origin and continuance" has been immensely successful.[78] Not only has it given back to Dresdners "prestige and common purpose" through the recreation of the historic city ensembles, but the resolute determination to protect their city from architectural harm, which many Dresdners collectively embrace, has marked the city with yet another label of exclusivity.[79] This legendarily unparalleled commitment has attracted tourists to the city as much as the rebuilt artifacts themselves.

The Other Destruction: Rebuilding Debates and the New Synagogue

The last chapter illustrated how the discourses about the bombing of Dresden and the experience of Jewish persecution are structured similarly, which allows the idea of a fellowship of victimhood and suffering. It also granted that historical rebuilding was and is presented as a sacred act and a symbolic offer for reconciliation. Yet despite the setting up of parallels and connections, the bombing narrative remains the defining force in understanding and presenting history in Dresden. Another look at the culture of remembrance surrounding the November Pogroms from 1938 illustrates this situation, in particular the public reactions to the plans of building a synagogue in the Old Town to replace the destroyed Semper Synagogue. While the Frauenkirche project immediately garnered much publicity and enthusiastic support, the building of a larger synagogue was received with less enthusiasm. The diverging attention paid to each project, the differing public and financial support, and the rise of a visual and verbal narrative about a fireman saving a Jewish artifact highlights poignantly how deep-seated the idea of victimhood and innocence of the general Dresden population has been written into the postwar discourse and how a lack of self-reflection still dominated the public post-reunification discussions in the city.

While the rebuilding of the Frauenkirche was underway immediately after the collapse of the GDR, a discussion about building the synagogue arose much more slowly. By the end of the socialist state, the Jewish congregation of Dresden had become extremely small and consisted mainly of older members, so that the little provisional synagogue from 1950 at the Jewish New Cemetery offered sufficient space. With the opening of the Eastern Bloc, however, the Jewish community experienced a significant revitalization through immigration. There was consequently a lot of interest in building a new synagogue that would be able to house all its members. The rebuilding plans for the Frauenkirche were enthusiastically supported by Dresden residents, but there was less excitement about the synagogue. Siegfried Reimann, a Protestant pastor who was also one of the founders of the working group "Begegnung mit dem Judentum" (Encounters with Judaism) in 1982 and a strong proponent of the synagogue building project, recounts that while there were repeated discussions in the early 1990s, silence and stagnation had taken over by 1995.[80] In a letter to the mayor, Reimann reminded the city of the responsibilities connected with the rebuilding of the Frauenkirche: "Considering the reconstruction of the Dresden Frauenkirche, it appears to me and also to the Jews of our city as increasingly oppressive that there is no public discussion of their house of worship, which had been taken from them through criminal pillage. I know that the city is talking about some plans to rebuild a synagogue. However, in contrast to the significant time and effort invested in the rebuilding of the Frauenkirche, these plans represent a point zero."[81]

Even though there were still initiatives by small groups and concerned citizens, most steps taken toward a wider and public reflective discourse on the National Socialist past and what occurred in Dresden had ceased. It was overpowered by the all-dominating rebuilding discussions of the 1990s and early 2000, with the goal to get key parts of Dresden back to its prewar shape. Eventually, the project gained stronger support due to political developments. The anniversaries of the Dresden bombing attracted more and more neo-Nazi groups, who gathered for a "mourning march" to commemorate the Dresden destruction and victims of what they call a "Bomben Holocaust."[82] Most city residents resent it when they feel that the Dresden destruction is (mis)used by others for their own agenda, just as they resisted the propagandistic remembrance in the GDR by developing their own rituals and symbols. A message given out to the population by then Dresden mayor Herbert Wagner concerning the remembrance activities of February 13, 2001, exemplifies this position. He reminded the Dresden citizens that they should unite more strongly "when forces try, try again and again, to disturb our day, our commemoration, and our mourning [. . .] of the destruction of the city, [. . .] for the dead of the war and in willingness to achieve reconciliation."[83] In addition, well aware of the optics of neo-Nazis marching through Dresden, the strong interest in attracting tourism to the city undoubtedly also played a significant role in the desire to counter these external movements.

Many Dresden residents view themselves as being in a unique position to grasp Jewish suffering due to their own losses. So rather than pitting one type of suffering against the other, they allege moral authority when speaking about the German past. This view is not changed, but rather strengthened when neo-Nazis from outside the city claim the anniversary of the bombing for their political ends. A renewed memorialization of the destruction of the synagogue took place, including support for the erection of a temple close to the location where the Semper Synagogue had stood. The discussions did not, however, form their own discourse, but instead the prominent rhetoric around the loss of the Frauenkirche and its rebuilding were widened to include the 1938 destruction of the synagogue. The image of the burning Semper Synagogue was increasingly evoked in speeches and commemorative events about the Frauenkirche's loss in 1945. The synagogue project was also referenced during calls for support of the church's rebuilding in the interest of signaling the importance of peace and reconciliation. As Herbert Wagner emphasized in his 2001 speech, both projects are expressions of reconciliation: "The building of the synagogue and the reconstruction of the Frauenkirche are now closely connected."[84] The Frauenkirche also became a site for the collection of donations for the new synagogue.

The pairing suggested a shared experience of Dresdners and Jews, which bolstered the idea of innocence and undeserved loss. Integrating Jewish loss into the loss of the Frauenkirche pushed aside the key differences and cut out questions about German guilt. Furthermore, by discussing the building of a new synagogue within the strong Christian framework that surrounded the Frauenkirche reconstruction, the distinct Jewish religion, history, and fate were suppressed and excluded.

The responsibility for the burning down of the synagogue was also still understood as solely lying with external fascist forces, not with the ordinary Dresden citizens. As we have seen, during the time of the GDR discussions and research about the Holocaust and the specific Jewish plight were discouraged. The rhetoric of a comparative fascism between Nazism and Western capitalism was also employed to downplay questions of responsibility for the Holocaust. In the last decade of the GDR, however, particularly in 1988, the Holocaust and Jewish suffering became a more central theme, which made it more difficult to avoid questions about responsibility in the population. After reunification, the deflective GDR narratives were no longer available at all. Regarding the discourse surrounding November 9, 1938, in Dresden, one observes that the fewer narratives about regular Germans as fascist victims were available, the more a new account arose to prominence that featured a heroic and courageous response by a Dresden resident to the events. This narrative revolves around a fireman, Alfred Neugebauer, who is said to have saved and hidden an original Star of David of the Semper Synagogue during the pogroms, in defiance of the given orders. The artifact was returned to the Jewish community in 1946 by Neugebauer and the captain of the fire brigade and subsequently installed on the newly built synagogue at the cemetery in 1950.[85] The narrative of the rescue of the Semper-designed Star of David is usually recounted in association with a photograph that had been taken on November 10, 1938. Despite the catastrophic fire, two Stars of David still ordained the ruins of the synagogue the next morning, as if the building were trying to defy the destruction of its significance as a place of Jewish identity. The image shows two firemen on a ladder removing the Star of David from one of the towers. Given the camera angle, it must have been taken not from the ground but from a higher vantage point.

As we have seen in the previous chapter, the wealth of materials, particularly visual ones, about the torching of the synagogue, its dismantling, and the abuse of the Jewish community leaders in Dresden is quite exceptional. Yet it is this picture that has become representative of the destruction of the synagogue in Dresden and stands for the events on November 9–10,

Fig. 56. Two firemen remove one of the Stars of David from the synagogue in Dresden on November 10, 1938. (Photographer unknown. Reprinted by permission of SLUB/Deutsche Fotothek.)

1938, as well as the Jewish persecution in general. The photograph is clearly an important document, since it depicts the state of the synagogue after the fire, but before any of the remaining ruins had been blasted. I would like to propose, however, that the reason why this particular picture remains much more dominant in the discourse surrounding the destruction of the Dresden synagogue lies with the suggestive symbolism that arises from the interaction between the narrative of the rescue of the Star of David and this image, even though it requires a misinterpretation of the pictured event.

The story of the rescue of the Star of David was shared in the *Nachrichtenblatt der jüdischen Gemeinde Groß-Berlin und des Verbandes der jüdischen Gemeinden der Deutschen Demokratischen Republik*, the newsletter published by the Association of the Jewish Congregations of the GDR, immediately after Alfred Neugebauer and the fire brigade captain had returned the artifact. Over the next decades, the account about the rescue was referenced repeatedly in the newsletter. The story also made it into the newspaper in an article discussing the opening of the new synagogue near the cemetery in 1950.[86] The Dresden Jewish Congregation appreciated the return of the important relic. At this point, the rescue is generalized as an act of the entire fire brigade. In a note from 1947 to the brigade, the congregation thanks the actions of the "courageous firefighters at the risk of their own lives and at the greatest danger, not shying away from the rescue despite the Nazi terror and the persecution associated with it."[87]

It is unclear where the photograph with the two firemen taking down the Star of David was stored or who owned it, but it came into possession of the Dresden Jewish Congregation some time before 1972, as was reported in the Jewish *Nachrichtenblatt* in December 1972. It was here that the photograph was publicly shared for the first time, even if only reaching the small audience of the Jewish congregations.[88] It is also at this time that the account of the rescue of the Star of David was associated with the image. Whether this association was suggested by whoever shared the image with the congregation or was simply an assumption is not clear.

As we know, the Dresden fire brigade did not try to save the burning synagogue, but only stood by to protect other houses the night of the pogrom. The next morning, however, they were actively assisting in preparing the remaining ruins for full destruction, which required the removal of the stars from the towers. The photograph pictures this very act in support of the clearing efforts. Afterwards, one of the Stars of David was taken to the fire house, most likely as a trophy. Here, Neugebauer said, he hid the star so that it would not be destroyed. Starting with the first publication of the photograph with the two firemen, the evidence of complicity shown on the image is instead read as a moment of resistance against the perpetrators. From then on, it has been repeatedly identified as depicting how the firemen in the photograph are saving the Star of David from the Nazis. At its first publication in 1972, the Dresden Jewish community already coded the image in such positive terms:

> We have often written [. . .] about how our small, beautiful synagogue in Fiedlerstrasse is adorned with the Mogen Dovid, that had already decorated the synagogue [. . .] which the Nazis destroyed during the infamous Kristallnacht of November 9–10, 1938. It was removed and saved by courageous firefighters on the night of the fire and given to us after 1945 so that it could once again crown the synagogue that was to be rebuilt. Our picture, which was recently given to us, shows the firefighters' actions.[89]

In the newsletter from December 1988, Hans Leupold, a member of the Jewish congregation, mentions the photographer for the first time. Leupold here reports on the history of the Star of David and its rescue at the occasion of the star's restoration. Leupold identifies Alfred Neugebauer as the one who rescued the Star of David and the photographer as the Jewish teacher Aron Höxter:

> It is thanks to the fireman Alfred Neugebauer that this Star of David has been preserved. There is also a photo of the removal of the star, which was taken by the Jewish teacher Höxter from the window of his apartment on an upper floor; he lived in the house at Zeughausstraße 1, which was very close to the synagogue.[90]

This circumstance would make the image an even scarcer document, since it would offer a rare victim's perspective on the events. It also elevates the rescue story about Neugebauer. The rescue is, according to this narrative, not only documented via a photograph, but in fact verified by a victim of the pogroms.

Leupold does not, however, offer a source for his comment. Some researchers have pointed out that a Dresden address book indeed shows Aron Höxter as residing on the third floor at Zeughausstraße 1, which would seem to support Leupold's statements about Höxter.[91] But many questions remain as to whether Höxter actually took the photograph. For one, the address book that lists Höxter at this address stems from the year 1940, when the former Jewish Congregation's community centers and apartments at the Zeughausstraße 1 and 3 had been turned into "Jew houses" by the city. Address books from 1938 and 1939 suggest an entirely different apartment building in another part of town as the home of the Höxter family. Here "Höxter Aron, Lehrer" ("teacher") is listed as residing on Stormstraße 2. Consequently, it is only after the Dresden "Jew houses" had been established and people were forced to move into them that he is listed as living on the third floor of Zeughausstraße 1. In 1938, three different names are listed for the apartments on the third floor at Zeughausstraße 1, among them Dr. Albert Wolf, who served as one of the rabbis for the Dresden congregation from 1920 to 1938, after 1936 as the head rabbi. We know that pictures were taken either directly by the SA and SD or with their knowledge, such as the photograph shown in chapter 4 in which the SD officer Johannes Clemens poses with the synagogue employees for the camera. The film that depicts the removal of the synagogue also contains scenes that indicate filming had started as early as the morning of November 10 and from various viewpoints.

While the film was made over a number of days, when the camera pans upward in the beginning of the film, the Star of David is still visible on top of the tower. The camera angles in this and other scenes suggests that some houses across from the synagogue were used to depict the dismantling of the building from a higher vantage point. A picture taken later in the day of November 10 by the soldier Helmut Hoffmann displays the towers without their stars. Could the rabbi's apartment have been of interest to the Nazi henchmen and the photograph of the removal of the Star of David instead be a perpetrator image documenting the beginning of the dismantling of the synagogue?

Further, Aron Höxter was among the Dresden Jews who were arrested during the pogrom and brought to Buchenwald around the 10th of November. Among the many Jewish people who were taken to the camp were also friends of Höxter from his former longtime teaching post in Bibra in Thuringia. They had, just like Höxter, been brought to the special area within Buchenwald that the SS had established for the Jews who had been taken into custody as part of the excesses during the November Pogrom. The Bibra men reported that they had met Aron Höxter in the camp when they arrived there.[92] His daughter Margot, the only survivor of the Höxter family, also confirmed his imprisonment when she told friends in Bibra after the war that her father was physically and psychologically broken after his release: "Papa could not walk for weeks."[93] The German Federal Archive Memorial Book of Jewish persecution in Germany also lists Aron Höxter as having been interned at Buchenwald starting November 10, 1938.[94] It is not clear how Aron Höxter was pinpointed as the photographer, but the circumstances suggest that it might be a misidentification.

For the fiftieth anniversary of the November Pogroms in 1988, the photograph became much more prominent in Dresden. Both the story of the rescue of the star and the picture were repeatedly highlighted during government-led events and were also part of the exhibit on Jewish life in Saxony shown in the Kreuzkirche. By this time, Alfred Neugebauer is named as the person rescuing the star. In the *Sächsische Zeitung*, an article on November 4, 1988, by the member of the board of directors of the Dresden Jewish Congregation, Dr. Herbert Lappe, outlines how Neugebauer saved the artifact. The article is supposedly based on Neugebauer's account that he had given Lappe during a recent visit, but it contains a number of inconsistencies about where the star was stored until it was returned after the war. The picture of the firemen with the Star of David was published in a separate article on November 9.[95] The Kreuzkirche exhibition used an altered version of the photograph, which appears to be a blown-up detail of the original image. In this photograph, the focus rests more closely on the two firemen, and their black uniforms stand out particularly strong in front of the white smoke. The firemen on their ladders appear to be rising high above any other buildings, which suggests even more clearly a heroic act of higher purpose instead of the true situation, namely an active part in the process of dismantling the synagogue. Since then, the picture and the narrative surrounding the rescue of the Star of David have received ever more attention, and the image and story have become standard elements when describing Jewish persecution in Dresden.[96]

When the photograph was exhibited in the Kreuzkirche, the description also identified the action of the firemen as rescuing the Star of David.[97] In the newspaper article about the photograph, the author does not imply that Neugebauer is on the ladder, but that these two firemen assisted Neugebauer with rescuing the artifact in an act of retribution, since "they had been forbidden from saving the burning Jewish house of worship on November 9, 1938."[98] According to Neugebauer's own description, he was part of the team standing by when the synagogue burned down the night of November 9 but was not present for removing the stars the next morning. Rather, he only later saw the Star of David after it had been brought to the fire station. Neugebauer was interested in artistic and cultural heritage and claims that he wanted to save the star as a cultural artifact from the Nazis.[99] Neugebauer is also cited as saying that he wanted to save the star because he was friendly with many Jews attending the synagogue.[100] There are several variations about where Neugebauer hid the star until the war was over. In the most widely shared story, Neugebauer moved it to the attic of the fire station and hid the artifact inside a large crate full of sand. When he was called up to serve in the Wehrmacht, he retrieved the star, wrapped it in blankets and carried it by bike to his father-in-law's house where it remained until the end of the war hidden in his attic or workshop, depending on who tells the story.[101] With a height of 84 cm (33 inches) and a width of 76 cm (30 inches), moving the star via bicycle must have been challenging, but it is possible. In 1946, Neugebauer returned the star to the Dresden Jewish community. The details of this rescue have never been closely scrutinized, but Neugebauer has been celebrated as a selfless hero who risked his life to save an important part of Dresden Jewish history.

It was also during this time that the picture was officially (and conveniently) attributed to Höxter. With a Jewish victim photographing an act of heroism and resistance by the non-Jewish Dresden resident and fireman

Neugebauer during gruesome antisemitic events in the city, the picture is an expression of opposition to the perpetrators. The photograph can thus serve as a building block and proof for the memories that were constructed around Jewish persecution in Dresden. Making this association of both shared victimhood and heroism acknowledges the Holocaust but allows responsibility to shift to an "other": the Nazi organizations and their leaders. These Nazi outsiders, it is suggested, did not share the actual societal beliefs and norms associated with Dresden and its residents. They lacked the true Dresden spirit, since people in Dresden were aware of the history and meaning of their exceptional cityscape and would never destroy a treasure such as a building designed by Gottfried Semper. According to this logic, the Nazis could not be real Dresdners since a Dresdner's identity rises out of the city's past: Dresdners are focused on conservation, preservation, and protection, not destruction. Making the picture and the rescue of the Star of David the foundation for the memorialization of the November Pogroms suggests that while the people of Dresden were unable to save the synagogue or the Jewish community, one in their midst was at least able to save a precious symbol of Jewish culture and religion. The Star of David, returned by a Dresdner to the Jewish congregation, then formed the basis for Jews to rebuild their community after the war was over.

So while such attention to the November Pogroms and the destruction of the synagogue appears to signal an intent to face the Holocaust and the responsibility of the Dresden residents, and commemorate the events accordingly, the narrative surrounding the Star of David's rescue and the photograph that accompanies it can draw attention away from the need to address Jewish persecution. Instead it centers on anti-Nazi heroics of Dresden residents, even pointing silently to a shared victimhood by destructive forces. The uplifting story of the return of the Star of David to the Dresden Jewish community served perfectly as a further justification for Dresden to call for peace, not just because of the experience of the Dresden bombing, but also because of the horrors the Nazis inflicted on the city from the start.

This story has become so ingrained in the Dresden narrative about the November Pogroms that Alfred Neugebauer's rescue of the Star of David is almost indivisibly linked to most accounts that refer to the 1938 destruction of the synagogue in Dresden. The photograph of the star removal often illustrates the story to support the notion of defiance and rescue. The two narratives, the destruction of the synagogue and Neugebauer's rescue, have become one of triumph reigning over misery and threat. For example, Dresden residents voted Alfred Neugebauer to be one of "The 100 Dresdners of the 20th Century," for a series by the newspaper *Dresden Neueste Nachrichten.* In a feature on the former fireman, the journalist Heidrun Hannusch turns Neugebauer into a cipher for Dresden's integrity. Under the heading "How a Fireman Saved Dresden's Honor,"[102] the journalist does not only tell Neugebauer's story of the star's rescue but emphasizes its lasting and powerful meaning. With an anecdote, she tries to underline the unquestionable significance and bravery of this act by showing how this rescue still serves as inspiration today, even to descendants of the victims of the Holocaust. She relays how an "upper class" "Jewish American" told her: "Do you know why I donated to the Dresden Synagogue [the New Synagogue, opened in 2001]? [. . .] Because of this man who saved the Star of David. That is an amazing story."[103]

Other publications feature similar approaches. In the catalogue accompanying the exhibition "Schuhe der Toten: Dresden und die Shoah" (Shoes of the Dead: Dresden and the Shoah) in the Dresden-based Military History Museum of the German Armed Forces, the photograph of the removal of the star from the tower is spread over two pages and leads into the chapter "Quiet Heroes in Dresden."[104] In the essay, the fireman Alfred Neugebauer is described as "one of the first 'Quiet Heroes' in Dresden [. . .]. The Firemen were not allowed to save the burning Synagogue, but Neugebauer saved the 'Mogen Dovid,' and returned it to the Jewish community after the war."[105] Over and over, various articles and mentions make a clear distinction between the perpetrators as "members of the SA" and Neugebauer as the "brave *Dresden* fireman" (emphasis added). In 2001, he was awarded the Saxon Order of Merit for "accomplishing an act with which he risked freedom and life."[106]

Had the Dresden Jewish congregation decided to reconstruct the historic Semper Synagogue and simply placed the Star of David back on its tower, there might have been more support by the public for the plans to build a new synagogue. It could have been integrated even more thoroughly into the discourse of shared victimhood and the symbolism of peace and reconciliation associated with the city's rebuilding of its heritage landmarks. The historic synagogue would be the fitting conclusion to a path toward harmony that started with the rescue of the Star of David and its subsequent return to the Jewish congregation. But while using part of the site where the original Semper Synagogue had stood, the Jewish community decided not to try to rebuild it in its original shape, but instead agreed on a contemporary design by the architectural office Wandel, Hoefer und Lorch & Hirsch.

Even though donations were significantly smaller for the synagogue

Fig. 57. New Synagogue in Dresden (completed in 2001). (Photograph by Susanne Vees-Gulani.)

than for the Frauenkirche and the project experienced repeated funding problems, construction was completed in 2001. The New Synagogue consists of two separate structures: the larger one, closer to the Elbe, serves for worship, while the other, toward Dresden's Old Town, houses a community center. The two blocks are connected by a courtyard. Here, parts of the original layout of the Semper Synagogue are made visible on the courtyard's floor, so that this space between temple and community center creates a "gap" in which the memory of the destruction of the former synagogue can unfold.[107] Since the terrain did not allow the traditional alignment of the New Synagogue toward the east, the allocated design contains a "twist": while the blocks are arranged in straight lines, cantilevered bricks at each corner orient the structure eastward.[108] With this decision, the Jewish community resisted the rhetoric of community, peace, and reconciliation evoked in the rebuilding discourse between the Frauenkirche and the synagogue project. They instead chose a design the architects of which specifically aimed to counteract such historical reconstructions, with which "not only a political, but also a spatial caesura is blocked," by suggesting an uninterrupted "continuity between past and present."[109] For the synagogue, with its distinct history, such continuity appeared inappropriate, and the Jewish congregation emphasized the need not to reconstruct it in its original form from before 1938. They agreed that after the Holocaust, one should not connect to the pre-Holocaust past as if nothing had happened.[110]

This decision provoked an outcry of anger in parts of the population. Such a reaction is a strong indication that rhetorical support for the synagogue's construction did not necessarily include a revisiting of Dresden's role in Nazi Germany and Jewish persecution. The resentment against the contemporary design was widely expressed at model exhibitions following the architectural design competition, where guest books contained numerous comments about "vain, career-driven architects" and the disfiguring of Dresden.[111] In the *Sächsische Zeitung*, a reader expressed her hope that such "creative attacks of God-like creators (also called architects) [. . .] will in the future immediately end up in the shredder."[112] By the time the New Synagogue celebrated its ten-year anniversary, opinions had become more varied, as the organization Zeitgenossen (Contemporaries), a group of young architects, concluded after an unofficial survey on the streets of Dresden. The answers they received to the question "Die Neue Synagoge ist für mich . . ." (The New Synagogue is for me . . .) swung between the overwhelmingly positive, such as the New Synagogue is "an architectural highlight," to the extreme negative: the New Synagogue is an "abomination." Overall, the main criticism shared with the group remained that the New Synagogue does not match with Dresden's historic cityscape.[113]

While Dresden residents have been continuously critical of contemporary architecture, the decision not to rebuild the synagogue according to Semper's design caused particular outrage. It appears to be based on two objections: that a modern structure is part of the city's Elbe panorama and that with the contemporary design of the synagogue there exists a widely visible memorial to the events of 1938. The building contrasts strongly with Dresden's self-view as an icon of peace and reconciliation that finds its material translation in re-establishing a harmonious architectural city center. Such doubt was also openly expressed when a resident questioned whether such a design could achieve the "tolerance and togetherness in harmony" that Dresden claims for itself.[114] Taken together with the concept of "reconciliation," the often-evoked term concerning both the rebuilt Frauenkirche and the New Synagogue, the distinct feeling of shared victimhood remained. The prominent discourse of peace and reconciliation, bound to the re-emergence of the Baroque cityscape in Dresden can erase distinctive differences of experiences of the past. Yet foregrounding harmony for the present and future is also coupled with a desire for homogeneity since the historic cityscape and peace and reconciliation are tightly framed within a restrictive Christian Western identity. Any intrusion into this discourse can consequently be understood as a threat to a carefully curated self-understanding of Dresden as victim, voice of caution, and peacemaker for the world. In response to such threats, many residents feel the need for action, which they understand as growing out of their exceptional past and special role within Germany. They thus become outspoken fierce protectors of the high culture as it is preserved in Dresden, they defy intrusions into the formed narratives, and they feel called upon to act as representative truth tellers.

With the contemporary design of the New Synagogue and the reconstructed Frauenkirche both in its city center, Dresden displays an interesting symbiosis of old and new, remembrance and forgetting, in its urban structure. Even though the emphasis is clearly on reconstruction, one might think that a workable relationship of Dresden to the Nazi past could develop through these two buildings and the rhetorical association that has been established between them. But the narrative framing of the post-reunification rebuilding projects in Dresden as a sacred journey to demonstrate and signal peace and reconciliation, to which the building of the synagogue was expected to conform, leaves little space to develop new, more complex structures of remembrance. As the next chapters will show, the Dresden narrative, the hesitation in engaging with questions about the responsibilities during the Nazi era, and the idea of being agents of truth that are called upon to proclaim "wrongs" can open up a fertile narrative space in which nationalist, nativist, and populist movements can plant and grow their rhetoric and support. With this shift to the right, opposition has grown to combat such singular views of culture and identity, particularly among the cultural institutions in Dresden. Cultural and artistic expression has become a major voice in the city to counter the established narrative and to offer alternative viewpoints. Yet the narrative that has ultimately led to the recreation of a historic urban structure, ideas about what it should mean to live in a city of such significance, and the wide national and international embrace of the victim story despite far-right political developments have proven to remain powerful protective shields against change.

CHAPTER 6

Dresden Memory Culture and the Success of the Far Right

For the residents who identify strongly with their Dresden heritage, living in their beloved city comes with the joy and pride of residing in a place of unique cultural significance, but also with obligations.[1] Dresden and its narrative of singular beauty, loss, and suffering must be protected from distortions. Events, building practices, or ideologies that could challenge Dresden's memory or perceived import are to be actively resisted. On the anniversaries of the bombing, many Dresdners insist on certain mourning rituals and ways of expressing grief. Depending on their political leanings, different forms are deemed appropriate to the memory of the city. As the previous chapter has shown, many residents view themselves as messengers for Dresden in this context and believe they have the duty to remind others of the costs of violence and war, while promoting Dresden as a sacred place and a beacon for peace and reconciliation.

Despite this emphasis on peace and reconciliation, though, Dresden has also become a leading center for far-right ideas and activities, particularly since 2014. This trend has been most publicly visible in the demonstrations in the old city center by the homegrown far-right protest movement Pegida (Patriotic Europeans against the Islamization of the Occident) and subsequent comparable organizations and the strong support by voters for the far-right party Alternative for Germany (AfD). Both Pegida and the AfD display the dominant characteristics of populist movements coupled with a nativist stance. Even though these developments have damaged Dresden's national and international reputation and can endanger Dresden's economically important tourist sector, support for the far right has remained robust.

I will show that to understand this exceptionally strong rise, it is necessary to go beyond regional assessments about the success of the AfD in eastern Germany or attribute the developments solely to the politics in the German Democratic Republic (GDR). The local culture and its dominant discourse that weaves together narratives of the city's exclusive cultural significance, its unparalleled loss, and its resurrection also play a key role in post-reunification developments. This discourse, as we have seen, decontextualizes the bombing, with the effect of highlighting the city and its residents as victims, and often precludes reflection upon past responsibilities or guilt. The Nazi era remains a blind spot in the Dresden bombing narrative, providing an opening for a variety of political discourses to appropriate it. I argue that this continued blind spot regarding the Nazi context plays an important part in explaining the current social and political situation. Such decontextualization turns the elements of the destruction narrative into floating signifiers receptive for political appropriations, even today. I propose that this support originates from the far-right rhetoric that links Dresdners' narrative of cultural losses to the far right's stated fear of losing a unique German identity and homeland, a form of "heritage populism."[2] Both stories and their performative assertions in the city center—Dresden's victim narrative concerning the destruction and rebuilding of the city and the far-right story concerning fears of losing a unique German way, culture, and quality of life based on its history of national achievements—can be seamlessly linked together to form a collaborative discourse pattern.

This looping discourse grounds, preserves, and deepens both views. Pegida, similarly aligned groups, and the Saxon AfD party claim to continue the mission of the anti-GDR Monday protests of the Peaceful Revolution of 1989. The Dresden population's identity as self-proclaimed guardians of culture and a bulwark against governmental intrusion easily dovetails with the far-right claims about threats against a German identity by "elite" German politicians and their views on refugees, multiculturalism, and inclusion. It makes Dresden a fertile place for far-right movements to form or to find a home and seemingly provides a foundation and history for far-right claims. Given Dresden's international reputation, the story of cultural loss propagated by the far right increases regional, national, and international attention for populist and nativist causes. To show these processes, the chapter first charts the history and rise of far-right political movements in Dresden since reunification up to the federal elections in February 2025, and the evolution of the dominant narrative surrounding Dresden's destruction and rebuilding. Examples from commemoration events since 2015 demonstrate how the incomplete contextualization of the Nazi era in Dresden links this narrative with those put forth by Pegida and the AfD, betraying an uncomfortable structural compatibility that eased the rise and establishment of such far-right movements. In the local arena of Dresden, the populist far-right groups use the bombing to assert what political scientist Jan-Werner Müller has called populists' claim to "exclusive moral representation" of the people.[3] The chapter also shows how these discourses were expanded to translate to protests regarding Covid-19 when the "enraged citizens" of Pegida and other groups transformed into campaigners decrying state-mandated health measures combatting the Covid-19 pandemic.[4]

The Post-Reunification Rise of the Far Right in Dresden

Dresden and the state of Saxony are known as home to a largely conservative population, particularly regarding members of the middle class, who value the traditions and history of its region. Saxony often characterizes itself within the Federal Republic as having a "unique political-cultural mentality," expressed in a special, (positive) "Saxon identity."[5] In a representative survey in 2016, 82.5 percent of the participants were proud to be from Saxony, more than 50 percent felt that Saxony offered more culturally and historically important sites than any other states of the former GDR and were convinced they were more successful economically, and 45.1 percent believed that Saxony's natural landscapes were more beautiful.[6] Such values have grown in subsequent surveys. In 2023, some similar questions were asked again. 86 percent reported that they were proud of what Saxony had achieved since 1990, and 63 percent saw Saxony as economically more successful than other states in Eastern Germany.[7] A significant number of Saxons thus perceive themselves and their Free State as superior and independent from the rest of the newer eastern German states.[8] After reunification, the right-centrist Christian Democrats (CDU) held an absolute majority in the state for more than a decade. Yet in 2004, the CDU lost this dominance when some of its voters shifted further to the right. The extreme-right National Democratic Party of Germany (NPD) managed to gain more than 9 percent of the vote and enter the parliament and city councils. But their influence remained limited, as the majority of Saxony's population, including in Dresden, rejected their openly neofascist program, and their party members were isolated and largely ignored.[9]

The NPD, with its long history as an extremist right-wing party in West Germany, thus never provided most East Germans, particularly its middle class, with a satisfying alternative to the mainstream parties.[10] When the so-called "refugee crisis" started to be a concern in Germany in 2014, the

NPD was replaced in the Saxon parliament by the newly formed Alternative for Germany (AfD). While operating on a conservative platform with anti-Islamic, xenophobic elements, the AfD denied far-right motives and presented itself as firmly democratic, but with room for patriotism and nationalism. In many ways, the AfD platform is similar to other European populist parties and movements and thus not a unique German phenomenon; rather it expresses "the political landscape of postindustrialism."[11]

Even though the party gained votes nationwide, support for their populist ideology is by far greater in the states of the former GDR.[12] Surveys have found a link between support for the AfD and sentiments mainly expressed by eastern German voters, which appear to stem from the emotional, social, and economic challenges surrounding reunification.[13] Even more than thirty years later, eastern German AfD voters mostly define their social identity in comparison to western Germans; they feel disadvantaged by them and viewed as "second-class citizens."[14] Politically, they judge the traditional party system in Germany as neglecting eastern German concerns.[15] The relatively newly founded AfD's lack of political history is perceived as an advantage despite its western German origins. Eastern German AfD voters now consider it a "party of the East" that successfully communicates their grievances.[16]

Since its founding, the AfD has increasingly moved further to the political right, in particular in the states of the former East Germany, by embracing the main talking points of such confirmed right extremists as Björn Höcke, Thuringia's AfD leader. At its core, his far-right ideology warns of an imminent loss of German culture and civilization: "against the backdrop of unprecedented migration, [. . . I want to] protect our Germany and our Europe from a cultural and civilizational rupture of historic proportions, indeed, a cultural meltdown."[17] In three states the party has been declared a "confirmed right-wing extremist organization" by their Domestic Intelligence Services (Landesverfassungsschutz), Thuringia in 2021, Saxony and Saxony-Anhalt in 2023.[18] Germany-wide, the Federal German Domestic Intelligence Services (Bundesverfassungsschutz) have been observing the AfD as a suspected right-wing extremist organization since 2021.[19] In May 2025, the Federal Domestic Intelligence Service moved to declare the AfD a "confirmed right-wing extremist organization," but pending court challenges have put a pause on the official classification.[20]

Yet Saxony is not only a reflection of a general trend of the former East German states but also represents an independent case in radicalization. Today, social science researchers identify Saxony as a center of right-wing extremism, also based on its long history of offering a home to the far right, which in turn attracts other far-right activists to the state.[21] The AfD radicalized increasingly over time and took its voters with them. The party received 9.7 percent in the 2014 Saxon state elections, growing to 27 percent during the 2017 federal election.[22] The 2019 state elections made the AfD the second strongest party in the Saxon parliament, with 27.5 percent of the vote, right behind the CDU. In the federal election in 2021 the AfD achieved 24.6 percent. While it received fewer votes than four years before, the CDU in that year lost considerably more voters and only reached 17.2 percent (SPD: 19.3 percent), making the AfD the most popular choice for conservatives in Saxony. In 2024 and 2025 the AfD was able to reach record results despite several large scandals that included staff members spying for China, secret ties to Russia, engaging in public revisionist history about the Nazi SS, and the AfD's links to far-right extremist hate groups whose members made secret plans to deport non-Germans.[23] In the elections for the European parliament in June 2024, the AfD was the strongest party in all eastern states; in Saxony, the party reached 31.8 percent. In the state elections, the AfD achieved its best result to date for Saxon elections with 30.6 percent of the votes. The election left the AfD with only one fewer seat than the CDU in the state's parliament. Finally, in the 2025 federal elections, the AfD received 37.3 percent of the vote in Saxony, a result only trumped by Thuringia, where 38.6 percent of voters chose the AfD. These results show that far-right extremism has arrived in the mainstream and has been able to root itself in Saxon institutions.[24]

As both a birthplace and home for far-right movements, Dresden overall has been standing out among larger cities, which do not often become centers of such wide support for far-right political activity.[25] More than 23 percent of Dresdners voted for the AfD in the 2017 federal elections, less than a percentage point behind the CDU, a result above all other cities of similar size, including in the former GDR. Four years later, Dresden still showed robust support for the AfD with 18.5 percent of the vote, which made it the strongest party in the city. In the state elections in 2019, the AfD received 20.7 percent, a rise of 12.5 percent since 2014 and again an unusually solid showing.[26] The AfD played a major role in Dresden's Europe and state elections in 2024 and achieved record highs in the 2025 federal election: 22.4 percent of Dresdners voted for the AfD for the European Parliament and in the state election the AfD was able to rise to 22 percent of votes in the city, making it the strongest party behind the CDU. In the federal election in February 2025, almost one third (26.7 percent) of Dresden residents voted for the AfD (the CDU followed with 18.8 percent).

In the 2024 local elections in Dresden, the AfD also expanded its influence. With 19.4 percent the party at this point occupies the most seats in the Dresden city council. The far-right Freie Sachsen (Free Saxons), with which the AfD associates, were also able to win one seat. It is true that the AfD has also been able to make bigger inroads into Leipzig, Saxony's largest city and the only place close in size to Dresden. Yet the voters in Leipzig display a stronger commitment to parties left of the center, particularly Die Linke (The Left), but also the Social Democratic Party of Germany (SPD) and Die Grünen (The Greens), which buffer the AfD's influence on the region. In the new 2024 Leipzig city council, the AfD received fewer votes than the CDU and Die Linke, and only slightly more than Die Grünen. In the 2025 federal election, similar trends can be observed. While the AfD received the second largest number of votes, the overall vote distribution was much more evenly split between right- and left-leaning parties. Die Linke achieved 22.5 percent, the AfD 21.9 percent, the CDU 16.6 percent, and Die Grünen and the SPD 13.6 and 10.7 percent respectively.[27]

The AfD's early growth in Dresden and Saxony occurred almost in parallel with the rise of the successful Dresden far-right protest movement, the Pegida, which was active from 2014 to 2024.[28] With their name, Pegida suggests that Islamophobia is the uniting force among the protesters, yet Islam is just one of a number of perceived threats.[29] The movement rather rested on the populist message of the increasing disenfranchisement of the ordinary German citizen of European background, which here needs to be understood as an ethnocultural claim denoting European (white and Christian) ancestry.[30] The term "Abendland" (Occident) in Pegida's name has been redefined from more traditional understandings by much of the far right. It has shifted geographically to highlight the role of the eastern states as leaders in recovering and protecting European culture.[31] Sabine Volk has noted in her ethnographic research into Pegida and the AfD that "far-right actors consider western Europe to be in 'cultural decline' due to higher levels of non-European immigration, [. . .], while praising eastern Europeans and their political leaders for defending the 'last bastion' of the Abendland."[32] The former East German states are seen as central in preserving and recovering high culture for the (Christian) Europe and Germany and protecting it from influences from the outside.

The AfD adds a more distinct national focus to these claims. According to the party's program, German traits are based on a "unique core inventory," which remains constant; the inclusion of other cultures is consequently considered a threat since it "puts on a par imported cultural trends with the indigenous culture, thereby degrading the value system of the latter," leading to a loss of social and cultural stability in Germany.[33] Similar to Pegida, the AfD maintains that it speaks for the common (German) people.[34] The rhetoric of Pegida focused on the idea that a governmental "elite," entirely removed from the people's grasp, tries to dictate societal attitudes counter to Germany's own cultural and national identity.[35] Their protests were thus framed as a performance of a patriotic duty: seeking to protect their homeland against internal and external threats.[36]

While Pegida expressed general fears for and about Germany, it framed its protests locally through Dresden's leading role in the 1989 Peaceful Revolution against the GDR. To make this connection, Pegida used several strong symbols. The protesters met on Mondays, so as to link their events to the 1989 Monday demonstrations. Each time they walked through the city imitating the peaceful protesters. Pegida had also adopted the leading slogan from 1989, "Wir sind das Volk" (we are the people), and compared the situation in the Federal Republic today to a GDR 2.0.[37] In this manner, Pegida could claim legitimacy by presenting themselves as the heirs of the Peaceful Revolution that brought down an oppressive top-down regime.[38] In 2019, the AfD, despite its western roots, also tapped into this successful linkage. One of their election posters in eastern Germany read: "Wende_2.0 Then and Now: We Are the People! 1989 | 2019: Complete the Wende!"[39] The idea of a political elite, uninterested in the concerns of the "regular" German citizens, and the perceived lack of freedom and democracy in today's Federal Republic is thus also a fundamental pillar for the AfD, which describes itself as an alternative to the established centrist parties in which these elites concentrate all control.[40]

With its rhetoric, the AfD paints a picture of the country under immediate threat from inside and outside the nation and revives the idea of protecting a "national body" (Volkskörper), a central metaphor during National Socialism.[41] This body, the party claims, is held together by a communal history of unparalleled cultural achievement, traditions, homogeneity, and the German language.[42] It can be upended by the idealization of multiculturalism, Islam, asylum seekers, and poor immigrants[43] who are accused of "plundering" the German social system,[44] increasing lawlessness,[45] far-left activists, the German guilt complex about the Nazi past,[46] and the European Union.[47] The AfD thus engages in "politics of fear" and a largely "symbolic nativism"[48] with a "civilizational discourse" that emphasizes defending a Judeo-Christian (white) heritage, maintaining national borders, and protecting what is understood as a distinct and collectively shared German identity.[49] Similar values and arguments characterized Pegida from its inception.

Within months, the Dresden Pegida grew from a few hundred in October 2014 to twenty-five thousand demonstrators in January 2015.[50] The large crowds with flags and provocative slogans triggered a decrease in tourism and fewer people moving to Dresden, particularly among young people.[51] Internal conflicts and scandals involving Pegida's founder Lutz Bachmann caused the numbers of protesters to fall quickly, but five years later, around a thousand people were still regularly participating.[52] On anniversaries or with special speakers, the numbers increased significantly. By February 2020, Pegida had demonstrated two hundred times in Dresden since its founding and had developed persisting protest rituals.

During the Covid-19 pandemic, many Pegida supporters joined ranks with the Querdenker (Contrarian or Lateral Thinkers) movement, which protested federal and local pandemic restrictions nationwide. The local Querdenker protesters evoked a similar set of grievances and incorporated the symbolic toolkit of Pegida so that the social movement of "Querdenken essentially absorbed Pegida."[53] They marched through the city on Mondays and claimed a lack of freedom comparable to living in the GDR and a loss of control of the individual against an overpowering governmental elite interested in manipulating the population. Accordingly, for those convinced that this was the state of the nation, the restrictions put in place during the pandemic only confirmed what Pegida and other groups had already emphasized before the pandemic, and it became cemented even more deeply in the protesters' consciousness: Germany was a dictatorship.[54] The victim discourse, prevalent before the pandemic in the rhetoric of Pegida and the AfD, took an even more radical turn nationwide when Querdenker protesters openly compared themselves to resistance fighters against the Nazi regime or to Jewish victims of the Holocaust. For example, they likened themselves to Sophie Scholl and Claus von Stauffenberg. Some wore yellow stars with the word "unvaccinated."[55] They thus stylized their protests as a moral obligation given German history while at the same time distorting the realities of the Nazi era and the gravity of the Holocaust.[56] In Dresden, such a link between a victim role and the claims of a moral obligation keep returning to the bombing narrative, which from its beginning as a Nazi propaganda campaign has been discussed within the parameters of moral and immoral behavior. It is thus not surprising that the Querdenker also appealed to Pegida sympathizers during the pandemic.

Around the same time, Pegida supporters had also started to join a number of other, more organized and more politically engaged groups that display similar concerns and rhetoric. The more radicalized wing of the AfD or the extreme-right Freie Sachsen, as well as various far-right splinter groups, have taken over Pegida's place in the political realm. The Freie Sachsen party was formed in 2021 and understands its role as offering a collective movement in which extremist and non-extremist actors, including from other groups, work together."[57] They have a strong social media presence and are able to mobilize significantly for their and other far-right and extremist groups' activities.[58] Pegida had served as a successful engine for creating a group dynamic, establishing grievances and desensitizing people to far-right ideas. It was able to embed its movement in the Dresden cityscape with positive connotations by suggesting a strong relationship between itself and the events surrounding the Peaceful Revolution and by utilizing the narratives revolving around Dresden's past. While the regional movement was successful, it had been unable, however, to translate its movement into a long-lasting national group or the more formal framework of a political party. At this point, the AfD, the Freie Sachen, and other far-right and extremist social protest groups also frequently organize or sponsor marches and demonstrations in Dresden. Pegida has consequently attracted fewer and fewer members to its solo events, and its leader Lutz Bachmann finally announced that the rally for the ten-year anniversary of Pegida, on October 20, 2024, would be the last Pegida event.[59]

So far, the literature on the far right in Germany has identified several possible reasons for Saxony and Dresden's strong support for far-right movements. Writing specifically on the emergence of Pegida, Fabian Virchow concludes that the conservative politics of Saxony led to established politicians engaging more commonly with Pegida, which gave their concerns more credence.[60] He also names the connection to the history of the successful protest during the Peaceful Revolution. Finally, he points to the high media coverage of Pegida within the famous rebuilt Old Town, which also inspired more people to join the protests. Julian Göpffarth focuses on the role of nostalgia to explain the support for the far right, in particular among local intellectuals.[61] Developing a concept of "multidirectional nostalgia," he sees the drive for political change arise through the activation of collective memories of the oppressive conditions in the GDR and the positive time of the Peaceful Revolution, when change seemed possible for the future. Some intellectuals now claim they experience Germany as being as oppressive as the GDR, where society expects conformity in beliefs and opinions. With Pegida and the AfD, they hoped to reactivate the memories of possible change and assert their right to a voice in shaping the country's identity. Sabine Volk points to the importance of not only external, but also internal dimensions for the persistence of nativist groups. She emphasizes the symbolic structures and the ritualization of movements as factors for their continuity.[62]

The following analysis adds another angle to these explorations that touches on both internal and external dimensions. It investigates how Dresden's established narrative about the city's significance, destruction, and revival, as well as how the already customary established ritualistic memory culture contribute, however inadvertently, to the exceptional rise of support for the far right. In addition, it will show how the bombing narrative lends itself to populist claims that define their group as the unique moral representation of the people. This assertion also encourages the idea that it is a moral duty to resist and speak up against the supposedly immoral and uncaring behavior of the state and the danger of subsequent societal loss. In particular, the discursive performances of both the Dresden master narrative and the far right's assertions about society reveal a strongly linked, collaborative affinity. As Dresden-born poet Durs Grünbein has put it polemically: "I'm not surprised that this diffuse feeling of threat broke out on the Elbe. The economic crisis, European politics, religious wars and refugee flows are also cutting into people's existence elsewhere. But only in Dresden do they also affect the soul."[63]

Of course, it should be stated again that there are considerable individual and social group variations among Dresden residents in regard to the city's history and far-right politics, which need to be acknowledged and which Grünbein here leaves aside. Yet there is a particularly tight-knit community of residents who define both their individual and their group identity strongly through their home city and its history. Their connection to Dresden is characterized by a deep emotional bond to a static image of the historical "true" Dresden that needs to be recreated, protected, and preserved. Often dominating public opinion, these residents share a stable, mostly homogeneous, deeply ingrained collective memory and symbolic vocabulary, and they engage in ritualized remembrance activities around Dresden's significance and loss. Such strong traditional place attachment as part of group identity has been shown to increase the feelings of threat against the character of one's city by outside groups, as well as a general distrust of change. These feelings can be passed on through generations.[64] Due to Dresden's history, such feelings carry particular power in this case. Beyond the local, beliefs and arguments linked to the often unchallenged Dresden narrative also hold immense signaling power and can influence how far feelings of a threat to one's culture will spread and be accepted.

Dresden Memory Culture and the Rise of Far-Right Movements

The creation and performance of both personal and public remembrance rituals around February 13 and the designation of memorials as physical placeholders for the lost sites enabled residents to preserve Dresden as an icon even before the city was rebuilt. Thousands still come together in the city center to mourn the victims: the dead, the built cityscape, and, to some extent, themselves. In post-reunification Germany, the remembrance of oppression and opposition in Dresden have also become part of the commemorations, performed via symbolic gestures such as the lighting of candles at the Frauenkirche and prayers for peace, both rituals that were performed during the 1989 protests in Dresden.

Despite reunification and the successful rebuilding projects, many Dresdners still see themselves as guardians of the memory of their city's past. In the 2000s, rising numbers of neo-Nazi groups, most from outside of Dresden, started to come to the city on the anniversaries to highlight German suffering, deny Nazi crimes, and relativize the Holocaust. By 2009, the events had attracted 6,500 neo-Nazis, making it one of the largest such gatherings in Germany since the end of the Second World War. Their marches past Dresden's rebuilt landmarks to commemorate what the groups call the "bombing terror" or "bombing holocaust" against the German population was nationally and internationally condemned.[65] This kind of appropriation of the bombing narrative, performed by outside groups specifically using Dresden as a symbolic platform for extreme-right politics, finally met widespread disapproval in Dresden.

A citizen's initiative (Interessengemeinschaft 13. Februar) was founded to combat the appropriation of the commemoration by extreme-right groups and to create guidelines for what they considered a suitable framing of the yearly events.[66] As part of the remembrance performances, they introduced a new symbol, the white rose, as a signal that Dresden is committed to overcoming "war, racism, and violence" caused by totalitarian regimes, and it has been integrated into the remembrance rituals.[67] Every year since 2010, a human chain has formed around the historic city center.[68] In 2015, on the seventieth anniversary of the bombing, the population was highly engaged in the project; at several points the rows had to be doubled up to accommodate the participants. The crowds were made up of a variety of people, from young families to bombing survivors, local and Saxon politicians from all parties, and representatives from the military and the federal government.

The mood was somber and disciplined. Many participants also had a small white cloth rose pinned to their coats.

The symbols reference tropes that are well-established in Germany's collective memory. The human chain was widely used during the peace movement in 1980s West Germany to demonstrate against the stationing of American Pershing II missiles, a concern BRD and GDR peace activists shared.[69] It also speaks to the feeling by many that being a Dresdner comes with a moral obligation: it has become their duty to warn the world about the absolute necessity of peace, a rhetoric already established during the GDR and carried forward into reunified Germany. For example, during the 2003 war with Iraq, Dresden peace activists distinctly referred to the experience and suffering under the bombing as a reason to oppose the war.[70] Blocking the neo-Nazis' access to the city and its narrative sends an even stronger signal of Dresden's innocence. As the enormous response and the somber mood shows, this message of peace can unify the various political forces in their remembrance. It also reveals, however, that such an approach can block necessary re-evaluations of the past. The widely used white rose symbol connects to the Munich-based White Rose resistance group against National Socialism. Dresdners see it as a way to oppose oppression, but also express kinship with, and a unique understanding of, other victims, including those of the National Socialist regime.

During a 2015 memorial event designed to remember the Holocaust in Dresden as part of the February 13 activities, the problematic nature of trying to fit Jewish suffering and persecution within a narrative that excludes questions about Dresdners' responsibility during the Nazi times, reveals itself. The citizen's group that had originally introduced the symbol of the white rose wanted to give space for the remembrance of the Dresden Jews and their suffering during the Holocaust while the seventieth anniversary of the bombings was commemorated. A small crowd, among them then-mayor Helma Orosz, visited the train station from which Dresden Jews had been deported. To mourn and honor the victims, white roses were placed onto the train tracks. Then the participants traveled to the Heidefriedhof, the cemetery where most bombing casualties are buried, and laid white roses on graves and memorials.[71] Most Dresdners do not intend to deny the Holocaust like the neo-Nazis that try to dominate the remembrance of February 13; in fact, the Shoah was clearly remembered in speeches both during the visit to the train station and the cemetery. The participants, however, did not question employing the symbol of a National Socialist resistance group to remember both the suffering of Holocaust victims and the dead of the Dres-

Fig. 58. White roses at the Dresden train station Leipziger Bahnhof in remembrance of the Jewish victims of the Holocaust (February 13, 2015). (Photograph by Susanne Vees-Gulani.)

den firestorm, blurring the boundaries between the meaning of the experience of persecution simply for one's cultural and religious background and the bombing of a German city during a war that was caused by Germany and which it refused to end.

The destruction of Dresden can thus be linked with a multitude of discourses and their political, social, and cultural goals. Absent reflections on responsibility and morality of comparison, the discourse has no clearly defined limits and can become compatible with the populist-nativist rhetoric of such groups as Pegida and the AfD, which claim to speak for the common people, to distinguish between a positive "us, the people," and a negative, demonized "other." It often includes strong anti-elite rhetoric.[72] In fact, Dresden can serve as a microcosm to explore the far right's claims about the circumstances that necessitate their actions and justify their demands. Dresden's destruction narrative and its manifestations can be read in parallel to the movement's populist and nativist approach. Both speak to the premises of a group identity characterized as unique and geographically and emotionally bound to a specific place and its history. In both cases they also attach a shared, exclusive high culture to this identity. Dresdners define themselves through their dedication to their home city; the AfD portrays itself as having arisen out of their attachment to the nation. A future destruction of Germany, they suggest, is possible, just as Dresden was unnecessarily destroyed by outside forces. Appealing to emotions over reason, the AfD conjures up their "defense of Germany," mirroring Dresdners' conviction that they must continuously protect Dresden and its cultural integrity. In their battle against what they consider the ongoing erosion of German values and cultural identity, the AfD and similar groups argue that such destruction is not only caused by outside forces, such as Muslim refugees, but also from the inside, namely the mainstream parties with their political elites, the press, and the far left and their prescriptive (multi)cultural ideas. Drawing an analogy with Dresden's historic opposition to the GDR resonates with residents who also make clear distinctions between themselves and others from whom Dresden has to be protected, be it the federal, state, or city government, building companies, or people questioning Dresden's significance and singularity. This opposition can even be found in the city itself; there are Dresden residents and there are "true Dresdners," namely those who connect their own identity with Dresden's memory.[73]

The narratives of Dresden and the far-right thus enter into a collaborative discourse in grounding, preserving, and protecting each other's understanding of the past and present. Far-right groups active in Dresden and the AfD present themselves as deeply engaged with the destiny of the city. They confirm through their discourse the validity of Dresden's self-appointed role in preserving German culture through memory. Dresden here functions as the prime example of the kind of fundamental cultural treasures that can be lost if Germany does not protect its cultural and national core, which in turn bolsters Dresdners' belief in the singularity of their city's cultural significance. The AfD not only confirms that Dresden is a "special place," but it also lifts up the people of Dresden and their actions as exemplary for the nation.[74] Thuringian AfD leader Björn Höcke emphasized Dresdners' key role in 2017: "Dresden is the capital of the courageous citizens [. . .] and when I consider the desolate internal and external situation of the German capital Berlin, then I think that Berlin should not actually be the German capital, but Dresden should."[75] Through these connections, key parts of the established, and generally unquestioned, Dresden destruction narrative—victimhood, moral authority, and promoting peace—become available for protest movements and political parties such as Pegida and the AfD to bind to their own agendas, using populism and nativism to connect even seemingly incompatible goals, such as opposing asylum seekers and calling for peace and reconciliation.

The Continued Integration of Far-Right Ideas into the Dresden Bombing Narrative

Several examples of events in Dresden since 2017 illustrate this tightening connection between the far-right discourse and the Dresden memory culture. While the AfD had not always seen eye to eye with Pegida,[76] AfD members from the beginning liked to hold rallies and meetings in Dresden or act as guest speakers at Pegida events, since supportive audiences, the baroque backdrop symbolizing traditional German culture, and Dresden's national standing guarantee wide media circulation.

In January 2017, Björn Höcke, a member of the right wing of the party (who has since gained increasing power within the organization), gave perhaps his most controversial speech in Dresden,[77] criticizing German Holocaust remembrance by labeling the Berlin Holocaust memorial a "memorial of shame."[78] Yet a different passage of his speech is more telling for pinpointing the AfD's affinity for Dresden:

> But I come from a family of displaced persons on both my mother's and father's side. My father told me very early on [. . .] what happened in Dresden at the end of the Second World War. The war had already been decided and the city was overcrowded with countless refugees from the German eastern territories. The majority of them were women, children and old people. There was no significant military infrastructure in Dresden [. . .] but Dresden had one of the most beautiful city centers of all German cities. That's why, as my father told me as a child, Dresden was always called the Florence on the Elbe. The bombing of Dresden and the subsequent firestorm destroyed the Florence on the Elbe and the people who lived there.

The passage echoes the fundamental parts of the Dresden destruction narrative as established early on by Nazi propaganda. By alluding to his own family background as German expellees from the east, Höcke embeds himself into the story by mentioning the refugees' presence in Dresden during the bombing. Earlier in his speech, Höcke emphasized growing up in West Germany while hearing about the destiny of Dresden, marking the Dresden bombing not only as a local, but a Germany-wide loss, an international atrocity, and a German trauma with a shared victimhood that is transferred from generation to generation.

Höcke makes a direct connection between the bombing of Dresden and what he describes as the threat to German culture and identity today, except that now the enemy comes from within the country in form of the established parties and their prescriptive view of the past:

> The bombing of Dresden was a war crime. It is comparable to the atomic bombs dropped on Hiroshima and Nagasaki. The bombing of Dresden and the other German cities was intended to do nothing other than rob us of our collective identity. They wanted to eradicate us root and branch, to pull us up by our roots. [. . .] There were no more German victims, only German perpetrators. We are, through today, not able to mourn our own victims. And instead of introducing our new generations to our great benefactors, [. . .] history, German history, is made to look terrible and ridiculous. It cannot, it must not go on like this."[79]

While criticizing the attitude to the past established by the mainstream parties, he applauds Dresden residents' stubborn will to rebuild their city with its historical façade and describes them as trailblazers in their continued attempts to preserve the highlights of the German past: The rebuilding of the Frauenkirche "was for us patriots a glimmer of hope that it still exists, the spark of a German self-assertion."[80] By interconnecting German history and culture with the destiny of Dresden and its residents, Höcke strengthens the idea that Dresdners need to lead the way in preserving culture. Höcke presents his xenophobic nationalist agenda as preventing Germany's destruction, which resonates with many Dresdners. With views in Dresden about society and high culture remaining frozen at the point of Dresden's destruction, there is much resistance to re-evaluating the victim narrative that has become part of their social identity. The idea of Dresden as a (lost and partially regained) unique representation of German cultural achievements also echoes the static definition of "German" in the AfD. Any change or wider inclusiveness is considered a threat.

The events arranged by the local Dresden chapter of the AfD for the commemorations of the seventy-fifth anniversary of the bombing in 2020 deepened the intertwined relationship between the AfD's agenda and Dresden. On February 13, they organized an information booth at the Altmarkt, as well as a wreath-laying ceremony. While the AfD did not, this time, openly downplay the Holocaust, they nevertheless pushed against established boundaries of a responsible framing of February 13 by distorting historical facts and highlighting their own far-right nativist agenda. Ahead of the commemorations, AfD cochairman and Saxon representative Tino Chrupalla inflated the number of those killed in the firestorm, casting doubt on the official death toll of twenty-five thousand, as had been definitively concluded by a commission of historians in 2010.[81] Claiming instead one hundred thousand victims, Chrupalla's reasoning resonated with many people in Dresden (and other parts of Germany) who believe in higher casualty numbers based on survivor stories.[82] In the face of contrary historical evidence, this claim suggests that the truth of an emotional reaction trumps factual assessments; in their eyes, the bombing is not a historical event that needs to be analyzed, but a matter of the heart, an experience that lives on in the emotional DNA of the city's residents through the generations.

Based on these sentiments, Chrupalla can easily reject any suggestion that he is trying to coopt the narrative to further the cause of the AfD, particularly since he places himself inside the bombing story. As he told the weekly *Der Spiegel* about February 13: "I do not need to mark this day in my calendar, the date is already inside of me. [. . .] My grandmother, my father, and other eyewitnesses have told me about streets full of people before the attacks, and piles of dead bodies after the bombing night." None of them, Chrupalla claims in the interview, believe the number of twenty-five thousand, which consequently makes him doubt it as well.[83] Since Chrupalla is part of the victim community due to his family's experiences, his statements carry legitimacy in the city. By declaring co-ownership of the February 13 narrative, Chrupalla can extend such legitimacy to the AfD as a victim of the establishment. In this vein, Chrupalla explains the absence of the AfD at the events with German president Frank-Walter Steinmeier for the seventy-fifth anniversary not as rejecting Steinmeier's call for openness and tolerance, but out of self-defense. He claimed that if the AfD attended, the president would politically instrumentalize the memory of the bombing against the AfD.[84] The AfD chairman thus reverses causalities. Since Dresdners are seldom confronted with questions about responsibility, such messages resonate in Dresden, where many feel misunderstood by established political structures.

This rhetoric continued at the AfD booth at the Altmarkt square on February 13, which informed visitors about "the truth of the events of that

Fig. 59. Large banners erected on the Altmarkt by the AfD (February 13, 2020). (Photograph by Sabine Volk, reprinted by permission.)

day."[85] With its motto "Remember Dresden with Dignity," the AfD suggests that many official rituals lack such dignity. The party, and with it other far-right activists that utilize the bombing, thus claim to have a monopoly on the appropriate remembrance of Dresden's past. The AfD focuses on the narrative's element of unjust suffering (and implied innocence) as the foundation for the AfD's commemoration strategies. Saxony's party leader Jörg Urban told a journalist at the booth that he wishes "'a more unique Dresden commemoration' [. . .] like Hiroshima" and in the process inflates the victim numbers as did Chrupalla, in this case by likening the Dresden bombing to the dropping of the atomic bomb: "In Hiroshima, there were also around 100,000."[86]

On Altmarkt square, several thousand corpses were cremated between the end of February and early March 1945, while the cemetery prepared more room for burials.[87] The gruesome scenes at the cremations at the Altmarkt were documented by the Dresden photographer Walter Hahn.[88] Next to its booth, the AfD erected large boards displaying two of Hahn's photographs. One of the larger-than-life-size banners showed the square full of dead bodies and a cremation area where corpses are burned in large piles, while horse carriages bring in more bodies. The other photo is a close-up of piled-up corpses awaiting cremation. It is difficult to read these enlarged photographs as a dignified path of remembrance. The pictures are from the same series that the GDR newspapers, in particular in the 1950s, repeatedly published from to underline their claim of the uncontrolled brutality of the Western Allies.

By claiming a need for an alternate discourse, the AfD uses the Dresden casualties to relativize Dresden's and Germany's past, drawing on the aesthetic similarity to well-known photographs from concentration camps. With this display, they follow the lead of far-right groups who frequently use these pictures that highlight the cruelty of the bombing as a way to displace the horror of German crimes in memory. The photographs usually go hand in hand with highly exaggerated casualty numbers. Both are employed in an effort to downplay the Holocaust,[89] but claim to counter the false public memory practiced elsewhere in the city.

Strangely, this striking setup at the AfD information booth was not mentioned in the press or by the leftist protesters. Their distinct misuse of the firebombing to relativize the Holocaust was rarely called out. The discourse about the singularity of Dresden's suffering and the unique horror of the events has been ingrained too deeply in the Dresden architecture of memory to realize the problematic nature of such approaches, which enable far-right ideas to be cloaked within an established, unchallenged narrative. Dresden residents have been accused of being complicit with fascist belief structures through their wide embrace of Pegida and the AfD, though such reproaches are firmly rejected by Dresdners, who counter by arguing that the innocent city, and by extension its residents, were also victims of the Nazis and thus cannot be National Socialists or right extremists themselves.[90] Yet it is exactly this understanding that makes it possible for Dresdners to embrace the AfD's messages and goals to protect German national history, identity, and values without questioning the party's legitimacy or concepts.[91]

Not surprisingly, the Altmarkt has remained the central place of remembrance within the Old Town for the AfD and other far-right groups, who deliberately separate themselves from the official remembrance activities in the city.[92] Even though the current mayor of Dresden, Dirk Hilbert (re-elected in 2022 for another seven-year term), and the CDU city council members traditionally visit the small memorial on the square in the morning of February 13 to lay down flowers for the bombing casualties that were cremated at the Altmarkt, the AfD has been organizing a separate vigil and

Fig. 60. The memorial of the cremation site on the Altmarkt (February 13, 2022). (Photograph by Susanne Vees-Gulani.)

wreath-laying ceremony at the same location. Symbolically, its ceremony is performed during the time that the first bombardment of the day took place. The event is a deliberate provocation that challenges official remembrance rituals, which at this time of the evening, after the human chain and during the second ringing of all church bells (they first ring during the human chain), was usually marked by silence. It carries strong political tensions and leads to confrontations with counterprotesters into what some would consider one of the most sacred parts of the remembrance rituals. The Dresden AfD is pushing for a more central role for the location during the remembrance of February 13 and calls for more dignity, which, however, the AfD connects with the suggestion that the official discourse of twenty-five thousand casualties is false. The party implies that the research team that determined the number was politically influenced to lower the number of dead. Consequently, the AfD, in their 2024 local election program, calls for a new investigation: "we want independent historical research into the events and victims of those days of bombing."[93] The yearly vigil is probably not supported by many locals, since it disrupts a moment long reserved for quiet reflection. With their performance, however, the far-right participants tell a story at the Altmarkt memorial that has grown out of the basic elements of the established, mostly unchallenged bombing narrative embraced by many.

According to Saxony's Domestic Intelligence Services, the number of right-extremist crimes has risen significantly in Dresden, and the incidents have become increasingly violent. The agency considers Dresden at this point a right-wing stronghold.[94] So does the right wing itself. For the extreme-right organizations, Pegida's continuous presence and the lack of consistent opposition by the middle class to the movement's activities, coupled with the large success of the AfD among voters, has turned Dresden into a "city of resistance."[95] Far-right groups have also referred to Dresden as the "capital of the patriotic movement," which inspires more extremist and New Right groups to get involved in city politics.[96] Dresdners have not entirely ignored these developments and there are many who oppose radical far-right ideas, but it has been difficult to motivate a consistent large-scale counterprotest movement. The far right has been successful with rhetorically grounding themselves in Dresden by activating key narratives closely connected with the way many residents define their identity: they assure the public that they are protecting true German culture and evoke Dresden's past as an ideal against which culture today needs to be measured. They strengthen the long-established narrative of insurmountable loss, suffering, and victimhood as a result of the bombing, and they identify a guilty party outside of Dresden, the Western Allies, for the destruction. They appeal to Dresdners to rise up again and demand a new political system as they did courageously during the Peaceful Revolution. For all these points, the cityscape repeatedly serves as a backdrop both during protests and as pictures on social media posts.

The success of this rhetoric based on weaving together the material, the idealized, and the wounded city with far-right ideas reveals that the present political developments cannot be explained without a complex contextualization. The GDR's ideology and its use of the Dresden destruction story and German victimhood, as well as its reluctance to discuss German guilt, clearly helped make people susceptible to far-right ideas about history. Yet the circumstances of the GDR are not enough to explain the situation. Rather, a much longer story has to be told to understand the ongoing discourses of retribution and resentment in Dresden, one that includes the centuries before 1945 and the three and a half decades since the East German state's demise. As we will see in the next chapter, this long story also significantly complicates counterprotests.

CHAPTER 7

Conclusions
Performing Counterprotest

Groups such as Pegida and the Alternative for Germany (AfD) define as one of their fundamental goals the protection of German society, culture, and values from what they perceive as internal and external threats. Up until 2021, the Merkel government was vilified, and after that the coalition under chancellor Olaf Scholz. Among the perceived external dangers to German society are refugees, foreigners, and the European Union. German (past) achievements in high culture, such as in architecture, art, music, and literature, are frequently highlighted as key building blocks of the traditions that form German identity and as proof that German culture is of invaluable significance for the world. These ideas are often represented in the intellectual output of the New Right and within the programs of far-right nativist groups. In the case of Dresden, the political right finds support among parts of the population who favor a static, nativist definition of German culture that is located in the past. In a city where historical reconstruction is a fundamental element of present self-understanding and where nostalgia for what was lost has led to substantial changes in the material environment, many are sympathetic to the argument that German culture is "under threat."[1] Such arguments play into the residents' self-understanding as "victims" through the losses of cultural heritage in 1945 and their fear of continued attempts by outside political and cultural forces to further damage Dresden through change. Consequently, the far right relies heavily on arguments surrounding a possible loss of "high culture." Not only is it represented as part of Dresden's unique significance, but also as a valuable and defining good for every German. This fundamental reliance on heritage culture for political gain in Dresden has also brought with it an urgency to find new ways of confronting the far right: the Dresden cityscape and its history of loss and recovery, including such performance and exhibition spaces as the Semper Opera House, the Baroque Zwinger with its galleries, or the State Theater in Dresden, have been utilized as effective backdrops for the political activities of Pegida, the AfD, the Querdenker (Contrarians) movement (which opposed national Covid-19 measures), the far-right groups Freie Sachsen (Free Saxons) and Identitäre (Identitarian Movement), and other extremist factions.

The national and international news reporting on Dresden politics has often included photographs of far-right demonstrations in front of the rebuilt historic Dresden cityscape. Yet while the engagement of the cityscape in far-right visual and textual rhetoric can be effective in communicating with supporters and sympathizers, the far right's claim on the Old Town has also had negative effects, such as impacting Dresden's reputation as a travel destination.[2] Since tourism is a key part of Dresden's economy, the adverse consequences for tourism have been a driving force for city officials who are not associated with the far right to try to regain control over the historic spaces. Furthermore, since nativist and far-right groups not only use Dresden's heritage sites as a backdrop but describe Dresden as quintessentially embodying German culture, the city's public cultural institutions have been forced to position themselves in relation to these groups. Grassroots organizations, often associated with leftist politics, also attempt to disrupt far-right movements and their co-opting of culture and heritage. In fact, as migrant studies researcher Carolin Müller has highlighted, "Dresden is a rather unusual research site apropos intercultural collaborative projects" since the protest culture displays "unique characteristics with regard to the establishment of collaborative left-wing mobilisation and its use of cultural heritage."[3] Müller refers to the way that in Dresden counterprotests are frequently conducted via artistic installations and cultural events in the Old Town, so that the premise of Dresden as an important cultural center, as frequently intoned by the far right, is not actually opposed in the protests. Still, these interventions have not been particularly successful in creating fruitful discussions. I propose that they are in fact based on definitions of contemporary cultural significance as a continued re-creation of culture within its temporal and societal context, while many of Dresden's residents build their identity on a narrative of cultural import that is perceived as originating in the past, as remaining unchanged, and in its essence immune to challenges.

The relatively uncontested narrative of loss and victimhood associated with Dresden—culturally, materially, and existentially—opens avenues for representatives of far-right groups to cite the city as a national example.

They highlight the enormity of the possible losses and the impact of German self-definition and values that would be at stake if German culture were lost. Many Dresdners share the idea that their "German Florence" plays an unrivaled role in Germany and indeed the world. Dresden's longtime self-marketing as a static cultural site, and the large positive response from the national and international audience to such marketing, repeatedly confirm this assessment. Travelers in particular value Dresden for its architectural heritage and its large collections of traditional masterpieces. This circumstance complicates the position of dynamic cultural interventions in the Dresden cityscape and its theaters and museums. They can signal to the outside that not all of Dresden clings to a streamlined definition of history and culture, yet at the same time they assert a definition of culture that lies outside of what most understand as Dresden's unique value. I assert that the rivalry for cultural attitudes that plays out in Dresden, one dynamic, the other static, does not in fact foster political and cultural dialogue and change, but instead fuels an increasing polarization that divides the population, Dresden artists, and intellectuals.

Contested Spaces: Artistic Interruptions in the Cityscape

The historic center with its highly recognizable buildings has been one of the contested spaces in Dresden for fathoming out the sociopolitical attitudes, identity, and culture from the 2010s to today. As political scientist Hans Vorländer diagnoses: "The 'street' in Dresden has become a space for collective outrage and self-affirmation."[4] The previous chapters have shown, however, that the close affinity between the Dresden population and the cityscape goes back to the very beginning of Dresden's rise as a city of European rank. Today, the famous silhouette, which many identify as an expression of German cultural achievement, appears to provide an affirming stage set for the nationalist politics of exclusion and the emphasis on "Germanness" propagated by protesters, who use the Old Town as a backdrop and a reference point in their speeches. In response, Dresden's cultural institutions and churches located in the Old Town at times in collaboration with grassroots movements, try to intervene in this "heritage mobilization" of the right with their own mobilization of culture.[5] The creative sphere has become a place to challenge the idea of culture propagated by the far right and a space to explore new pathways for identity within a society whose composition is transforming.

Some of the interventions have been based on reclaiming the visual realm. Theaters and museums put up large banners covering parts of their buildings with slogans supporting a society practicing tolerance for various cultures and experiences. The Semper Opera flew flags and installed signs with inscriptions such as "Open Your Eyes," "Open Your Hearts," "Open Your Doors," to counter the message of Germany under threat and to loosen the far-right groups' claim on German culture. In other examples, the State Theater used a declarative format: "For a Cosmopolitan Dresden—Refugees Welcome Here" and "Human Dignity Is Sacrosanct," a fundamental passage from the Federal Republic's constitution. At another time, the opera turned off the lights so that the building disappeared out of sight during the Pegida protest marches on Monday nights.[6]

More recently, the opera has put forward a dynamic definition of art with flags on two sides of the Theaterplatz that emphasize "For art and tolerance" and "More than 30 nations." These inscriptions stress a collaborative process and universal values in art. On one side of the square, the flags display messages in German, on the other they are translated into English. The large banners on buildings and squares can visibly signal that not all of Dresden agrees with the approach propagated by the far-right groups and New Right theories. The visual markers can interrupt the suggested unity of the crowds with their anti-immigrant, antigovernment stance and the sea of flags representing the various groups and their opinions in the historic cityscape. Both protesters and public organizations are aware of the media attention and stage their interventions accordingly. With their signs, the institutions hope to portray culture in Dresden as dynamic and engaged, in contrast to the static, limited nativist view emphasized by the AfD, Pegida, Querdenker, and various other groups. The English signage is also a reminder that while the cultural institutions and the city are certainly sincere in their efforts, they are also dependent on the income from national and international tourism. There is an incentive to make sure that this message of opposition to the protest movements is recognized around the world.

The dichotomy in approach to art and culture between part of the population and the institutions also arises from their differing relationship to Dresden, which we have seen play out on various levels in the previous chapters. Those whose families have long lived in Dresden, often for several generations, and who feel deeply connected to the city, identify particularly strongly with the static elements of Dresden's culture. It is experienced as having continually offered stability even during difficult political and cultural times when Dresden's traditional city and artistic scape was challenged. There is a level of suspicion among some members of this group toward others who moved to Dresden later, and they frequently divide the population

Fig. 61. English-language flags on the Theaterplatz with messages of multiculturalism and acceptance. (Photograph by Annika Gulani and Susanne Vees-Gulani.)

into "Old Dresdners" and "New Dresdners."[7] Most leaders of the cultural institutions are "newcomers," since they have only arrived in the city after 1990, usually from West Germany. Further, the artists, musicians, and actors performing in Dresden comprise many different backgrounds, cultures, and nationalities, a circumstance also emphasized with the flag's message of "30 nations" on the Theaterplatz.

Dresden's cultural institutions hope to convey with their signage that the far-right groups in fact close themselves off to culture by only valuing specific art. As public organizations of the city and the state of Saxony, they understand the challenging of traditional static views of culture as part of their mission. In 2015, at the height of the Pegida movement, the State Theater director at the time, Wilfried Schulz, insisted on political activity as part of the institution's scope: to oppose the far right and their "nonsense" was utterly indispensable since a fruitful and necessary public discourse in politics was not possible any longer.[8] Others, like Marion Ackermann, director of Dresden's art museums, sends a more muted public message. She pits a dynamic understanding of art against the far-right protesters as part of the museum's "educational mission." "We are actually turning it around: Dresden is currently a stage for right-wing populist movements, and we want to use it as a stage and model case to show what can be done from the artistic side to reflect these things more strongly and deal with them critically."[9] Consequently, the emphasis on openness on the signage is not only to imply that Dresden is indeed welcoming to others, but also that public institutions are open for discussion and a multitude of viewpoints, as long as basic human rights are respected.

Grassroots organizations against the right-wing movements also use the space of the Old Town to engage in protest via unique cultural spectacles. For instance, such groups as "Dresden für alle" (Dresden for All) and "Banda Internationale" organize marches with musical performances, encourage active participation from onlookers, and use artistic installations to introduce an alternative to the static understanding of culture that dominates in Dresden. Banda Internationale is a loosely organized brass ensemble in which musicians of all backgrounds come together to play and protest against xenophobia. The group does not just object to far-right and nativist views, but with its multicultural makeup, including refugees, it also tries to exemplify in its organization and its actions the success of an open society and the positive cultural return it offers.[10]

In March 2015, Banda Internationale and Dresden für alle organized one of their most elaborate spectacles, the "Prozession der Angsthasen" (Scaredy-Bunny Procession).[11] Happening shortly before Easter, the satirical march played on the German term "Angsthase," literally "scaredy rabbit/bunny." Labeling it a procession, the organizers alluded to the religious Easter processions of Holy Week, which remembers the suffering of Christ on his way to the cross. It also referenced the Procession of Princes, a famous 102-meter mosaic in the Old Town that celebrates Dresden's past as the capital of the Electorate of Saxony. Finally, it stood in opposition to Pegida's Monday demonstrations, which concluded with a so-called "stroll" through the city that symbolically marked the city as their territory and situated them as in line with the Monday protests of the Peaceful Revolution. Many Pegida participants also displayed a cult-like commitment to their group.

The Angsthasen march tried to counter with its ironic spectacle the irrational fearmongering against foreigners by far-right politics, call attention to the daily fears minorities experience while trying to navigate a hostile environment in Dresden, and take back the city as a realm in which to give voice to diverse cultural expressions. All participants were encouraged to bring or dress up in "bunny paraphernalia" and to walk and dance accompa-

Fig. 62. Sculpture by Heinz Schmöller at rebuilt Frauenkirche during "Angsthasenprozession" (2015, still image). (From Banda Comunale / https://www.youtube.com/@BandaComunaleVideo)

nied by the music of the marching band through the city. The motto of the event was "Let's pool our fears. Everyone bring one."[12] In front of the Frauenkirche on the Neumarkt, the Dresden artist Heinz Schmöller had installed a six-meter-high sculpture of a rabbit to which the participants were then symbolically sacrificing their fears.

The spectacle hit a nerve; Pegida felt so provoked that their leader Lutz Bachmann called upon his supporters to bring carrots to their Pegida march so that they could use them "to shut up the ugly little Antifa-rabbits by shoving them into their little mouths."[13] Yet the number of protesters in the procession was disappointing, since only nine hundred people came out to oppose the at that time vastly bigger Pegida demonstrations.[14] In a study on the effectiveness of counterprotests in containing right-wing popular movements, based on data collected on Pegida as a test case, researchers Johannes Füllers and Sebastian Hellmeier "found no evidence for a preventive effect of counter-demonstrations." In fact, "larger counter-protests are associated with more turnout at subsequent Pegida protests."[15] In the Dresden setting, when a protest is in its very form challenging fundamental ideas, it might provoke such reactions even more forcefully. So, while new approaches to culture have been used both to criticize the rise of the far right and to demonstrate and sketch out possible alternatives for society, it has been difficult to reach a wide audience or convince people to oppose far-right cultural attitudes with these performances.

Dresden's issue with contemporary dynamic cultural approaches was on display in 2017, when the temporary installation *Monument* by Manaf Halbouni was erected in front of the Frauenkirche as part of a culture festival under the heading "Am Fluss/At the River: Zu Kulturen des Ankommens/On Cultures of Arrival."[16] The Syrian German artist, who had studied at the Dresden Art Academy, called attention to the Syrian war by recreating part of a widely shared image from Aleppo, in which civilians were protected from sniper fire by three buses that had been propped up vertically as a barricade in a residential quarter. Halbouni installed three buses on the Neumarkt in front of the Frauenkirche in the same fashion. The artist hoped to draw attention to the suffering in Syria by connecting this monument to the horrors of war with the iconic Dresden monument to the bombing, the Frauenkirche. Halbouni encouraged viewers to associate the events in the Middle East with those in Europe's past. He aimed to build bridges of understanding about suffering and loss and the hope for rebuilding and peace.[17] For Halbouni, art was "just the right way to talk to each other," as it could offer an appropriate place for "friction and contact."[18] Sarah Dornhof in her reading of Halbouni's *Monument* also emphasizes how the work "might have been able to create multidirectional connections, references and associations around the physical space and its layers of memory as a way to open other possible orientations and interpretations."[19]

Yet despite Halbouni's wish to stir conversation and his direct link to Dresden's bombing narrative and the subsequent peace and reconciliation discourse, such comparisons caused an outrage among a significant number of Dresdners. It was seen as offensive to install a large contemporary art piece in front of Dresden's most revered Baroque symbol and beacon of peace. Instead of forming relations between the two symbols, the links between the experiences of Syrian civilians and their own, many felt Dresden's bombing victims were belittled and their cultural heritage dishonored with the contemporary installation.[20] Despite the mayor's support for the project, a vocal number of residents saw the work as a provocation or simply "absolute nonsense" and described it as "a complete scandal."[21] Its unveiling was disturbed by crowds screaming "Schande" (shame), a word that in this context is reminiscent of National Socialism's usage. In Nazi Germany, it decried the relationship between Germans and those considered to be racially inferior, which was seen as an affront against "Germanness." The mayor even received death threats for supporting the project.[22]

Fig. 63. The installation *Monument* near the rebuilt Frauenkirche by Syrian-German artist Manaf Halbouni (2017). (Photograph by Thomas Skowron / CC 4.0 International, reprinted by permission.)

But while the *Monument* was attacked for its political stance by Pegida followers, the main objections in the general population concentrated on the supposed lack of artistic value of the installation. Halbouni's work was experienced as a challenge to what many Dresdners understand as the central symbol of their city's cultural significance, its population's greatest achievement, and the basis for Dresdners' self-view as members of a unique culture, as victims, and as peacemakers. The Frauenkirche is understood as a static symbol, not a dynamic one, which signals its meaning exactly because of this stability. Even after destruction and years of neglect by the socialist government, it rose again to return as a safe anchor for identity. According to the widely supported narrative, Dresden residents reclaimed it as a symbol through their perseverance and their unchanging commitment to their cultural heritage.

The *Monument*'s physical location was perceived as blocking the Frauenkirche's symbolic role as a beacon of peace as well as Dresden's message of cultural import. Acknowledging the possibility of interaction between the *Monument* and the Frauenkirche would have given the *Monu-*

ment its own signaling power and turned Dresden's important symbol into a dynamic cultural artifact. This multidirectional possibility of the *Monument* could have destabilized the permanence of the role of Dresden as a cultural treasure and a static symbol for peace.[23] Even many Dresden citizens who do not support the far-right movement or the AfD thus probably agreed with the criticism brought forth by the AfD that described *Monument* as "an 'abuse of artistic freedom' deliberately designed to 'snub the citizens of Dresden'" and as "overshadowing the central symbol of Dresden's post-reunification revival with 'scrap metal.'"[24] This example reveals how a dynamic understanding of culture will be hard-pressed to counter the long-lasting support for a static view.

Sociologist Karl Mannheim in his lecture "Die Bedeutung der Konkurrenz im Gebiete des Geistigen" (The Meaning of Competition in the Area of the Intellectual) explores this very interrelationship of diverging social and cultural beliefs within a society.[25] He points out that "historical thinking, like existence related thinking in general, is a competition between different parties with the same objective." Such rivalry has the "tendency to degenerate into conflict, to turn into struggle or to be transformed into a relationship of togetherness."[26] As discussed above, the proponents of a dynamic understanding of art and culture often mention the wish to provoke such a fruitful friction in the cultural realm that can build bridges. But as Mannheim also emphasizes, this balance is hard to achieve since "all historical, ideological and sociological knowledge [is] embedded and supported by the drive for power and the craving for recognition of certain specific groups who want to make their interpretation of the world the general interpretation of the world."[27]

There are several reasons why approaches based on dynamic art will most likely be seen as a challenge and not as an offer for conversation among the group of citizens who draw on Dresden for their identity and self-worth. With the destruction in 1945, the image of Dresden, already idealized, became even more frozen in time. While some historical rebuilding took place during the GDR, it was particularly after reunification that many Dresdners felt they could finally take charge of their own city and recreate the permanence of their objects of identification by recreating them in their historic images. This emotional process moved the construction, particularly of the Frauenkirche, into the realm of the sacred. Anything that would be seen as trying to diminish or challenge the permanence and meaning of the sacred shrine would be answered with an even stronger demonstration of one's beliefs.

New ideas concerning the definition of culture, predominantly brought forward by "newcomers," are also rejected. As Dresden political scientist Hans Vorländer diagnoses the situation, there is a feeling that "New Dresdners" try to push new cultural approaches onto "Old Dresdners" because they feel superior to the longtime population.[28] In addition, many residents believe it is their duty to defend their city against further destruction. Since Dresdners, due to their narrative of destruction, see their local experiences and opinions as significant for the nation and the world, groups that could carry their feelings and concerns into the open can become attractive allies in what is experienced as continued challenges to Dresden's cultural essence. Even if many may not actively participate, tolerating the far right could lend support in shutting down rivaling understandings of art and culture.

There is also the question of how far proponents of art as a dynamic form do indeed wish dialogue or whether they are not also engaging in posturing in their rivalry with those insisting on art as a static product. In a study conducted in Dresden on the role of cultural institutions in the polarization of a city and framed by Mannheim's theory of rivalry, the researchers analyzed forums that had been organized by the city or institutions as places of dialogue, such as a discussion regarding Halbouni's *Monument* installation.[29] They found that most events were not characterized by an exchange of ideas and the search for common ground, but simply a way for each party to signal their viewpoint. They concluded that such events with representatives from opposing sides "are not only addressed to an audience but also made for an audience."[30] Similarly, the far-right protests in Dresden, as well as the opposing counterprotests by the cultural institutions or grassroots action groups, are consciously staged in opposition to each other and to announce their stand. While there is nothing wrong with this approach and it can be key in communicating to extremist groups that they will face competition in their pursuit to become the dominant force, it is important to recognize that such interactions reinforce polarizations rather than solve them.

Consequently, since a static view of culture has become the solid basis for the city's and many of its citizens' identity, introducing dynamic elements of meaning into the city's main artifact is often understood as an attempt to deconstruct self-definitions formed and communicated over generations. Challenging the far right in Dresden's cityscape with dynamic cultural productions will help to express a variety of opinions and perhaps signal to the world that Dresden is not a monolith, but it cannot counter the far right's cultural arguments or make people rethink their ideas of Dresden's cultural significance. For those Dresdners who are emotionally deeply attached to the cultural and architectural environment, one they even rebuilt for themselves from historic models, such dynamic cultural representations function as a provocation of cultural ideas rather than an invitation to dialogue.

Staging Criticism: Volker Lösch's Protest Plays

The Saxon State Theater in Dresden has not only challenged and criticized the emergence and rise of Pegida, the AfD, and other far-right groups in Dresden and Saxony with signage in the cityscape, but also with producing contemporary plays that defy traditional cultural assumptions. In particular, two plays directed by the (West German) Volker Lösch, *Graf Öderland–Wir sind das Volk* (Count Öderland–We Are the People) in 2015 and *Das Blaue Wunder* (The Blue Wonder) in 2019, confront the recent local political environment.[31] Already in 2009, Lösch directed *Die Wunde Dresden* (The Dresden Wound), in which he tried to splice Dresden's memory culture and commemoration rituals with Dresden history. The collage of original texts of a vast spectrum from Goethe to a bombing survivor's letter to a loved one, the often ironic representation, characters resembling caricatures on the stage, and at times carnivalistic elements did not convince most critics or the audience. Even though it was a solid attempt to try to question the Dresden myth, as critics conceded, the message was mainly lost.[32] While in 2009 Lösch aimed to disqualify the idea of the "innocent city" by looking into the past, in his plays from 2015 and 2019 Lösch reacts to the political movements arising from within the city. Comparing the two productions from 2015 and 2019 provides a look at the increasing unease with the Dresden developments among cultural agents, particularly also those who, such as Lösch, come into the city as outsiders. The attempts at understanding, dialogue, and humor in parts of *Öderland* give way to a view that has darkened considerably by 2019. In *Das blaue Wunder*, the AfD fully takes over the stage, and the audience descends with the party into a violent grotesque whose force overpowers any glimpses of hope to hold back a crushing wave of far-right extremism.

Graf Öderland—Wir sind das Volk is based on the Swiss writer Max Frisch's play *Graf Öderland*, in which Frisch explores questions of individual autonomy and fulfillment within society and the entanglement of authority, cruelty, and freedom. A central question revolves around the amount of power that mesmerized followers offer their leaders in exchange for supposed redemption from their current lives. The plot focuses on a prosecutor who starts identifying with a murderer he is supposed to convict. The killer claims that he simply does not know why he murdered an innocent person, thus breaking entirely with societal norms. This act inspires the prosecutor to leave behind his rule-bound bourgeois existence and profession and to adopt the persona of the mythical Count Öderland, who wanders the forests with an ax and kills people. This role frees him from the constraints of a society ruled by law. Soon he finds followers who also start carrying axes and rebelling against society. In the end, Öderland betrays his own people but in turn gains sole authoritative power over the country.

Lösch amalgamates these aspects of the postwar play with the post-reunification situation in Dresden from the demonstrations during the Peaceful Revolution in 1989–90 to the rise of the Pegida movement in the city in 2014. Such merging of concerns is not simply inferred by the added second part of the title, "Wir sind das Volk," but brought onto the stage by altering and adding scenes to the original play. A chorus shouts out arguments and phrases embraced by Pegida, while in other scenes it proclaims counterarguments. Individuals also narrate experiences that they characterize as "typical" in the post-reunification period: the feeling of being forced into the West German system in 1990, the fears of bottoming out in society, magnified by the many refugees entering the country, a sense of uncertainty caused by political inaction. These accounts are contrasted with other stories, such as that of a young Syrian refugee who talks about his flight, or expressions of personal anger against the lack of involvement of the Dresden middle class in taking a stance against Pegida, uttered by the actors who at this point step out of their roles and speak in their own voice.

With the merging of these various levels, Lösch wants to show how such far-right movements as Pegida can rise—often unexpectedly and suddenly—out of the midst of society. As Sonja Rüegg already concludes in reference to the original play by Frisch: it "makes the audience aware of the 'Öderlandic' hidden in everyone [. . .]. The Öderlandic, a product of bourgeois society, is latent in the present and can rise to the surface at any time."[33] Before bringing his production to the theater, Lösch and his team talked to Pegida supporters and included their concerns in the staging of the play. *Graf Öderland—Wir sind das Volk* is consequently an invitation for Dresdners to engage in the discourse playing out in the city and to work on the causes that have triggered such yearning for nativist and isolationist changes in opposition to the post-reunification society and its values. As Lösch says about the play, "we wanted to encourage people to act, to get more involved." He optimistically predicts that the kind of engagement he is calling for will also secure "that others do not solely look at [Dresden] through the Pegida lens any longer, but rather experience it as the kind of city that [Dresden] actually constitutes—a liberal city."[34] In other words, the noninvolved Dresden residents simply must be motivated into action to end the Pegida "nightmare" they underestimated early on.[35]

Despite this optimistic approach, however, the call for engagement takes on increasing urgency throughout the play, and Lösch's proclaimed positive characterization of Dresden starts to be negated by the intensifying force of the original source material used in the production. The expanding brutality of the plot and chorus unfolding on the stage becomes more and more daunting and overpowering. The Pegida chorus descends from telling a variation of stories and feelings to a chilling communal shouting of slogans culminating in the repeated screams of "deport, deport, deport." The play ends with the German national anthem sung to a triumphant Count Öderland, who rules over the ax carriers. While Lösch claims the play is simply motivating Dresden residents to express the opposition they already feel against Pegida, the production that resulted instead surges at the audience as an electric shock to intervene strongly and immediately to save Dresden from itself. Even though the director describes Dresden as fundamentally a liberal city in interviews, his play creates a scenery that is ready to implode at any time. *Öderland* develops its own dynamic, revealing more clearly the rifts and dangers in the conflict about whether the rest of Dresden can reclaim the "we" in the Peaceful Revolution's "We Are the People." This state is particularly obvious when looking at the play in hindsight, aware of the political developments in the city. While standing ovations at its premiere seemed to indicate a successful call to action, counteractivity to far-right protest groups has, as we have seen, remained limited. The play has not been able to create awareness outside of the circle of the progressive realm of shared values between theater maker and audience.

In 2019, the year of the state elections in Saxony, Lösch returned to Dresden again to offer direct commentary on the political situation. Lösch's attitude to Dresden has darkened since 2015. In *Das blaue Wunder*, he even more directly comments on the local conditions. As Lösch insists, the situation is now "beyond talking" and understanding.[36] It is not enough for the director to reconfigure and supplement an existing play to explore Dresden politics. Instead, he asked the authors Thomas Freyer and Ulf Schmidt to create a new text for the production. In *Das blaue Wunder*, the director puts on stage a vision of the way the world would look like if Saxony kept strongly supporting the AfD in the upcoming election. The title refers to the blue party color associated with the AfD and also to the 1893 Loschwitzer blue steel bridge in Dresden, which received the nickname "Blue Wonder" for its technologically novel design and its blue color, as well as to the German idiom that describes the experience of an unpleasant surprise. The title thus already indicates the main protagonist (the AfD), the location (the Saxon state capital Dresden), and the horrifying outcome of the play.

In *Öderland*, Lösch and his writers composed texts based on what they heard from Pegida protesters. In *Das blaue Wunder*, political goals of the AfD are included as direct citations of leading party figures of the far-right branch of the party, such as Alexander Gauland, at the time the party leader of the AfD, and Björn Höcke, the chair of the AfD Thuringia. They are collaged into the plot as quotations from the play's central reference point, the so-called "Blue Book," which guides the people on stage in their thinking and actions. Following the increasingly chilling demands of the Blue Book leads the group to slide more and more into debased behavior.

The plot starts out with a number of dissatisfied citizens from various societal backgrounds. They complain about the same issues the Pegida chorus in *Öderland* intoned, except that they have now moved on to finding their salvation within the AfD. They are a typical collection of what in Germany has been coined "Wutbürger," or "enraged citizens" (which then morphed into the "Querdenker" movement during the Covid-19 pandemic).[37] They claim to be victims of the way German politics and society have developed. They feel unrepresented and marginalized in contemporary Germany but are unwilling to reflect on their situation or move away from their claim of victimization. They then follow leaders who assure them that they will change the current societal order and values that exclude them and who promise to create a world in which they can feel heard and powerful.

The enraged citizens are encouraged not to see themselves as angry "Wutbürger" (enraged citizens) any longer, but instead as heroic "Mutbürger" (courageous citizens), those speaking truth to power about what they describe as Germany's path into its own destruction, an expression coined by Björn Höcke.[38] All travel together on a ship, which the group around the Blue Book claims will save them from going under in contrast to those of contemporary German society who do not prescribe to the Blue Book rules. The group's ark occupies the stage and is made up of the skeleton of a vessel thirteen meters long and more than seven meters high. The three-level structure is intimidatingly large and stays in motion during the performance.[39] In the play, the ship leaves via the Elbe by making a sharp turn "starboard," thus swinging toward the right, to carry their reactionary message "into a new future, as into a long-forgotten country."[40] Soon, however, the initial idyll fades. From the start, the ship's society is united by their self-identification as innocent victims and by their fears of further losing their identity to foreigners, refugees, and elites they consider to be out of touch.

They also share a nostalgia for an idealized view of a national Germany of distinction and power in politics and culture. Their new values, however, are mostly defined by degrading others. Lösch signals the doom of the seemingly positive and egalitarian developments on the ship from the beginning, since its society is built on the exclusion and enslavement of people; foreigners with "oil faces" are kept hidden as "machine people" far below deck (and invisible to the audience), where they work to keep the engine running. The skeleton representation of the ship's body metaphorically implies the hollowness of the societal vision; the void is filled only by the screaming of innumerable phrases from the Blue Book by the crew and passengers, which drown out any possible doubt.

As the leaders grow more radical and militarized, their voices become even louder to silence growing doubts or challenges to their program. In this climate, a ship full of refugees in need of help is rejected with the screams, "Absaufen, absaufen" (drown, drown), a direct quote from a Pegida rally in 2018 where supporters loudly called for refugees to drown on their passage to Europe and raged against relief agencies trying to save them.[41] The rallying call from 2015, "abschieben" (deport), which was intoned as a terrifying battle scream in *Öderland*, has thus turned into a call for the refugees' deaths.

Since no port welcomes the ship with its Blue Book philosophy, the group returns down the Elbe to their starting point. They are holding course directly for Dresden and the seat of the Saxon state government and are ready to cause war and destruction in order to take over. It turns out, however, that in Dresden no force is needed to gain power, and it happily surrenders to the passengers. As predicted by Björn Höcke's quote that "Dresden is the city of the courageous citizens . . . not actually Berlin, but Dresden should be the German capital," the city is portrayed as the ideal place for the new German vision of the AfD.[42] This idea is confirmed when a local form of the "Deutsche Michel" ("Michael the German"), the "Dresden Michel," appears on the stage to talk to the rebels. He represents the typical Dresden middle-class resident who is, according to the play, a naïve and complacent follower. The "courageous" citizens Höcke refers to in his comments are looking for leaders who promise them a world in which they belong and feel secure without having to change their attitudes or worldview.

Lösch criticizes the lack of sympathy for war refugees in a city that represents itself as a place of peace due to its violent past. Instead, he implies, the former East Germans hold on to the feeling of victimization they have internalized with the Dresden narrative. First, the West Germans treated them badly, even though they were fellow countrymen, and then, as if to double down on the humiliation, Germany's "Welcome Culture" under Angela Merkel again did not consider their opinions or needs.[43]

The choruses in *Das blaue Wunder* bring actual Dresden activists on stage. They range from Antifascists (who are masked during the performance) to an organization that rescues refugees at sea, but most are part of groups that try to use creative public spectacles on Dresden's streets to oppose Pegida and the AfD. The group "tolerave" holds parties and rave dances in support of tolerance, and others have organized performances, such as the ironic Angsthasen demonstration, or have assembled a big band or drum circle that play to drown out the speeches and demonstrations by Pegida and the AfD. Many actions utilize again the contemporary cultural creative realm, which acts as a space of resistance against the right-wing trend. The organizations and groups identify the residents' warped relationship to the past and their self-identification as victims, including their focus on Dresden's destruction in 1945, as a major hurdle in reaching them with their message.[44] As one chorus member shares, "My wish is that we leave the victim role behind, that we reflect on the time before and after 1945 and [instead of mourning] draw courage from it."[45]

The often negative reaction by the Dresden public to the protesters who oppose organizations such as Pegida and the AfD party thus appears twofold: On the one hand, they are challenged to change their firmly established identities that emphasize their role as innocent victims, and on the other hand, they are asked to accept political protest characterized by the use of irony, the grotesque, contemporary music, and spectacles as valid expressions of culture and dissent. Yet such requests run counter to the narrative of suffering, to the static definition of culture, and to established rituals of commemoration that have shaped the city and many of its citizens for decades. Lösch leaves it up to the Dresdners to mold their future: with the play ending after the fourth act instead of the Aristotelian fifth, it falls to the audience to "write" the last act with their actions in light of the election.[46] According to Lösch, the decision for the future of Dresden and Saxony thus lies with the citizens and their choice at the ballot box. Either the action can rise upward for a happy ending, or fall to turn into a (bourgeois) tragedy when widespread support for the AfD could push the entire state further to the political right.

Since Lösch let some of the activists tell their own stories, he gave them a stage within the established cultural realm in Dresden. In addition, Lösch offered the various groups a space to meet, interact, and exchange ideas with each other in an open, nonthreatening environment. In this sense the play also directly took part in the sociopolitical and cultural conversations in Dresden and linked both realms more strongly under a cultural umbrella. In contrast, the influence of the actual performance on the political situation was limited. Lösch is widely recognized as producing left-leaning political theater. In the past, he had attracted even in Dresden a more diverse audience when he worked with well-known plays by established authors. With *Das blaue Wunder*, Lösch presented a new piece specifically written to critique the AfD and Dresden, which only appealed to an already select viewership critical of the party. The play consequently functioned as an echo chamber and only reconfirmed opinions the audience members already held. Even if the performance of the play itself was meant largely as a provocation, it did not cause as much outrage as one might have expected. The AfD's reaction was relatively muted. The party homed in on dismissing political drama from being considered art and criticized that public money was spent on a production that they did not view as a contribution to culture but characterized as a political campaign.[47]

While the play most likely did not change people's politics, it added to the debate about the contested definition and value of culture, such as what is and is not allowed in the cultural sphere and which art should be supported by state funding. As is typical for populist approaches, cultural opinions reveal double standards; while the AfD criticizes the freedom given to the cultural domain, they continuously complain that their party members are censored and robbed of their freedom of expression. In Dresden, however, such an approach is not necessarily considered contradictory, but rather mirrors a lingering worldview among a segment of Dresden's population. The fear of being suppressed, of not being heard, and of being robbed of their identity based on past values is deeply ingrained in some residents' mentality, which can make them particularly susceptible to such arguments.

At the same time, since many Dresdners subscribe to the idea that Dresden and its Baroque past are the cultural gold standard, they view themselves as excellent judges of what constitutes a cultural contribution. With their traditional stance, plays such as *Das blaue Wunder* or politically relevant artistic installations in the city are widely dismissed and are instead considered attacks on the cultural integrity of Dresden. Yet the play offers more than just Lösch's attempt to stir general opposition to the AfD. For one, Lösch firmly roots the play in the local situation. Not only with the play's title, but also in its ending, Lösch emphasizes "Dresden" as the issue since the ship is not welcome anywhere else. He encourages natives of Dresden to reflect on the conflicts as local ones. This approach can serve to connect their situation to the specific circumstances of the local history without elevating them to a national dynamic.

Das blaue Wunder explores the causes, reasoning, and goals with which both the Blue Book group/the AfD and the activists explain their political paths. It turns out that while there are two opposing responses, the reference points for the political right and the left-leaning groups are remarkably similar. In both cases, Dresden is recognized as a place that is unique, but paradoxically also functions as a national model, which raises the stakes in the fight for acceptance. In their argumentation, proponents and opponents of the nativist, far-right political wave in Dresden emphasize the importance of Dresden's past and the city's destruction for their self-understanding. Both also send a message that the continued victimization of the city and its residents, which has destroyed traditional paths for identity, needs to be stopped by turning victims into active agents for themselves, their city, and the nation. For this transformation from victim to agent, each group calls upon an inherent "courage" that is won by reframing the negative past experiences embedded in the collective memory of the city.

The application of such courage, however, differs for the right and left. Far-right groups such as the AfD find bravery in people's open support of their agenda, despite the many detractors that try, they repeatedly claim, to suppress their "straight talk." The Blue Book/AfD community emphasizes that it is exactly the Dresden residents' past suffering, their strength in continued resistance against outside forces, and their commitment to protecting Dresden's cultural distinction that makes them the chosen people to lead the rest of the nation in their active commitment to the values of the right. The AfD fans the local fear that Dresden is always under threat from the outside and preach not just a continued, but heightened resistance to dynamic changes to avoid further losses. Standing with Pegida and the AfD is the natural way, the groups insist, to continue the protests against the suppressive system of the GDR in the 1989 Monday demonstrations and protect the values and cultural treasures Dresden rebuilt for itself after its repeated victimizations. As we have seen, this strategy has worked well so far. The slogan "We are the people" has been successfully rebranded to represent the voices of xenophobic nativist groups as that of the common man and to justify the protests as a protection of their past, present, and future from erasure, this time by fighting the Berlin government and by defending Dresden (and all of Germany) and German culture against refugees.

Similarly, most leftist activists also acknowledge that Dresden has experienced significant events in the past that will influence current beliefs and actions. They also try to encourage a way to overcome the victim role that Dresden and its residents have been captured in and assign Dresden a particularly weighty part in the fight against the far right because of its unique significance as a national cultural leader. But in contrast to the entities on the political right, the left activists hope to raise awareness for the need to contextualize the past beyond mourning rituals and to find new ways to build a local and national identity. They also appeal to the idea that Dresden is under threat, yet in this case they identify the far right, which is trying to take over the city, as the danger. Courage would then be expressed by stepping outside the victim identity and taking action against the far-right political developments for a better future. Similar to Pegida and the AfD, they also identify the importance of the 1989 revolution in their path. In their view, however, demonstrators stood up against discrimination and for personal freedoms to make the country an open entity, not a closed one. For each group the revolution against the GDR is essential to realize Dresden's self-understanding as a national beacon for peace and unity, but the ways these values are defined for society are diametrically opposed.

The play does not consciously thematize the parallels in the paths of the right and its countermovements in Dresden when arriving at one conviction or the other. It does also not thematize the way culture can be defined in numerous ways. It does acknowledge, however, that this is inherently a Dresden problem and should be solved locally. Yet as visitors to the city, while Lösch, Freyer, and Schmidt are able to duplicate the Dresden far-right rhetoric and give the counteractivists space on the stage, they seem to underestimate the deep grounding of feelings, behaviors, and beliefs on specific views of Dresden's past among the local population, no matter their political leanings.

Uwe Tellkamp and Durs Grünbein's Public Writers' Debate

The previous examples suggest that in Dresden those who produce and exhibit culture favor art to be contextualized and engaged, be it by performing contemporary art or by setting classical works into a dynamic relationship with present societal concerns. Despite some attempts to engage in conversation to find common ground with traditional audiences, cultural polarizations remain prevalent. It would be wrong, however, to assume that these polarizations are partially caused by the opposition between those who create culture and those who consume it. In 2017, well-known writer Uwe Tellkamp came out in opposition to what he identifies as the left politics that dominate the cultural establishment, and he has repeated his criticism ever since. When his novel *Der Turm: Geschichte aus einem versunkenen Land* (The Tower: Tales from a Lost Country) was published in 2008, it was widely read and praised as a critique of the conservative bourgeoisie and its nostalgia.[48] There was some surprise when nine years later, the author became an outspoken critic of what he felt were cultural and political prescriptions for artists. Since then, the discussion has been circling around the thesis of a cultural taboo propagated by the left. The Dresden native joined Susanne Dagen, owner of an eclectic Dresden bookstore and facilitator of a literary salon, in this line of argument. They claim that leftist politics have entirely taken over the cultural realm, disqualifying and censoring any cultural (or other) contributions that do not fit into the leftist agenda.

Susanne Dagen is a Dresden public intellectual who has been a staple in Dresden's literary scene and had been in opposition to the GDR government, but in the past decade has made headlines with her close relationship to Pegida and the AfD and her collaborations with the New Right publisher Antaios. While not a member of the AfD, Dagen, as an independent elected representative for the Dresden City Council, helped the party to become the strongest council force in 2024 by joining the AfD faction.[49] Her opinions became widely known when Dagen authored the so-called "Charta 2017." The document was addressed to the German Publishers' and Booksellers' Association, which organizes the large Leipzig and Frankfurt Book Fairs. It criticized the way New Right publishers and AfD speakers at the 2017 Frankfurt Fair had not been given the protection from protests or the room they deserved to present their positions. Uwe Tellkamp was one of the first to sign, which made public their shared beliefs.[50] In the Charta, Dagen diagnoses what she calls an "opinion corridor" ("Gesinnungskorridor") in the association, since it had encouraged critics of the New Right publishers' presence to express their opposition, which Dagen calls out as a way of limiting artistic freedom. She speaks about an impending "dictatorship of conviction" ("Gesinnungsdiktatur") in German society and concludes the letter with the quotation, "Beware the Beginnings" ("Wehret den Anfängen"), implying that the situation resembles the rise of a totalitarian regime, such as the Nazis' in the 1920s.[51]

The Charta 2017 made a national claim that caused a stir in the German newspaper culture sections and put Dresden again in the spotlight regarding questions about the political leanings and cultural developments in the city.

Many critics suggested that Dagen and the undersigned bought into the victim myth perpetuated by the far right. Dagen, however, already earlier that year, had explained in the weekly *Die Zeit* that her defensive stance for the ideas of far-right thinkers is simply a continuation of the need to protect her ideals, which are defined by the "fear of foreign control" as she had already experienced when, according to Dagen, East Germans and Dresdners were disenfranchised after reunification: "'We do not want to be forced into something again that has nothing to do with us.' [. . .] And the reason for some East Germans protesting with Pegida is that they do not want something like this to happen to them again. 'I hear over and over again: The East Germans do not want to be f***ed again.'"[52]

Disappointed by the left and by the main parties, they recognize themselves in the ideas of the far right with their self-proclaimed disenfranchisement by the establishment, and they embrace the conviction that if they do not speak up, they will be entirely driven out by internal and external influences. Any doubt about these arguments and their possible consequences, and the human toll they might take, are pushed aside by their positive self-labeling as dissidents who act as true guardians of democracy and culture. They propose that they are performing a necessary act of preserving free speech, saving democracy from being undermined, and keeping cultural values alive.

In opposition to these arguments, other intellectuals have criticized this idea of the sidelined far right's stance as baseless. In their opinion, instead of supporting democracy, their ideas serve as a platform for spreading inhumane, xenophobic, and antidemocratic views. Another group of Dresden writers and intellectuals, who count among their signatories the well-known poet and Dresden native Durs Grünbein and the novelist Marcel Beyer, who has been living in Dresden since the mid-1990s, countered the Charta 2017 with their own document.[53] In this declaration, the term "dictatorship of conviction" is highly criticized as a "defamation," a "verbal gaffe," that denigrates the actual situation in the Federal Republic as well as all those who as true dissidents have fought for democratic freedoms in dictatorial regimes.[54] The declaration denies the Charta's argument that it is simply fostering open discussion between different sociopolitical and cultural camps; rather, they claim, this stance collaborates in suppressing fruitful debate and helps with spreading the victim myth perpetuated by far-right intellectuals and their outlets: "The emphatic call for democracy and tolerance turns into a contradiction when this call comes in defense of authors and texts that question the basic democratic order, that disdain pluralistic societies and base their arguments on racist reasoning."[55]

Given the vast interest in the discussed issues, the Dresden newspaper *Sächsische Zeitung* organized a roundtable, a "citizen's dialogue," between the two Dresden writers Uwe Tellkamp and Durs Grünbein under the heading: "Streitbar! Wie frei sind wir mit unseren Meinungen?" (Debatable! How Free Are We in Our Speech?). It drew such a large crowd that the location had to be moved twice to increasingly bigger venues. Finally, about eight hundred people followed the discussion between the two writers, among them many culture journalists. Yet the issue of freedom of expression quickly faded into the background and instead a discussion ensued about how to define a German political, social, and cultural identity. Since then, the authors, particularly Tellkamp, have repeatedly echoed their views.

During the dialogue with Grünbein, Tellkamp displays a strong sense of duty to speak up about the political and cultural restrictions that he feels are not only limiting culture, but also threatening its established form and quality. Yet even though Tellkamp formulates his critique as a national concern, I propose that substantial parts of the debate are rooted in distinctly local experiences and sentiments that are transposed onto the national stage. Tellkamp speaks from within the Dresden narrative in which he feels at home. This narrative offers the building blocks for Tellkamp's arguments: It emphasizes victimhood, both personally and culturally, which is also intertwined with a continuous feeling of threat to both the city itself and those whose identity is closely connected to it. Further, it fosters a sense of static culture as high culture and the insurmountable loss involved in its destruction. In addition, the unique suffering of the city and its people by the catastrophe of the bombing has encouraged the belief that Dresdners have been given unique insight into questions of culture. These experiences have assigned them the duty to warn others of the debilitating consequences of the destruction of culture and urge them to act against such attacks. Tellkamp's political and cultural stance is thus inseparably intertwined with the relationship the artist has carved out for himself over time to Dresden and its history, as well as a sense of special "ownership" over the cultural domain.

This close connection to Dresden is also visible in Tellkamp's work. *Der Turm* already contains the primary elements of his later stance. The novel takes place in the part of Dresden where Tellkamp grew up. The author was raised on the "Weiße Hirsch," the once exclusive residential area of Dresden located on top of the slope of the river Elbe that was home to the eclectic spa hospitals described in chapter 2. Situated in a beautiful natural setting, it was a sought-after area by industrialists and other well-to-do and well-educated burghers, artists, and scholars who lived there in secluded villas starting in the second half of the nineteenth century. After 1945, in accordance with socialist policy, the owners were dispossessed and most villas were divided into several individual apartments to provide living spaces in the heavily destroyed city. Unlike Dresden's center, the Weiße Hirsch had remained entirely untouched by the bombs. Yet more importantly, the affluent quiet neighborhood and its elite and bohemian inhabitants stood for everything that the socialist societal model wanted to do away with. Despite these changes, though, the neighborhood continued to be a haven where the educated, bourgeois population found some seclusion.

Der Turm describes this world on the "Weiße Hirsch" in the 1980s, the last decade of the GDR. It shows how the Weiße Hirsch society is continuing its attempt to retreat from the pressures of the GDR realities into a bubble of high culture and academic pursuit. In their historic villas high above the main city, three generations of Dresdners aim to preserve a semblance of the life of the nineteenth-century educated burgher class, in which sons and daughters learn classical instruments and people read literature, attend the opera and the theater, and get together in a salon setting to discuss the arts and philosophy. In addition, particularly among the war generation, they communally mourn the loss of the old Baroque Dresden, destroyed by the Western Allies' bombs and then subsequently by the rule of the socialist regime.

Tellkamp does not portray the Weiße Hirsch and its society as a fully successful paradisial island immune to the challenging world of the GDR. He does reveal that the impulse of the residents to try to keep the realities of East Germany entirely out of their lives is flawed, as it must ignore a substantial part of daily experiences. On an intellectual level, Tellkamp channels these convictions through one of the main characters, Meno Rhode, an editor, researcher, and writer who reflects on the difference between idea and reality in the world of the residents in his diary entries. The melancholic Meno is particularly disturbed by the contrast between the Dresden cityscape and culture conjured up among the inhabitants of the Weiße Hirsch, who diligently study the Dresden "Bible," Fritz Löffler's art history book *Das alte Dresden*, and the actual surroundings they live in. Meno compares the alternate universe of the Baroque past with the rundown villas on the Weiße Hirsch and the crumbling and decaying buildings of Dresden's center: "and that was something I knew from the whole city, this bullet-riddled Baroque boat in the bathtub of the Elbe Valley, this shimmering fetus trapped in the womb of its own, parallel time; everywhere I went it was the same: tables set for coffee, Eierschecke, DAS ALTE DRESDEN."[56] He compares this continuous presence of the lost city to the repeating melody of a musical clock that keeps playing "Dresden . . . in the muses' nests / the sweet sickness of yesteryear rests."[57]

Other characters, such as Tellkamp's 1980s alter ego Christian, Meno's nephew, cannot escape the brutal demands of the GDR regime on the individual despite his family's attempt to offer him educational respite, particularly through music. While his father is still able to work as a physician, a profession that allows him a certain level of autonomy and ability to keep retreating into the world of the educated burgher class, Christian's future is entirely in the hands of the state and its demands. With his father's educational standing and the family's reserved attitude regarding the Socialist Party, he is targeted and faces repercussions that deny him the opportunity to study medicine and follow in his father's footsteps. The Weiße Hirsch society thus cannot fully protect its residents from the power of the state or isolate them from the hopelessness, despair, and near destruction the GDR causes for a person with high intellectual goals and passions.

Tellkamp published *Der Turm* in 2008, describing the last decade of the GDR almost twenty years after reunification. The novel was hailed by critics as a brilliant Wenderoman, an honest look back at a country that eroded the essence of culture, society, and the individual. Meno muses repeatedly on the bourgeois attachment to the Old Dresden that did not exist any longer and about the inability or refusal of the burghers to see the world of the GDR. Too focused on the past, this attitude was unfit to deal with the destructive realities of East Germany and was unable to preserve cultural achievements such as Dresden's cityscape except within their memories.

But *Der Turm* must also be understood from the temporal distance to the described events. The author presents a historical period in which the GDR moved closer to its demise and the counterworld of the Weiße Hirsch was starting to unravel under the pressures of a destructive regime desperate to hold on to power. In contrast, by 2008, Dresden, almost twenty years after reunification, was in the process of rebuilding and renovating its Baroque history and thus its cultural significance. In the novel, Tellkamp complains via the character Meno about the predominantly formulaic nostalgia for the Old Dresden and questions the future of the traditional lifestyle based on humanistic tradition with which the Weiße Hirsch society tries to isolate itself. He underlies the novel with the anger he himself must have felt growing up in an inhumane world in which he was not allowed to follow his passions and with the melancholy caused by seeing a once great city of unique cultural significance crumbling and deteriorating.

Yet by 2008, the subculture of the educated bourgeois had in fact turned out to have survived the GDR. In other words, high up on the mountain in the parallel world of the Weiße Hirsch, Dresden's true self and identity as center of high culture had taken exile. While at times clumsy, nostalgic, and out of touch with the growing threat to their societal bubble, they did after all succeed and save the cultural elements of the city so that they could return to the mainstream. The Dresden cityscape was rising in its renewed Baroque glory and Dresden was once again establishing its image as an important center for the arts.

By remembering in 2008 the threat to the city and the educated burgher class's plight during the GDR, the author points to the need to continue to care and preserve German high culture against possible threats. Tellkamp is caught in a pattern of perpetual suspicion of an impending attack on the culture he values and sees reflected in Dresden. This is the culture he understands as the essence of Dresden and himself, which he projects to the nation. Any societal change activates suspicion and fear. As he states in an essay published in the monthly of the New Right think tank Institut für Staatspolitik (Institute for State Politics, IfS), "home and culture" provide him with the "necessary anchors in time. It helps to survive."[58] Since many in Dresden feel that their role goes beyond protecting their own city to protecting culture in general, as well as warning others to be vigilant against (cultural) destruction, the specifically local dimension of the struggles about what constitutes and does not constitute true culture is not explored. The idea propagated by the far right of a culture under threat simply validates already existing persuasions, feelings of victimhood, and the fear of impending destruction and doom, which the Dresden narrative has nurtured for decades.

In contrast to Uwe Tellkamp, Durs Grünbein, while also born and raised in Dresden and only slightly older than Tellkamp, left the city for good and moved to East Berlin in his early twenties (1985). Still, Grünbein repeatedly returns to the topic of Dresden in his oeuvre, and this relationship has been formative. Early in his career, the poet distances himself from the city to find his own personal and literary voice. In his 1991 "Gedicht über Dresden" (Poem about Dresden), he labels his hometown the "seemingly dead city, Baroque wreck on the Elbe" that lives off a past aura that works as a "narcotic" on its citizens:[59]

> The best depressant is the genius loci
> In a place fattened with memories
> Dry rot, beautifully tinted as nostalgia
> Lulling like the psychotropic iams
> *The Anglo-Saxon version of nevermore*[60]

By 2005, three years before Tellkamp's *Der Turm*, the poet published a stand-alone work on Dresden that strives for a more contemplative approach. The long poem *Porzellan: Poem vom Untergang meiner Stadt* (Porcelain: Poem on the Downfall of My City) contains reflections on Dresden during various historical, political, and societal periods.[61] The two texts share some overall themes. Similar to Tellkamp's *Der Turm*, *Porzellan* reveals how deeply Dresden's history and identity have influenced Grünbein's ideas of culture and how they have informed his worldview. Both authors claim ownership of the subject matter, with Grünbein even indicating so in the subtitle by using the possessive: "*My City*." They also both hark back to traditional literary forms to try to capture the city and its meaning. Grünbein utilizes the form of the long poem, the traditional verse epic that dates back to classical antiquity, while Tellkamp writes in a late nineteenth-century style inspired by the novels of Theodor Fontane and Thomas Mann.

Yet their ideas of Dresden put the two authors on opposing trajectories for understanding reality: While Tellkamp's view of the value of culture and the world he developed in his relationship to Dresden is deeply rooted in a static cultural past that is easily endangered by a changing society, Grünbein advanced his approach to culture and the world through the repeated friction with Dresden's established identity and nostalgic focus on the past. Grünbein emphasizes that even though he is deeply appreciative of the past, culture includes development and motion, not stasis: "It is always about not standing still. This is particularly true for artists. One has to set off to be able to return again one day like Odysseus."[62] Over time, Tellkamp has been retreating more and more into the idea of German culture under threat: from warfare, the GDR, refugees, immigrants, established politics, the mainstream press, and most intellectuals. In Tellkamp's view, only the far right at this point shows openness to representing his concerns about protecting high culture. Grünbein instead draws different lessons from Dresden and the way its past is being revised from what he considers an unreflected victim discourse and singular idea about culture; these processes rather highlight the very importance of advocating for openness and multi-perspectivity when trying to grasp the world. New ideas and new situations, he suggests, do not destroy German culture, but simply become part of creation.

Grünbein already outlines these convictions in *Porzellan*. By utilizing traditional form, he acknowledges the meaning and power of the previous rich artistic achievements, which have also been important identity markers for Dresden, yet he contrasts it with content that necessarily problematizes the relationship of cultural tradition with Dresden's (and Germany's) past, particularly regarding its National Socialist and socialist history. *Por-*

zellan is a constant balancing act in both content and form, piecing together poem shards to a new, though fragile whole. Grünbein does not feed an illusion of complete harmonious and cultural unity as Dresden's essence. The individual stanzas are placed at different locations on the paper and are separated from each other by empty spaces, and some of the pages are left blank. A number of stanzas include quotations from a wide selection of texts. The poem combines a multitude of perspectives, opinions, and angles seen through the eyes of shifting subjects and addressing various objects: the lyrical "I," different unnamed third-person references, and direct addresses to characters of the poems or the readers. There are no voids as vast as the empty lots so characteristic of the Dresden Grünbein grew up in, but there still are cracks and gaps comparable to what can be found on an antique vase that has been carefully reconstructed out of its broken fragments many centuries later.

The text underlies the premise that it is the poet's role to reflect by embracing different viewpoints and bringing in various historical experiences:

> Such fragile forms.
> What's all this for?—Someone's
> listening to hear the daughters of Mnemosyne dictating.
> Changing places, times, dimensions as he goes—goes on—
> *creating.*"[63]

Grünbein portrays how the part of Dresden's identity that refuses to accept the destruction of Dresden and the way it was rebuilt during the GDR leaves the residents stagnant and unable to live fully in the present. This state can be oppressive to others:

> And what the people hear in everything
> —Papageno, Papagena stuttering—
> is the echo of that triad, the same old refrain,
> *destruction. The hated theme hangs heavy in the air.*[64]

In *Porzellan*, no views are allowed to overtake the text completely. Rather, it is the author's goal to present and explore the ambiguous nature of the events, the multilayered dimensions, ideas, and cultural contributions that can grow out of the gaps and fragments of Dresden's history if they are not made invisible via a nostalgically imagined cityscape of harmony.

When Tellkamp and Grünbein came together in their hometown to engage in a discussion, it quickly became clear that they approached the state of German culture and the political situation in Germany from two angles that did not have much in common despite some of their biographical similarities. In fact, the experience of growing up in Dresden led to fundamentally different views of the world, of what constitutes culture, and what role it plays in a changing society. The conversation between Tellkamp and Grünbein did not engage with different aspects of one issue, namely what exactly freedom of expression looks like, but rather became a confrontation between two constructions of reality that revealed a deep divide about how to understand the world, its society, culture, and identity.[65]

Outlook

The protests and counterprotests that have defined Dresden's past decades have also been clashes of two different definitions of culture. While often identified as national issues, in Dresden these concerns are very much bound to the local. The Dresden narrative of artistic distinction, loss, and victimhood leads many Dresdners to concentrate on the past as the foundation for Dresden's contemporary cultural significance; they see Dresden's exceptionality as based on its architectural and artistic history and view it as completed. According to this view, newer cultural developments that do not replicate heritage cannot compete in quality with the Baroque Dresden and are in fact considered part of the destruction of the city's cultural meaning. In contrast to this static concept, many artistic agents and grassroots movements define the cultural import of Dresden, while based on a long history of achievements, as dynamic. In this view, Dresden stays significant not because it is a museum-like vessel of heritage culture, but because it is a center for continuously "creating" art. This dynamic understanding focuses on change, development, and openness to the new. The confrontations between these two ideas have led to increasing polarization.

The continued societal split in Dresden suggests that while the confrontation of the far right with a dynamic form of culture can be a good path to signal disagreement with their opinions, it is not necessarily an effective way to break their support, since their agenda regarding the protection of German culture can be easily integrated into the widely embraced, dominant Dresden narrative. As we have seen, despite the work of historians, artistic agents, intellectuals, and many others to dig deep into the blank spaces between the prevailing images of Dresden's past, it has proved difficult to challenge the Dresden narrative more broadly. Many Dresden residents experienced that no matter the political changes from Nazism to the socialist GDR to today's Federal Republic, a stable set of values remained associated with Dresden. This position was also not challenged internationally. The city was confirmed as an exceptional locale that also held universal historical and symbolic significance. It granted the city and its population a special position to chime in as particular experts on culture, loss, peace, and reconciliation.

Considering the more recent political developments in Dresden, some have tried to introduce another theme that shows Dresden as dynamic, colorful, and diverse, also in an attempt to escape a tainted reputation that could scare away travelers. At the same time, Dresden's touristic success lies exactly in its insistence on an unwavering embrace of Dresden's unchanged cultural worth nourished by tradition and the identification of the city as a historic masterpiece. So when drawing on their experience, self-proclaimed "Old Dresdners" often conclude that they do best if they continue to oppose change, build their future on their cultural past, and do not break with the narratives that have served them well. Even if they do not fully support all positions of the far right, they will be less inclined to protest against politicians who seem to value Dresden's role and express a strong desire to protect their city from harm.

But even though Dresden natives' intense focus on the past is an integral part of the rise of the far right in the city, this past is also the most promising topic that could lead to opening up a dialogue. The city is still defined by the postwar before-and-after structure of the undestroyed and the destroyed. The GDR expanded the diptych to a triptych that featured the socialist city as the final iteration of Dresden. Much of the population, however, understood rebuilding during the GDR as a second destruction if it did not include historic reconstruction. While after reunification not everything could be reversed to the image of the Baroque Dresden, enough has been reclaimed to view it as a corrective. Yet such an understanding of history based on static images excludes the dynamic developments that would contextualize the depicted static views of the city. Exploring the excluded in-betweens of the past could add the complexity and self-exploration needed to move away from the one-dimensional views propagated by populist and nativist groups and help bridge the gap that has so deeply split Dresden society.

As an example of a possible move forward, beyond the divide of static and dynamic understandings of culture and society, I would like to return to the iconic Richard Peter photograph from the town hall tower in which the viewer is guided by the figure of kindness to take in the vast ruinscape of the destroyed Dresden. Between 2005 and 2007, the German artist Andreas Rosenthal made the sculpture of the image the main focus of his inquiry into the motif. In his cycle of paintings ". . . Facing Kindness" (. . . angesichts der Güte) (first exhibited in 2008), the perspective is often reversed; instead of the viewer looking through the gaze of the figure upon the ruins, Rosenthal breaks down the various planes of the image and offers "effectively the perspective of the destruction" upwards onto the sculpture.[66]

Rosenthal has long been fascinated by Peter's photograph, which he had encountered in a magazine article in the mid-1980s. He severed the picture from the article and pinned the illustration to the wall of his atelier, even repeatedly taking it down and putting it back up when moving to new workspaces.[67] While for many artists before him, Dresden itself had served as a muse for their artistic production, Rosenthal found his in the Schreitmüller sculpture. Rosenthal does not reconfirm the Dresden narrative of suffering, but rather breaks open the myth by destroying and newly recreating its most iconic image and representation. He forces apart what seems, in Barthes's term, "naturally" connected: the destruction below, the stone figure, and the stone figure's mediating role between onlooker and the rubbled cityscape. Rosenthal thus dissolves the elements of Peter's photograph, a process the artist describes as "zer-zeichnen," or "de-drawing," which in turn severs the connections between the Dresden myth and the picture that appears to confirm it.[68] By separating out the background, the destroyed city, and the figure itself, a reassessment becomes viable for the viewer since the elements can be arranged together in new ways, with new nuances, and with new perspectives.

To achieve this goal, Rosenthal first countered Peter's photograph with his own. Going up on the Dresden town hall tower, he reversed the established photographic perspective. Mounting a camera on a long pole, he took a picture back toward the platform of the tower, capturing the sculpture's front and revealing the figure's face and the welcoming gesture created by both outstretched arms.[69] It is this new photograph that serves as the basis for Rosenthal's reflections on the iconic picture, which he portrays with a technique he developed that brings together two distinct drawings in a unique, often surprising way. By placing two drawings together and then treating them with wax, they become transparent and both drawings start to form one. These specially processed works reveal various views of the Schreitmüller sculpture or its individual parts, often resembling drawing studies of the motif. They are combined with line patterns and blocks, some more geometrical, reminiscent of the building ruins and their window holes,

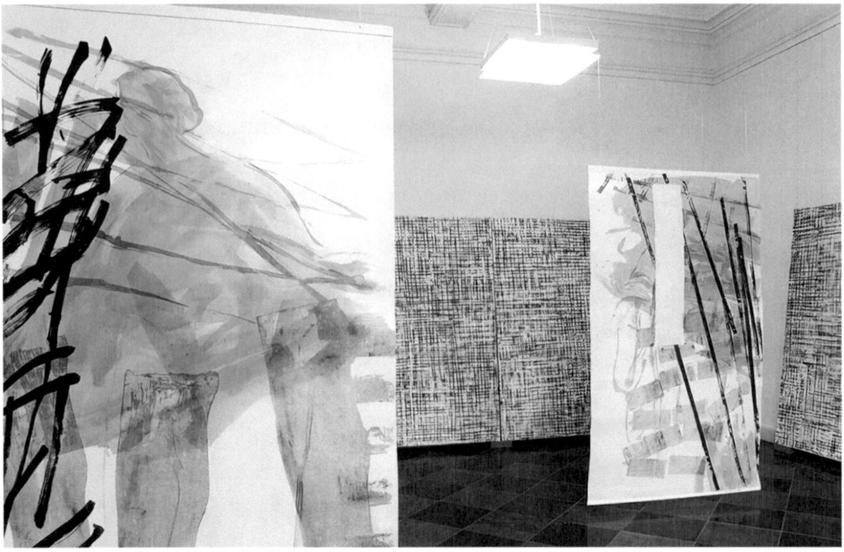

Fig. 64. Andreas Rosenthal, . . . *angesichts der Güte*, exhibition in Aachen, Germany (2009). (Reproduced by permission of Andreas Rosenthal.)

others wild and chaotic, reminding one of the flames of the firestorm. Other patterns suggest lines of bombs descending downwards or placement markers for the attacks. Some of the transparent drawings also contain the word "guide print" and the indication of distance measurements, such as "1500 YDS." Repeatedly, wide black bars cover the face of the sculpture as if it were censored. These special paper drawings are not exhibited traditionally on walls, but instead are hung from the ceiling in the exhibition space, so that they can be seen from all sides.

Rosenthal's representation of the Dresden ruins is also multiplied into several independent works. The destroyed cityscape arises over and over in patterns of lines on large wooden boards that lean on the walls of the exhibition space. The artist reduces the ruins to their basic components by emphasizing their dominant shapes, such as the rectangles and squares of bricks or the empty window holes. They are transformed into grids of white, gray, and black, some of these carved into the wooden surfaces, which give the pictures plasticity. They also duplicate the material changes caused by the firestorm to the built environment.

With this setup, Rosenthal allows the visitors to the exhibit to "exist in the midst of the drawing."[70] They themselves become actors and creators; the iconic image is reconceived in new terms as the visitors themselves take over the interpretive space between sculpture and destroyed city, a state similar to the one the artist is relenting to when he combines two individual drawings into one, as if they were on a "blind date," as the artist explains his process.[71] With this technique, Rosenthal stands in stark contrast to the original creator, Richard Peter. While Peter strove to hide his directorial power of the shot to suggest absolute objectivity but firmly guided the viewer's gaze via the Schreitmüller figure's gesture, Rosenthal creates endless possibilities to combine and view the depicted parts. Yet the painter does not give up his power entirely, even if he, and this is similar to Peter, hopes to suggest so. By introducing elements of alienation and abstraction—such as including words on the drawings or blocking out the face or eyes of the sculpture—he effectively impedes the audience from arriving at traditional interpretations of the iconic image. Viewers cannot see the destruction, the historic moment, through the eyes of the onlooking sculpture, but they must choose their own viewpoint.

Rosenthal's approach to the photograph, which breaks the image down into individual parts and places the viewer in a position to observe its construction, dissolves the strong bonds of seemingly natural connections the picture has formed with the Dresden destruction story. With his installation, Rosenthal offers the opportunity to reassess and to explore Dresden's historical blind spots through visual and spatial experiences, sensory experiences that, as this study has shown, have been inseparably linked to Dresden as the city of art, architecture, and culture for centuries. Similarly, Rosenthal's use of the iconic Peter photograph models how static and dynamic states are not mutually exclusive.

The technique of "de-drawing" is not limited to the artist's studio. While Dresden most prominently has rebuilt itself in its own image, the local cityscape contains obvious markers that speak to Dresden as a city with a diverse history and a continuously changing face. From late nineteenth- and early twentieth-century architecture, Nazi buildings, GDR apartment complexes, and the New Synagogue, to contemporary infrastructure projects such as a bridge whose realization caused the withdrawal of the Elbe Valley's designation as a World Heritage Site, Dresden offers a multitude of spaces that break open the imagined harmonious cityscape and invite reflection. A re-evaluation from within of what represents culture, paired with a more comprehensive contextualization of Dresden's history, constitutes a possible way forward. It could help decouple far-right rhetoric about German culture and history from Dresden and would allow Dresdners to honor the city's past and present cultural significance and remember the detriment of the bombing without the need to distort it. With its unique place in German and international memory, Dresden indeed holds strong signaling power, but it is time for Dresdners to look inwards at the deeply ingrained narratives passed down from generation to generation if they want to overcome the societal divide that has been characterizing the city. A model for a new approach can be found in Dresden's architectural composition. When opening up the focus onto the cityscape beyond the Old Town, we find endless examples of oppositions, contrasts, and novel combinations, which together, despite their disparities, still constitute an urban unit called Dresden.

Notes

Introduction

1. Dietmar Süß, *Death from the Skies: How the British and Germans Survived Bombing in World War II* (New York: Oxford University Press, 2014), 6; Richard Overy, *The Bombers and the Bombed: Allied Air War Over Europe, 1940–1945* (New York: Penguin, 2014), 27.

2. Richard Overy, for example, in his foundational work *The Air War 1939–1945* (London: Europa, 1980) argues that air warfare was a critical factor in deciding the outcome of the Second World War. In *The Bombing War: Europe, 1939–1945* (London: Allen Lane, 2013), he speaks more specifically to bombing Dresden and other such attacks at the end of the war, showing how Dresden had been on the target list since 1944 and had carried definite military significance during the point of the advancement toward Germany. In his eyes the question is rather whether these air raids needed to be of such extreme dimension. The first critical history solely concerned with Dresden was Götz Bergander's *Dresden im Luftkrieg* (Köln: Böhlau, 1977). Bergander was particularly concerned with presenting a factual account, including Dresden's military significance. Frederick Taylor, in *Dresden: Tuesday 13 February 1945* (New York: HarperCollins, 2004), leaves no doubt that Dresden was a justified military target but sees the bombing mainly as the logical consequence of the total, uncompromising war that was fought in the Second World War. Marshall De Bruhl, in *Firestorm: Allied Air Power and the Destruction of Dresden* (New York: Random House, 2006), firmly supports the decision to bomb Dresden. While, as De Bruhl states, in hindsight the war was most likely decided by this point, he calls attention to the understanding of the British government that the war would still go on for at least another six months in early 1945. In addition, he emphasizes that "in the week of the Dresden raids, Germans launched the greatest number of rockets against England of any week since the beginning of the vengeance-weapon campaign." A. C. Grayling, in *Among the Dead Cities* (New York: Walker, 2006), in contrast, clearly condemns any large-area bombings at any time of the war. Grayling emphasizes that they were indecisive for winning and that only target bombing actually made a difference in the course of the war. He thus insists that all area bombing was unnecessary, out of proportion, and very wrong. The most recent book-length work on the

bombing of Dresden, Sinclair McKay's *The Fire and the Darkness: The Bombing of Dresden, 1945* (New York: St. Martin's Press, 2020), is a popular history that aims to describe in lyrical terms the complex drama and anguish of Dresden's destruction by emphasizing the emotional toll of architectural and human losses, but also of the pilots and bomber crews who dropped the bombs. Among German military historians, Horst Boog sees the bombing of civilians in large-area raids of such cities as Dresden as inhumane "terror bombing," but he also acknowledges that they did necessarily slow down the war effort in Germany ("Der strategische Bombenkrieg der Alliierten gegen Deutschland 1939–1945. Ein Überblick," in *Alliierter Bombenkrieg: Das Beispiel Dresden*, ed. Lothar Fritze and Thomas Widera [Göttingen: Vandenhoeck & Ruprecht Unipress, 2005]). Rolf-Dieter Müller, in *Der Bombenkrieg 1939–1945* (Berlin: Links Verlag, 2004), appeals to the readers to understand the air war not as individual destinies of cities that were decided case by case, which clouds judgment, but as an overall strategy that already started during the First World War and is still valid today: the use of the air war to avoid fighting on the ground. According to Müller, Dresden is one of the high points of this development in a war in which large-area bombing had become an important tool. He acknowledges that through the relentless use of the strategy, moral and logical limits were overstepped, but also points out that war on the ground was in no way less bloody or cruel. In the Second World War, Müller asserts, the distinction between combatant and civilians was thoroughly erased. Dietmar Süß, in *Death from the Skies*, concentrates instead on the way the air war affected the people on the ground both physically and psychologically, the policies put in place to protect them, and the effectiveness of these measures. For an in-depth analysis of the air war discourse among German historians, see Bas von Benda-Beckmann, *German Historians and the Bombing of German Cities: The Contested Air War* (Amsterdam: Amsterdam University Press, 2015).

3. See, for example, Tony Joel on the use of the Dresden bombing as a political tool in *The Dresden Firebombing: Memory and the Politics of Commemorating Destruction* (London: Tauris, 2013), literary scholar Anne Fuchs' *After the Dresden Bombing: Pathways of Memory, 1945 to the Present* (New York: Palgrave, 2012), which looks at cultural memory formation, and Elizabeth A. Ten Dyke, *Dresden: Paradoxes of Memory in History* (London: Routledge, 2001) for an anthropological approach. For a comparative memory discourse of Hamburg and Dresden, see Gilad Margalit, *Guilt, Suffering, and Memory: Germany Remembers Its Dead of World War II* (Bloomington: Indiana University Press, 2010). For a detailed survey of the memory discourse regarding the bombing of German cities that arose in the 1990s and 2000s, see Mary Nolan, "Germans as Victims during World War II: Air Wars, Memory Wars," *Central European History* 38, no. 7 (2005): 7–40, https://doi.org/10.1163/1569161053623651, and Jeffry Diefendorf, "Memories of the Bombing of German Cities in World War II," *German History* 32, no. 4 (2014): 615–32, https://doi.org/10.1093/gerhis/ghu108

4. Ali Cheshmehzangi, *Identity of Cities and City of Identities* (Singapore: Springer Nature, 2020).

5. René König, "Die soziale Struktur der Stadt," in *Soziologische Studien zu Gruppe und Gemeinde. René König: Schriften*, ed. Kurt Hammerich (Wiesbaden: Springer, 2006), 355. "ein ästhetisches Bild ihrer Stadtgemeinde im Kopf, dem sie sich alle mehr oder weniger verbunden fühlen. Darum erhalten auch gewisse zentrale

Gebäude in der Stadt eine so hervorragende symbolische Bedeutung." All translations from the German are mine unless an English translation has been published.

6. Krista E. Paulsen, "Place," in *The Wiley-Blackwell Encyclopedia of Urban and Regional Studies*, ed. Anthony M. Orum and Dennis R. Judd (Oxford: Wiley-Blackwell, 2019), 1461–70.

7. Martina Löw, *Soziologie der Städte* (Frankfurt: Suhrkamp, 2008), 80. "Orte [entwickeln] als sozial konstruierte Phänomene Eigenlogiken, welche sich auf die Erfahrungsmuster derer, die in ihnen leben, auswirken."

8. Daniel R. Williams, "'Beyond the Commodity Metaphor,' Revisited," in *Place Attachment: Advances in Theory, Methods and Applications*, ed. Lynne C. Manzo and Patrick Devine-Wright (London: Routledge, 2014), 94; see also Cheshmehzangi, *Identity of Cities and City of Identities*, 15–16.

9. Marco Lalli, "Urban Related Identity: Theory, Measurement and Empirical Findings," *Journal of Environmental Psychology* 12 (1992): 285–303.

10. It should be mentioned that these interviews were conducted before some of the more controversial developments in recent Dresden history. Still, the cohesion of the reported elements of identity suggests that they are of lasting validity. For details see Gabriela Christmann, "Städtische Identität als kommunikative Konstruktion," *Institut für höhere Studien* (2003), https://www.researchgate.net/publication/48667110_Stadtische_Identitat_als_kommunikative_Konstruktion, and Gabriela Christmann, *Dresdens Glanz, Stolz der Dresdner: Lokale Kommunikation, Stadtkultur und städtische Identität* (Wiesbaden: Deutscher Universitätsverlag, 2004).

11. The city government of Dresden publishes results on its city website. https://www.dresden.de/de/leben/stadtportrait/statistik/publikationen/umfragen/kbu/archiv.php. For the results and analysis of a variety of surveys before 2021, see Karl-Heinz Reuband, ed., *Dresden im Wandel: Kulturelle Repräsentationen und soziale Transformationen* (Dresden: Thelem, 2022).

12. See Statistisches Amt Stadt Dresden, *Kommunale Bürgerumfrage 2024 Hauptaussagen* (2024), https://www.dresden.de/de/leben/stadtportrait/statistik/publikationen/umfragen/kbu/2024.php; Statistisches Amt Stadt Dresden, *Kommunale Bürgerumfrage 2022 Hauptaussagen* (2022), https://www.dresden.de/de/leben/stadtportrait/statistik/publikationen/umfragen/kbu/archiv.php

13. Bernd Raffelhüschen, *SKL Glücksatlas 2023* (München: Penguin, 2023), https://www.skl-gluecksatlas.de/artikel/staedteranking-2023/dresden.html

14. Michael Häder and Sabine Häder, "Die Architekturwahrnehmung prägt in Dresden das Verbundenheitsgefühl mit dem Wohnort: Ergebnisse einer kommunalen Umfrage und der ALLBUS-Befragung," *Informationsdienst Soziale Indikatoren* 63 (2019): 1–5, https://doi.org/10.15464/isi.63.2019.1-5

15. Wulf Kansteiner, "Finding Meaning in Memory: A Methodological Critique of Collective Memory Studies," *History and Theory* 41, no. 2 (2002): 179–97. Kansteiner emphasizes the importance of visual media for collective memory studies.

16. Robert Hariman and John Louis Lucaites, "Public Identity and Collective Memory in US Iconic Photography: The Image of 'Accidental Napalm,'" *Critical Studies in Media Communication* 20, no. 1 (2003): 35–66.

17. Roland Barthes, *Image, Music, Text* (New York: Hill and Wang, 1977).

18. Francesca Weil, Uwe Hirschfeld, Jonas Kühne, and Fruzsina Müller, "Editorial," *Totalitarismus und Demokratie* 18 (2021): 149, https://doi.org/10.13109/tode.2021.18.2.147

19. Weil et al., "Editorial," 149–50.

20. The GDR historian Helmut Eschwege was one of the few researchers who was able to work on the topic extensively, albeit with difficulty.

21. This book draws on the approaches of some recent examples of these studies, such as Paul Stangl's *Risen from Ruins: The Cultural Politics of Rebuilding in East Berlin* (Stanford: Stanford University Press, 2018) and Eli Rubin's book on East Berlin architecture, *Amnesiopolis: Modernity, Space and Memory in East Germany* (Oxford: Oxford University Press, 2016), both concerning East Berlin, as well as Andrew Demshuk's comparative work *Three Cities after Hitler: Redemptive Reconstruction Across Cold War Borders* (Pittsburgh: University of Pittsburgh Press, 2021), which includes an in-depth study of Leipzig. Some other important works that include less well-studied cities from the GDR are Jörg Arnold, *The Allied Air War and Urban Memory: The Legacy of Strategic Bombing in Germany* (Cambridge: Cambridge University Press, 2011), which compares the East German city of Magdeburg with the West German Göttingen, and anthropologist Jason James's *Preservation and National Belonging in Eastern Germany: Heritage Fetishism and Redeeming Germanness* (Hampshire: Palgrave Macmillan, 2012) on the city of Eisenach.

22. A number of case studies have explored identity formation, nationalism, and image formation, as well as memorialization through city planning and architecture in West German cities. For example, in *Nuremburg: The Imaginary Capital* (Rochester, NY: Camden House, 2006) Stephen Brockmann looks at the development of a city identity for Nuremburg starting in 1500, showing how a city is as much a construct of the imagination as it is of brick and mortar. Geographer Joshua Hagen in *Preservation, Tourism, Nationalism: The Jewel of the German Past* (New York: Routledge, 2006) investigates the cultural politics of historical preservation and tourism by looking at the city of Rothenburg ob der Tauber. In *Munich and Memory: Architecture, Monuments, and the Legacy of the Third Reich* (Berkeley: University of California Press, 2000) Gavriel D. Rosenfeld explores how the Nazi past has been dealt with and remembered in Munich through rebuilding and other city planning decisions.

23. Some of the earlier representations of the Dresden bombing include one of the most important and most widely read novels on Dresden, Kurt Vonnegut's *Slaughterhouse-Five* (New York: Delacorte, 1969), based on the writer's own experience as a prisoner of war in Dresden during the bombardment. Other examples for international representations are Dutch writer Harry Mulisch, *Het Stenen Bruidsbed* (1959) on the inner and outer destructive force of war violence, and French writer Henri Coulognes' melodramatic bombing survival story *L'Adieu à la femme sauvage* (1979). All three are discussed in Susanne Vees-Gulani, *Trauma and Guilt: Literature of Wartime Bombing in Germany* (New York: De Gruyter, 2003). Newer international novels include Jonathan Safran Foer, *Extremely Loud and Incredibly Close* (2005), which explores the experiences of the terrorist attack on the World Trade Center in New York and the firebombing of Dresden, as well as Jonathan Lethem's *The Garden of Dissidents* (2013), which focuses on the air attack's appropriation by East Germany to use as propaganda against the West. In the German author Martin Walser's *Verteidigung der Kindheit* (1991), the protagonist's relationship to his hometown of Dresden is used to explore questions about conserving and recovering a lost German past. Walter Kempowski's *Der rote Hahn: Dresden* (2001) represents the bombing as a

collage of various authentic materials, and Marcel Beyer in *Kaltenbach* (2008) explores the grip of the experience on a survivor. Sven Hanuschek, in *Wir leben noch* (2018), imagines Kurt Vonnegut and Ida Kästner, the Dresden writer Erich Kästner's mother, during the bombing. Ingo Schulze, in the novel *Die rechtschaffenen Mörder* (2020), looks at the changes of intellectual life and belief structures after reunification. In 2021, Schulze also published a small collection of newspaper articles and speeches he had written about Dresden as *Dresden wieder sehen.* The poet Durs Grünbein (whose long poem *Porzellan* (2005) is discussed in chapter 7 alongside Uwe Tellkamp's Dresden novel *Der Turm* (2008)) has recently published two books on the history of his family in Dresden: *Die Jahre im Zoo* (2015) and *Der Komet* (2023). Other Dresden poets have also reflected on Dresden, such as Heinz Czechowski, Volker Braun, and Karl Mickel, who all lived through the bombing. Autobiographical texts include Victor Klemperer's journals *Ich will Zeugnis ablegen bis zum letzten* (I Shall Bear Witness) (1995) and Henny Brenner's memoir *The Song Is Over: A Jewish Girl in Dresden* (2010), both discussed in chapter 5, the painter Otto Griebel's *Ich war ein Mann der Straße* (1986), and the poet Heinz Czechowski's *Die Pole der Erinnerung* (2006). The journalist and writer Peter Richter reflects on his hometown from a distance as a US correspondent in *Dresden Revisited* (2016). For other examples of Dresden literature, in particular earlier ones, see Thomas C. Fox, "Writing Dresden Across the Generations," in *Victims and Perpetrators: 1933–1945: (Re)Presenting the Past in Post-Unification Culture*, ed. Lauren Cohen-Pfister and Dagmar Wienroder-Skinner (Berlin: De Gruyter, 2006), 136–53. For a collection of artistic works on Dresden, see Walter Schmitz, ed., *Die Zerstörung Dresdens: Antworten der Künste* (Dresden: Thelem, 2005). On the television melodrama *Dresden* (2006), see Susanne Vees-Gulani, "The Ruined Picture Postcard: Dresden's Visually Encoded History and the Television Drama Dresden," *New German Critique* 38, no. 1 (2011): 85–113, https://doi.org/10.1215/0094033X-2010-024

24. For further reading on the Military History Museum in Dresden, see Stephan Jaeger, *The Second World War in the Twenty-First-Century Museum: From Narrative, Memory, and Experience to Experientiality* (Berlin: De Gruyter, 2020), https://doi.org/10.1515/9783110664416

25. Franco Bianchini, "Introduction: European Urban Mindscapes: Concepts, Cultural Representations and Policy Applications," in *Urban Mindscapes of Europe*, ed. Godela Weiss-Sussex and Franco Bianchini (Leiden: Brill, 2006), 13–31.

Chapter 1

1. Richard Peter, *Dresden: eine Kamera klagt an* (Dresden: Dresdener Verlagsgesellschaft, 1950).

2. Wolfgang Hesse, "Der 'Engel' von Dresden: Trümmerfotografie und visuelles Narrativ der Hoffnung," in *Das Jahrhundert der Bilder 1900 bis 1949*, ed. Gerhard Paul (Göttingen: Vandenhoeck & Ruprecht, 2008), 732.

3. The number of dead as a consequence of the Dresden raids has been contested ever since they occurred, with some estimates claiming more than 200,000 victims. To settle the discussions, a historical working group was formed in 2004, which painstakingly investigated all sources. The study was completed in 2010 and

concluded that up to 25,000 people lost their lives in Dresden during the February bombing. Rolf-Dieter Müller, Nicole Schönherr, and Thomas Widera, *Die Zerstörung Dresdens 13. bis 15. Februar 1945: Gutachten und Ergebnisse der Dresdner Historikerkommission zur Ermittlung der Opferzahlen* (Göttingen: Vandenhoeck & Ruprecht Unipress, 2010).

4. Erving Goffman, *Frame Analysis: An Essay on the Organization of Experience* (Cambridge, MA: Harvard University Press, 1974).

5. Manfred Kunz, "Chronik: Stadtgeschichte—Militärgeschichte," *Militärhistorisches Museum der Bundeswehr in Dresden 10: Dresden und das Militär* (2006): 6–8.

6. Roland Gräfe, "Die Entstehung und Entwicklung der Albertstadt," *Dresdner Hefte* 53, 2nd ed. (2012): 22; Matthias Rogg, "Der historische Ort," in *Militärhistorisches Museum Dresden: Ausstellungsführer*, ed. Gorch Pieken and Matthias Rogg (Dresden: Sandstein Verlag, 2011), 7; Manfred Kunz, "Ein Stück von Sachsens Glanz—das Arsenal in der Dresdner Albertstadt," *Militärhistorisches Museum der Bundeswehr in Dresden 5: Arsenal und Museum* (2003): 5–6.

7. Kunz, "Chronik: Stadtgeschichte—Militärgeschichte," 7–8.

8. Hermann Rahne, "Zur Geschichte der Dresdner Garnison im Zweiten Weltkrieg 1939 bis 1945," in *Verbrannt bis zur Unkenntlichkeit: Die Zerstörung Dresdens 1945*, ed. Stadtmuseum Dresden (Dresden: DZA Verlag, 1994), 121.

9. Hermann Rahne, "Zur Geschichte der Dresdner Garnison im Zweiten Weltkrieg 1939 bis 1945," 125.

10. According to the census from May 17, 1939. Statistisches Reichsamt, *Statistisches Jahrbuch für das Deutsche Reich, 1939–1940* (Berlin: 1940).

11. Heinz Schulz, "Die Herstellung von militärhistorischem Bedarf in Dresden (1900–1920)," in *Dresdner Geschichtsbuch 11* (2005), 171.

12. Holger Starke, "Vom Werkstättenareal zum Industriegelände," in *Dresdner Geschichtsbuch 5* (1999), 164.

13. Starke, "Vom Werkstättenareal zum Industriegelände," 176.

14. Heinz Schulz, "Der Rüstungsstandort Dresden 1933–1945," in *Sachsen im Bombenkrieg—und nun auch Dresden*, ed. Militärhistorisches Museum Dresden (Dresden: Militärhistorisches Museum Dresden, 2005), 23–26; Rahne, "Zur Geschichte der Dresdner Garnison im Zweiten Weltkrieg 1939 bis 1945," 132; Frederick Taylor, *Dresden, Tuesday, February 13, 1945*, 1st ed. (New York: HarperCollins, 2004), 148–50; Marshall De Bruhl, *Firestorm: Allied Airpower and the Destruction of Dresden* (New York: Random House, 2006), 281.

15. Götz Bergander, "Vom unattraktiven zum besonders lohnenden Ziel: Dresden in den Luftkriegsplanungen der Alliierten," in *Das rote Leuchten: Dresden und der Bombenkrieg*, ed. Matthias Neutzner, Oliver Reinhard, and Wolfgang Hesse (Dresden: Edition Sächsische Zeitung, 2005), 52.

16. Rolf-Dieter Müller, "Die militärische Bedeutung Dresdens im Frühjahr 1945 und die Auswirkungen der alliierten Luftangriffe," in *Die Zerstörung Dresdens 13. bis 15. Februar 1945*, ed. Rolf-Dieter Müller, Nicole Schönherr, and Thomas Widera (Göttingen: Vandenhoeck & Ruprecht Unipress, 2010), 76.

17. Hermann Rahne, "Die 'Festung Dresden' von 1945," *Dresdner Hefte* 41 (1995): 19–20.

18. Bergander, "Vom unattraktiven zum besonders lohnenden Ziel," 54–55.

19. Christian Groh, "Was Pforzheim angetan wurde: Erinnerungsorte und Denkmäler zum Luftkrieg," in *Luftkrieg: Erinnerungen in Deutschland und Europa*, ed. Jörg Arnold, Dietmar Süß and Malte Thießen (Göttingen: Wallstein 2009), 183–99.

20. Malte Thießen, *Eingebrannt ins Gedächnis: Hamburgs Gedenken an Luftkrieg und Kriegsende 1943 bis 2005* (Hamburg: Dölling und Galitz, 2007).

21. Sönke Neitzel, "The City under Attack," in *Firestorm: The Bombing of Dresden, 1945*, ed. Paul Addison and Jeremy A. Crang (Chicago: I. R. Dee, 2006), 77.

22. In this context, historian Matthias Neutzner has called the narrative a "cipher" ["Chiffre"]: "The narrative began as a selective reflection of the events, which were defined by established interpretations and were then generalized in symbolic form. The narrative thus established itself quickly as a way to frame the remembrance." ("Die Erzählung entstand als selektive Reflektion der Ereignisse, die von fest gefügten Wertungen eingefasst und symbolhaft verallgemeinert wurde. So etablierte sie sich rasch als Erinnerungsrahmen"). Matthias Neutzner, "Vom Alltäglichen zum Exemplarischen: Dresden als Chiffre für den Luftkrieg der Alliierten," in *Das rote Leuchten: Dresden und der Bombenkrieg*, ed. Oliver Reinhard, Matthias Neutzner, and Wolfgang Hesse (Dresden: Edition Sächsische Zeitung, 2005), 110.

23. Thomas Widera, "Gefangene Erinnerung: Die politische Instrumentalisierung der Bombardierung Dresdens," in *Alliierter Bombenkrieg. Das Beispiel Dresden*, ed. Thomas Widera and Lothar Fritze (Göttingen: Vandenhoeck & Ruprecht Unipress, 2005), 118.

24. This assertion has not been substantiated. When studying the number of dead in Dresden, the historical commission determined that the number of refugees was relatively small given the housing restrictions in Dresden. Furthermore, the casualties among refugees were already included in the available statistics. Müller, Schönherr, and Widera, *Die Zerstörung Dresdens 13. bis 15. Februar 1945.*

25. Neutzner, "Vom Alltäglichen zum Exemplarischen," 117; Taylor, *Dresden*, 369; Richard Overy, *The Bombers and the Bombed: Allied Air War Over Europe, 1940–1945* (New York: Penguin, 2014), 214–15.

26. Taylor, *Dresden*, 370.

27. Neutzner, "Vom Alltäglichen zum Exemplarischen," 115–20; Taylor, *Dresden*, 369–70.

28. Gladwin Hill, "Rail City Blasted," *New York Times*, February 16, 1945, 1.

29. Norbert Frei and Johannes Schmitz, *Journalismus im Dritten Reich* (München: Beck, 1989), 109–10. For his contributions, Goebbels collected 2000 reichsmarks each.

30. Hans Dieter Müller, "Hoch über Grab und Gram und Tod und Qual. 'Das Reich'—Porträt einer deutschen Wochenzeitung," *Der Spiegel*, August 19, 1964, 32.

31. Frei and Schmitz, *Journalismus im Dritten Reich*, 108–9.

32. Rudolf Sparing, "Der Tod von Dresden. Ein Leuchtzeichen des Widerstandes," *Das Reich*, March 4, 1945.

33. Müller, "Hoch über Grab und Gram," 38.

34. Sparing, "Der Tod von Dresden." "[. . .] daß die Dresdener Katastrophe beispiellos ist."

35. Sparing, "Der Tod von Dresden." "die abendländische Kultur selbtzerstörerisch preisgegeben [wurde]."

36. Sparing, "Der Tod von Dresden." "Eine Stadtsilhouette von vollendeter Harmonie ist vom europäischen Himmel gelöscht."

37. Sparing, "Der Tod von Dresden." "Wann wird die Welt erkennen, was es auch für sie bedeutet, daß man von dem, was den Begriff Dresden ausmacht, nur noch in der Vergangenheitsform sprechen kann? Daß im Zwingerhof keine Abendmusik mehr erklingen wird, daß das Haus am Altmarkt, in dem Weber den Freischütz komponierte, und die Kreuzschule, in die Theodor Körner ging, nicht mehr stehen, daß George Bährs Frauenkirchenkuppel, der die rechthaberischen Statiker vor dem Bau den Einsturz prophezeiten, nicht weitere Jahrhunderte überdauern kann, daß die Brühlsche Terrasse mit ihren Sammlungen und Galerien ein Bombenkrater geworden ist? Dresden übte eine Trauhänderschaft über all das aus, es war ein von dieser Stadt gehüteter abendländischer Gemeinbesitz."

38. Sparing, "Der Tod von Dresden." "Wer diese Trümmer sah, dem muß es sinnlos erscheinen, mit den Engländern und den Amerikanern darüber zu rechten, was für militärische Ziele sie in der Brühlschen Terrasse, im Zwinger, in den Gewölben der Frauenkirche, den Bühnen- und Zuschauerräumen der Staatstheater, den Bücherbeständen des Japanischen Palais [suchten]."

39. Helmut Schnatz has extensively researched the possible presence of strafing planes in the Dresden raids. He has concluded that this type of attack was not used in the bombardments of the city, despite the numerous claims by eyewitnesses. Helmut Schnatz, *Tiefflieger über Dresden?: Legenden und Wirklichkeit* (Köln: Böhlau, 2000).

40. "Dresden, Once Reich Pride, Erased by Bombs, German Radio Asserts," *New York Times*, March 5, 1945, 1.

41. "Dresden Leveled, Nazi Says," *Chicago Daily Tribune*, March 5, 1945, 1.

42. "Total Annihilation of Dresden from Air Admitted by Nazis," *Washington Post*, March 5, 1945, 4.

43. Charles E. Egan, "Dresden Blasted from Europe; Not a Soul Left, Berlin Claims," *Gazette (Montreal)*, March 5, 1945, 10.

44. Mark Connelli, "Britain and the Debate over RAF Bomber Command's Role in the Second World War," in *H-Soz-Kult*, June 28, 2004, www.hsozkult.de/debate/id/diskussionen-492; Taylor, *Dresden*, 271–72, 375–79; Neutzner, "Vom Alltäglichen zum Exemplarischen," 123–24.

45. "Dresden Raid Killed 300,000, Say Ex-Captives," *Chicago Daily Tribune*, May 3, 1945, 3; "300,000 Reported Dead in 14-Hour Dresden Air Raid," *Washington Post*, May 4, 1945, 5.

46. "300,000 Reported Dead in 14-Hour Dresden Air Raid," *Washington Post*, May 4, 1945, 5.

47. Neutzner, "Vom Alltäglichen zum Exemplarischen," 126–27.

48. Neutzner, "Vom Alltäglichen zum Exemplarischen," 127.

49. Roland Barthes, *Mythologies* (New York: Hill and Wang 1972), 131.

50. Barthes, *Mythologies*, 129.

51. Barthes, *Mythologies*, 131.

52. Barthes, *Mythologies*, 131.

53. Barthes, *Mythologies*, 143.

54. Thomas E. Nelson, Zoe M. Oxley, and Rosalee A. Clawson, "Toward a Psychology of Framing Effects," *Political Behavior* 19 (1997): 221–46.

55. Dennis Chong and James N. Druckman, "Framing Theory," *Annual Review of Political Science* 10 (2007): 103–26.

56. Gilad Margalit, "Der Luftangriff auf Dresden, Seine Bedeutung für die Erinnerungspolitik der DDR und für die Herauskristallisierung einer historischen Kriegserinnerung im Westen," in *Narrative der Shoah. Repräsentationen der Vergangenheit in Historiographie, Kunst und Politik*, ed. Susanne Düwell and Mathias Schmidt (Paderborn: Schöningh 2002), 189–207.

57. Susanne Vees-Gulani, "The Politics of New Beginnings: The Continued Exclusion of the Nazi Past in Dresden's Cityscape," in *Beyond Berlin: Twelve German Cities Confront the Nazi Past*, ed. Gavriel Rosenfeld and Paul B. Jaskot (Ann Arbor: University of Michigan Press, 2008), 25–47.

58. Will Lang, "Fun, Culture and Rebuilding in the Other Germany," *Life Special Issue: Germany: A Giant Awakened*, May 10, 1954, 44–50.

59. Lang, "Fun, Culture and Rebuilding in the Other Germany," 50. This claim has been disproven. As Richard Overy states in *The Bombing War: Europe 1939–1945*, during the discussions at Yalta, Marshal Aleksei Antonov only mentioned Berlin and Leipzig to the Western Allies. According to Overy, "Though Harris later argued at the height of the Cold War that the request to bomb Dresden had come 'from the other side of the Iron Curtain', there can be no doubt that the plan was always a Western one. Overy, *The Bombing War*, 394.

60. Gilad Margalit, *Guilt, Suffering, and Memory: Germany Remembers Its Dead of World War II* (Bloomington: Indiana University Press, 2010), 183.

61. Jan Assmann, *Cultural Memory and Early Civilization: Writing, Remembrance, and Political Imagination* (New York: Cambridge University Press, 2011 [1992]); Aleida Assmann, *Cultural Memory and Western Civilization: Functions, Media, Archives* (New York: Cambridge University Press, 2011 [1999]).

62. Robert Hariman and John Louis Lucaites, *No Captions Needed: Iconic Photographs, Public Culture, and Liberal Democracy* (Chicago: University of Chicago Press, 2007), 1–2.

63. Richard Peter, "Gute Fotos kosten Zeit und Mühe," *fotografie* 4 (1960): 149–51. See also Ursula Breymayer, "Der engagierte Dokumentarist: Richard Peter Senior," in *Ende und Anfang: Photographen in Deutschland um 1945*, ed. Klaus Honnef, Ursula Breymayer, and Deutsches Historisches Museum (Berlin: Deutsches Historisches Museum, 1995), 184–87.

64. Hariman and Lucaites, *No Captions Needed*, 29–30.

65. Paul-Georg Fickus, "Richard Peter sen.—Fotografien aus dem zerstörten Dresden" (Master's thesis: Köln, 1995), 29.

66. Ludwig Meidner, "Anleitung zum Malen von Großstadtbildern," *Das neue Programm. Kunst und Künstler* 12, no. 5 (1914): 312–14. "ein Bombardement von zischenden Fensterreihen, sausenden Lichtkegeln zwischen Fuhrwerken aller Art und tausend hüpfenden Kugeln, Menschenfetzen."

67. Peter, *Dresden: Eine Kamera klagt an.*

68. Raymond Tallis, *Michelangelo's Finger: An Exploration of Everyday Transcendence* (New Haven: Yale University Press, 2010), 104.

69. Hariman and Lucaites, *No Captions Needed*, 32.

70. John Milton, "On the Morning of Christ's Nativity," 1629, *Poems of Mr. John Milton* (London: 1645).

71. Hermann Claasen, *Gesang im Feuerofen* (Düsseldorf: L. Schwann, 1947).

72. Hesse, "Der 'Engel' von Dresden, 733; Ludger Derenthal, *Bilder der Trümmer- und Aufbaujahre: Fotografie im sich teilenden Deutschland* (Marburg: Jonas Verlag 1999), 48.

73. Hans Erich Nossack, *Der Untergang* (Berlin: Suhrkamp, 2021 [1948]); Hans Erich Nossack, *The End: Hamburg 1943* (Chicago: University of Chicago Press, 2004).

74. Arnold Hauser, *The Social History of Art* (New York: Routledge, 1999 [1951]), 62.

75. Brad Prager, "Air War and Allegory," in *Bombs Away! Representing the Air War over Europe and Japan*, ed. William Rasch and Wilfried Wilms (Amsterdam: Amsterdamer Beiträge zur neueren Germanistik, 2006), 27.

76. Joseph Leo Koerner, *Caspar David Friedrich and the Subject of Landscape* (London: Reaktion Books, 1990), 166.

77. Clive Scott, *Spoken Image: Photography and Language* (London: Reaktion Books 1999), 34.

78. Michael Griffin has identified these elements as typical for high-impact war photography. Even though Peter's photograph does not picture battlefield scenes and projects rather a state than an action, it certainly shares in these symbolically constructed scenes. Michael Griffin, "The Great War Photographs: Constructing Myth and History of Photojournalism," in *Picturing the Past: Media, History and Photography*, ed. Bonnie Brennen and Hanno Hardt (Urbana: University of Illinois Press, 1999), 122–57.

79. W. J. T. Mitchell, *Picture Theory* (Chicago: University of Chicago Press, 1995), 83–109.

80. Photographer and theorist Victor Burgin emphasizes that the political realm is an aspect that necessarily arises and influences the way photographs are read. Victor Burgin, "Art, Common Sense and Photography," *Camerawork* 3 (1976): 86–91.

81. Robert Dale, "Visualizing the Red Army's Demobilization: Photography, Reconstructing Community and Creating Post-War Memory," *Journal of War and Culture Studies* 15, no. 2 (2022): 177.

82. The photojournalist Erich Höhne reported in an interview how he repeatedly ran into fellow photographers such as Richard Peter and Walter Hahn (as well as painters like Wilhelm Rudolph, who produced a series of woodcuts of the destroyed Dresden) at some of the "prominent ruins" in Dresden shortly after the war. Photographers from other cities also came to Dresden to photograph the destruction, another example for the shared interest in Dresden's destiny. Derenthal, *Bilder der Trümmer- und Aufbaujahre*, 63.

83. Walter Hahn, *Über den Dächern von Dresden*, ed. Jens Bove (Leipzig: Lehmstedt 2008), 8–10, 30. The photographs are part of the collection of the Deutsche Fotothek.

84. There is also a montage version of the photo that contains an embedded swastika. See Wolfgang Hesse, "Bild-Geschichte(n): Dresden 1939 bis 1945—die

Kriegszeit in Fotografien und Filmen," in *Das rote Leuchten: Dresden und der Bombenkrieg*, ed. Oliver Reinhard, Matthias Neutzner, and Wolfgang Hesse (Dresden: Edition Sächsische Zeitung, 2005), 240.

85. Hesse, "Bild-Geschichte(n)," 240.

86. In contrast, German historians largely remained silent on Dresden and the air war for a significant time after the war. Bas von Benda-Beckmann, *German Historians and the Bombing of German Cities: The Contested Air War* (Amsterdam: Amsterdam University Press 2015), 121.

87. Max Seydewitz, *Zerstörung und Wiederaufbau von Dresden* (Berlin: Kongress 1955); renamed *Die unbesiegbare Stadt* starting with the third edition.

88. Max Seydewitz, *Die unbesiegbare Stadt*, 5th ed. (Berlin: Kongress 1962), 13–14.

89. Seydewitz, *Die unbesiegbare Stadt*, 13. "[die] herrlich[e] Silhouette der Stadt am Strom."

90. Seydewitz, *Die unbesiegbare Stadt*, 30. "Ein Glanz lag über der Schönheit dieser Stadt, die menschliche Arbeit und höchste Kunst in Jahrhunderten hatten erstehen lassen. Dresden, herrliche Stadt am Strom . . . Am Rathaus vorbei zog grölend eine SA-Kolonne. Ihr Heil Gebrüll, das die friedliche Stille zerstörte, drang bis zum Rathausturm herauf. [. . .] Die marschierenden SA-Kolonnen erinnerten nur zu deutlich daran, daß auf all die an diesem klaren Januartag hell erstrahlende Schönheit der Kultur- und Kunststadt Dresden unheilverkündend der dunkle Schatten des Hakenkreuzes fiel."

91. Seydewitz, *Zerstörung und Wiederaufbau*, 428.

92. Seydewitz, *Zerstörung und Wiederaufbau*, 428. "schöner aufzubauen, als sie jemals war."

93. Seydewitz, *Die unbesiegbare Stadt*, 371–372. "schöne Neubauten [. . .] stehen an breiten Straßen; sie sind von schönen Grünflächen umgeben, so dass Luft, Licht und Sonne in die modernen Wohnungen eindringen können."

94. Walter Weidauer, *Inferno Dresden: Über Lügen und Legenden um die Aktion "Donnerschlag,"* 4th ed. (Berlin (East): Dietz 1982 [1965]).

95. Weidauer, *Inferno Dresden*, 20. "Die Zerstörung Dresdens sollte, wie Churchill formulierte, 'ein Donnerschlag' sein und die Sowjetunion heftig erschrecken. Alle Tatsachen beweisen, daß die englische und die amerikanische Regierung mit der Zerstörung Dresdens tatsächlich nicht die Hitlerfaschisten, sondern in erster Linie ihre sowjetischen Bundesgenossen treffen wollten / Die Aktion diente offensichtlich nicht der militärischen Niederschlagung Hitlerdeutschlands, sondern mit ihr wurden von den Imperialisten weitgesteckte Ziele verfolgt."

96. Von Benda-Beckmann, *German Historians and the Bombing of German Cities*, 93.

97. Axel Rodenberger, *Der Tod von Dresden* (Dortmund: Landverlag, 1951).

98. Introduction to the 1951 edition, quoted in the eighth edition: Axel Rodenberger, *Der Tod von Dresden*, 8th ed. (Frankfurt a. M.: Müller-Rodenberger, 1963), 10. All quotations refer to the eighth edition from 1963. https://digital.slub-dresden.de/werkansicht/dlf/362674/1. "Dresden! Elbflorenz! Stadt der Museen und der Künste. Dresden, Stadt zahlloser weltberühmter Bauten. Dresden, die Stadt, die wie keine

zweite das Ziel der Reisenden aus aller Herren Ländern war, ist nicht mehr. Dresden starb, es zerschmolz in der Flammenglut, es zerbarst unter den Explosionen der Bomben. . . . Schutzlos waren [die Einwohner und Flüchtlinge] dem Verderben ausgesetzt."

99. Rodenberger, *Der Tod von Dresden*, 198.

100. Rodenberger, *Der Tod von Dresden*, 192. "Der Tod von Dresden sollte ein ewiges Mahnmal bleiben. Eine Warnung an die Menschheit, alles zu tun, um eine Wiederholung von Kriegen und derartigen Katastrophen zu verhindern."

101. Rodenberger, *Der Tod von Dresden*, 136.

102. Rodenberger, *Der Tod von Dresden*, 139.

103. Rodenberger, *Der Tod von Dresden*, 10.

104. Rodenberger, *Der Tod von Dresden*, 12.

105. Rodenberger, *Der Tod von Dresden*, Bildanhang, 209. "Ein trostloser Anblick."

106. Rodenberger, *Der Tod von Dresden*, 12. "Der Bericht ist völlig frei von Tendenzen."

107. Jörn Glasenapp, *Die deutsche Nachkriegsfotografie. Eine Mentalitätsgeschichte in Bildern* (Paderborn: Wilhelm Fink, 2008), 122.

108. David Irving, *The Destruction of Dresden* (London: W. Kimber 1963). The book was first published as a serial in the West German magazine *Neue Illustrierte*.

109. In later editions, the picture is also found on the cover.

110. Irving, *The Destruction of Dresden*, 92.

111. Irving, *The Destruction of Dresden*, 210.

112. Irving, *The Destruction of Dresden*, 234.

113. Irving, *The Destruction of Dresden*, 76.

114. See Susanne Vees-Gulani, "Diagnosing Billy Pilgrim: A Psychiatric Approach to Kurt Vonnegut's *Slaughterhouse-Five*," *Critique: Studies in Contemporary Fiction* 44, no. 2 (Winter 2003): 175–84.

115. Kurt Vonnegut, *Slaughterhouse-Five* (New York: Delacorte 1969), 191.

116. Vonnegut, *Slaughterhouse-Five*, 12.

117. Kurt Vonnegut, *Armageddon in Retrospect* (New York: Putnam 2008), 12.

118. Vonnegut, *Armageddon in Retrospect*, 36.

119. Academic study is, of course, not entirely free of the legends of the popular Dresden narrative or political staging. Dagmar Barnouw, for example, uncritically repeats the basic tropes so long connected with the Dresden destruction narrative in *The War in the Empty Air* (2005), claiming that "Dresden [. . .] had no war-related importance" (120), was housing "hundreds of thousands of refugees" (133), and that there were "the feared Mustang fighters flying low and gunning the riverbanks and the Grosser Garten area, killing the survivors of the firestorms of the first two attacks, panicked women, children, animals rushing around in their futile search for shelter" (134). Barnouw, in 2005, still draws upon David Irving's book on Dresden as a source and supports his estimate of the death toll of 135,000 civilians from the bombing (279, note 64). Yet a closer look reveals that Barnouw never truly leaves the realm of the personal and symbolic; she structures her evidence around a story deeply rooted in her childhood experiences in Dresden during and after the war. Dagmar Barnouw, *The War in the Empty Air: Victims, Perpetrators, and Postwar Germans* (Bloomington: Indiana University Press, 2005).

Chapter 2

1. Kirsten Wagner, "Die visuelle Ordnung der Stadt. Das Bild der Stadt bei Kevin Lynch," *H-Soz-Kult*, September 14, 2006, www.hsozkult.de/debate/id/fddebate-13 2142

2. Kevin Lynch, *The Image of the City* (Cambridge, MA: MIT Press, 1960), 1–14.

3. Markus A. Castor, "Rocco di Linar und die Mathematica Militaris der Dresdner Fortifikation in italienischer Manier. Städteplanung von der Bild- zur Raumordnung," in *Elbflorenz: Italienische Präsenz in Dresden 16.-19. Jahrhundert*, ed. Barbara Marx (Dresden: Verlag der Kunst, 2000), 108, 111.

4. Castor, "Rocco di Linar und die Mathematica Militaris," 111–15.

5. Dresdner Geschichtsverein, *Dresden: die Geschichte der Stadt* (Dresden: Junius, 2005), 44–45.

6. Barbara Marx, "Vorwort," in *Elbflorenz: Italienische Präsenz in Dresden 16.-19. Jahrhundert*, ed. Barbara Marx (Dresden: Verlag der Kunst, 2000), 5.

7. The notion of the ideal city was an important theoretical and practical concept in the Renaissance. It referred to a city that was carefully planned out on the drawing board, offering symmetry and harmony, and was, due to its design, infused with certain idealized manners and culture. This view of the city was necessarily attractive for the Saxon leaders, who tried to imitate and translate some of these ideals in Dresden to increase their reputation, their prestige, and their representative power.

8. Peter J. M. Nas et al., "Introduction: Variety of Symbols," in *Cities Full of Symbols: A Theory of Urban Space and Culture*, ed. Peter Nas (Leiden: Leiden University Press, 2011), 20.

9. Beatrix Busse, Ingo Warnke, and Jennifer Smith, eds., *Place-Making in the Declarative City* (Berlin: De Gruyter, 2020), 6–9.

10. Nas et al., "Introduction," 9.

11. Katrin Nitzschke, *Dresden: Literarische Spaziergänge* (Frankfurt a. M.: Insel, 1999), 67. "Die Stadt Dresden scheint gleichsam nur ein bloßes Lustgebäude zu sein, worin sich alle Erfindungen der Baukünste angenehm miteinander vermischen, und doch besonders betrachten lassen."

12. Reiner Groß, "Ratsregiment und Stadtverwaltung," in *Geschichte der Stadt Dresden: Vom Ende des Dreißigjährigen Krieges bis zur Reichsgründung*, ed. Reiner Groß and Uwe John (Stuttgart: Theiss, 2005), 65.

13. Much of the city on this side of the Elbe had been destroyed by a fire in 1685, which paved the way for such a radical redesign.

14. Moritz Bonenehr, 1733, quoted in Heinrich Magirius, "Die Augustusbrücke," *Dresdner Hefte* 94 (2008): 27. "herrlich geziert[e] Elbbrücke."

15. The Augustus Bridge today is, however, not identical to the one designed by Pöppelmann; the increase in shipping traffic as well as traffic on the bridge, including streetcars, made it necessary to take down the old bridge in 1907. The Augustus Bridge in its current design, a construction in reinforced concrete hidden under a covering of sandstone blocks, was completed in 1910. Two arches were blown up in 1945 but quickly rebuilt in their 1910 design. For more information see Ulrich Hübner, "Der Neubau der Augustusbrücke von 1910," in *Dresdner Hefte* 94 (2008): 35–43.

16. Maria Lieber, "Die italienische Präsenz am Hofe August des Starken und seiner Söhne—Erste Überlegungen," in *Elbflorenz: Italienische Präsenz in Dresden 16.-19. Jahrhundert*, ed. Barbara Marx (Dresden: Verlag der Kunst, 2000), 144.

17. Klaus Bergdolt, "Dresden und Venedig," *Dresdner Hefte* 40 (1994): 66.

18. Barbara Marx and Andreas Hennig, *Venedig-Dresden: Begegnung zweier Kunststädte* (Leipzig: Seemann 2010), 7; Klaus Bergdolt, *Deutsche in Venedig* (Darmstadt: Primus, 2011), 124.

19. Anke Fröhlich, "Kunst, Kultur und Bildung: Höfische Festkultur im Augusteischen Dresden," in *Geschichte der Stadt Dresden: Vom Ende des Dreißigjährigen Krieges bis zur Reichsgründung*, ed. Reiner Groß und Uwe John (Stuttgart: Theiss, 2005), 204–13.

20. Bergdolt, *Deutsche in Venedig*, 124–25.

21. Fröhlich, "Kunst, Kultur und Bildung," 208–9.

22. Lieber, "Die italienische Präsenz am Hofe August des Starken," 154.

23. Barbara Marx, "Diplomaten, Agenten, Abenteurer im Dienst der Künste: Kunstbeziehungen zwischen Dresden und Venedig," in *Venedig—Dresden: Begegnung zweier Kulturstädte*, ed. Barbara Marx and Andreas Henning (Leipzig: Seemann, 2010), 21.

24. Gregor J. M. Weber, "Die Galerie als Kunstwerk: Die Hängung italienischer Gemälde in der Dresdener Galerie 1754" in *Elbflorenz: Italienische Präsenz in Dresden 16.-19. Jahrhundert*, ed. Barbara Marx (Dresden: Verlag der Kunst, 2000), 231–32.

25. Weber, "Die Galerie als Kunstwerk," 234–36.

26. For additional thoughts about understanding Dresden as a Gesamtkunstwerk see Janna Düringer and Rainette Lange, "Dresden bleibt Dresden—die Stadt in der Reiseliteratur," in *Dresden. Ethnografische Erkundungen einer Residenzstadt*, ed. Rolf Lindner and Johannes Moser (Leipzig: Leipziger Universitätsverlag 2006), 36–74 (particularly 42–48), and Rolf J. Goebel, "Gesamtkunstwerk Dresden: Official Urban Discourse and Durs Grünbein's Poetic Critique," *German Quarterly* 80, no. 4 (2007): 492–510.

27. Richard Wagner, *Das Kunstwerk der Zukunft* (Leipzig, 1850), 32–33, https://www.deutschestextarchiv.de/wagner_zukunft_1850

28. For a detailed account of Wagner's time in Dresden, see Thomas S. Grey, "Dresden," in *Wagner in Context*, ed. David Trippett (Cambridge: Cambridge University Press, 2024), 20–30.

29. Gottfried Semper was a fellow revolutionary, but, as we will see in chapter 4, he did not share Wagner's antisemitic beliefs.

30. Odo Marquard, "Gesamtkunstwerk und Identitätssystem: Überlegungen im Anschluss an Hegels Schellingkritik," in *Der Hang zum Gesamtkunstwerk*, ed. Harald Szeemann (Frankfurt a. M.: Sauerländer Verlag 1983), 43-44.

31. Marquard, "Gesamtkunstwerk," 40.

32. Marquard, "Gesamtkunstwerk," 46–48.

33. Peter J. M. Nas and Annemarie Samuels, eds., *Hypercity: The Symbolic Side of Urbanism* (New York: Kegan Paul, 2006), 8.

34. Nas and Samuels, *Hypercity*, 9.

35. Richard Sennett, *Flesh and Stone: The Body and the City in Western Civilization* (New York: Norton, 1994).

36. Andreas Beyer, "Bernardo Bellotto (Canaletto) und die Skyline von Dresden: Zur Bildkarriere einer Stadt," in *Mythos Dresden: Eine kulturhistorische Revue*, ed. Deutsches Hygiene-Museum Dresden (Köln: Böhlau, 2006), 48–49.

37. Düringer and Lange, "Dresden bleibt Dresden," 51.

38. Caroline Lucius, "Briefwechsel mit Christian Fürchtegott Gellert in Leipzig, 1764," reprinted in *Dresden in alten und neuen Reisebeschreibungen*, ed. Wolfgang Paul (Düsseldorf: Droste, 1990), 22. "Die Raketen sahen schön aus, aber sie klingen mir abscheulich, sie rauschen und zischen wie Karkassen und Bomben in der Belagerung, wenn sie in der Luft über dem Hause hinflogen."

39. Fritz Löffler, *Bernardo Bellotto genannt Canaletto: Dresden im 18. Jahrhundert* (Leipzig: Koehler und Amelang, 1985), 23.

40. James Buzard, "The Grand Tour and After (1660–1840)," in *The Cambridge Companion to Travel Writing*, ed. Peter Hulme and Tim Youngs (Cambridge: Cambridge University Press, 2002), 39. Buzard quotes the Earl of Chesterfield.

41. Philip Dormer Stanhope, Earl of Chesterfield, *The Letters of Philip Dormer Stanhope, Earl of Chesterfield*, ed. John Bradshaw (London: Allen, 1913).

42. Letter from June 21, 1748. In Chesterfield, *The Letters of Philip Dormer Stanhope, Earl of Chesterfield*, 118.

43. Franco Bianchini, "Introduction. European Urban Mindscapes: Concepts, Cultural Representations and Policy Applications," in *Urban Mindscapes of Europe*, ed. Godela Weiss-Sussex and Franco Bianchini (Amsterdam: Rodopi, 2006), 13–14.

44. Dean MacCannell, *The Tourist: A New Theory of the Leisure Class* (Berkeley: University of California Press, 1999 [1976]), 43–48.

45. Johann Wolfgang Goethe, *Autobiography: Truth and Fiction Relating to My Life*, trans. John Oxenford, vol. 1 (Philadelphia: J. H. Moore, 1902), available at http://www.gutenberg.org/cache/epub/5733/pg5733-images.html

46. Johann Wolfgang Goethe, *Autobiography*, vol. 2, eighth book. The translation is slightly adjusted. http://www.gutenberg.org/cache/epub/5733/pg5733-images.html; "Goethes erster Besuch in Dresden, 1768" in *Johann Wolfgang Goethe, Dichtung und Wahrheit: Erster und zweiter Teil* (Leipzig: Tempel Verlag, 1811–1812) Buch 8, Gutenberg.spiegel.de. http://gutenberg.spiegel.de/buch/dichtung-und-wahrheit-erster-und-zweiter-teil-7130/10. "Diese köstlichen, Geist und Sinn zur wahren Kunst vorbereitenden Erfahrungen wurden jedoch durch einen der traurigsten Anblicke unterbrochen und gedämpft, durch den zerstörten und verödeten Zustand so mancher Straßen Dresdens, durch die ich meinen Weg nahm. Die Mohrenstraße im Schutt, sowie die Kreuzkirche mit ihrem geborstenen Turm, drückten sich mir tief ein und stehen noch wie ein dunkler Fleck in meiner Einbildungskraft. Von der Kuppel der Frauenkirche sah ich diese leidigen Trümmer zwischen die schöne städtische Ordnung hineingesät."

47. One of the most important publishers of such *Städtebücher* was Matthäus Merian the Older, a Swiss copperplate engraver who, through his own publishing house, sold illustrated books on various cities. It is no accident that a travel magazine in Germany carries the same name, emphasizing the close relationship of *Städtebücher* to travel guides and magazines.

48. Wolfgang Behringer, "Die großen Städtebücher und ihre Voraussetzungen," in *Das Bild der Stadt in der Neuzeit, 1400–1800*, ed. Wolfgang Behringer and Bernd Roeck (München: C. H. Beck-Verlag, 1999), 1–92.

49. Bianchini, "Introduction," 14.

50. Patricia C. Albers and William R. James, "Travel Photography: A Methodological Approach," *Annals of Tourism Research* 15, no. 1 (1988): 140.

51. Rudy Koshar, *German Travel Cultures* (Oxford: Berg, 2000), 22.

52. *Beschreibung der Königlich Sächsischen Residenzstadt Dresden und der umliegenden Gegend. Für Fremde bearbeitet* (Dresden: Walther, 1807).

53. Johann Gottlob August Kläbe, *Neuester Dresdner Wegweiser für Fremde und Einheimische* (Dresden: Hilschersche Buchhandlung, 1797).

54. Johann Gottfried Herder, "Kunstsammlungen in Dresden" *Adrastea* (1802), http://gutenberg.spiegel.de/buch/adrastea-6371/38. "deutsches Florenz" . . . "Colonien der Kunst, [die] als Vorbereitungen zu betrachten [sind], die den Schüler über die Alpen hinleiten."

55. August Wilhelm von Schlegel, "Die Gemälde," in *August Wilhelm von Schlegel's vermischte und kritische Schriften*, ed. Eduard Böcking, vol. 3 (Leipzig: Weidmann'sche Buchhandlung, 1846), 3–101.

56. For more information on this circle of friends, see Klaus Günzel, *Romantik in Dresden* (Frankfurt: Insel, 1997), 28–46.

57. For Friedrich Schleiermacher's theory of "Geselligkeit," see Günter Meckenstock, "Schleiermachers Theorie der Geselligkeit [2006]," in *Protestantismus und Moderne: Studien zu Theologie, Philosophie und Ethik*, ed. Anette Hagan, Michael Pietsch, and Dirk Schmid (Berlin: De Gruyter, 2022), 193–208, https://doi.org/10.1515/9783110745498-015

58. Schlegel, "Die Gemälde," 17. "Wir können keinen bequemeren und anmuthigeren Sitz finden. Vor uns der ruhige Fluß; jenseits erhebt sich hinter dem grünen Ufer die Ebne in weichen Wellen, dort unten spiegelt sich die Stadt mit der Kuppel der Frauenkirche im Waßer, oberhalb ziehen sich Rebenhügel dicht an der Krümmung hin, mit Landhäusern besäht und oben mit Nadelholz bedeckt."

59. Schlegel, "Die Gemälde," 3. "Gewühl gaffender Fremden."

60. Schlegel, "Die Gemälde," 24. "Seit ich mich mit diesen Dingen [Kunst] viel beschäftige, sehe ich eine wirkliche Gegend mehr als Gemälde, und ein Landschaftsstück suche ich mir zu einer wahren Aussicht zu machen."

61. Heinrich von Kleist, "An Wilhelmine von Zenge (Leipzig, 21.05.1801)," in *Briefe* (Munich: Hanser Verlag, 1961), http://gutenberg.spiegel.de/buch/briefe-7043/3

62. *Neue Ansicht von Dresden: Für Reisende von einem Reisenden* (Leipzig: Leo, 1799), 18. "Wer übrigens einmal in seinem Leben, der entzückenden Aussicht von der Dresdner Brücke genossen hat, der wird es nicht unnatürlich finden, wenn jemand seine Tage in dieser Stadt zuzubringen wünscht."

63. W. U. Lindau, *Neues Gemählde von Dresden* (Dresden: Arnoldische Buchhandlung, 1817).

64. Hans Christian Andersen, *Andersen's Works: Pictures of Travel* (Boston: Houghton, Mifflin and Company, 1871), 74.

65. Printed in Karin Kolb, Gilbert Lupfer, Martin Roth, *Zukunft seit 1560. Die Anthologie* (Dresden: Staatliche Kunstsammlungen, 2010), 134. "Die Gegend ist paradiesisch. [. . .] Ich weiß nicht, war es die Gewohnheit der letzten Tage, in Galerien heimisch zu sein, oder liegt es im eigentümlichen der hiesigen Natur, daß jede einzelne Aussicht sich mir so sehr als ein Gemälde darstellte. Ich habe das wohl nie in so hohem Grade erfahren."

66. Brad Prager, *Aesthetic Vision and German Romanticism: Writing Images* (Rochester, NY: Camden House, 2007), 99.

67. Prager, *Aesthetic Vision and German Romanticism*, 100.

68. Kaspar Friedrich Gottschalck, *Dresden, seine Umgebungen und die Sächsische Schweiz: ein Taschenbuch für Reisende* (Dresden: H. M. Gottschalck, 1842), 10. "Wo vereinigen sich auch Kunst und Natur zu einem so herrlichen Bunde wie hier! Wo böte letztere so liebliche Bilder, so reizende Landschaften, daß den schönern man den Namen "Schweiz" beilegen durfte, während der Erstern Schätze, durch die Munifizenz der Regenten des Landes, in solchen Massen hier angehäuft wurden, daß ihrem Wohnsitze der Beiname "Elbflorenz" ward." For a similar sentiment, see also the *Illustrirter Dresden-Prager-Führer* from 1852, which emphasizes how the wonderful "Lage" (location) of the city makes up for its "Mangel an hervorragenden alterthümlichen Werken der Baukunst" (lack of outstanding classical architectural works). *Illustrirter Dresden-Prager-Führer: Malerische Beschreibung von Dresden, der Sächsischen Schweiz mit Teplitz, der Dresden-Prager Eisenbahn und Prag* (Leipzig: Weber, 1852), 1.

69. Heinrich Klemm, *Vollständiger illustrirter Führer durch ganz Dresden, seine Umgebung und die Sächsisch-Böhmische Schweiz* (Dresden: Klemm, 1858), 26.

70. For example, one of Klemm's illustrations of the second part of his two-part guidebook from 1858, the Felsenthor im Uttewalder Grund (45), is also found in *Cray's Reiseführer: Dresden und die Sächsische Schweiz* (Berlin: Berliner Verlagsanstalt, 1890), 13.

71. It is interesting that the area is often referred to as Saxon-Bohemian or Bohemian-Saxon in travel guides and other writings, as if there were no border between the two areas. This designation even continues after German national unification in 1871. Caitlin Murdock in her essay on tourism and identity in this area of Saxony has shown that the borderlands were indeed treated "as a unified landscape, in spite of the political border between Germany and Habsburg Austria," which confirmed the idea that the German nation continued beyond its established borders. Caitlin Murdock, "Tourist Landscapes and Regional Identities in Saxony, 1878–1938" *Central European History* 40 (2007): 600.

72. Ewald Christian Victorin Dietrich, *Der treue Führer in der Böhmisch-Sächsischen Schweiz* (Prag, Leitmeritz, Teplitz: Medau, 1839), 5. "Seit mehr als dreißig Jahren ist die böhmisch-sächsische Schweiz oder das böhmisch-sächsische Elbehochland der Gegenstand der Bewunderung des In- und Auslandes geworden.// Sie zu besuchen, gehört jetzt, so zu sagen, zum Tone der großen Welt."

73. Murdock, "Tourist Landscapes," 596.

74. Illustration in Dietrich, *Der treue Führer*, 96–97.

75. Staatsbetrieb Sachsenforst, "Der Nationalpark Sächsische Schweiz als regionaler Wirschaftsfaktor," *Schriftenreihe des Nationalparks Sächsische Schweiz* 6 (2010): 16.

76. William Makepeace Thackeray, *The Newcomes* (1854). Chapter 35, "Across the Alps," http://www.gutenberg.org/files/7467/7467-h/7467-h.htm#link2HCH0035; in the novel, two stereotypical international Dresden favorites are also mentioned, pointing to the start of the kitschification of the location and its treasures: the Sixteen Madonna (chapter 30) and Dresden porcelain knick-knacks, fiercely collected by Mrs. Clive: "What corner cupboards there were filled with Dresden gimcracks,

which it was a part of this little woman's business in life to purchase!" (chapter 63). See also James Buzard, *The Beaten Track: European Tourism, Literature, and the Ways to "Culture," 1800–1918* (Oxford: Oxford University Press, 1993), 88.

77. Henry Adams, "To Charles Francis Adams, Jr., Dresden. June 7, 1859," *The Letters of Henry Adams, 1858–1892* (Massachusetts Historical Society, 1982), 46.

78. Susanne Gänshirt-Heinemann, "'Fremde' in Dresden," in *Geschichte der Stadt Dresden: Von der Reichsgründung bis zur Gegenwart*, ed. Holger Starke (Stuttgart: Theiss, 2006), 234–42; Ralf Richter, "Die Geschichte der 'Englischen Kolonie' in Dresden," *Dresdner Hefte* 70 (2002): 47–55; Valerija Schälike, "Die Russisch-Orthodoxe Kirche in Dresden und ihre Gemeinde," *Dresdner Hefte* 74 (2003): 72–77.

79. Henry M. Field, *Summer Pictures: From Copenhagen to Venice* (New York: Sheldon, 1859), 182–83.

80. John Quincy Adams, *Memoirs of John Quincy Adams*, vol. 1 (Philadelphia: Lippincott, 1874), 229.

81. Adams, *Memoirs*, 235.

82. Washington Irving, *The Journals of Washington Irving*, vol. 1, ed. William Trent and George Hellman (Boston: The Bibliophile Society, 1919), 175, 151, 160.

83. Irving, *The Journals*, 142, 189.

84. Irving, *The Journals*, 145. Jean Paul (Johann Paul Friedrich Richter) was actually fifty-nine at the time of this encounter. The writer was very close to his dog, the poodle Ponto.

85. Irving, *The Journals*, 134, 155, 196.

86. Wayne Franklin, *James Fenimore Cooper: The Early Years* (New Haven: Yale University Press, 2007), 395.

87. Entry from November 22, 1835. Quoted in Thomas Adam and Gisela Mettele, eds., *Two Boston Brahmins in Goethe's Germany: The Travel Journals of Anna and George Ticknor* (Plymouth: Lexington Books, 2009), 103–4.

88. Eberhard Brüning, "Saxony Is a Prosperous and Happy Country," in *Traveling Between Worlds: German-American Encounters*, ed. Thomas Adam and Ruth Gross (Arlington: University of Texas Press, 2006), 20–50.

89. Entry from May 11, 1845, in J. Bayard Taylor, *Views Afoot* (New York: Wiley and Putnam, 1846), http://www.gutenberg.org/cache/epub/11535/pg11535-images.html

90. Thomas Adam, "Travel, Gender, and Identity," in *Crossing the Atlantic: Travel and Travel Writing in Modern Times*, ed. Thomas Adam and Nils Roemer (College Station: Texas A&M Press, 2011), 204–5.

91. *Dr. Lahmann's Sanatorium Weisser Hirsch in Weisser Hirsch bei Dresden: Prospekt und Jahresbericht*, 29th edition (1912), 7, 14. "Lebensreform," "Schäden einer 'unnatürlichen und naturwidrigen' Lebensweise."

92. Andrea Dietrich, "Die Entwicklung der Stadt Dresden zu einer Tourismusmetropole von den Anfängen bis zum Vorabend des Ersten Weltkriegs" (PhD diss., Hochschule für Verkehrswesen, Leipzig, 1992), 208–10.

93. Gustav Schumann, *Dresden. Der lustige Baedeker*, vol. 2 (Stuttgart: Schwabacher'sche Verlagsbuchhandlung, 1888), 65–66.

94. Sigmund Freud, "Aus einem Brief an Martha Bernays vom 20.12.1883," in

Zukunft seit 1560. Die Anthologie, ed. Karin Kolb, Gilbert Lupfer, and Martin Roth (Dresden: Staatliche Kunstsammlungen, 2010), 180. "Ich hätte es gerne mitgenommen, aber es waren zu viel Leute da, Engländerinnen, die kopierten, Engländerinnen, die saßen und leise sprachen, Engländerinnen, die gingen und schauten."

95. Gänshirt-Heinemann, "'Fremde' in Dresden," 235.

96. Gänshirt-Heinemann, "'Fremde' in Dresden," 236.

97. *Letter from Theodore Roosevelt to Theodore Roosevelt*, July 12, 1873. Theodore Roosevelt Collection. MS Am 1834.1 (338A). Houghton Library, Harvard University, Theodore Roosevelt Digital Library, Dickinson State University, http://www.theodorerooseveltcenter.org/Research/Digital-Library/Record.aspx?libID=o283140

98. *Letter from Theodore Roosevelt to Theodore Roosevelt*, July 12, 1873, and July 20, 1873, Theodore Roosevelt Collection. MS Am 1785.2 (114A). Houghton Library, Harvard University, Theodore Roosevelt Digital Library, Dickinson State University, http://www.theodorerooseveltcenter.org/Research/Digital-Library/Record.aspx?libID=o280757

99. *Letter from Theodore Roosevelt to Mr. Godey*, September 23, 1873, Theodore Roosevelt Collection. MS Am 1540 (358). Houghton Library, Harvard University. Theodore Roosevelt Digital Library. Dickinson State University, http://www.theodorerooseveltcenter.org/Research/Digital-Library/Record.aspx?libID=o280113

100. Verein zur Förderung Dresdens und des Fremdenverkehrs, 1898–1912, Ref. Nr. 8.58–116, Stadtarchiv Dresden, http://archiv.dresden.de/detail.aspx?ID=1274008

101. For an in-depth description of the Dresden Steamship Company and its development, see the publication *Elbeschifffahrt und Weiße Flotte, Dresdner Hefte* 105 (2011).

102. *175 Jahre Leipzig-Dresdner Eisenbahn, Dresdner Hefte* 117 (2014); see particularly the contributions by Joachim Breuninger and Dana Runge.

103. By 1880 the Kleindeutsche Reich owned 33,838 km of tracks, which by 1910 had increased to 61,209 km in the German Reich. Rüdiger Hachtmann, *Tourismusgeschichte* (Göttingen: UTB Vandenhoeck & Ruprecht, 2007), 72.

104. Hachtmann, *Tourismusgeschichte*, 75.

105. *Illustrirter Dresden-Prager-Führer*, 264. "Die Bedeutung dieser Bahn ist in kommerzieller, strategischer und kulturgeschichtlicher Beziehung von der umfassendsten Wichtigkeit. [. . .] Sie befördert die Verschmelzung der beiderseitigen Interessen Sachsens und Österreichs und macht insbesondere Sachsen zum Mittelgliede einer großartigen Verbindung zwischen dem Norden und Süden, zwischen dem Oriente und dem fernen Amerika."

106. Susanne Müller, *Die Welt des Baedekers: Eine Medienkulturgeschichte des Reiseführers 1830–1945* (Frankfurt: Campus, 2012), 144. The philosopher Dolf Sternberger saw this emphasis on the panoramic view as a typical development of the nineteenth century, and the historian Wolfgang Schivelbusch has directly linked this perception to the rise of train travel during this time. Dolf Sternberger, *Panorama oder Ansichten vom 19. Jahrhundert* (Hamburg: Goverts Verlag, 1938); Wolfgang Schivelbusch, *The Railway Journey* (Oakland: University of California Press, 1986).

107. Gabriela Christmann, *Dresdens Glanz, Stolz der Dresdner* (Wiesbaden: Springer 2004), 130.

108. Christmann, *Dresdens Glanz*, 131. Christmann refers to the text by Schumann (1903), *Dresden als Kunst-, Industrie und Fremdenstadt.*

109. Christmann, *Dresdens Glanz*, 84–85.

110. Otto Richter, *Dresden sonst und jetzt*, 1905 (Dresden: Edition Sächsische Zeitung, 2007).

111. Otto Richter, *Dresden sonst und jetzt*, no page numbers. "Möge das Werkchen die Einsicht verbreiten helfen, daß es eine dankbare Aufgabe unsers Geschlechts ist, die Schöpfungen der Vorfahren zu hüten und gegenüber dem Ansturme neuzeitlicher Bedürfnisse den geschichtlichen Charakter unserer Stadt nach Möglichkeit zu wahren."

112. The numbers were published by the Statistisches Bureau Dresden, later Statistisches Amt der Stadt Dresden. The yearly publications changed titles and formats several times: *Statistischer Jahresbericht der Stadt Dresden, Statistisches Jahrbuch der Stadt Dresden* (1899–1924), *Dresden in Zahlen* (1925–1937; 1956–1964; 1965–1968; 1992–2002). Numbers marked with "*" stem from reports by the Förderverein. *Rechenschaftsbericht des Vereins zur Förderung Dresdens und des Fremdenverkehrs in Dresden.* For the indicated years, the club had received them from the Statistische Bureau der Stadt Dresden, later called Statistisches Amt der Stadt Dresden. In Ref. Nr. 8.58–116, Stadtarchiv Dresden.

113. Verein zur Förderung Dresdens und des Fremdenverkehrs, *Rechenschaftsbericht des Vereins zur Förderung Dresdens und des Fremdenverkehrs in Dresden auf die Zeit von 1. April 1901 bis 31. März 1902* (Dresden, 1902), 7–8. In Ref. Nr. 8.58–116, Stadtarchiv Dresden.

114. In 1906, ads were put into the *New York Herald*, which included a variety of pictures. Verein zur Förderung Dresdens und des Fremdenverkehrs, *Rechenschaftsbericht des Vereins zur Förderung Dresdens und des Fremdenverkehrs in Dresden auf die Zeit von 1. April 1906 bis 31. März 1907* (Dresden, 1907), 4. In Ref. Nr. 8.58–116, Stadtarchiv Dresden.

115. Verein zur Förderung Dresdens und des Fremdenverkehrs, *Rechenschaftsbericht des Vereins zur Förderung Dresdens und des Fremdenverkehrs in Dresden auf die Zeit von 1. April 1902 bis 31. März 1903* (Dresden 1903), 13. In Ref. Nr. 8.58–116, Stadtarchiv Dresden.

116. Statistisches Amt der Stadt Dresden, *Die Verwaltung der Stadt Dresden 1927* (Dresden: Statistisches Amt, 1929), 28.

117. Statistisches Amt der Stadt Dresden, *Die Verwaltung der Stadt Dresden 1933* (Dresden: Statistisches Amt, 1935), 26; Verein zur Förderung Dresdens und des Fremdenverkehrs, 1898–1912, Ref. Nr. 8.58–116, Stadtarchiv Dresden.

118. Leaflets designed by Prof. Paul Naumann, 1906. Verein zur Förderung Dresdens und des Fremdenverkehrs, 1898–1912, Ref. Nr. 8.58–116, Stadtarchiv Dresden.

119. Peter Leuter, "Gruss aus Dresden: Verlage, Themen, Künstler, Dokumente," *Dresdner Geschichtsbuch* 4 (1998): 195.

120. Peter Leuter, "Gruss aus Dresden," 196.

121. Marion Marwick, "Postcards from Malta: Image, Consumption, Context" *Annals of Tourism Research* 28, no. 2 (2001): 417.

122. Christina Bonarou refers to this process as a "poetics of travel" (44). Christina Bonarou, "The Poetics of Travel through Unravelling Visual Representations on Postcards: A Critical Semiotics Analysis," *Journal of Tourism, Heritage & Services Marketing* 7, no. 1 (2021): 44–53, 44, https://doi.org/10.5281/zenodo.4519317

123. John Urry, *The Tourist Gaze: Leisure and Travel in Contemporary Societies* (London: Sage, 1990).

124. Claire Colomb and Ares Kalandides, "The 'be Berlin' Campaign: Old Wine in New Bottles or Innovative Form of Participatory Place Branding?," in *Towards Effective Place Brand Management: Branding European Cities and Regions*, ed. Gregory John Ashworth and Mihalis Kavaratzis (Cheltenham: Edward Elgar, 2010), 173–90.

125. Rat der Stadt Dresden, *Das Buch der Stadt Dresden* (Dresden: Industrie- und Verkehrsverlag, 1924–1930).

126. Statistisches Amt der Landeshauptstadt Dresden, *Dresden in Zahlen 1937* (Dresden: Statistisches Amt der Landeshauptstadt Dresden, 1939), 72.

127. Kristin Semmens in *Seeing Hitler's Germany: Tourism in the Third Reich* (New York: Palgrave, 2005), 43–46, points out how brochures and leaflets were more and more centrally regulated. The emphasis on National Socialist symbols and specific National Socialist tourist sites, however, depended very much on the individual place. Munich, Nuremberg, and Berlin, for example, started to build specific tourist reputations for the history of the National Socialist movement and its institutions. In the case of Dresden, however, this connection was less emphasized and National Socialist insignia were not used as frequently.

128. See chapter 4 for a more detailed analysis of Dresden's National Socialist past.

129. Jan Schenk, "Verbrannte Orte. Idee, Ziele und Entwicklungen des Citizen-Science-Projekts zu den Bücherverbrennungen 1933," in *Erinnerungskultur digital: Herausforderungen und Chancen für die historische und politische Bildung*, ed. Thomas Bürger and Roland Löffler (Dresden: Sächsische Landeszentrale für Politische Bildung, 2024), 251, https://doi.org/10.25366/2024.90

130. "Dresdens doppelte Bücherverbrennung? Oliver Reinhard im Gespräch mit Mike Schmeitzner," posted March 5, 2021, by Stadtbibliothek Dresden, youtube.com, https://www.youtube.com/watch?v=U6aOxDCO8_U&list=PLhJAj5cU5qWEf_-frr0xyU6ALn274qsAB&index=5

131. Norbert Haase, "Bücherverbrennung und 'Säuberung' Dresdner Bibliotheken," *Dresdner Hefte* 77 (2004): 52–53.

132. Christoph Zuschlag, "Die Dresdner Ausstellung 'Entartete Kunst' 1933 bis 1937," in *Geschichte der Stadt Dresden: Von der Reichsgründung bis zur Gegenwart*, ed. Holger Starke (Stuttgart: Thiessen, 2006): 482–83.

133. Die Deutsche Arbeitsfront, *Urlaubsfahrten und Wanderungen 1938* (Stuttgart: N.S. Gemeinschaft "Kraft durch Freude" Gau Württemberg-Hohenzollern, 1938), 3. "[Kraft durch Freude] erschließt ihm sein Vaterland, bringt ihm dessen Schönheit, seine Kulturdenkmäler nahe und erzieht ihn so zum Stolz und zur Liebe seiner Heimat gegenüber."

134. Die Deutsche Arbeitsfront, *Urlaubsfahrten und Wanderungen 1938*, 112.

135. Die Deutsche Arbeitsfront, *Urlaubsfahrten und Wanderungen 1938*, 110.

136. Statistisches Amt der Stadt Dresden, *Verwaltung der Stadt Dresden, 1933*, 60. "Gräuelpropaganda über Deutschland."

137. Semmens, *Seeing Hitler's Germany*, 18–19.

138. Reich Committee for Tourist Travel, *Germany: Periodical for Scenery, Travel, and Touring* (Berlin: Reich Committee for Tourist Travel, 1934).

139. Verkehrsamt der Stadt Dresden, *Berlin-Dresden in 1 ½ Stunden* (Dresden: Dr. Güntzsche Stiftung, 1936).

140. Statistisches Amt der Landeshauptstadt Dresden, *Dresden in Zahlen 1937*, 72. Rudy Koshar reports that the number of international visitors to Germany more than doubled between 1931 and 1938. In Dresden the situation looks to be different. A dip in international tourism can be observed in 1933–35, with 32,140 at its lowest in 1933. By 1936 the numbers of international travelers resemble again those of 1930–31. Koshar, *German Travel Cultures*, 129.

141. Deutscher Organisationsausschuß des Weltkongresses für Freizeit und Erholung, *Amtlicher Führer zum Weltkongress Freizeit und Erholung: Hamburg 23.-30. Juli 1936* (1936), 140. "In all diesen genialen Männern obersächsischen Geblütes spiegelt sich ein Stück Deutschtum, ein Stück art- und volksgebundener Schöpfung wider." Not all the listed artists were born or grew up in Saxony, but this fact is neglected in the description.

142. *Deutschland—Zeitschrift für Industrie, Handel und Schiffahrt* 3, no. 8 (Hamburg: Adolf Ernst Schultze Verlag, 1940), 33. "die Stadt [hat] sich alle jene Vorzüge zu bewahren gewußt, die ihr ihre anerkannte internationale Geltung eingetragen haben. Weder der Anmut ihres einzigartigen Stadtbildes noch der unvergleichlichen Schönheit ihrer Umgebung hat der Aufstieg zur Industriestadt irgendwie Abbruch zu tun vermocht. [. . .] Industrie einerseits und wissenschaftliche wie künstlerische Leistung andererseits [. . . können] als verschiedene Regungen und Fähigkeiten ein und desselben Körpers harmonisch zur Entfaltung kommen."

143. *Deutschland—Zeitschrift für Industrie, Handel und Schiffahrt*, 56. "Die Romantik des schwärmerischen Seufzers, der von der Elbe aus das Land, wo die Zitrone blüht, mit der Seele sucht, ist so zeitlos wie ursprünglich. Es ist jenes Gefühl beglückten Sichhingebens an ein vollkommenes Schönes, das früher oder später jeden Wanderer durch Dresden erfüllt, auch heute noch, da ein anderers Banner über den Türmen dieser wundersamen Stadt weht."

144. "Dresden," Deutsche Wochenschau Nr. 586, 49/1941; Zensur 26.11.1941. Internet Archive, https://archive.org/details/grmnnr/The+German+Newsreel+-+Die+Deutsche+Wochenschau+(1939-1945)/German+Newsreel+586+-+November+26%2C+1941.mp4

145. Kay Hoffmann, "Sinfonie des Krieges: Die Deutsche Wochenschau im Zweiten Weltkrieg," in *Geschichte des dokumentarischen Films in Deutschland, Band 3 "Drittes Reich" 1933–1945*, ed. Peter Zimmermann and Kay Hoffmann (Stuttgart: Reclam, 2005), 646–47.

Chapter 3

1. For example: Anne Fuchs in *After the Dresden Bombing: Pathways of Memory, 1945 to the Present* (London: Palgrave, 2012), 8; David Crew, *Bodies and Ruins* (Ann Arbor: University of Michigan Press, 2017), 156ff.

2. Historian Daniel Fischer points to the importance of looking beyond the of-

ficial discourses in the GDR and their general mandates from above. One needs to explore the local realizations of these specifications from below. This approach reveals tensions in these relationships which led to local variations. Daniel Fischer, *Stadtbürgerlicher Eigensinn in der DDR?* (Leipzig: Leipziger Universitätsverlag, 2022), 13.

3. Kurt Schaarschuch, *Bilddokument Dresden, 1933–1945* (Dresden: Rat der Stadt Dresden, 1945).

4. See Sylvia Ziegner, "Der Bildband *Dresden—eine Kamera klagt* an von Richard Peter senior. Teil der Erinnerungskultur Dresden" (PhD diss., Marburg an der Lahn, 2012), and Friedrich Reichert, *Foto Schaarschuch—Dresden: Bildbericht 1927 bis 1955* (Dresden: Stadtmuseum Dresden, 1996). Since Schaarschuch had never officially joined the National Socialist Party, he was able to receive a work permit as a photographer by the Soviet occupation forces as early as June 1945, which allowed him to undertake the work on the photo book. From 1933 to 1945, Schaarschuch was officially registered as an advertisement photographer, and several of the pictures of the photo book had been used for materials put together for Nazi institutions. For instance, Schaarschuch provided the Dresden photographs for an advertisement brochure on Dresden from 1937. It had been ordered by the local chapter of the German Labor Front, which was the umbrella organization for such subgroups as the Kraft durch Freude (Strength through Joy) program. In addition, Ludger Derenthal has established that Schaarschuch also worked on the National Socialist picture book by Kurt Herzog, *Wir marschierten nach Nürnberg* (We Marched to Nuremburg) (Dresden: Kommunalverlag Sachsen, 1938). Ludger Derenthal, *Bilder der Trümmer- und Aufbaujahre* (Marburg: Jonas Verlag, 1999), 67.

5. Reichert, *Foto Schaarschuch*, 11. In the case of the Frauenkirche, the photograph of the undestroyed church with Luther statue was taken most likely as late as 1940 or 1941, after the war had begun.

6. Schaarschuch, *Bilddokument*, no page numbers. "Nazikriegstreiber."

7. Schaarschuch, *Bilddokument*, no page numbers. "Die Trümmer einer der schönsten Städte der Welt rufen die aufbauwilligen Kräfte zum Neuaufbau."

8. Schaarschuch, *Bilddokument*, no page numbers. "dennoch Wiederaufbau 1945."

9. For a publication history see Reichert, *Foto Schaarschuch*, 5, 14–15.

10. Tom Allbeson, *Photography, Reconstruction and the Cultural History of the Postwar European City* (London: Routledge, 2021), 23.

11. Kate Palmer Albers and Jordan Bear, "Photography's Time Zones," in *Before-and-After Photography: Histories and Contexts*, ed. Jordan Bear and Kate Palmer Albers (London: Bloomsbury, 2017), 4.

12. See also Crew, *Bodies and Ruins*, 149; Derenthal, *Bilder der Trümmer und Aufbaujahre*, 66.

13. Paul Morgan, "Towards a Developmental Theory of Place Attachment," *Journal of Environmental Psychology* 30, no. 1 (2010): 20.

14. Arijit Sen and Lisa Silverman, *Making Place: Space and Embodiment in the City* (Bloomington: Indiana University Press, 2013), 8.

15. Melinda Milligan, "Displacement and Identity Discontinuity: The Role of Nostalgia in Establishing New Identity Categories," *Symbolic Interactions* 26, no. 3 (2003): 382.

16. See also Susanne Vees-Gulani, "The Ruined Picture Postcard: Dresden's Visually Encoded History and the Television Drama *Dresden*," *New German Critique* 38, no. 1 (2011): 85–113.

17. Derenthal, *Bilder der Trümmer und Aufbaujahre*, 65.

18. Schaarschuch, *Bilddokument*, no page numbers. "Dresdens Maler."

19. Pictured is the painter Ernst Schöne (1902–1952). Ziegner, "Der Bildband Dresden," 66.

20. Derenthal, *Bilder der Trümmer und Aufbaujahre*, 67–68. See also Jörn Glasenapp, "Nach dem Brand: Überlegungen zur deutschen Trümmerfotografie," *Fotogeschichte* 91 (2004): 47–64.

21. Allbeson, *Photography*, 63.

22. See, for example, "Dresden mahnt zum verstärkten Kampf um den Frieden" *Sächsische Zeitung*, February 11, 1950, 1; "Gemeinsamer Kampf gegen die Verbrecher Deutschlands" *Sächsische Zeitung*, February 13, 1950, 1; "Einheit bedeutet Frieden und Aufbau" *Sächsische Zeitung*, February 9, 1951, 1. In 1951, the slogan "Prevent a new February 13, 1945: Germans from East and West Come Together" ("Verhindert einen neuen 13. Februar 1945: Deutsche aus Ost und West an einen Tisch") was used consistently during the commemoration events as well as in newspapers (*Sächsische Zeitung*, February 7, 1951, 1).

23. Richard Peter, *Dresden: Eine Kamera klagt an* (Dresden: Dresdener Verlagsgesellschaft, 1950). Overall, the volume sold well, although Peter's claim that the entire edition was sold out within two and a half years is one of the many embellishments of the past in Peter's memoirs. In reality, the first edition became only unavailable by the end of 1956. Sylvia Ziegner and Jens Bove: "Beruf Arbeiterfotograf: Zum Werk und zur Rezeption von Richard Peter sen," in *Die Eroberung der beobachtenden Maschinen: Zur Arbeiterfotografie der Weimarer Republik*, ed. Wolfgang Hesse (Leipzig: Leipziger Universitätsverlag 2012), 355.

24. See chapter 1 for more detail.

25. Peter, *Dresden: Eine Kamera klagt an*, no page numbers. "Aufbau."

26. When Peter's work was reissued in 1980, the final section on rebuilding was significantly expanded with fourteen additional photographs from the years 1956 through 1973. The focus of the work thus shifted some of the attention away from the destruction to emphasize more strongly the new beginnings, the achievements in rebuilding and reimagining Dresden's cityscape, as well as its political landscape. In addition, this edition showed Peter's "View from the Town Hall Tower" on its cover, responding to the iconic status the photograph had achieved. In 1982, the photobook was reissued again, unchanged. Jens Bove and Sebastian Lux, "Erlösung durch Sozialismus: Der Bildband *Dresden—Eine Kamera klagt an* von Richard Peter sen," in *1945-Köln und Dresden: Fotografien von Hermann Claasen und Richard Peter, sen*, ed. LVR-Landesmuseum Bonn and Deutsche Fotothek in der SLUB Dresden (Bonn: Landschaftsverband Rheinland, 2015), 43–46.

27. Rat der Stadt Dresden, *Du und Deine Stadt: 5 Jahre Aufbauarbeit der Stadtverwaltung Dresden* (Dresden: Dresdener Verlagsgesellschaft, 1950).

28. Andrew Demshuk, *Three Cities after Hitler: Redemptive Reconstruction Across Cold War Borders* (Pittsburgh: University of Pittsburgh Press, 2021), 59–60.

29. Rat der Stadt Dresden, *Du und Deine Stadt*, 1.

30. Rat der Stadt Dresden, *Du und Deine Stadt*, 1. "Dresden im Spiel der Lichter."

31. Rat der Stadt Dresden, *Du und Deine Stadt*, 6–13.

32. Kalevi Korpela, "Place-Identity as a Product of Environmental Self-Regulation," *Journal of Environmental Psychology* 9 (1989): 241–56.

33. Eleanor Ratcliffe and Kalevi M. Korpela, "Memory and Place Attachment as Predictors of Imagined Restorative Perceptions of Favourite Places," *Journal of Environmental Psychology* 48 (2016): 129.

34. Komitee für die 750-Jahr-Feier der Stadt Dresden, *Thesen und Rahmenplan für die 750-Jahr-Feier der Stadt Dresden* (Dresden: 1955), 7.

35. Komitee für die 750-Jahr-Feier, *Thesen und Rahmenplan*, 6. "*Was einst der fortschrittliche Teil unserer Bürger zu allen Zeiten der Geschichte erhofft und ersehnt, wofür sie gekämpft und geopfert haben, ist in der Deutschen Demokratischen Republik, ist im Dresden der Arbeiter- und Bauernmacht, Wirklichkeit geworden.*"

36. Friedrich Reichert, "750-Jahr-Feier Dresdens im Juni 1956," in *Dresdner Geschichtsbuch* 1, ed. Stadtmuseum Dresden (Dresden: DZA Verlag, 1995), 195. "Flucht in die Vergangenheit."

37. Komitee für die 750-Jahr-Feier der Stadt Dresden, *Thesen und Rahmenplan*, 3; see also Fischer, *Stadtbürgerlicher Eigensinn*, 67.

38. Fischer, *Stadtbürgerlicher Eigensinn*, 71–73.

39. Ulrich Rosseaux, "Das ambivalente Jubiläum: die 750-Jahr-Feier Dresdens 1956," *Dresdner Hefte* 87 (2006): 52–55.

40. Rosseaux, "Das ambivalente Jubiläum," 50–59.

41. Portfolio-Höhne-Pohl-750-Jahr-Feier-Dresden, Deutsche Fotothek, 1956, http://www.deutschefotothek.de/documents/obj/90012588

42. Quoted in Reichert, "750-Jahr-Feier Dresdens im Juni 1956," 202. "dass der erwartete Gästestrom nicht eingetreten ist."

43. Harald Marx, "Dresden und die Wiedereröffnung der Gemäldegalerie 1956," in *Geschichte der Stadt Dresden*, vol. 3, ed. Holger Starke (Stuttgart: Theiss, 2006), 688–690. The west wing was completed by 1960.

44. The *New York Times* reports under the heading, "Dresden Holds a Fete: East German Art Center Is Marking 750th Anniversary" on Dresden's "month-long" celebration, but only highlights the opening of the rebuilt gallery with the returned paintings. *New York Times*, June 3, 1956, 26.

45. April Eisman, "Symbolic Erasures and Populist Discontent: The Post-War Rebuilding of Historic Dresden" *Monatshefte* 114, no. 1 (2022): 33–34.

46. Eisman, "Symbolic Erasures," 34.

47. Haley Schneider, "Deliberative Topoi and the Pull of the Future: Bridging Disparate Visions of Dresden Elbe Valley," *Rhetoric Society Quarterly* 49, no. 5 (2019): 498. These negotiations between past and future in Dresden did not stop with the end of the GDR. Schneider here discusses the building of a bridge in Dresden that led to the withdrawal of UNESCO's designation of the Elbe Valley as World Cultural Heritage site. Even though the parties argued from the same vantage point, Dresden's significant past, they envisioned different futures for the site as a consequence of Dresden's history.

48. Lothar Kempe, "Introduction," in *Dresden*, Referat Fremdenverkehr beim Rat der Stadt Dresden (Dresden: VEB Landesdruckerei Sachsen, 1961), no page numbers. Quoted is the English language text of the booklet.

49. Kempe, "Introduction," no page numbers.

50. "Dresden lebt—und ganz Deutschland wird leben," *Neues Deutschland*, February 13, 1955, 1. "unersetzliche, der ganzen Welt heilige Kulturwerte."

51. *Dresden. Fotografiert von Willy Pritsche und anderen. Mit einem Geleitwort von Ludwig Renn* (Dresden: Sachsenverlag Dresden, 1958).

52. *Dresden* (1958), 21–22.

53. *Dresden* (1958), 21.

54. Ludwig Renn, "Geleitwort," in *Dresden. Fotografiert von Willy Pritsche und anderen* (Dresden: Sachsenverlag Dresden, 1958), 8–10. "Dresden, du gründurchschlungene Stadt, in der man über der Mühe nie die Kunst des Lebens vergaß, du wirst dich weiterplagen, aber auch Freuden genießen und Fremden Wertvolles reichen [. . .] Nur Frieden mußt du haben, um wieder zu blühen, vielleicht sogar schöner, sicher aber gesünder, als du je warst"; "Ihr Betrachter dieses Buches, tragt seine Bilder in alle Welt, nicht nur vom besseren Geiste Deutschlands Zeugnis, auch, um bescheiden und liebenswert den Fremden zu erfreuen."

55. Referat Fremdenverkehr beim Rat der Stadt Dresden, *Dresden* (Dresden: VEB Landesdruckerei Sachsen, 1961), no page numbers.

56. Referat Fremdenverkehr, *Dresden* (1961), no page numbers. Quoted is the English text of the brochure.

57. Rat der Stadt Dresden, *Dresden, Kleine Städtereihe 14* (Leipzig: Brockhaus, 1965), 20. Quoted is the English text of the guide.

58. Referat Fremdenverkehr, *Dresden* (1961), no page numbers.

59. Referat Fremdenverkehr, *Dresden* (1961), no page numbers.

60. "Bericht über den Stand der Arbeiten auf dem Gebiete des FREMDENVERKEHRS vom Rat der Stadt Dresden Abteilung Fremdenverkehr," April 21, 1965, Abteilung Internationale Beziehungen und Tourismus Ref Nr. 4.2.12, Sig. 36, Stadtarchiv Dresden.

61. Ref Nr. 4.2.12, Sig. 36, Stadtarchiv Dresden.

62. Rat der Stadt Dresden, *Dresden*, Kleine Städtereihe (1965), 20.

63. Herbert Wotte, Wolfgang Göthel, and Siegfried Hoyer, *Brockhaus Stadtführer Dresden* (Leipzig: Brockhaus, 1968) 30; *Brockhaus-Stadtführer Dresden* (Leipzig: Brockhaus, 1975) 10. "Jahr für Jahr zwei Millionen Touristen [. . .], unter ihnen Tausende ausländische Gäste."

64. Even if one takes into consideration that some guests stayed in private accommodations, it is impossible that the hotels in Dresden, both those for national and those for international tourists, were able to accommodate such a high number of overnight stays, at least before the Interhotels (for foreign guests only) on the Prager Straße were completed. By 1970, the hotel guide for Dresden lists 640 beds for the Interhotel Newa, which had just been opened at one of the corners of the Prager Straße, and 1,917 beds for the Interhotel Prager Straße, the ensemble of three high rises completed shortly before in 1969. Most other hotels offered significantly fewer than 100 beds. Hauptdirektion des volkseigenen Einzelhandels, *Hotelführer der DDR 1970* (Konsum Verlag: Karl-Marx Stadt, 1970), 48–50.

65. Seymus Baloglu and Ken W. McCleary, "A Model of Destination Image Formation," *Annals of Tourism Research* 26, no. 4 (1999): 868–97.

66. Sabrina Francesconi, "Images and Writing in Tourist Brochures," *Journal of Tourism and Cultural Change* 9, no. 4 (2011): 349.

67. Rat der Stadt Dresden, *Dresden* (Dresden: Grafischer Großbetrieb Völkerfreundschaft Dresden, 1960s).

68. For example, according to reports on the city government meetings in Dresden, the Commission for Tourism and Vacation reported that it "inspected and worked through" the Dresden volume in the Kleine Städtereihe (1965) before it was to be printed by the Brockhaus publisher in Leipzig. The representatives also mention their preparation of another city guide, which most likely refers to the Brockhaus Stadtführer Dresden. Ref Nr. 4.2.12, Sig. 36, Stadtarchiv Dresden.

69. Rat der Stadt Dresden, *Dresden, Kleine Städtereihe.*

70. Wotte, Göthel, and Hoyer, *Brockhaus Stadtführer Dresden.*

71. Wotte, Göthel, and Hoyer, *Brockhaus Stadtführer Dresden*, 74.

72. Matthias Lerm, *Abschied vom alten Dresden: Verluste historischer Bausubstanz nach 1945* (Rostock: Hintsorff Verlag, 2000). Lerm here offers details on the decade-long discourse about the removal of the Sophienkirche.

73. Quoted in Lerm, *Abschied vom alten Dresden*, 187. "Wir haben eine sozialistische Stadt und da muß die Sophienkirche fallen."

74. Matthias Lerm, *Abschied vom alten Dresden*, 186–87, 208–11.

75. Quoted in Lerm, *Abschied vom alten Dresden*, 186–87. "Ich erinnere nur daran, wo Walter Ulbricht in Dresden war und sagte, wenn ich mit meinem Auto an der Sophienkirche vorbeifahre, möchte ich das Ding am liebsten umfahren."

76. Matthias Lerm, *Abschied vom alten Dresden*, 186–87, 208–11.

77. Paul Stangl, *Risen from Ruins: The Cultural Politics of Rebuilding East Berlin* (Stanford: Stanford University Press, 2017).

78. It was experienced as a "Schandfleck." See, for example, the newspaper articles by Luisa Schlitter "So war's damals im Fresswürfel," *Bild Regional: Dresden*, April 4, 2012, https://www.bild.de/regional/dresden/ddr/so-wars-damals-im-fresswuerfel-23486988.bild.html; Lars Kühl in sächsische.de, "Lieblingskneipe am Postplatz," December 17, 2017, https://www.saechsische.de/lieblingskneipe-am-postplatz-3566975.html; Holger Naumann, "Das Ende des Fresswürfels," saechsische.de, February 18, 2017, https://www.saechsische.de/das-ende-des-fresswuerfels-3616313.html

79. Fritz Löffler, *Das alte Dresden: Geschichte seiner Bauten* (Dresden: Sachsenverlag, 1955).

80. Throughout the 1950s and 1960s, Löffler was repeatedly attacked by mayor and local politician Walter Weidauer, who was a long-time critic of the preservationist, for his lack of commitment to socialist ideas and interpretations. For one example, see "Öffentliche Sitzung der Stadtverordnetenversammlung," Beschluss-Nr.: 94/67—113/67 Ref. Nr. 4.2.1–138, January 26, 1967. Stadtarchiv Dresden. Despite these attacks, Löffler was able to remain in his position and published in East and West Germany about Dresden's past cityscape.

81. Renatus Deckert and Michael Wüstefeld, "Gespräch mit Michael Wüstefeld," in *Die wüste Stadt: Sieben Dichter über Dresden*, ed. Renatus Deckert (Frankfurt: Insel Verlag, 2005), 168. "Es ist eine Dresdner Eigenheit, ungebrochen auf der Geschichte der Stadt zu beharren und allen Neuheiten [. . .] mit Skepsis oder gar Ablehnung zu begegnen."

82. Deckert and Wüstefeld, "Gespräch mit Michael Wüstefeld," 161.

83. Renatus Deckert and Thomas Rosenlöcher, "Gespräch mit Thomas Rosen-

löcher," in *Die wüste Stadt: Sieben Dichter über Dresden*, ed. Renatus Deckert (Frankfurt: Insel Verlag, 2005), 128–29. For a detailed look at Löffler's book and its influence, see Ingrid Wenzkat, "Fritz Löffler: Das alte Dresden," in *Geschichte der Stadt Dresden*, vol. 3, ed. Holger Starke (Stuttgart: Theiss, 2005), 629–34.

84. Gerhard Schill, "Perle des Aufbaus—dem Frieden verpflichtet," *Sächsische Zeitung*, Beilage zur festlichen Wiedereröffnung der Semperoper, February 14, 1985.

85. Erich Honecker, "Ehrendes Gedenken für die Toten des 13. Februar 1945 in Dresden," *Sächsische Zeitung*, February 14, 1985, 3. "Heute ist Dresden eine blühende aufstrebende Stadt. [. . .]. Am heutigen Abend werden wir nun mit der neuen Semperoper eines der traditionsreichsten Opernhäuser Europas wiedereröffnen. [. . .] Es kündet von dem hohen Rang der Kultur in unserem Lande."

86. Gerhard Marx, "Tätigkeitsbericht," February 1, 1985, Ständige Kommission für Erholung und Tourismus, Ref. Nr. 4.2.5. Sig. 32N, Stadtarchiv Dresden.

87. *Merian* was originally published in the Hoffmann und Campe Verlag. Since the year 2000, the magazine is part of the Jahreszeiten Verlag.

88. *Dresden, Merian* 1, no. 12 (Hamburg: Hoffmann und Campe, 1949); *Dresden, Merian* 20, no. 10 (Hamburg: Hoffmann und Campe, 1967); *Dresden, Merian* 48, no. 1 (Hamburg: Hoffmann und Campe, 1995).

89. Grete Swensen and Karoline Daugstad, "Travels in Imaginary Landscapes: An Analysis of Four Cultural Historic Guidebooks," *Belgeo* 3 (2012): 2, http://journals.openedition.org/belgeo/7219

90. Alica Buck, "Reisemagazine im Anthropozän: *Merian* und die Darstellung der Natur," in *Handbuch Zeitschriftenforschung*, ed. Oliver Scheiding and Sabina Fazli (transcript, 2022), 539, 541.

91. Martin Raschke, "Einladung an einen Freund," *Merian* 1, no. 12 (1949): 3–5. "Lieber Freund, wärest Du nur erst hier und könntest all das Schöne, mit mir teilen! So aber kann ich nichts anderes, als Dich bitten, mit mir wenigstens in Gedanken auf einen der Türme zu steigen, um Nähe und Ferne zu betrachten. Spürst Du den Wind? . . . Sieh Dich um! Sieh Dich um! [. . .].
Glaub mir, ich kannte einen Mann, der meinte, hier sei der Mittelpunkt der Welt. Er zeigte mir die Stadt, wie sie sich nachts mit ihren Lichtern im Wasser spiegelte, und den Geruch des sommerlich brackigen Wassers einatmend sagte er: 'Erinnert das nicht an Venedig?'"

92. The text was published even though Raschke had been a convinced National Socialist; not surprisingly the 1938 destruction of the synagogue built by the famous architect Gottfried Semper does not feature in his text.

93. Fritz Diettrich, "Kindheit in Dresden," *Merian* 1, no. 12 (1949): 6. "Was mit einer quälenden Realistik die Kamera tut, darf der denkende Mensch nicht nachahmen, weder beginnen noch vollenden. So möchte ich denn alle, die diese Blätter zur Hand nehmen, nicht betrüben, und mit vordergründigen Darstellungen verstören, sondern behutsam versuchen, durch lose gefügte Erinnerungen eine Fata Morgana zu erzeugen, in der die geliebte Stadt mit ihren noblen Konturen wieder erscheint."

94. Gottfried Fischer-Gravelius, "Begegnungen und Gestalten," *Merian* 12 (1949): 40. "Wir fühlten [. . .] Trauer um das Verlorene, aber auch die Gewißheit, daß auch das Gewesene und Vergangene in einem geheimen Seelenraume der Welt bewahrt und unvergänglich behütet sei."

95. Rolf Engert, "Der Untergang" *Merian* 1, no. 12 (1949): 49–55.

96. Engert, "Der Untergang," 54–55.

97. Ludwig Grote, "Abschied von der Sixtinischen Madonna," *Merian* 1, no. 12 (1949): 93.

98. Grote, "Abschied," 93. "Wir haben mit der Sixtinischen Madonna nicht nur das berühmteste Gemälde der Dresdner Galerie verloren, nicht nur eines der kostbarsten Meisterwerke der Malerei [. . .]. Uns Deutschen war sie noch viel mehr. Sie war ein Gnadenbild [. . .]. Wir haben ihm die göttliche Aura verliehen, die aus der Tiefe unserer Seele, aus unserer Glaubens- und Erlebniskraft geflossen ist."

99. Fritz Löffler, "Das jetzige Stadtbild," *Merian* 1, no. 12 (1949): 76. "Rettet Dresden!"

100. It is important to remember, however, that while some progress was made, rebuilding in East Germany continued far into the time after reunification. It had been hampered throughout by the lack of funds, materials, and changing planning concepts. In contrast, West Germany's rebuilding had generally been completed by the early 1960s.

101. Volker Skierka, the editor-in chief of the *Merian* magazines from 1992 to 1997, tells this story in an address to the readers in the 1995 post-reunification *Merian* on Dresden (*Merian* 48, no. 1 (1995): 3).

102. Sigfried Asche, "Die Residenz der Wettiner," *Merian* 20, no. 10 (1967): 24. "Das blieb so bis 1945. Da erloschen die Lichter."

103. Dorothea Stein, "Figuren aus Meißen," *Merian* 20, no. 10 (1967): 91. "Die Erinnerung ist das einzige Paradies, aus welchem wir nicht getrieben werden können."

104. Peter Härtling, "Eine eingebildete Landschaft," *Merian* 20, no. 10 (1967): 60–61.

105. Härtling, "Eine eingebildete Landschaft," 61. "Es ist keine Stadt, sondern eine eingebildete Landschaft. Im Nachhinein entspringt ihr eine Musik, die ihn mit Heimweh erfüllt. [. . .] Es ist eine Stadt, von der er erzählen kann, die nur er sieht, kein anderer mehr, auch die Cousinen nicht, die aus Dresden schreiben: 'Der Zwinger ist wieder so herrlich wie früher.'"

106. Brigitte Jeremias, "Für die Menschen von Morgen," *Merian* 20, no. 10 (1967): 25–34.

107. Jeremias, "Für die Menschen von Morgen," 26. "nicht gerade glücklich wiederaufgebaut."

108. Jeremias, "Für die Menschen von Morgen," 30. "fremd in dieser Zementöde."

109. Jeremias, "Für die Menschen von Morgen," 30. "vielleicht schaut darum Luther, auf seinem Sockel vor dem Trümmerhaufen am Neumarkt, so unwillig."

110. *Merian* 20, no. 10 (1967): 33.

111. Durs Grünbein, "Corso," *Merian* 20, no. 10 (1995): 7. "Die Aufbauschäden nach dem Krieg mit überbreiten Straßen sind bitter schwer zu korrigieren."

112. Herbert Riehl-Heyse, "Der Aufbau," *Merian* 48, no. 1 (1995): 52. "Ein paar [. . .] Häuser sind [. . .] zustande gekommen, angesichts derer jeder Dresden-Freund nur noch sein Haupt verhüllen kann vor Scham—das hätte den Vorteil, daß er dann nicht sehen müßte, wie von der Brühlschen Terrasse her der wunderbare Blick auf die Elbe an der Carola-Brücke durch zwei hässliche Kolosse verstellt wird."

113. Riehl-Heyse, "Der Aufbau," 53.

114. "Sachsens Glanz," *Merian* 48, no 1 (1995): 17. "Dresden war eine Perle des Barocks und eine große europäische Kulturmetropole. Und schickt sich an—nach Jahrzehnten im Abseits—wieder in die erste Reihe der deutschen Städte zu rücken."

115. Volker Skierka, "Das neue alte Elbflorenz," *Merian* 48, no. 1 (1995): 3. "entstand dagegen in harmonischer ost-/westdeutscher Kooperation von Autoren und Fotografen."

116. Friedrich Karl Fromme, "Land und Leute," *Merian* 48, no. 1 (1995): 101. "Die meisten Dresdener nehmen daran inneren Anteil, viele sind froh, daß ihre Stadt, die in einen kleinen, künstlichen Denkmalbezirk und in eine Wohnstadt geteilt zu sein schien, wieder das wird, was sie war: eine Einheit. Für sie ist die Stadt ein beseeltes Gebilde."

117. Grünbein, "Corso," 13–14. "Die altsächsischen Bürgerhäuser im neuen Glanz machen die Plattenbauten von gestern vergessen. Ob Brühlsche Terrasse oder Italienisches Dörfchen—bis in die Einzelheiten wird demnächst das linke Elbufer die alten Veduten aufs Neue als urbane Traumbilder wiederbeleben. Und so sind es die Zeitformen, unmerklich, die sich als erste verwirren. Plusquamperfekt und Futur schieben sich verkehrt ineinander, mit dem Präsens gleitet die Gegenwart an restaurierten Fassaden ab. Schnell, schnell, als sollte ein ganzer Kriegsfilm nun rückwärts laufen, finden die Steine an ihre alten Plätze, richten die Mauern sich wieder auf zu den alten Gebäuden, den neuesten Museumsstücken."

Chapter 4

1. Alexander Walther, "Jewish Anti-Fascism? 'Kristallnacht' Remembrance in the GDR between Propaganda and Jewish Self-Assertion," in *New Perspectives on Kristallnacht: After 80 Years, the Nazi Pogrom in Global Comparison*, ed. Steven J. Ross, Wolf Gruner, and Lisa Ansell (West Lafayette: Purdue University Press, 2019), 259–82.

2. Sven Brajer, *Am Rande Dresdens: Das völkisch-nationale Spektrum einer 'konservativen Kulturstadt' 1879–1933* (Dresden/München: Thelem, 2022), 14. Christine Pieper, "Juden in Sachsen 1933 bis 1945: Ein defizitäres Forschungsfeld," *Medaon* 15 (2014), http://www.medaon.de/pdf/MEDAON_15_Pieper.pdf

3. For a more comprehensive analysis of the reemergence and rebuilding of Jewish Congregations and Jewish Life from 1945 to 1953 in West and East Germany, see Jay Howard Geller, *Jews in Post-Holocaust Germany, 1945-1953* (Cambridge: Cambridge University Press, 2005).

4. Gunda Ulbricht, "Geschichte der Jüdischen Gemeinde im vergleichenden Überblick zu sächsischer und deutscher Geschichte von 1697 bis 1872," in *Der alte jüdische Friedhof in Dresden*, ed. HATiKVA e. V. (Berlin: Hentrich und Hentrich, 2002), 285.

5. Joachim Albrecht, "Konzessionierte und connivendo geduldete Juden—von der Gnade einer Aufenthaltsgenehmigung für Juden im Dresden des 18. Jahrhunderts," in *Der alte jüdische Friedhof in Dresden*, ed. HATiKVA e. V. (Berlin: Hentrich und Hentrich, 2002), 62–75.

6. For a description of the situation in Dresden, see Emil Lehmann, "Der polnische Resident Berend Lehmann, der Stammvater der israelitischen Religionsge-

meinde zu Dresden," in *Emil Lehmann Gesammelte Schriften* (Berlin: Herman, 1899), 116–53.

7. Albrecht, "Konzessionierte und connivendo geduldete Juden," 62–65.

8. Simone Lässig, "Vom Mittelalter in die Moderne? Anfänge der Emanzipation der Juden in Sachsen," *Dresdner Hefte* 45 (2000): 11.

9. Adolf Diamant, *Chronik der Juden in Dresden: Von den ersten Juden bis zur Blüte der Gemeinde und deren Ausrottung* (Darmstadt: Agora, 1973), 30–31.

10. Ingrid Kirsch, "Das Ringen um die rechtliche Gleichstellung der Dresdner Juden und ihrer Religionsgemeinde von 1830 bis 1871," *Dresdner Hefte* 22 (2000): 19–26.

11. Emil Lehmann, *Ein Halbjahrhundert in der israelitischen Religionsgemeinschaft zu Dresden: Erlebtes und Erlesenes* (Dresden: Salomon, 1890), https://www.diss-duisburg.de/Internetbibliothek/Artikel/Lehmann%20Dresden%20.pdf

12. This was the original theater building designed by Semper, which burned down in its entirety in 1869. While Semper also designed the replacement building, he had to do so from a distance. After his involvement in the 1848–49 revolution in Dresden, he had been banned from Saxony and even in 1869 was still not allowed to return. His son Manfred oversaw its actual building at the Theaterplatz in his stead.

13. Harold Hammer-Schenk, *Synagogen in Deutschland* (Hamburg: Hans Christians Verlag, 1981), 130; Hannelore Künzl, *Islamische Stilelemente im Synagogenhau des 19. und frühen 20. Jahrhunderts* (Frankfurt am Main, P. Lang, 1984), 182–83.

14. Gerald Kolditz, "Zur Entwicklung des Antisemitismus in Dresden während des Kaiserreichs," *Dresdner Hefte* 45 (1996): 40.

15. Büro für Statistik der Juden, Berlin-Halensee, *Zeitschrift für Demographie und Statistik der Juden* 4, no. 9 (1908): 142.

16. Emil Lehmann, "Schutz und Förderung jeder redlichen Arbeit," in *Emil Lehmann Gesammelte Schriften* (Berlin: Herman, 1899), 288. "Ihr politischer Einfluss ist Null. Weder in den Kammern, noch in den Kreis- und Bezirksausschüssen, weder im Stadtrat oder im Stadtverordnetenkollegium, noch in der Handelskammer, nicht als Schöffen, nicht als Geschworene, nicht als Handelsrichter sind Bekenner des jüdischen Glaubens in Sachsen tätig [. . .] Wo ist da in Sachsen der Jude?"

17. Pinkert published it under the pseudonym Egon Waldegg. Egon Waldegg, *Die Judenfrage gegenüber Handel und Gewerbe: Ein Manifest an die deutsche Nation* (Dresden: von Grumbkow, 1879). The Saxon State Library lists in total five editions for the text. For more detail see Matthias Piefel, *Antisemitismus und völkische Bewegung im Königreich Sachsen 1879–1914* (Göttingen: Vandenhoeck & Ruprecht Unipress, 2004), 22; Brajer, *Am Rande Dresdens*, 27; 275–97.

18. Brajer, *Am Rande Dresdens*, 309.

19. Brajer, *Am Rande Dresdens*, 310.

20. Piefel, *Antisemitismus und völkische Bewegung*, 47.

21. Piefel, *Antisemitismus und völkische Bewegung*, 48–50.

22. Brajer, *Am Rande Dresdens*, 342.

23. Ingrid Kirsch, "Die Israelitische Religionsgemeinschaft zu Dresden während der Zeit der Weimarer Republik," in *Einst und jetzt: Zur Geschichte der Dresdner Synagoge und ihrer Gemeinde*, ed. Jüdische Gemeinde Dresden (Dresden: Ddp Goldenbogen, 2001), 80–81.

24. Franz Walter, "Sachsen—Ein Stammland der Sozialdemokratie?" *Politische Vierteljahresschrift* 32, no. 2 (1991): 207–31, http://www.jstor.org/stable/24196320

25. Ina Jessen, *Ein deutscher Maler: Otto Dix und der Nationalsozialismus* (Berlin: De Gruyter, 2022), 418.

26. Uwe M. Schneede, *Otto Dix* (München: Beck, 2019), 23.

27. Schneede, *Otto Dix*, 24.

28. For an assessment of "workarounds" in Dix's war paintings, see Kathrin Fehringer, "Workaround am eigenen Leib. Prothetik bei Otto Dix und in der französischen Gegenwartsliteratur" in *ilinx—Berliner Beiträge zur Kulturwissenschaft 4: Workarounds. Praktiken des Umwegs* (2017), 24–40.

29. Schneede, *Otto Dix*, 20.

30. "Meinen Zeitgenossen gewidmet."

31. Andreas Peschel, "Die Entwicklung der Dresdner NSDAP bis 1933," *Dresdner Geschichtsbuch* 18 (2013): 151.

32. Mike Schmeitzner, *Der Fall Mutschmann: Sachsens Gauleiter vor Stalins Tribunal* (Markkleeberg: Sax-Verlag, 2011), 21, 26.

33. Gunda Ulbricht, "Sie waren es nicht? Bürgerlicher Konsens im Nationalsozialismus" *Dresdner Hefte* 93, no. 1 (2008): 55–64.

34. For a detailed analysis of Mutschmann's struggles with the Dresden party leadership, see Stephan Dehn, "Mutschmanns Machtkampf gegen Anton Groß," *Neues Archiv für sächsische Geschichte* 86 (2015): 225–40.

35. Andreas Wagner, *Machtergreifung in Sachsen* (Köln: Böhlau, 2004), 381.

36. Mike Schmeitzner: "Tödlicher Hass: Antisemitismus und Judenverfolgung in Dresden 1933–1945," *Medaon* 10 (2016): 4–6, http://www.medaon.de/pdf/medaon_19_Schmeitzner.pdf

37. Steffen Held, "Von der Entrechtung zur Deportation: Juden in Sachsen," in *Sachsen in der NS-Zeit*, ed. Clemens Vollnhals (Leipzig: Kiepenheuer, 2002), 202.

38. Marcus Gryglewski, "Zur Geschichte der nationalsozialistischen Judenverfolgung in Dresden 1933–1945," in *Die Erinnerung hat ein Gesicht. Fotografien und Dokumente zur Nationalsozialistischen Judenverfolgung in Dresden 1933–1945*, ed. Norbert Haase, Stefi Jersch-Wenzel, Hermann Simon, Marcus Gryglewski (Leipzig: Kiepenheuer, 1998), 110.

39. Gryglewski, "Zur Geschichte der nationalsozialistischen Judenverfolgung," 112.

40. She credits this circumstance to one of the other tenants in her building, Köhler, who, according to Frischmann, was part of the NSDAP leadership and involved in Jewish persecution. Hans-Peter Lühr and Ilse Frischmann, "Das war die absolute Ausgrenzung," in *Dresdner Hefte* 35, no. 3 (1993): 27–33.

41. Gryglewski, "Zur Geschichte der nationalsozialistischen Judenverfolgung," 113.

42. For an extensive first-time analysis of Nazi propaganda in Saxony, see Stephan Dehn, "Die nationalsozialistische Propaganda in Sachsen 1921–1945" (PhD thesis, Universität Leipzig, 2016), https://core.ac.uk/download/pdf/351712164.pdf. For specific information about Mutschmann's anti-Jewish campaigns after 1933, see pages 280–84.

43. "Wir kennen nur eine deutsche Kunst! Die Rede des Reichsministers Dr.

Goebbels zur Eröffnung der Reichstheaterwoche," *Der Freiheitskampf*, May 28, 1934, 3.

44. "'Entartete Kunst'—Ausstellung im Lichthofe des neuen Rathauses," *Dresdner Neueste Nachrichten*, September 24, 1933, 2.

45. "'Entartete Kunst,'" 2.

46. "'Entartete Kunst,'" 2. "bietet in der Tat ein abschreckendes Beispiel"; "das natürliche Empfinden des Volkes sich angewidert [abwendet]"; "das Niedrige, Gemeine, Erbärmliche."

47. "'Entartete Kunst,'" 2. "überwunden."

48. Christoph Zuschlag, "Die Dresdner Ausstellung 'entartete Kunst' 1933–1937," *Dresdner Hefte* 77 (2008): 17–25.

49. Hartmut Ellrich, *Dresden 1933–1945: Der historische Reiseführer* (Berlin: Ch. Links Verlag, 2008), 3.

50. Heinrich Magirius, "Stadtbild- und Denkmalpflege" *Geschichte der Stadt Dresden*, vol. 3, ed. Holger Starke (Stuttgart: Theiss, 2005), 324–25.

51. Gilbert Lupfer, "Planungen für das Gauforum Dresden," in *Führerschule, Thingplatz, "Judenhaus": Orte und Gebäude der nationalsozialistischen Diktatur in Sachsen*, ed. Konstantin Hermann (Dresden: Sandstein Verlag, 2014), 95.

52. Paul Wolf, "Historische Stadtform und künftige Gestaltung der Stadt Dresden," *Deutsche Bauzeitung* 42, no. 72 (1938): B1143.

53. Joshua Hagen, "Historic Preservation in Nazi Germany: Practices, Patterns, and Politics," in *Heritage at the Interface: Interpretation and Identity*, ed. Glenn Hooper (Gainesville: University Press of Florida, 2018), 57, https://doi.org/10.2307/j.ctvx06znr.9

54. Andrew Demshuk, *Three Cities after Hitler: Redemptive Reconstruction Across Cold War Borders* (Pittsburgh: University of Pittsburgh Press, 2021), 27.

55. Wolf, "Historische Stadtform," B1143. "Aufgaben besonders schwieriger Art bietet in Dresden das Gebiet der Altstadtgesundung. [. . . Es] treten hier Fragen der Baugestaltung der Gesundungsviertel um so stärker in die Erscheinung.
Von größter Bedeutung aber ist der Plan für die Neugestaltung der Dresdner Innenstadt, der eine Reihe von Straßendurchbrüchen in Verbindung mit Promenaden vorsieht und auf der Grundlage der historischen Gegebenheiten, und diese sinngemäß weiter entwickelnd, bedeutsame Zukunftsmöglichkeiten eröffnet."

56. Lupfer, "Planungen für das Gauforum Dresden," 96.

57. "Erster Spatenstich zum Gauhaus," *Der Freiheitskampf 69*, March 10, 1939, 1.

58. "Erster Spatenstich zum Gauhaus," 1.

59. Matthias Donath, *Architektur in Dresden 1939–1945* (Meißen: Elbland, 2016), 24–27. Other examples include the offices of the Saxon Air District Command (Luftgaukommando), the house of the Saxon Farmers' Association (Landesbauernschaft) near the main train station, and the Air War Training School (Luftkriegsschule) with airport. Yet these buildings are rarely talked about in their historical context (19).

60. Konstantin Hermann, "Der Führerbesuch 1934 und die Treuekundgebung 1944 in Dresden," in *Führerschule, Thingplatz, "Judenhaus": Orte und Gebäude der nationalsozialistischen Diktatur in Sachsen*, ed. Konstantin Hermann (Dresden: Sandstein Verlag, 2014), 76–77. In a recent study, historian Francesca Weil has analyzed the reflections, feelings, and attitudes of thirty-one representative Saxon residents

during 1943–45. Despite the differences between the individuals and their circumstances, and the disastrous situation in the last war years, the loyalty to the National Socialist regime remained unbroken. Francesca Weil, *Uns geht es scheinbar wie dem Führer . . . Zur späten sächsischen Kriegsgesellschaft (1943–1945)* (Göttingen: Vandenhoeck & Ruprecht Unipress, 2020).

61. Quoted in Konstantin Hermann, "Der Führerbesuch 1934," 75. "das Volk rast."

62. Nora Goldenbogen, "Nationalsozialistische Judenverfolgung in Dresden seit 1938-ein Überblick," *Dresdner Hefte* 45 (2000): 77; Gryglewski, "Zur Geschichte der nationalsozialistischen Judenverfolgung," 113.

63. The events were most likely organized by the NSDAP Kreisleiter in Dresden, Hellmut Walter. Daniel Ristau, *Bruch/Stücke: Die Novemberpogrome in Sachsen 1938* (Berlin: Hentrich & Hentrich, 2018), 125. Also: Gryglewski, "Zur Geschichte der nationalsozialistischen Judenverfolgung," 107–8.

64. "25 bis 30 Leute"; "starrten auf die Flammen. Kaum jemand sprach ein Wort."

65. Hans Schneider shared his memories in a letter to the editor to the *Sächsische Zeitung* in November 1998. Quoted in Ristau, *Bruch/Stücke*, 69. "Ja die Feuerwehr war wohl da, aber die haben bloß so bissel getan und waren im Übrigen in der Hauptsache damit beschäftigt, erst mal eine große Bresche in die Mauer zu schlagen."

66. "Einsätze, die Geschichte schrieben," in *Berufsfeuerwehr Dresden 1868–2018*, Stadtfeuerwehrverband Dresden e.V. (Erfurt: Sutton Verlag, 2018).

67. Leo Jehuda Schornstein, "Erlebnisbericht aus Dresden," in *Chronik der Juden in Dresden: Von den ersten Juden bis zur Blüte der Gemeinde und deren Ausrottung*, ed. Adolf Diamant (Darmstadt: Agora, 1973): 405–7.

68. "Bevor man uns auf die Straße brachte, zog man uns Thoramäntel über den Kopf, band uns Schürzen der Kinder des dort befindlichen Kinderhortes um den Hals und stülpte uns Zylinderhüte der Synagogenvorsteher auf den Kopf, indem man mit einem Schlag die Hüte zusammendrückte, was einen makaberen, seltsamen und erniedrigenden Eindruck darstellte."

69. Ristau, *Bruch/Stücke*, 164–65. The photograph is part of the archive of the Jüdische Gemeinde in Dresden, but it was Daniel Ristau's excellent work on the November Pogroms that drew attention to its existence.

70. Helmut Hoffmann, *Nachbelichtet* (Dresden: Ddp Goldenbogen, 2001).

71. Photographs are part of the Helmut Hoffmann Nachlass, Niedersächsisches Landesarchiv Oldenburg. A selection was published in Helmut Hoffmann, *Nachbelichtet.*

72. Henny Brenner, *Das Lied ist aus* (Zürich: Pendo Verlag, 2001).

73. Brenner, *Das Lied ist aus*, 52–53. "als die Bahn am Zeughausplatz vorbeikam, sah man von weitem schon eine Menschenmenge versammelt und Rauch aufsteigen: 'Die Synagoge brennt,' hieß es da plötzlich. [. . .] In ein paar Stunden hatten die Nazis es nicht nur geschafft, den Mittelpunkt der traditionsreichen Dresdner jüdischen Gemeinde zu zerstören, sondern die Stadt auch um eines ihrer imposantesten Bauwerke zu berauben."

74. Ristau, *Bruch/Stücke*, 75–76.

75. Nora Goldenbogen, *Die Dresdner Synagoge: Geschichte und Geschichten* (Teetz: Hentrich and Hentrich, 2004), 37.

76. "Beseitigung der Brandruine der Dresdner Synagoge unter Mitwirkung der

Technischen Nothilfe Ortsgruppe Dresden," 1938. Filmwerk ID: 42434 | Sig.: B-2038, Bundesarchiv Berlin.

77. Günter Wittenbecher, director, "Als die Synagogen brannten—Pogromnacht 1938," DDR RF, 1988. Available at Deutsches Rundfunkarchiv, https://www.dra.de/de/

78. "Die Schmach auf Zelluoid gebannt," *Berliner Zeitung*, November 10, 1988.

79. Dieter Hildebrandt, director, "Der gelbe Stern. Die Judenverfolgung 1933–1945," documentary, Germany, 1980. The documentary was nominated for an Oscar in 1981.

80. The slides are part of the archive of the Jüdische Gemeinde Dresden. See also Ristau, *Bruch/Stücke*, 77.

81. It has been assumed that the film was produced as a training video for the Technical Emergency Agency (Tobias Ebbrecht, "Bilder, die es nicht geben dürfte," *Filmblatt* 112, no. 44 (2010/2011): 48). The film indeed offers meticulous details, but historian Daniel Ristau in his 2018 study on the November Pogroms in Saxony points out that the film materials originally might have been filmed for propaganda purposes since they included sequences from November 10 in the beginning before the Stars of David were removed (Ristau, *Bruch/Stücke*).

82. "Zusammenlegung der letzten Juden in Dresden in das Lager am Hellerberg am 23./24. Nov. 1942."

83. In a public viewing and discussion of the film in 2017 Hirsch talks about these events. VORHIN—Erinnerungskultur im Zentralwerk, "Folge 3: Tagesmarsch zur Judenabteilung," 17. Oktober 2017, https://www.youtube.com/watch?v=iDl321U5VMc&t=6054s; also Holger Starke, "Das Judenlager Hellerberg," in *Geschichte der Stadt Dresden*, vol. 3, ed. Holger Starke (Stuttgart: Theiss, 2005), 495–96.

84. Starke, "Das Judenlager Hellerberg," 495–96.

85. This fact is also confirmed by Victor Klemperer's wife Eva, who comments on the operation to her husband, which he records subsequently in his diary on November 24, 1942: "Eva said this new kind of evacuation is so shameless because everything happens so openly" (Victor Klemperer, *I Will Bear Witness: 1942–1945* [New York: Random House, 1999], 168).

86. Irina Suttner and Gunda Ulbricht, "Henry Schmidt: Leiter des Judendezernats der Dresdner Gestapo," in *Braune Karrieren*, ed. Christine Pieper, Mike Schmeitzner, and Gerhard Naser (Dresden: Sandstein, 2012), 75.

87. It is not entirely clear how far the cameraman actively directs the actions of the people he films. It is obvious that the forced laborers were aware of being filmed, and the way some scenes play out they appear to indicate that they were given directives of what to do for the camera.

88. Klemperer, *I Will Bear Witness: 1942–1945*, 169–70.

89. Gesellschaft für Christlich-Jüdische Zusammenarbeit Dresden, Arbeitskreis Gedenkbuch, *Buch der Erinnerung: Juden in Dresden; deportiert, ermordet, verschollen; 1933–1945* (Dresden: Thelem, 2006).

90. Stadtleitung Dresden der SED, *Patrioten gegen Barbaren: Aus der Chronik des Kampfes gegen Faschismus und Krieg in Dresden in den Jahren 1933–1945* (Dresden: Stadtleitung Dresden der SED, 1985), 10.

91. Siegmund Rotstein, "Vorwort," in *Lebenslänglich für den Gestapokommissar*, by Horst Busse und Udo Krause (Berlin: Staatsverlag der DDR, 1989), 8.

92. Peter Monteath, "A Day to Remember: East Germany's Day of Remembrance for the Victims of Fascism," *German History* 26, no. 2 (2008): 197.

93. Monteath, "A Day to Remember," 204.

94. Monteath, "A Day to Remember," 210.

95. See for example the speeches and their titles in the publication for the fortieth anniversary of the November Pogroms, such as "The Socialist German State Has Become a Homeland for the Citizens of Jewish Belief," "We Can Be Proud of Our Socialist German Democratic Republic," or "We Found Our Home in the GDR." Verband der Jüdischen Gemeinden in der Deutschen Demokratischen Republik, *Gedenke! Vergiß Nie!: 40. Jahrestag des Faschistischen "Kristallnacht"-Pogroms; Eine Dokumentation* (Berlin: Union-Verlag, 1979).

96. Herfried Münkler, "Antifaschismus als Gründungsmythos der DDR: Abgrenzungsinstrument nach Westen und Herrschaftsmittel nach innen," in *Der missbrauchte Antifaschismus. DDR-Staatsdoktrin und Lebenslüge der deutschen Linken*, ed. Manfred Agethen et al. (Freiburg: Herder, 2002), 79–99.

97. Andrea Sinn, "Returning to Stay? Jews in East and West Germany after the Holocaust," *Central European History* 53 (2020): 398–99.

98. Gabriel Berger, "War die DDR antisemitisch?," in *Bpb Deutschland Archiv*, March 18, 2021, www.bpb.de/328430; Karin Hartewig, *Zurückgekehrt: Die Geschichte der jüdischen Kommunisten in der DDR* (Köln: Böhlau, 2000).

99. Berger, "War die DDR antisemitisch?"

100. Matthias Neutzner, "Vom Anklagen zum Erinnern," in *Das rote Leuchten: Dresden und der Bombenkrieg*, edited by Oliver Reinhard, Matthias Neutzner, and Wolfgang Hesse (Dresden: Edition Sächsische Zeitung, 2005), 157.

101. For an overview of the GDR's relationship to Israel, see David Tompkins, "Israel as Friend and Foe: Shaping East German Society through Freund- and Feindbilder," in *Becoming East German: Socialist Structures and Sensibilities after Hitler*, ed. Mary Fulbrock and Andrew I. Port (Oxford: Berghahn, 2013), 219–36.

102. Before, public memory was almost entirely reserved for celebrating the November Revolution from 1918.

103. Walther, "Jewish Anti-Fascism?," 264.

104. Historian Steffen Heidrich (Dresden) points out the key role of the congregation in initiating the memorial in his forthcoming book: *Neuanfang und Konsolidierung des Jüdischen im geteilten Deutschland: Jüdische Gemeinden in Dresden und Würzburg*.

105. City representative Meinecke, quoted in "Eine Grünanlage am Rathenauplatz," *Sächsische Zeitung*, December 1946 (precise date unknown; newspaper excerpt is part of the archive of the Judische Gemeinde Dresden). "Meine Fraktion hält es für ihre Ehrenpflicht mit diesem Antrag einen Teil zur Wiedergutmachung eines Verbrechens und einer Kulturschande beizutragen."

106. "Vor vier Jahren sank Dresden in Asche," *Neues Deutschland* 37, February 13, 1949, 3. "Die Gestapo ließ die Leichenberge auf dem Marktplatz verbrennen."

107. For the misinformation in connection with these cremations not just in popular or propagandistic sources, but also in scholarly sources, see Christoph D. Weber, "'A Blemish on the History of the Twentieth Century'? Legends and Fabrications

Surrounding the Mass Cremations in the Wake of the Dresden Air Raids, February 1945," *Oxford German Studies* 47, no. 4 (2018): 486–504.

108. "Entschlossener Kampf, um den Weltfrieden zu erhalten," *Sächsische Zeitung*, February 13, 1950, 1. "Opfer des Hitlerkrieges."

109. Erich Honecker, "Ehrendes Gedenken für die Toten des 13. Februar 1945 in Dresden," *Sächsische Zeitung*, February 14, 1985, 3. "Coventry und Dresden, Leningrad und Stalingrad, Oradour und Lidice, Warschau und Rotterdam, Maidanek und Auschwitz, Buchenwald und Dachau, Bergen-Belsen und Ravensbrück, Hiroshima und Nagasaki—all diese Namen, und man müßte noch viele andere nennen, stehen heute für ein Programm für den Frieden der Welt."

110. The VVN was resolved in 1953, even though it still followed a communist political line and its leadership was made up of SED functionaries. Its focus on Nazi antisemitism, however, was not understood as aligned with the political situation and messaging in the Soviet Union or the GDR. Walther, "Jewish Anti-Fascism?," 262.

111. "Wir stehen an der Seite der Dresdner Bevölkerung," *Sächsische Zeitung*, February 13, 1950. "Wir stehen an der Seite der Dresdner Bevölkerung," "schwergeprüfte Einwohner der Stadt Dresden für ein freies und schönes Deutschland."

112. *Sächsische Zeitung*, February 14, 1950, 1. "eines der schwersten Verbrechen des vergangenen Krieges."

113. "Dresden mahnt Deutschland!" *Neues Deutschland* 36, February 13, 1951, 6. "ungeheuerlicher Akt der Unmenschlichkeit," "barbarisch," "bestialische Ermordung," "verbrecherisches Vernichtungswerk."

114. Walter Weidauer, "Damit das Leben Perspektive hat: Nie wieder ein Inferno Dresden" *Sächsische Zeitung*, February 13, 1985, 4. "Die Brutalität kannte keine Grenzen," "barbarisch," "Verbrechen."

115. Eberhard Günther, "Grabstätten sind Zeugen der Vergangenheit einer Stadt" *Sächsische Zeitung*, October 28, 1988. "eines der größten Verbrechen," "barbarische[] Grausamkeit[], "Vernichtung." Eberhard Günther, "Warum brannten die Synagogen? Vier Jahrzehnte nach der schmachvollen Kristallnacht" *Sächsische Zeitung*, November 4–5, 1978. "bestialisch ermordet."

116. "Ehrendes Gedenken für die Toten des 13. Februar 1945 in Dresden," *Sächsische Zeitung*, February 14, 1985, 2; "mahnen die Lebenden zum Kampf für Frieden und Glück der Menschheit;" "Auf Sandsteinquadern liegen kleine Bilder—gemalt von Schülern einer dritten Klasse [. . .];" "ihr Spiel im neuen Dresden. 'Wir wollen im Frieden leben' schrieben sie dazu."

117. "50 Jahre Novemberpogrom: Jüdisches Zentrum und Stätte der Mahnung," *Sächsische Zeitung*, October 27, 1988, 3; "Jüdische Gemeinde gedachte ihrer Opfer des Pogroms: Neuweihe der rekonstruierten Synagoge in Dresden" *Sächsische Zeitung*, November 7, 1988, 1, 2. "Stätte der Mahnung."

118. "Jüdische Gemeinde gedachte ihrer Opfer des Pogroms: Neuweihe der rekonstruierten Synagoge in Dresden," 1, 2.

119. "Ehrendes Gedenken für Opfer der antisemitischen Pogrome," *Sächsische Zeitung*, November 9–10, 1985, 2.

120. "Nie wieder einen 13. Februar." "Never Again Kristallnacht" was used as the title of the commemoration event held in the Hygiene Museum in 1968 that is pictured on the photograph. "Nie wieder Kristallnacht."

121. For example, in 1965: Walter Weidauer, "Dresden ruft: Nationaler Widerstand gegen Bonner Atomkriegspläne," *Sächsische Zeitung*, February 13, 1965, 3. The politics of the day also influenced the way the past was reported and which parts were emphasized. In 1975, thirty-five years after the pogroms, the *Sächsische Zeitung* remembers the "Kristallnacht" and antisemitism, but it is represented as if it had been undertaken to make the German population ready for war. These actions are then compared to Israel's supposed imperialism and racism against the Arab peoples. G. Kirsch and S. Pfeiffer, "Kristallnacht," *Sächsiche Zeitung*, November 9, 1973.

122. "Kristallnacht. 30 Jahre danach: Judenverfolgungen in Westdeutschland," *Sächsische Zeitung*, November 9, 1968, 8.

123. Eberhard Günther, "Warum brannten die Synagogen? Vier Jahrzehnte nach der schmachvollen Kristallnacht," *Sächsische Zeitung*, November 4–5, 1978, 3. "die Kristallnacht war auch der Anfang der Vernichtung Dresdens."

124. Günther, "Warum brannten die Synagogen?," 3. "Ausbeutergesellschaft."

125. Stadtarchiv Dresden, 17.6.1-SP 009/1.

126. In preparation for possible bombardments of the city, a place for ten thousand graves had been prepared on the cemetery in 1943–44. Matthias Neutzner, "Heidefriedhof: Lernen am konfliktbeladenen Ort," *Dresdner Hefte* 127 (2016): 76. These actions show that there were indeed preparations against air raids going on in Dresden. It also indicates, however, that the possible effects of the bombings were underestimated.

127. "Ehrenhain vollendet," *Sächsische Zeitung*, September 9, 1965.

128. "Wieviele starben? Wer kennt die Zahl? / An Deinen Wunden sieht man die Qual / Der Namenlosen, die hier verbrannt / Im Höllenfeuer aus Menschenhand."

129. Neutzner, "Heidefriedhof," 78.

130. Christiane Hertel, "Dis/Continuities in Dresden's Dance of Death," *Art Bulletin* 82, no. 1 (2000): 83–116.

131. "Meldung vom 13.02.2022: Skulptur Trauerndes Mädchen am 'Tränenmeer' auf Heidefriedhof zurück," Dresden.de, February 13, 2022, https://www.dresden.de/de/rathaus/aktuelles/pressemitteilungen/2022/02/pm_036.php

132. Małgorzata Chodakowska, "Trauerndes Mädchen am Tränenmeer," Heidefriedhof Dresden (2010), Dresden.de

133. The *Sächsische Zeitung* also published specific instructions for where and how to gather. In the case of the commemoration of February 13, the events often started with wreath layings at the cemetery and then continued in the city center with further proclamations. Similarly, the September and November commemorations for the Victims of Fascism or November 9 also included wreath layings at the Heidefriedhof Memorial Park. *Sächsische Zeitung*, February 13, 1965, 3: "Dresden ruft: Nationaler Widerstand gegen Bonner Atomkriegspläne." *Sächsische Zeitung*, September 11, 1965, 2: "Kampfkundgebung gegen die westdeutsche Atomkriegspolitik." *Sächsische Zeitung*, February, 13 1985, 1: "Dresden—das ist eine Mahnung und Verpflichtung: Alle Kräfte für den Kampf um den Frieden vereinen." *Sächsische Zeitung*, September 9, 1985, 3: "Antifaschistisches Vermächtnis lebt in unseren Taten für den Sozialismus und den Frieden," "Tag des Gedenkens—ein Tag der Verpflichtung," "Erhaltung des Friendens ist wichtigste Aufgabe."

134. Kurt Hager, "Antifaschistisches Vermächtnis lebt in unseren Taten für den Sozialismus und den Frieden," *Sächsische Zeitung*, September 9, 1985, 3. "Zerstörung Hiroshimas und Nagasakis, Dresdens und Magdeburg."

135. For a collection of memorials in Dresden, see Herbert Goldhammer and Karin Jeschke, *Dresdner Gedenkorte für die Opfer des NS-Regimes* (Dresden: Ddp Goldenbogen, 2002, 2006).

136. Georg Joachimsthal, "Einweihung der neuen Synagoge in Dresden," *Der Weg: Zeitschrift für Fragen des Judentums* 5, no. 25 (1950): 7.

137. "Ansprache des Herrn Bürgermeister Wagner anlässlich der Einweihungsfeierlichkeiten der Jüdischen Gemeinde am 18. Juni 1950." Archive of the Jüdische Gemeinde Dresden.

138. "Neue jüdische Synagoge in Dresden," *Sächsische Zeitung*, June 20, 1950.

139. "Ansprache des Herrn Julius Meyer, Berlin, anlässlich der Einweihungsfeierlichkeiten der Jüdischen Gemeinde zu Dresden am 18. Juni 1950," Archive of the Jüdische Gemeinde Dresden.

140. Volkmar Lehnert, "Symboldispositiv und Affektwirkung: Architektursoziologie der Synagoge in Dresden" (MS Thesis/Diplomarbeit, Technische Universität Dresden, 2011), 76.

141. Lehnert, "Symboldispositiv und Affektwirkung," 76.

142. Jürgen Helfricht, *Die Synagoge zu Dresden* (Taucha: Tauchaer Verlag, 2001), 63. "Zur Erinnerung an die Toten und als Mahnmal für die Lebenden hat die Jüdische Gemeinde zu Dresden im Jahre 1950 diese Tafel ihren zahlreichen Brüdern und Schwestern geweiht, die von 1933–1945 der Mörderhand des Faschismus erlagen."

143. Jüdische Gemeinde Dresden, *Einst und jetzt*, 120; Gesellschaft für christlich-jüdische Zusammenarbeit Dresden e. V., *Juden in Sachsen: Ihr Leben und Leiden*, 106.

144. Jeffrey Herf, *Divided Memory: The Nazi Past in the Two Germanys* (Cambridge, MA: Harvard University Press, 1997), 133.

145. "Für ein gemeinsames Erinnern: Gespräch der Dresdner Hefte mit Vertretern der Jüdischen Gemeinde in Dresden," *Dresdner Hefte* 45, 2nd ed. (2000): 95.

146. Angelika Timm, "The Burdened Relationship," *Israel Studies* 2, no. 1 (1997): 23.

147. Uwe Ullrich, *Zur Geschichte der Juden in Dresden* (Dresden: Hille, 2001), 42.

148. Goldenbogen, *Die Dresdner Synagoge*, 53.

149. For example, Philipp Bammes, "Wiederaufbau der Carolabrücke nach historischem Vorbild," *Dresden.de*, https://www.dresden.de/de/leben/gesellschaft/buergebeteiligung/epetition.php?extForwardUrl=https%3A//apps.dresden.de/ords/f%3Fp%3D1610%3A3%3A%3A%3ANO%3A%3AP3_P_ID%3A23184. As depicted in chapter 2, Otto Richter in 1905 chose the Carolabrücke from 1895 as an example of city developments that negatively affected Dresden's cityscape.

150. Wolf, "Historische Stadtform und Gestaltung der Stadt Dresden," B1139, B1141, B1143.

151. Joachim Fischer, "Rekonstruktivismus als soziale Bewegung. Die revolutionäre Rückkehr der okzidentalen Stadt." *Geographische Revue* 14 (2012): 31.

152. Fischer, "Rekonstruktivismus als soziale Bewegung," 31–34.

153. "Hier stand die 1838–1840 von Gottfried Semper erbaute, durch Oberrab-

biner Dr. Zacharias Frankel geweihte und am 9. November 1938 von den Faschisten zerstörte Synagoge der Israelitischen Religionsgemeinde zu Dresden."

154. Verband der Jüdischen Gemeinden in der Deutschen Demokratischen Republik, ed, *Gedenke! Vergiß Nie!: 40. Jahrestag des Faschistischen "Kristallnacht"-Pogroms; Eine Dokumentation* (Berlin: Union-Verlag, 1979).

155. Gerhard Schill, "Rassenhaß als Bestandteil imperialistischer Politik," in *Gedenke! Vergiß Nie!: 40. Jahrestag des Faschistischen "Kristallnacht"-Pogroms; Eine Dokumentation*, ed. Verband der Jüdischen Gemeinden in der Deutschen Demokratischen Republik (Berlin: Union-Verlag, 1979), 50. "Vor 140 Jahren, 1838, trafen sich hier Dresdner Bürger, um die Grundsteinlegung für den Bau einer Synagoge [. . .] zu erleben. [. . .] genau 100 Jahre später, in der Nacht vom 9. zum 10. November, sank das Bauwerk, im Zuge einer organisierten verbrecherischen Aktion der Hitlerfaschisten, in Schutt und Asche."

156. Thomas Fache, "DDR Antifaschismus und das Gedenken an die November Pogrome 1938," *Medea* 2 (2008): 8.

157. The group was originally founded in the 1950s in West Germany by the Protestant Church. When East German members were unable to participate with their West German counterparts, they kept working in their own group.

158. Fache, "DDR Antifaschismus," 11–12.

159. Beate Meyer, "'Der Eichmann von Dresden,' 'Justizielle Bewältigung' von NS-Verbrechen in der DDR am Beispiel des Verfahrens gegen Henry Schmidt," in *Deutsche, Juden, Völkermord. Der Holocaust als Geschichte und Gegenwart*, ed. Jürgen Matthäus and Klaus-Michael Mallmann (Darmstadt: WBG, 2006), 285.

160. Róża Berger-Fiedler, director, *Herr Schmidt von der Gestapo: filmische Dokumentation einer Beamtenkarriere*, Berlin: DEFA, 1987; Horst Busse und Udo Krause, *Lebenslänglich für den Gestapokommissar* (Berlin: Staatsverlag der DDR, 1989).

161. Meyer, "Der Eichmann von Dresden," 281.

162. Meyer, "Der Eichmann von Dresden," 284.

163. Mike Dennis and Norman LaPorte, *State and Minorities in Communist East Germany* (Oxford: Berghahn, 2011), 28–60.

164. "Jüdische Gemeinde zu Dresden," *Nachrichtenblatt des Verbandes der Jüdischen Gemeinden in der Deutschen Demokratischen Republik*, December 12, 1987, 23. "Zehntausende Dresdner gedenken öffentlich der Zerstörung ihrer Stadt. Wo sind die öffentlichen Hinweise auf die Verfolgung ihrer Mitbürger zu finden? Und wer erinnert an die tapferen nicht-jüdischen Ehepartner, die alles zur Rettung jüdischer Angehöriger wagten?"

165. "In Scham und Trauer gedenken Christen der jüdischen Bürger dieser Stadt. [. . .] Wir schwiegen, als ihre Gotteshäuser verbrannt, als Juden entrechtet, vertrieben und ermordet wurden. Wir erkannten in ihnen unsere Brüder und Schwestern nicht. Wir bitten um Vergebung und Schalom."

166. A catalogue of the exhibition of the same title, which traveled for several years in Saxony, including after reunification, was published in 1994 by the Gesellschaft für christlich-jüdische Zusammenarbeit Dresden e. V. (Leipzig: evangelische Verlagsanstalt, 1994).

167. The slides are part of the archive of the Jüdische Gemeinde in Dresden.

Chapter 5

1. Pierre Nora, "Between Memory and History: Les Lieux de Mémoire," *Representations* 26 (1989): 7–24; https://www.jstor.org/stable/2928520; Aldo Rossi, *The Architecture of the City* (Cambridge, MA: MIT Press, 1982 [1966]).

2. Rossi, *The Architecture of the City*, 103, 106.

3. For the idea of a tourist site as shrine and repository of signification, see M. Pretes' analysis of the meaning of Mount Rushmore for American tourists in "Tourism and Nationalism," *Annals of Tourism Research* 30, no. 1 (2003): 125–42.

4. For a detailed analysis of the rebuilding of the Frauenkirche, the claims of authenticity, and a contextualization within postwar rebuilding debates, see Susanne Vees-Gulani, "From Frankfurt's Goethehaus to Dresden's Frauenkirche: Architecture, German Identity, and Historical Memory after 1945," *The Germanic Review: Literature, Culture, Theory*, 80, no. 2 (2005): 143–63; for rebuilding and the idea of undoing loss, see Jason James, "Undoing Trauma: Reconstructing the Church of Our Lady in Dresden." *Ethos* 34, no. 2 (2006): 244–72.

5. Rossi, *The Architecture of the City*, 127.

6. Vees-Gulani, "From Frankfurt's Goethehaus to Dresden's Frauenkirche," 143–63, 151; see also Tony Joel, *The Dresden Firebombing: Memory and the Politics of Commemorating Destruction* (London: Tauris, 2013), 107.

7. Commemoration events at the Frauenkirche were not restricted to February 13, but also took place during other citywide events, for example during the 750-year-anniversary festivities in 1956. At the same time, the Frauenkirche ruins were not the site of large demonstrations on every anniversary of the bombing, also due to clearing and construction projects at the Neumarkt.

8. Bundeszentrale für politische Bildung, "Jugendorganisationen der DDR: Friedensgebete und Montagsdemonstrationen" (2022), www.jugendopposition.de/14 5465. Wonneberger moved to Leipzig in 1985 where he established similar events. Wonneberger was an important voice in the Peaceful Revolution. Recently, Wonneberger has been involved in protests again, however, under a different political banner. In 2020, Wonneberger became a speaker during one of the large antimasking protests during the Covid-19 pandemic in Leipzig (the group calls itself "Querdenker" (Contrarian Thinkers). With his appearance at the protest, he seemed to support the idea, pushed by the participants, that the activities of the "Querdenker" were in the tradition of the 1989 Peaceful Revolution against state control and for freedom and democracy, even though the protests were largely organized and carried out by far-right, antidemocratic groups. See chapters 6 and 7 for a discussion on the rise of far-right voices and movements in Dresden and the way they similarly claim the 1989 protests as a precursor to their actions, as well as the support they receive from former 1989 leading freedom demonstrators in trying to legitimize their stance.

9. Bundeszentrale für politische Bildung and Robert-Havemann-Gesellschaft e.V., "Dresden und die Gruppe Wolfspelz" (2019). www.jugendopposition.de/145413

10. Gedenkversammlung am 13. Februar 1982 an der Ruine der Frauenkirche in Dresden," January 5, 1982, Stasi Unterlagen Archiv, Sig: BArch, MfS, BV Dresden, AKG, Nr. 11389, Bl. 1–8, 1. https://www.stasi-mediathek.de/medien/information-ue ber-eine-geplante-gedenkveranstaltung-am-13-februar-1982-an-der-ruine-der-frau

enkirche-in-dresden/blatt/1/; Emanuel Eckhardt, "Das Wunder von Dresden," *Die Zeit* 43 (2005), October, 20, 2005. https://www.zeit.de/2005/43/Dresdner_Frauenkirche. Stephan Fritz, a theology student and participant, here describes to the journalist how such a step was a monumental turning point since it meant that the church could not grant protection for them any longer.

11. Sabrina P. Ramet, *Social Currents in Eastern Europe: The Sources and Consequences of the Great Transformation* (Durham: Duke University Press, 1995), 64; Barbara Lubich, director, *Come Together: Dresden und der 13. Februar*, documentary (Hechtfilm, 2012). See also: http://www.dresdner.nu/interviews/Lebendige-Geschichtsstunde-Die-Macher-des-Films-Come-Together-Dresden-und-der-Februar-im-Interview.511A0D31.61B5.html.php

12. The event was not only discussed in the West German media but received an international echo. See, for example, the article in the *New York Times* prominently placed on page three: John Tagliabue, "4,000 East Germans Dispute Official Defense Policy," *New York Times*, February 15, 1982, 3 (section A).

13. "Information über die Durchführung eines Friedensforums in der Kreuzkirche Dresden," 19.02.1982. Stasi Unterlagen Archiv, Sig: BStU, MfS, BV Dresden, AKG, Nr. 7917, Bl. 1–20, 10. https://www.stasi-mediathek.de/medien/information-ueber-die-durchfuehrung-eines-friedensforums-in-der-kreuzkirche-dresden/blatt/1/. "rechtzeitige Einleitung entsprechender Sicherungsmaßnahmen": "Gegen 21.45 Uhr begab sich ein geringerer Teil der Besucher zur Ruine der Frauenkirche, an der sich insgesamt ca. 400–500 Jugendliche [. . .] versammelt hatten. Sie zündeten Kerzen (ca. 50 Stück) an und sangen Lieder [. . .] und legten Blumen nieder. Eine sechsköpfige Personengruppe stellte an der Ruine ein aus Kistenbrettern gefertigtes Kreuz (Höhe 0.70 m.), versehen mit der Aufschrift '35 000 Tote—warum?,' auf. Gegen 23.00 Uhr löste sich die Ansammlung ruhig und diszipliniert auf."

14. Karl-Siegbert Rehberg and Matthias Neutzner, "The Dresden Frauenkirche as a Contested Symbol: The Architecture of Remembrance after War," in *War and Cultural Heritage: Biographies of Place*, ed. Marie Louise Stig Sorenson and Dacia Viejo-Rose (Cambridge: Cambridge University Press, 2015), 108.

15. "7. Pioniertreffen 1982 in Dresden," YouTube, shared by Ernst Steiger, October 5, 2009, https://www.youtube.com/watch?v=rW98LVme-AM

16. Erich Honecker, "Der heutigen und kommenden Generation den Frieden zu bewahren—dafür kämpfen wir," *Neues Deutschland*, August 23, 1982, 1. "Das schöne Dresden," "eine Stadt froher und glücklicher Kinder." https://www.nd-archiv.de/artikel/391671.der-heutigen-und-kommenden-genetutionen-den-frieden-zu-bewahren-dafuer-kaempfen-wir.html

17. Tony Joel, *The Dresden Firebombing*, 114.

18. "Dresdner Manifestation für sichere Zukunft der Jugend," *Neues Deutschland*, August 28, 1982, 1–2. https://www.nd-archiv.de/ausgabe/1982-08-18. The plaque is now part of the collection of the Stadtmuseum Dresden. "Die Frauenkirche Dresden—im Februar 1945 zerstört durch anglo-amerikanische Bomber. Ihre Ruine erinnert an Zehntausende Tote und mahnt die Lebenden zum Kampf gegen imperialistische Barbarei für Frieden und Glück der Menschheit."

19. Quoted in "Dresdner Manifestation," 1–2. "Sprengköpfe sind dann auf uns gerichtet."

20. Quoted in "Dresdner Manifestation," 1–2. "Was der Imperialismus zerstörte, hat der Sozialismus zu neuer Blüte geführt."

21. Quoted in "Dresdner Manifestation," 1–2. "Das Geschaffene zu erhalten, immer schöner zu gestalten und nicht zuzulassen, daß es jemals wieder in einem Krieg zerstört wird."

22. Einar Haugen, "The Implementation of Corpus Planning Theory and Practice," in *Progress in Language Planning*, ed. Juan Cobarrubias and Joshua A. Fishman (Berlin: Mouton, 1983), 269–89.

23. Natalie Braber, "The German Language and Reunification 1990: The Effect of Emotion on the Use of Modal Particles in East and West Berlin" (PhD diss., St Andrews University, 2001).

24. For the multitude of meaning of heritage sites as well as their possible restrictions in the European city, see G. J. Ashcroft, "The Conserved European City as Cultural Symbol: The Meaning of the Text," in *Modern Europe: Place, Culture, and Identity*, ed. Brian J. Graham (New York: Arnold, 1998), 261–86.

25. Foucault understands such shifts in meaning as a fundamental characteristic of discourses, since the idea of the legitimacy of a discourse, or what we perceive as knowledge, are in fact linked to the perspectives of the world projected by the political and societal powers. Michel Foucault, *The Archaeology of Knowledge* (New York: Pantheon Books, 1972 [1969]).

26. Emmanuel Droit, "Frieden," in *Erinnerungsorte der DDR*, ed. Martin Sabrow (München: Beck, 2009), 154.

27. Droit, "Frieden," 154. "bewaffneter Frieden."

28. Droit, "Frieden," 160.

29. Michael Silverstein, "'Cultural' Concepts and the Language-Culture Nexus," *Current Anthropology* 45, no. 5 (2004): 621–52.

30. For the role of analogy as a way to translate the specialized language of urban planning to the lay person, see Karl Kropf, "Urbanism, Politics, and Language: The Role of Urban Morphology," *Urban Morphology* 1 (2011): 159.

31. Markus Driftmann, "Mythos Dresden: Symbolische Politik und deutsche Einheit," *Politik und Geschichte* 21, no. 22 (2009), https://www.bpb.de/apuz/31986/mythos-dresden-symbolische-politik-und-deutsche-einheit

32. Helmut Kohl, "Rede des Bundeskanzlers auf der Kundgebung vor der Frauenkirche in Dresden," *Die Bundesregierung: Bulletin 150*, December 22, 1989. https://www.bundesregierung.de/breg-de/service/bulletin/rede-des-bundeskanzlers-auf-der-kundgebung-vor-der-frauenkirche-in-dresden-790762. "Auf diesem traditionsreichen Platz."

33. Kohl, "Rede des Bundeskanzlers." "Das 'Haus Deutschland'—unser gemeinsames Haus—muß unter einem europäischen Dach gebaut werden. Das muß das Ziel unserer Politik sein. [I]n wenigen Tagen [. . .] beginnt das letzte Jahrzehnt dieses Jahrhunderts. Es ist ein Jahrhundert, das vor allem in Europa und auch bei uns in Deutschland viel Not, viel Elend, viele Tote, viel Leid gesehen hat—ein Jahrhundert, das auch uns Deutschen eine besondere Verantwortung auferlegt hat—angesichts des Schlimmen, das geschah. Hier vor der Ruine der Frauenkirche in Dresden, am Mahnmal für die Toten von Dresden, habe ich gerade ein Blumengebinde niedergelegt—auch in der Erinnerung an das Leid und an die Toten dieser wunderschönen alten deutschen Stadt."

34. Driftmann, "Mythos Dresden." The myth of the spontaneous speech has integrated itself strongly into the discourse surrounding Dresden and reunification, and it is often repeated, for example in Tony Joel's study *The Dresden Firebombing*.

35. Kohl, "Rede des Bundeskanzlers." "Von deutschem Boden muß in Zukunft immer Frieden ausgehen—das ist das Ziel unserer Gemeinsamkeit!"

36. Kohl, "Rede des Bundeskanzlers." "Fest des Friedens"

37. Patricia Clough, *Helmut Kohl, Ein Porträt der Macht* (Munich: Dtv, 1998), 195–97.

38. Driftmann, "Mythos Dresden."

39. Driftmann, "Mythos Dresden."

40. Ludwig Güttler et al., "Ruf aus Dresden," February 12, 1990, https://www.frauenkirche-dresden.de/foerdergesellschaft/wie-alles-begann. The English translation is also found on the website.

41. Güttler et al., "Ruf aus Dresden."

42. Güttler et al., "Ruf aus Dresden." For a different approach, see Tony Joel, *The Dresden Firebombing*, 29. The historian identifies the speech and rebuilding debate as the beginning of what he calls a "BRDDR memory hybridisation."

43. See Colossian 1:19–21 (King James Version): "For it pleased *the Father* that in him should all fulness dwell; And, having made peace through the blood of his cross, by him to reconcile all things unto himself; by him, *I say*, whether *they be* things in earth, or things in heaven. And you, that were sometime alienated and enemies in *your* mind by wicked works, yet now hath he reconciled. In the body of his flesh through death, to present you holy and unblameable and unreproveable in his sight." 1 Peter 1:19 (King James Version): "But with the precious blood of Christ, as of a lamb without blemish and without spot." Johannes 20:19ff (King James Version): "Then the same day at evening, being the first day of the week, when the doors were shut where the disciples were assembled for fear of the Jews, came Jesus and stood in the midst, and saith unto them, Peace be unto you. And when he had so said, he shewed unto them his hands and his side. Then were the disciples glad, when they saw the Lord. Then said Jesus to them again, Peace be unto you: as my Father hath sent me, even so send I you. And when he had said this, he breathed on them, and saith unto them, Receive ye the Holy Ghost: Whose soever sins ye remit, they are remitted unto them; and whose soever sins ye retain, they are retained."

44. Güttler et al., "Ruf aus Dresden."

45. 1 Peter 2:24: "Who his own self bare our sins in his own body on the tree, that we, being dead to sins, should live unto righteousness: by whose stripes ye were healed."

46. In *Three Cities after Hitler*, historian Andrew Demshuk has coined the term "redemptive reconstruction" for postwar city planning of destroyed urban places in which mainly modernist building decisions are moderated by rebuilding individual historic landmarks which are then available for the residents for identity formation. While on the one hand characteristic for such rebuilding ideas, on the other hand Dresden was a special case due to the mythologizing strength of the Dresden architectural and subsequent bombing narrative. With its state of having been neither cleared nor rebuilt during the GDR period, the Frauenkirche holds an exceptional position in postwar city planning symptomatic of the Dresden situation.

47. A further association also suggests the re-emergence of confidence in eastern Germany after reunification; the phrasing is a nod to what is known as "the Miracle of Bern," when the Federal Republic of Germany, for the first time eligible to participate after 1945, won the 1954 World Cup in soccer. It felt to many as the beginning of a new German self-confidence on the world stage after the Second World War.

48. Claudia Jerzak, "Sakralisierte Räume und die Institutionalisierung multiperspektivischer Erzählung," in *Erinnern wozu? Beiträge zur politisch-historischen Bildung*, ed. Uwe Hirschfeld (Berlin: Lit Verlag, 2015), 141.

49. Michael Batty and Paul Longley, *Fractal Cities—A Geometry of Form and Function* (London: Academic Press, 1994).

50. Dean MacCannell, *The Tourist* (Berkley: University of California Press, 2013 [1976]), 45.

51. MacCannell, *The Tourist*, 45.

52. MacCannell, *The Tourist*, 45.

53. John Urry and Jonas Larsen, *The Tourist Gaze 3.0* (London: Sage, 2011).

54. Raymond W. K. Lau, "Tourist Sights as Semiotic Signs: A Critical Commentary," *Annals of Tourism Research* 32, no. 2 (2011): 711–14.

55. Magdalena Roszczynska-Kurasinska, Anna Domaradzka, Anna Wnuk, and Tomasz Oleksy, "Intrinsic Value and Perceived Essentialism of Culture Heritage Sites as Tools for Planning Interventions," *Sustainability* 13 (2021): 5078. https://doi.org/10.3390/su13095078

56. For a more detailed discussion of authenticity and rebuilding, see Vees-Gulani, "From Frankfurt's Goethehaus to Dresden's Frauenkirche," 143–63. See also James, "Undoing Trauma," 244–72.

57. Vera Kämper. "Dresdens Herz schlägt wieder," *Spiegel Online*, October 30, 2005, http://www.spiegel.de

58. David Lowenthal, *The Past Is a Foreign Country—Revisited* (Cambridge: Cambridge University Press, 2015), 503.

59. Horst Köhler, "Was uns eint," Ansprache von Bundespräsident Horst Köhler zur Eröffnung der Dresdner Frauenkirche, Dresden, October 30, 2005. https://www.bundespraesident.de/SharedDocs/Reden/DE/Horst-Koehler/Reden/2005/10/20051030_Rede.html. "Der Wiederaufbau der Frauenkirche ist in einzigartiger Weise Ausdruck des Guten, das in einer Bürgergesellschaft und ihren Bürgern steckt und das darauf wartet, geweckt zu werden. [. . .] Frieden ist ein Geschenk, für das man aber immer wieder arbeiten muss, und manchmal grenzt das, was Versöhnung bewirken kann, an ein Wunder. Die Dresdner Frauenkirche kann uns Kraft geben, uns gemeinsam und grenzenlos noch stärker für Frieden und Versöhnung einzusetzen."

60. Jürgen Paul, Thomas Kantschew, and Uwe Kröger, *Der Wiederaufbau der Frauenkirche zu Dresden*, 3rd ed. (Dresden: Gesellschaft zur Förderung des Wiederaufbaus der Frauenkirch Dresden e.V., 1997), 20.

61. Jürgen Trimborn, "Das 'Wunder von Dresden': Der Wiederaufbau der Frauenkirche; Ein kritischer Blick auf das größte Rekonstruktionsprojekt des Jahrhunderts," *Die Alte Stadt* 97 (1997): 127. "ein Neubau des Dresdner Wahrzeichens in der alten Form." See also Eberhard Burger, "The Reconstruction of the Frauenkirche in Dresden," in *Revival of Dresden*, ed. Wolfram Jäger and C. A. Brebbia (Ashurst: WIT Press, 2000), 141–44.

62. Achatz von Müller, “Monumentaler Nippes,” *Die Zeit*, July 29, 2004.

63. Hans Joachim Neidhardt, “Wozu eine ‘Gesellschaft Historischer Neumarkt Dresden e. V.,’” in *Der Wiederaufbau des Neumarkts: Herz und Seele der Stadt*, ed. Gesellschaft Historischer Neumarkt e. V., Dresden (Dresden: Michael Imhof Verlag, 2019), 9. “Die Bürger dieser Stadt haben aber in unserer 1989 nach langer Zeit der Entmündigung erkämpften Demokratie das Recht und die Pflicht, mitzureden und mitzuentscheiden, wenn es um die Gestaltung ihres Stadtzentrums geht.”

64. “Entwürfe und Wirklichkeit am Neumarkt: Beispiele für Entwürfe für Neumarkthäuser und was am Ende entstanden ist,” *Dresdner Neueste Nachrichten*, April 26, 2019, https://www.dnn.de/lokales/dresden/entwuerfe-und-wirklichkeit-am-neumarkt-VSL7TUGYAWWM5RH5ZRDHWMS3RQ.html

65. Norbert Göller, “Droht die ‘dritte’ Zerstörung Dresdens?” *Sächsische Zeitung*, August 23, 1997, http://www.sz-online.de/archiv

66. Gesellschaft Historischer Neumarkt e. V., *Dresden: Der Wiederaufbau des Neumarkts: Herz und Seele der Stadt* (Dresden: Michael Imhof Verlag: 2019), 15. “Die Rückgewinnung des wunderbaren Stadtbildes.”

67. Already in the 1980s, Dresden had started to develop plans for additional buildings on the Neumarkt, which even considered the possibility of the historical rebuilding of some of the burgher houses. As so often happened, however, no plans were realized, be it from a lack of materials, money, or political will.

68. Heinrich Magirius, “Der Wiederaufbau des Dresdner Neumarkts aus der Sicht eines Denkmalpflegers,” in *Dresden: Der Wiederaufbau des Neumarkts: Herz und Seele der Stadt*, ed. Gesellschaft Historischer Neumarkt e. V (Dresden: Michael Imhof Verlag, 2019), 23–34, 24. “Kunstempfinden.”

69. Torsten Kulke, “Rekonstruktion im Zeitalter der Moderne—Dresden als Zentrum städtebaulicher und architektonischer Debatten,” in *Dresden: Der Wiederaufbau des Neumarkts: Herz und Seele der Stadt*, ed. Gesellschaft Historischer Neumarkt e. V. (Dresden: Michael Imhof Verlag, 2019), 96.

70. For more details, see Katja Marek, “Rekonstruktion und Kulturgesellschaft: Stadtbildreparatur in Dresden, Frankfurt am Main und Berlin als Ausdruck der zeitgenössischen Suche nach Identität” (PhD diss, Universität Kassel, 2009).

71. The website of the society offers further information on their activities and their various surveys. https://www.neumarkt-dresden.de/

72. “DNN-Barometer: Nur 14 Prozent fehlt moderne Architektur,” *Dresdner Neueste Nachrichten*, July 6, 2018, https://www.dnn.de/Dresden/Lokales/DNN-Barometer-Nur-14-Prozent-fehlt-moderne-Architektur

73. Joachim Fischer, “Prager Straße in Dresden: Zur Architektur-Soziologie eines utopischen Stadtensembles,” *Ausdruck und Gebrauch* 5 (2004): 13.

74. “Begründung zum Bebauungsplan Nr. 155 Dresden-Altstadt I Nr. 28, Prager Straße/Nord-West Einkaufszentrum,” *Dresdner Amtsblatt* 5 (2006): 6.

75. Landeshauptstadt Dresden, “Tourismus,” dresden.de (last updated January 4, 2024). https://www.dresden.de/de/leben/stadtportrait/statistik/wirtschaft-finanzen/tourismus.php

76. Dresden Marketing GmbH, *Tourismusentwicklung Dresden-Elbland* (Dresden, February 2023), https://mediaserver.dresden.de/overview/media/4190; Dresden Marketing GmbH, *Tourismusentwicklung Dresden-Elbland* (Dresden, March 2025), https://mediaserver.dresden.de/collections/6/media/1997663523

77. Dresden Marketing GmbH, "Markt und Trendforschung," https://dmg.dresden.de/de/marketing/mafo/startseite-marktforschung.php. Amounts reflect gross earnings.

78. Lowenthal, *The Past Is a Foreign Country—Revisited*, 505.

79. Lowenthal, *The Past Is a Foreign Country—Revisited*, 505.

80. Siegfried Reimann, "Der 'Förderverein Bau der Synagoge Dresden e. V.'—Seine Entstehung und seine Ziele," *Dresdner Hefte* 45 (2000): 86–87.

81. Reimann, "Der 'Förderverein Bau der Synagoge Dresden e. V.,'" 87. "Angesichts des Wiederaufbaus der Dresdner Frauenkirche wirkt es auf mich und auch auf die Juden unserer Stadt zunehmend beklemmend, dass von ihrem durch räuberischen Brandschatzung genommenen Gotteshaus in der Öffentlichkeit keine Rede ist. Zwar ist mir bekannt, daß es städteplanerische Überlegungen gibt, eine Synagoge wieder aufzubauen. Aber gegenüber dem großen Aufwand des Wiederaufbaus der Frauenkirche stellen diese planerischen Arbeiten einen Nullwert dar."

82. This term gained particular notoriety when members of the Saxon parliament, the far-right National Democratic Party of Germany (NPD) representatives Holger Apfel and Jürgen Gansel, refused to take part in a moment of silence to commemorate the victims of the Holocaust in 2005, a custom for Holocaust Remembrance Day in all of Germany. In their speeches, the NPD representatives pointed to the duty to commemorate instead the victims of what they referred to as the Dresden "Bomben-Holocaust."

83. Quoted in "Es ist der Tag der Dresdner," *Sächsische Zeitung*, February 13, 2001, http://www.sz-online.de/archiv

84. "Es ist der Tag der Dresdner."

85. Repeatedly, the return has been dated as occurring in 1950, but a letter by the Dresden Jewish Congregation from February 11, 1947, thanks the Dresden city fire brigade for the return of the Star of David the previous year. Archive of the Jüdische Gemeinde Dresden.

86. "Neue jüdische Synagoge in Dresden," *Sächsische Zeitung*, June 20, 1950.

87. Quoted in a letter by the Dresden Jewish Congregation from February 11, 1947. Archive of the Jüdische Gemeinde Dresden. "beherzte Feuerwehr unter Hintanstellung ihrer Person und unter größter Gefahr, nicht scheuend des Naziterrors und der damit verbundenen Verfolgungen gerettet haben."

88. *Nachrichtenblatt der jüdischen Gemeinde Groß-Berlin und des Verbandes der jüdischen Gemeinden der Deutschen Demokratischen Republik*, December 1972, 17; see also Daniel Ristau, *Bruch/Stücke* (Berlin: Hentrich und Hentrich, 2018), 166.

89. *Nachrichtenblatt* 1972, 17. "Wir haben schon oft darüber geschrieben [. . .], daß auf unserer kleinen, wunderschönen Synagoge in der Fiedlerstraße der Mogen Dovid angebracht ist, der schon unsere in der berüchtigten Kristallnacht vom 9./10. November 1938 von den Nazis zerstörte Synagoge [. . .] verzierte. Er wurde in der Brandnacht von mutigen Feuerwehrleuten abmontiert und gerettet und uns nach 1945 übergeben, damit er auch die neu zu erbauende Synagoge wieder krönt. Unser Bild, das uns vor kurzem übergeben wurde, zeigt die Tat der Feuerwehrleute."

90. Hans Leupold, "Ein Davidstern Gottfried Sempers," *Nachrichtenblatt der jüdischen Gemeinde Groß-Berlin und des Verbandes der jüdischen Gemeinden der Deutschen Demokratischen Republik*, December 1988. "Es ist dem Feuerwehrmann Alfred Neugebauer zu verdanken, daß dieser Davidsstern erhalten geblieben ist. Von

der Abnahme des Sternes gibt es noch ein Foto, das der jüdische Lehrer Höxter vom Fenster seiner hochgelegenen Wohnung aus aufgenommen hatte, er wohnte im Haus Zeughausstraße 1, das der Synagoge sehr nahe stand." In a draft of the article, Leupold described the rescue of the Star of David in more detail: "er [Neugebauer] hatte ihn abmontiert und im Keller der Feuerwehr Louisenstraße heimlich aufbewahrt" (he [Neugebauer] had removed it [from the tower] and had secretly stored it in the cellar of the Louisenstraße fire station). This account is not correct. The draft is located in the archive of the Jüdische Gemeinde Dresden.

91. Daniel Ristau, "Ein Foto und seine Geschichte (3): Die Abnahme eines Davidsterns von der Dresdner Synagogenruine als Bildikone," February 10, 2018, https://bruchstuecke1938.de/ein-foto-und-seine-geschichte-3-die-abnahme-eines-davidsterns-von-der-dresdner-synagogenruine-als-bildikone/

92. Arbeitskreis gegen das Vergessen Bibra, *Juden in Bibra, unvergessen: Tage der Begegnung in Bibra vom 17.-20. Mai 2007* (Bibra, 2008), 22. "Am 9. November 1938, zur Pogromnacht, wurde Aaron [*sic*] Höxter von Dresden nach Buchenwald verschleppt. Dort traf er alle jüdischen Bibraer Männer [. . .]."

93. Quoted in Dimitrana Floßmann and Hartwig Floßmann, "Bibra (Ein Rückblick auf 300 Jahre jüdisches Leben)," in *Juden in Südthüringen geschützt und gejagt: Eine Sammlumng jüdischer Lokalchroniken*, vol. 3, ed. Hans Nothnagel (Suhl: Verlag Buchhaus Suhl, 1999), 147. "Papa konnte wochenlang nicht laufen."

94. Bundesarchiv Deutschland, *Memorial Book: Victims of the Persecution of Jews under the National Socialist Tyranny in Germany 1933–1945*, last accessed November 27, 2024, https://www.bundesarchiv.de/gedenkbuch/en942384

95. Herbert Lappe, "Die Rettung des Davidsterns der Semper-Synagoge," *Sächsische Zeitung*, November 4, 1988, 2; C.-U. Stäglich, "Gedanken zu einem einmaligen Bilddokument: Keiner darf je wegsehen," *Sächsische Zeitung*, November 9, 1988, 4.

96. Ristau sees the photograph at this point as having reached iconic standing. *Bruch/Stücke*, 166.

97. Gesellschaft für christlich-jüdische Zusammenarbeit Dresden, e. V., *Juden in Sachsen: Ihr Leben und Leiden* (Leipzig: Evangelische Verlagsanstalt, 1994): 77. The catalogue was only published after reunification.

98. Stäglich, "Gedanken zu einem einmaligen Bilddokument," 4; "das brennende jüdische Gotteshaus hatten sie an jenem 9. November des Jahres 1938 nicht retten dürfen."

99. Herbert Lappe, "Die Rettung des Davidsterns der Dresdner Semper-Synagoge. Mit freundlicher Unterstützung von Herrn Alfred Neugebauer." Archive of the Jüdische Gemeinde Dresden. Undated. This write-up appears to be a draft for Lappe's final article in the *Sächsische Zeitung* in 1988.

100. Lappe, "Die Rettung des Davidsterns," *Sächsische Zeitung*, 2.

101. Susann Mayer, "Feuerwehrmann und Kunstliebhaber," *Jüdisches Leben: Facetten der Geschichte und Gegenwart, Universitätsjournal-Sonderausgabe* (1999): 24.

102. Heidrun Hannusch, "Wie ein Feuerwehrmann die Ehre Dresdens rettete," *Dresden Neueste Nachrichten*, August 15, 2000, 14.

103. Hannusch, "Feuerwehrmann," 14. "'Wissen Sie, warum ich für die Dresden Synagoge spende?,' [. . .] 'Wegen dieses Mannes, der den David-Stern gerettet hat.' Das ist eine 'amazing story.'"

104. Regina Scheer, "'Stille Helden' in Dresden," in *Die Schuhe der Toten*, ed. Gorch Pieken (Dresden: Sandstein, 2014), 158–59.

105. Regina Scheer, "'Stille Helden' in Dresden," 162. "die brennende Synagoge retten durften die Feuerwehrleute nicht, aber den Magen David bewahrte Neugebauer auf und gab ihn nach Kriegsende der Jüdischen Gemeinde zurück."

106. "Verleihung des Sächsischen Verdienstordens an Bürgerinnen und Bürger," October 12, 2001. https://www.medienservice.sachsen.de/medien/news/152167. "eine Tat vollbracht, bei der er Freiheit und Leben riskierte."

107. Wandel et al, "Zur Architektur der Neuen Synagoge in Dresden," *Dresdner Hefte* 45 (2000): 90.

108. Wandel et al., "Zur Architektur der Neuen Synagoge in Dresden," 90.

109. Wandel et al., "Zur Architektur der Neuen Synagoge in Dresden," 90.

110. Birgit Hilbig, "Moderne Synagoge mit einer Drehung gen Osten," *Sächsische Zeitung*, August 23, 1997, http://www.sz-online.de/archiv

111. Göller, "Droht die 'dritte' Zerstörung."

112. Julia Tews, "Ideen für den Reißwolf," *Sächsische Zeitung*, May 14, 1999, http://www.sz-online.de/archiv

113. Zeitgenossen e. V. and Jüdische Gemeinde Dresden, "Die neue Synagoge ist für mich . . . ," (Dresden, 2011), http://zeitgenossen-dresden.de/die-neue-synagoge-ist-fur-mich/

114. "Entwürfe umstritten," *Sächsische Zeitung*, July 15, 1997, http://www.szonline.de/archiv

Chapter 6

1. Parts of this chapter are based on Susanne Vees-Gulani, "Symbol of Reconciliation and Far-Right Stronghold? Pegida, AfD and Memory Culture in Dresden," *German Politics and Society* 39, no. 1 (2021): 56–78.

2. Dominique Reynié, "'Heritage Populism' and France's National Front," *Journal of Democracy* 27, no. 4 (2016): 47–57. Reynié characterizes general heritage populism as emphasizing "the protection of heritage, whether tangible (living standards) or intangible (ways of life). [It] combines hostility toward elites with opposition to the European Union, immigrants, and Islam" (47–48).

3. Jan-Werner Müller, *What Is Populism?* (Philadelphia: University of Pennsylvania Press, 2016), 38.

4. The term "Wutbürger," or "enraged citizen," arose first in connection with the demonstrations against the large-scale redesign of the Stuttgart train station as part of the project Stuttgart 21. It was used in an essay in *Der Spiegel* by Dirk Kurbjuweit titled "Wutbürger" (October 11, 2010), https://www.spiegel.de/spiegel/a-724587.html

5. Eckhard Jesse, Thomas Schubert, Tom Thieme, *Politik in Sachsen* (Wiesbaden: Springer Verlag, 2014), 297, 335.

6. "Umfrage: Sachsenstolz ist ungebrochen," sachsen-fernsehen.de, May 25, 2016, https://www.sachsen-fernsehen.de/umfrage-sachsenstolz-ist-ungebrochen-35239/

7. Sächsische Staatskanzlei, *Sachsen-Monitor 2023*, sachsen.de, January 23, 2024, https://www.staatsregierung.sachsen.de/sachsen-monitor-5656.html

8. Jesse, Schubert, and Thieme show that while Saxony displays great confidence in its own uniqueness, in reality there are only some minor political and conceptual differences. *Politik in Sachsen,* 332–37.

9. Tino Moritz and Toralf Staud, "Rechtsaußen, mittendrin," in *Unter Sachsen,* ed. Heike Kleffner and Matthias Hausner (Berlin: Ch. Links Verlag, 2017), 59–60.

10. Jay Julian Rosellini, *The German New Right* (London: Hurst, 2019), 90.

11. Barbara Donavan, "Populist Rhetoric and Nativist Alarmism: The AfD in Comparative Perspective," *German Politics and Society* 38, no. 1 (2020): 69, https://doi.org/10.3167/gps.2020.380104

12. Jennifer A. Yoder, "'Revenge of the East'? The AfD's Appeal in Eastern Germany and Mainstream Parties' Responses," *German Politics and Society* 38, no. 2 (2020): 35–58.

13. Hans-Georg Betz and Fabian Habersack, "Regional Nativism in East Germany: The Case of the AfD," in *The People and the Nation: Populism and Ethno-territorial Politics in Europe,* ed. Reinhard Heinisch, Emanuele Massetti, and Oscar Mazzoleni (New York: Routledge, 2019), 110–35.

14. Betz and Habersack, "Regional Nativism in East Germany," 123; Manès Weisskircher, "The Strength of Far-Right AfD in Eastern Germany: The East-West Divide and the Multiple Causes behind 'Populism,'" *Political Quarterly* 91, no. 3 (2020): 2.

15. Betz and Habersack, "Regional Nativism in East Germany," 118.

16. Betz and Habersack, "Regional Nativism in East Germany," 127.

17. Quoted in "BfV-Pressekonferenz vom 12. März 2020 zum Stand der Bekämpfung des Rechtsextremismus," *www.verfassungsschutz.de,* March 12, 2020, https://www.verfassungsschutz.de/SharedDocs/statements/DE/2020/statement-haldenwang-presekonferenz-stand-der-bekaempfung-des-rechtsextremismus.html. "vor dem Hintergrund einer nie dagewesenen Migration, [. . .] unser Deutschland und unser Europa vor einem Kultur- und Zivilisationsbruch historischen Ausmaßes, ja, einer kulturellen Kernschmelze [bewahren]."

18. Thüringer Ministerium für Inneres und Kommunales, *Verfassungsschutzbericht 2023 Freistaat Thüringen* (Erfurt, 2024), 14–21; Staatsministerium des Inneren und Sächsischer Verfassungsschutz, *Sächsischer Verfassungsbericht 2023* (Dresden, 2024), 53; Ministerium für Inneres und Sport des Landes Sachsen-Anhalt, *Verfassungsschutzbericht 2023* (Magdeburg, 2024), 33.

19. Bundesinnenministerium des Innern und für die Heimat, *Verfassungsschutzbericht 2023: Fakten und Tendenzen* (Berlin, 2024), 28–29.

20. Friederike Haupt, "AfD klagt gegen Hochstufung durch Verfassungsschutz," faz.net, May 8, 2025, https://www.faz.net/aktuell/politik/inland/wegen-hochstufung-afd-reicht-klage-gegen-verfassungsschutz-ein-110456341.html

21. Stefan Garsztecki, Thomas Laux, and Marian Nebelin, eds., *Brennpunkte der "neuen" Rechten: Globale Entwicklungen und die Lage in Sachsen* (Bielefeld: Transcript Verlag, 2023), 25.

22. State and local election results: sachsen.de. Federal election results: bundeswahlleiter.de. Specific Dresden results: dresden.de.

23. Many of these scandals involve, among others, the representative to the European Parliament Maximilian Krah from Saxony. Nevertheless, he was able to defend his parliament seat in the Europe election. While the AfD has partially dis-

tanced itself from Krah, he remains a strong figure in the party, but particularly in Saxon party politics.

24. Garsztecki, Laux, and Nebelin, *Brennpunkte der "neuen" Rechten*, 25.

25. Nitzan Shoshan, "Spatial Configerations of Right-Wing Populism in Contemporary Germany," *International Journal of Urban and Regional Research* (2019), https://www.ijurr.org/spotlight-on/political-geographies-of-right-wing-populism/spatial-configurations-of-right-wing-populism-in-contemporary-germany/

26. As a comparison, in Leipzig, Saxony's largest city, the AfD received 18.3 percent and 17.3 percent, respectively. While also high, a strong showing of the left parties of Die Linke, SPD, and the Greens buffered the AfD's influence on the region. Leipzig is also a hotspot for left extremism. Election results: leipzig.de

27. Election results: leipzig.de

28. Rosellini, *The German New Right*, 90.

29. Hans Vorländer, Maik Herold, and Steven Schäller, *PEGIDA and New Right-Wing Populism in Germany* (London: Palgrave Macmillan, 2018): 2.

30. Sabine Volk, "'Wir sind das Volk.' Representative Claim-Making and Populist Style in the PEGIDA Movement's Discourse," *German Politics* 29, no. 4 (2020): 609, https://doi.org/10.1080/09644008.2020.1742325

31. Sabine Volk, "Conceptualising Europe from the Far Right: The Mobilisation of Intellectual Heritage in Germany," *Journal of European Studies*, 52, no. 3–4 (2022): 245–46, https://doi.org/10.1177/00472441221115564

32. Volk, "Conceptualising Europe from the Far Right," 246.

33. Alternative für Deutschland (AfD), *Manifesto for Germany: The Political Programme of the Alternative for Germany* (Stuttgart: AfD, 2016), 45–46.

34. Volk, "Wir sind das Volk!," 601.

35. Ruth Wodak, *The Politics of Fear: What Right-Wing Populist Discourses Mean* (London: Sage, 2015), 26. Cas Mudde and Cristóbal Rovira Kaltwasser, *Populism: A Very Short Introduction* (Oxford: Oxford University Press, 2017), emphasizes the importance of the negatively viewed "elite," which does not represent what the populist groups would define as the "common will" (5).

36. Volk, "Wir sind das Volk," 609–10.

37. Bruni Reitzenstein, *Mein Dresden: Die zerrissene Stadt*, aired June 26, 2019, ZDF, https://www.zdf.de/dokumentation/dokumentation-sonstige/mein-dresden-die-zerrissene-stadt-100.html

38. Volk, "Wir sind das Volk," 607.

39. Yoder, "Revenge of the East?", 46–47. These slogans did cause criticism among some of the participants of the Peaceful Revolution in 1989. See their statement from August 20, 2019: "Nicht mit uns: Gegen den Missbrauch der Friedlichen Revolution 1989 im Wahlkampf" (Not with us: Against the misuse of the Peaceful Revolution 1989 in the election campaign), https://www.havemann-gesellschaft.de/beitraege/nicht-mit-uns-gegen-den-missbrauch-der-friedlichen-revolution-1989-im-wahlkampf/. Some East German intellectuals, however, agree with the idea that today's Federal Republic can be compared to the GDR. See Julian Göpffarth, "Activating the Socialist Past for a Nativist Future: Far-Right Intellectuals and the Prefigurative Power of Multidirectional Nostalgia in Dresden," *Social Movement Studies* 20, no. 1 (2021): 57–74.

40. AfD, *Manifesto for Germany*, 7.

41. For the use of body metaphors and body politics in National Socialism, see Andreas Musolff, *Metaphor, Nation and the Holocaust: The Concept of Body Politics* (New York: Routledge, 2010); "AfD-Politiker Gauland fabuliert vom 'Volkskörper,'" *Spiegel Online*, January 8, 2016, https://www.spiegel.de/politik/deutschland/afd-alexander-gauland-fabuliert-vom-volkskoerper-a-1071101.html

42. Jasper von Altenbockum, "Was ist Deutsch?" *Frankfurter Allgemeine Zeitung*, June 1, 2016, https://www.faz.net/aktuell/politik/harte-bretter/programm-der-afd-und-die-deutsche-identitaet-14262312.html

43. AfD, *Manifesto for Germany*, 47–49, 57–64.

44. See for example the comments by the AfD parliamentary group's spokesperson for labor and social policy, René Springer. AfD Bundestag Fraktion, "Presseerklärung: René Springer: Plünderung unserer Sozialkassen beenden," afdbundestag.de, November 15, 2023, https://afdbundestag.de/rene-springer-pluenderung-unserer-sozialkassen-beenden/

45. AfD, *Manifesto for Germany*, 25.

46. AfD, *Manifesto for Germany*, 47.

47. AfD, *Manifesto for Germany*, 7; Justus Bender, *Was will die AfD? Eine Partei verändert Deutschland* (München: Pantheon, 2017), 45–47; Melanie Amann, *Angst für Deutschland* (München: Dröhmer, 2017), 37–38.

48. Hans Georg Betz, "Facets of Nativism: A Heuristic Exploration," *Patterns of Prejudice* 53 (2019): 111–35; Wodak, *The Politics of Fear*, 21–22.

49. Rogers Brubaker, "Between Nationalism and Civilizationism: The European Populist Moment in Comparative Perspective," *Ethnic and Racial Studies* 40, no. 8 (2017): 1193. See also Donavan, "Populist Rhetoric and Nativist Alarmism," 55–76.

50. Vorländer, Herold, and Schäller, *PEGIDA*, 1.

51. Erdinç Çakmak and Laura Gorlero, "The Pegida Movement and Social Conflict in Dresden, Germany," in *Tourism and Hospitality in Conflict-Ridden Destinations*, ed. Rami K. Isaac, Erdinç Çakmak, and Richard Butler (New York: Routledge, 2019), 153; Enzo Brox and Tommy Krieger, "Weniger Zuzug nach Dresden: Rechte Proteste verschrecken junge Leute!," *ifo Dresden berichtet* 28, no. 4 (2021): 12–17.

52. Vorländer, Herold, and Schäller, *PEGIDA*, 9. During my field work, which consisted of regular observations of Pegida protests from 2015 to 2024 (with some interruptions during the Covid-19 pandemic), I noticed that while the crowds had become smaller since 2015, the large engagement of the participants did not, even though the content of the speeches and the order of events—first speeches and then a walk through parts of the city—barely changed from week to week. Many seemed to arrive in groups and know each other. The events appeared as the performance of identity-confirming ritualistic acts within a community.

53. Maximilia Zehring and Eseme Domahidi, "German Corona Protest Mobilizers on Telegram and Their Relations to the Far Right: A Network and Topic Analysis," *Social Media and Society* 9, no. 1 (2023), https://doi.org/10.1177/20563051231155106

54. Sabine Volk and Manès Weisskircher, "Defending Democracy against the 'Corona Dictatorship'? Far-Right PEGIDA during the COVID-19 Pandemic," *Social Movement Studies* 23 no. 6 (2024), https://doi.org/10.1080/14742837.2023.2171385

55. Vanessa Prattes. "'Inzidenz bei 1933': Visuelle Inszenierungs- und Emotion-

alisierungsstrategien des Opfer- und Widerstandsmythos in der 'Querdenken-Bewegung,'" *Zeitschrift für Kultur- und Kollektivwissenschaft* 9, no. 1 (2023): 82–184, https://doi.org/10.14361/zkkw-2023-090108

56. Prattes, "Inzidenz bei 1933," 192.

57. Staatsministerium des Inneren und Sächsischer Verfassungsschutz, *Sächsischer Verfassungsbericht 2023*, 42.

58. Staatsministerium des Inneren und Sächsischer Verfassungsschutz, *Sächsischer Verfassungsbericht 2023*, 43.

59. Christoph Pengel, "Lutz Bachmann verkündet Aus von Pegida-Demos in Dresden," *Dresdner Neueste Nachrichten*, October 14, 2024, https://www.dnn.de/lokales/dresden/pegida-in-dresden-lutz-bachmann-verkuendet-aus-OAUJIVSPUJDUTC4SBV6QLHDITY.html

60. Fabian Virchow, "PEGIDA: Understanding the Emergence and Essence of Nativist Protest in Dresden," *Journal of Intercultural Studies* 37, no. 6 (2016): 541–55, https://doi.org/10.1080/07256868.2016.1235026

61. Göpffarth, "Activating the Socialist Past."

62. Sabine Volk, "Explaining PEGIDA's 'strange survival': An Ethnographic Approach to Far-Right Protest Rituals," *Political Research Exchange* 4, no. 1 (2022), https://doi.org/10.1080/2474736X.2022.2136036

63. Durs Grünbein, "Das Volk, dieses Monster," zeit.de, February 12, 2015, https://www.zeit.de/2015/07/dresden-seele-pegida-demos-durs-gruenbein. "Es wundert mich nicht, daß es an der Elbe ausbrach, dies diffuse Gefühl der Bedrohung. Auch woanders schneiden Wirtschaftskrise, Europolitik, Glaubenskriege und Flüchtlingsströme in die Existenz. Aber nur in Dresden schlagen sie auch aufs Gemüt."

64. Anna Wnuk, Tomasz Oleksy, and Maria Lewicka, "Attached to Place, Threatened by Newcomers? The Threat to a Place's Cultural Continuity as a Mediator Between Place Attachment and Attitudes Towards War Refugees," *Journal of Environmental Psychology* 92 (2023), https://doi.org/10.1016/j.jenvp.2023.102182

65. For a detailed analysis of the neo-Nazi presence in Dresden, as well as the counterprotests from the left and remembrance culture on February 13, see Stephan Petzold, "Challenging the Politics of German Victimhood: Memory Activism and the Contested Anniversary of the Dresden Bombing since 2005," *German Life and Letters* 73, no. 3 (2020): 441–63.

66. For thoughts about theoretically framing appropriate remembering versus appropriation of memory, see Susannah Eckersley, "Between Appropriation and Appropriateness: Instrumentalizing Dark Heritage in Populism and Memory?," in *European Memory in Populism*, ed. Chiara De Cesari and Ayhan Kaya (London: Routledge, 2020), 210–38.

67. Dpa, "Hintergrund: Weiße Rose zum Dresdner Gedenken," *Dresdner Neueste Nachrichten*, September 9, 2015, https://www.dnn.de/Dresden/Stadtpolitik/Hintergrund-Weisse-Rose-zum-Dresdner-Gedenken

68. The human chain was initiated by the Working Group February 13 under the leadership of the city government and with representatives from politics, cultural institutions, and residents. During the Covid-19 pandemic, the human chain was performed virtually. https://13februar.dresden.de/de/ag/ag-13.-februar.php

69. In fact, the peace movements of East and West Germany were exchanging letters, had meetings, and supported each other's work. Helmut Hoffmann, who took the pictures at the Dresden synagogue on the day after it had been set on fire (chapter 4), was active in these circles because of his war experiences. He was also in contact with the Dresden peace community. See the documents and comments in Helmut Hoffmann, *Nachbelichtet* (Dresden: Ddp Goldenbogen, 2001).

70. Richard Bernstein, "Germans Revisit War's Agony, Ending a Taboo," nytimes.com, March 15, 2003, https://www.nytimes.com/2003/03/15/world/germans-revisit-war-s-agony-ending-a-taboo.html

71. The description of the events is based on my qualitative observations.

72. Wodak, *The Politics of Fear*, 26. Wodak identifies these three points as central to all theoretical approaches in the debate on right-wing populism. Cas Mudde and Cristóbal Rovira Kaltwasser emphasize the importance of the negatively viewed "elite," which does not represent what the populist groups would define as the "common will." Mudde and Kaltwasser, *Populism: A Very Short Introduction*, 5.

73. Anne Hähnig, Susanne Kailitz, Martin Machowecz, "Wie glücklich ist . . . Dresden?," zeit.de, June 26, 2017, https://www.zeit.de/2017/26/ostdeutschland-dresden-zufriedenheit-glueck

74. Konstantin Nowotny, "Höcke-Rede im Wortlaut: 'Gemütszustand eines total besiegten Volkes,'" tagesspiegel.de, January 19, 2017, https://www.tagesspiegel.de/politik/gemutszustand-eines-total-besiegten-volkes-5488489.html. "Dresden ist eine ganz besondere Stadt."

75. Nowotny, "Höcke-Rede im Wortlaut." "Dresden ist die Hauptstadt der Mutbürger [. . .] und wenn ich mir jetzt die desolate innere und äußere Lage der Bundeshauptstadt Berlin vor Augen führe, dann meine ich, eigentlich dürfte nicht Berlin, eigentlich müsste Dresden die deutsche Hauptstadt [sein]."

76. Hubert Kleinert, *Die AfD und ihre Mitglieder* (Wiesbaden: Springer, 2018), 45–46.

77. Björn Höcke, "Dresdner Gespräche mit Björn Höcke," You Tube video, posted by compacttv, January 17, 2017, https://www.youtube.com/watch?v=sti51c8abaw&feature=youtu.be&t=6225

78. Sascha Lobo, "Schauen Sie diese Rede," *Der Spiegel*, January 18, 2017, https://www.spiegel.de/netzwelt/web/bjoern-hoecke-rede-offenbart-gesinnung-kolumne-von-sascha-lobo-a-1130551.html

79. Nowotny, "Höcke-Rede im Wortlaut."

80. Nowotny, "Höcke-Rede im Wortlaut."

81. Rolf-Dieter Müller, Nicole Schönherr, and Thomas Widera, eds., *Die Zerstörung Dresdens 13.-15. Februar 1945* (Göttingen: Vandenhoeck & Ruprecht Unipress, 2010).

82. Marco Bertolaso, "'Wir manipulieren nicht, wir zitieren Historiker,'" deutschlandfunk.de, February 13, 2016, https://www.deutschlandfunk.de/die-zahl-der-opfer-von-dresden-1945-wir-manipulieren-nicht.2626.de.html?dram:article_id=345493; Sven Felix Kellerhoff, "Warum genügen 25000 Tote von Dresden nicht," Welt.de, February 7, 2015, https://www.welt.de/geschichte/zweiter-weltkrieg/article137184137/Warum-genuegen-25-000-Tote-von-Dresden-nicht.html. Several books dismiss the study's results as being too low. For example, Wolfgang Schaarschmitt, *Daten-Fakten-Opfer*, Manfred Böttcher, *Dresdens Tote.*

83. Susanne Beyer, et al., "Die missbrauchte Tragödie," spiegel.de, February 10, 2020, https://www.spiegel.de/politik/deutschland/bombardement-auf-dresden-1945-die-missbrauchte-tragoedie-a-00000000-0002-0001-0000-000169356858

84. Beyer, "Die missbrauchte Tragödie."

85. Beyer, "Die missbrauchte Tragödie."

86. Quoted in Doreen Reinhard, "Das belastete Datum," Zeit.de, February 13, 2020, https://www.zeit.de/gesellschaft/zeitgeschehen/2020-02/dresden-13-februar-gedenken-bombardierung. "'ein einzigartigeres Dresdner Gedenken.'" "'so wie Hiroshima.'" "'In Hiroshima sind es auch um die 100.000 gewesen.'"

87. Matthias Neutzner, "Die Bergung, Registratur und Bestattung der Dresdner Luftkriegstoten," Dresden.de, March 17, 2010: 6–7, https://www.dresden.de/media/pdf/stadtarchiv/Historikerkommission_Dresden1945_Bericht_TP1_V1_0.pdf

88. Walter Hahn has claimed that he photographed without permission. Many pictures, however, are close-ups, including some of the personnel. The pictures suggest that Hahn was freely walking around on the square, possibly documenting the scenes for the Nazi regime. Deutsche Fotothek, "Zu Leben und Werk," https://www.slub-dresden.de/sammlungen/deutsche-fotothek/fotografen/hahn/zu-leben-und-werk/

89. For example, Konrad Badenheuer, "Kein Ende der Debatte," *Preußische Allgemeine*, March 24, 2010, https://www.preussische-allgemeine.de/nachrichten/artikel/kein-ende-der-debatte.html

90. Werner J. Patzelt, "Pegida-Demonstranten und Deutschlands Demokratie," *Zeitschrift für Parlamentsfragen* 49, no. 1 (2018): 112–13. Patzelt and his team have shown that Pegida protesters see themselves as democrats. Patzelt has since become active in right-conservative to far-right circles. The study results, however, are independent of his own involvement.

91. Rosellini, *The German New Right*, 92–93, 95.

92. The vigil has become a yearly event. I was able to observe the vigil and the counterprotests on the Altmarkt in their entirety on February 13, 2022.

93. AfD Kreisverband Dresden, *Kommunalwahlprogramm 2024* (2024), https://afd-dd.de/kommunalwahlprogramm-2024/. "eine freie historische Forschung zu den Ereignissen und Opfern jener Tage der Bombenangriffe."

94. Staatsministerium des Inneren und Sächsischer Verfassungsschutz, *Sächsischer Verfassungsbericht 2023*, 118.

95. "Neue Rechte will Dresden erobern," *taz*, August 4, 2019, https://taz.de/Rechtsextremismus-im-Osten/!5610832/. "Stadt des Widerstands."

96. Quoted in Uwe Backes and Steffen Kailitz, "Ergebnisse," in *Sachsen—eine Hochburg des Rechtsextremismus?*, ed. Uwe Backes and Steffen Kailitz (Göttingen: Vandenhoeck & Ruprecht, 2020), 392. "'Hauptstadt der patriotischen Bewegung.'"

Chapter 7

1. Regarding the role of nostalgia as a way of activating support for populist and nativist political stances, see Hans-Georg Betz and Fabian Habersack, "Regional Nativism in East Germany: The Case of the AfD," in *The People and the Nation: Populism and Ethno-Territorial Politics in Europe*, ed. Reinhard Heinisch, Emanuele Mas-

setti and Oscar Mazzoleni (New York, Routledge, 2020), https://doi.org/10.4324/9781351265560

2. Erdinç Çakmak and Laura Gorlero, "The PEGIDA Movement and Social Conflict in Dresden, Germany: An Investigation of the Impacts of Far-Right Populism on Tourism in Europe," in *Tourism and Hospitality in Conflict-Ridden Destinations*, ed. Rami K. Isaac, Erdinç Çakmak, and Richard Butler (Oxon: Routledge, 2019). 153–67.

3. Carolin Müller, "Heritage Mobilisation as Radical Politics in a Left-Wing Social Movement," *Journal of Intercultural Studies* 45, no. 1 (2024): 129, https://www.tandfonline.com/doi/full/10.1080/07256868.2023.2268001?src=

4. Hans Vorländer, "Zerrissene Stadt: Kulturkampf in Dresden," *APuZ: Dresden* (2016), https://www.bpb.de/shop/zeitschriften/apuz/219407/zerrissene-stadt/#footnote-target-5. "Die 'Straße' ist in Dresden zu einem Raum kollektiver Empörung und Selbstvergewisserung geworden."

5. Müller, "Heritage Mobilisation," 127.

6. "Semperoper schaltet das Licht aus," *Die Sueddeutsche*, December 22, 2014, https://www.sueddeutsche.de/politik/gegenveranstaltungen-semperoper-schaltet-pegida-das-licht-aus-1.2279428

7. Felicitas Galinat, "Das Bürgerforum: die Dresdner und das 'Monument': ein Stück in 4 Akten," *cybersax.de* (2017), https://www.cybersax.de/stadtgespraech/details/article/das-buergerforum/; Vorländer, "Zerrissene Stadt."

8. "Erfolgssaison bei Staatsschauspiel Dresden wird überschattet von Pegida," *Dresdner Neueste Nachrichten*, September 9, 2015, https://www.dnn.de/Nachrichten/Kultur/Regional/Erfolgssaison-bei-Staatsschauspiel-Dresden-wird-ueberschattet-von-Pegida

9. Marion Ackermann, "Hilft politische Kunst gegen Populismus," *deutschlandfunk.de*, May 17, 2017, https://www.deutschlandfunkkultur.de/dresden-hilft-politische-kunst-gegen-populismus-100.html. "Bildungsauftrag"; "Wir drehen es eigentlich um: Dresden ist gerade eine Bühne für rechtspopulistische Bewegungen, und wir wollen es umgekehrt nutzen als Bühne und Modellfall, um auch zu zeigen, was man tun kann von künstlerischer Seite, um diese Dinge stärker zu reflektieren und kritisch damit umzugehen."

10. For a detailed analysis of the group, see Carolin Müller, "From Musical Activism to Musical Citizenship: Dresden's Banda Internationale" (PhD diss., Ohio State University, 2020).

11. Netzwerk Kultur Dresden, "Postplatzkonzert am 23. März: Angst—Prozession der Angsthasen," netzwerk-kultur-dresden.de, March 23, 2015, https://netzwerk-kultur-dresden.de/postplatzkonzert-am-23-maerz-angst-prozession-der-angsthasen/

12. Netzwerk Kultur Dresden, "Prozession der Angsthasen." "Nehmt eure Angst zusammen. Jeder bringt eine mit."

13. Simone Rafael, "Pegida-Anhänger_innen bewerfen Gegendemo mit toten Küken," *Belltower News*, March 30, 2015, https://www.belltower.news/pegida-anhaenger_innen-bewerfen-gegendemo-mit-toten-kueken-39350/. "den hässlichen Antifa-Häschen das Mäulchen zu stopfen."

14. Thomas Schade, "Pegida Möhrchen für die Angsthasen" *Sächsische Zeitung*, March 23, 2015, https://www.saechsische.de/pegida-moehrchen-fuer-die-angsthasen-3065793.html?utm_source=szonline

15. Johannes Vüllers and Sebastian Hellmeier, "Does Counter-Mobilization Contain Right-Wing Populist Movements? Evidence from Germany," *European Journal of Political Research* 61 (2022): 21–45, https://doi.org/10.1111/1475-6765.12439

16. Kunsthaus Dresden, "Am Fluss/At the River," https://amfluss.tumblr.com/

17. "Manaf Halbouni im Gespräch mit Sigrid Brinkmann," deutschlandfunk.de, February 7, 2017, https://www.deutschlandfunkkultur.de/manaf-halbounis-kunstprojekt-in-dresden-mahnend-gegen-den-100.html; Julia Lefeber, "Interview—Monument—Manaf Halbuni," *NDSM*, July 22, 2022, https://www.ndsm.nl/en/story/interview-monument-manaf-halbouni/

18. Quoted in "Morddrohungen wegen Aleppo-Kunstwerk in Dresden," *Redaktions Netzwerk Deutschland*, rnd.de, February 6, 2017, https://www.rnd.de/kultur/morddrohungen-wegen-aleppo-kunstwerk-in-dresden-OOSXNWCWRG3KMYNCFLNZYOOQ7U.html. "genau der richtige Weg, um miteinander zu reden," "Reibung und den Kontakt."

19. Sarah Dornhof, "Manaf Halbouni's 'Monument' Installation in Dresden (2017)," in *Public Space Democracy: Performative, Visual and Normative Dimensions of Politics in a Global Age*, ed. Nilüfer Göle (London: Routledge, 2022), 136.

20. Bastian Brandau, "Streit um das Gedenken" deutschlandfunk.de, February 13, 2017, https://www.deutschlandfunk.de/jahrestag-der-bombardierung-dresdens-streit-um-das-gedenken-100.html

21. Quoted in Philip Oltermann, "Dresden's Bitter Divide over Aleppo-Inspired Bus Barricade Sculpture," theguardian.com, February 7, 2017, https://www.theguardian.com/world/2017/feb/07/dresdens-bitter-divide-over-aleppo-inspired-bus-barricade-sculpture

22. Doreen Reinhard, "Tumultartige Trauerarbeit," zeit.de, February 8, 2017, https://www.zeit.de/gesellschaft/zeitgeschehen/2017-02/dresden-gedenken-13-februar-tumulte-einweihung-skulptur-monument-manaf-halbouni

23. For the idea of multidirectional memory, see Michael Rothberg, *Multidirectional Memory: Remembering the Holocaust in the Age of Decolonization* (Stanford: Stanford University Press, 2009).

24. Oltermann, "Dresden's Bitter Divide."

25. Karl Mannheim, "Die Bedeutung der Konkurrenz im Gebiete des Geistigen," in *Verhandlungen des 6. Deutschen Soziologentages vom 17. bis 19. September 1928 in Zürich: Vorträge und Diskussionen in der Hauptversammlung und in den Sitzungen der Untergruppen* (Tübingen: Mohr Siebeck, 1929), 35–83, https://nbn-resolving.org/urn:nbn:de:0168-ssoar-188028

26. Mannheim, "Die Bedeutung der Konkurrenz," 45. "daß es sich beim historischen Denken wie beim seinsverbundenen Denken überhaupt um einen Wettbewerb verschiedener Parteien mit der gleichen Zielsetzung handelt;" "Tendenz in Konflikt auszuarten, in Kampf umzuschlagen oder aber in eine Beziehung des Miteinander sich umzuwandeln."

27. Mannheim, "Die Bedeutung der Konkurrenz," 45. "jedes historische, weltanschauliche, soziologische Wissen [ist] eingebettet und getragen vom Macht- und Geltungstrieb bestimmter konkreter Gruppen, die ihre Weltauslegung zur öffentlichen Weltauslegung machen wollen."

28. Vorländer, "Zerrissene Stadt."

29. Viktoria Rösch, et al., "Kunst und Kultur in der polarisierten Stadt. Dresdner Kultureinrichtungen als Vermittelnde zwischen 'Diversität' und 'Ethnopluralismus'?" *Theoretische Beiträge des Zentrums für Integrationsstudien* 2 (2020): 41.

30. Rösch, et al., "Kunst und Kultur in der polarisierten Stadt," 41. "Das Publikum ist nicht nur der primäre Adressat, es ist auch das Hauptmotiv für die Veranstaltung."

31. Max Frisch, *Graf Öderland* (Frankfurt: Suhrkamp, 1963 [1951]); Volker Lösch, "Graf Öderland—Wir sind das Volk," first performed November 28, 2015, Staatsschauspiel Dresden, Director: Volker Lösch; Thomas Schreyer and Ulf Schmidt, *Das blaue Wunder* (Hamburg: Rowohlt Theater Verlag, 2019). First performed January 26, 2019, Staatsschauspiel Dresden, Director: Volker Lösch.

32. For example, Reinhard Wengierek in "Dresden war beides barock und braun," *Die Welt*, February 16, 2009, https://www.welt.de/kultur/article3211587/Dresden-war-beides-barock-und-braun.html, or Irene Bazinger, "Blick zurück nach vorn," faz.net, February 16, 2009, https://www.faz.net/aktuell/feuilleton/buehne-und-konzert/theater-blick-zurueck-nach-vorn-1768506.html

33. Sonja Rüegg, *Ich hasse nicht die Schweiz, sondern die Verlogenheit: das Schweiz-Bild in Max Frischs Werken "Graf Öderland," "Stiller" und "Achtung, die Schweiz" und ihre zeitgenössische Kritik* (Switzerland: Chronos, 1998), 174. "soll den LeserInnen bewusst machen, dass auch in ihnen etwas 'Öderländisches' steckt [. . .]. Das Öderländische, Produkt der bürgerlichen Gesellschaft, ist in der Realität latent vorhanden und kann jederzeit ausbrechen."

34. "dass wir Mut machen möchten, sich zu verhalten. Mischt euch ein;" "und dann wird es, glaube ich, sehr schnell so sein, dass diese Stadt nicht mehr nur in dem Licht von Pegida gesehen wird, sondern als eine Stadt empfunden wird, wie sie sie eigentlich auch ist, als eine offene Stadt."

35. "Graf Öderland/Wir sind das Volk," youtube.com, posted by Staatsschauspiel Dresden, December 11, 2015, https://www.youtube.com/watch?v=tr3_6R5LpIw

36. Martin Machowecz, "Genug gespielt: Jetzt wird's Ernst," *Zeit Online*, January 24, 2019, https://www.zeit.de/2019/05/blaue-wunder-theaterstueck-afd-kampf-dresden-staatsschauspiel

37. The term "Wutbürger" was coined by the Spiegel author Dirk Kurbjuweit and became instantly widely used. Dirk Kurbjuweit, "Der Wutbürger. Stuttgart 21 und Sarrazin-Debatte: Warum die Deutschen so viel protestieren," *Spiegel Magazin*, October 11, 2010, https://www.spiegel.de/spiegel/a-724587.html

38. Björn Höcke, quoted in *Das blaue Wunder*, Act IV, 15.

39. Hubert Eckart, "Brennpunkt Theater—kippt Dresden," *Bühnentechnische Rundschau* 2 (2019): 64, https://www.der-theaterverlag.de/buehnentechnische-rundschau/aktuelles-heft/artikel/brennpunkt-theater-kippt-dresden/

40. *Das blaue Wunder*, "in eine neue Zukunft, wie in ein längst vergessenes Land," Act I, 4.

41. *Das blaue Wunder*, Act II, 6.

42. "Dresden ist die Stadt der Mutbürger . . . eigentlich dürfte nicht Berlin, eigentlich müsste Dresden die deutsche Hauptstadt sein." Björn Höcke, quoted in *Das blaue Wunder*, Act IV, 15. See also chapter 6 for Björn Höcke's statements about Dresden.

43. Kaya Ayhan, "The Use of the Past by the Alternative for Germany and the Front National: Heritage Populism, Ostalgia and Jeanne D'Arc," *Journal of Contem-*

porary European Studies 31, no. 2 (2023): 1–14, https://doi.org/10.1080/14782804.2021.1981835

44. *Das blaue Wunder,* Act IV, 4.

45. *Das blaue Wunder,* Act IV, 14. "Ich wünsche mir, dass man rauskommt aus der Opferrolle, dass man sich mit der Geschichte vor und nach 1945 auseinandersetzt und [statt zu trauern] daraus Mut entwickelt." Some of the lines appear to have been changed from the manuscript for the performance. While I use the manuscript for most quotations in this discussion, in this case, I marked the addition of text in the performance in parenthesis, since it significantly sharpens and clarifies the message.

46. Hans-Joachim Hahn, "PEGIDA auf der Bühne. Volker Löschs *Das Blaue Wunder* in Dresden," *Monatshefte* 12, no. 2 (2020): 274–94.

47. See for example Karin Wilke "Staatsbürgerkunde im Staatstheater," karinwilke.de, January 25, 2019, http://karinwilke.de/staatstheater-hetzt-mit-steuermitteln-gegen-die-afd/. Karin Wilke was a representative for the AfD in the Saxon State Parlament from 2015 to 2019.

48. Uwe Tellkamp, *Der Turm: Geschichte aus einem versunkenen Land* (Frankfurt: Suhrkamp, 2008). Translated as: *The Tower: Tales from a Lost Country* (Penguin, 2014 [2008]), 365. See for example reviews by Sabine Franke *Frankfurter Rundschau,* September 25, 2008, Beatrix Langner, *Neue Zürcher Zeitung,* October 11, 2008. In literary criticism, see for example Anne Fuchs, "Psychotopography and Ethnopoetic Realism in Uwe Tellkamp's 'Der Turm,'" *New German Critique* 116 (2012): 126, http://www.jstor.org/stable/23259406

49. Elias Hantzsch, "Susanne Dagen geht zur AfD-Fraktion im Dresdner Stadtrat," *Dresdner Neueste Nachrichten,* August 8, 2024, https://www.dnn.de/lokales/dresden/dresden-afd-fraktion-im-stadtrat-nimmt-susanne-dagen-auf-NWX3VTCXAJGLNI5WPBLSUN35S4.html

50. The name alludes to the Charta 77, which was originally a 1977 protest letter by intellectuals in Czechoslovakia denouncing the communist government's human rights violations.

51. Susanne Dagen, "Charta 2017—Zu den Vorkommnissen auf der Frankfurter Buchmesse 2017," first published at kulturhaus-loschwitz.de. The text has since been removed, but can be found at "Charta 2017—Zu den Vorkommnissen auf der Frankfurter Buchmesse 2017," October 16, 2017, https://www.openpetition.de/petition/online/charta-2017-zu-den-vorkommnissen-auf-der-frankfurter-buchmesse-2017

52. Maria Timtschenko, "Wut im Buch," *Die Zeit,* March 23, 2017, https://www.zeit.de/2017/13/susanne-dagen-dresden-pegida-buchhaendlerin-buergertum/komplettansicht. "Wir wollen uns im Osten nicht wieder etwas aufdrücken lassen, das mit uns nichts zu tun hat;" "Ich höre immer wieder: Die Ossis wollen sich heute nicht wieder verscheißern lassen."

53. "Aufruf von Dresdner Autoren," literaturner.de, December 4, 2017, https://literaturner.de/aufruf-von-dresdner-autoren/

54. "Aufruf von Dresdner Autoren." "Diffamierung," "verbale Entgleisung."

55. "Aufruf von Dresdner Autoren." "Das emphatische Einfordern von Demokratie und Toleranz gerät dort zum Widerspruch, wo dadurch Autorinnen und Autoren sowie Texte verteidigt werden, welche die demokratische Grundordnung in Frage stellen, die liberale, pluralistische Gesellschaftsentwürfe verachten oder rassistisch argumentieren."

56. Tellkamp, *The Tower*, 365. Translation slightly adjusted.

57. Tellkamp, *The Tower*, 364.

58. Uwe Tellkamp, "Das späte Atlantis: Dresdner Aufzeichnungen" *Sezession* 90 (2019): 47. "Man muß Anker haben in der Zeit. Es hilft zu überleben." In 2023, the German Domestic Intelligence Services (Bundesamt für Verfassungsschutz) classified the IfS as a confirmed right-wing extremist organization. The IfS subsequently dissolved in April 2024 but continues its political activities via a number of newly founded organizations, https://www.verfassungsschutz.de/SharedDocs/hintergruende/DE/rechtsextremismus/das-netzwerk-der-neuen-rechten.html

59. Durs Grünbein, "Gedicht über Dresden," in *Schädelbasislektion* (Frankfurt: Suhrkamp, 2020 [1991]), 112. "Scheintote Stadt, Barockwrack an der Elbe."

60. Grünbein, "Gedicht über Dresden"; my translation does not replicate the iambic rhythm of the stanza. With "*nevermore*," Grünbein refers to the Edgar Allan Poe poem "The Raven." "Das beste Depressivum ist der genius loci / An einem Ort, gemästet mit Erinnerungen / Schwammfäule, schön getönt als Nostalgie / Narkotisch wie die psychotropen Jamben / Die anglo-sächsische Version von *nevermore*."

61. Durs Grünbein, *Porzellan: Poem vom Untergang meiner Stadt* (Frankfurt: Suhrkamp, 2005). Translated by Karen Leeder as *Porcelain: Poem on the Downfall of My City* (New York: Seagull, 2020). See a note after stanza 49.

62. Renatus Deckert, ed., *Die wüste Stadt: Sieben Dichter über Dresden* (Frankfurt a. M.: Insel, 2005), 189. "Es geht immer darum, nicht stehenzubleiben. Für den Künstler gilt das in ganz besonderem Maße. Man muß aufbrechen, um wie Odysseus eines Tages wiederkehren zu können."

63. Grünbein, *Porzellan*, stanza 49. Translation slightly adjusted from *Porcelain*. "Diese heiklen Formen. Worum geht's hier?—Einer lauscht, / Was die Töchter Mnemosynes ihm diktieren. / Und er tauscht die Zeiten, Räume, Maße, tauscht und tauscht."

64. Grünbein, *Porzellan*, stanza 11. "Aus allem hören / Die Leute hier—wie Papageno stotternd, Papagena, / Den Dreiklang noch, den ewiggestrigen: Zerstörung. / Und in der Luft liegt, süßlich, das verhaßte Thema."

65. Lisa Marie Porsch and Marie-Theres Ueberlein, "'Streitbar! Wie frei sind wir mit unseren Meinungen?'—Uwe Tellkamp und Durs Grünbein im Dresdner Kulturpalast," in *Bürgerdialoge in Zeiten der Krise*, ed. Cathleen Bochmann (Wiesbaden: Springer Nature, 2022), 77–131.

66. Gerd Andersen, "Ein kleiner Papierschnipsel oder Nullpunkt der Räumlichkeit," in *Andreas Rosenthal, . . . angesichts der Güte*, ed. Kunsthaus Kloster Gravenhorst (Wuppertal: J. Abels, 2008), 11.

67. Jennifer Abels, ". . . angesichts der Güte," in *Andreas Rosenthal, . . . angesichts der Güte*, ed. Kunsthaus Kloster Gravenhorst (Wuppertal: J. Abels, 2008), 22; Andersen, "Ein kleiner Papierschnipsel," 9.

68. Quoted in Helga Bittner, "Transparenz und Masse," *Neuß-Grevenbroicher Zeitung*, July 6, 2011, https://rp-online.de/nrw/staedte/neuss/transparenz-und-masse_aid-13406963

69. Abels, ". . . angesichts der Güte," 23.

70. Quoted in Bittner, "Transparenz und Masse." "mitten in der Zeichnung stehen."

71. Quoted in Bittner, "Transparenz und Masse."

Bibliography

Archives and Libraries

Archiv der Jüdischen Gemeinde Dresden
Archiv des Stadtmuseums Dresden
Deutsche Fotothek, Dresden
Deutsches Bundesarchiv
Deutsches Rundfunkarchiv
Historisches Archiv Tourismus, Technische Hochschule Berlin
Massachusetts Historical Society
Niedersächsisches Landesarchiv/ Staatsarchiv Oldenburg
Sächsische Landes- und Universitätsbibliothek Dresden
Stadtarchiv Dresden
Stasi-Unterlagen-Archiv
Württembergische Landesbibliothek Stuttgart

Works

Abels, Jennifer. ". . . angesichts der Güte." In *Andreas Rosenthal . . . angesichts der Güte*, edited by Kunsthaus Kloster Gravenhorst. Wuppertal: J. Abels, 2008.

Ackermann, Marion. "Hilft politische Kunst gegen Populismus." *Deutschlandfunk Kultur*, May 17, 2017. https://www.deutschlandfunkkultur.de/dresden-hilft-politische-kunst-gegen-populismus-100.html

Adam, Thomas. "Travel, Gender, and Identity." In *Crossing the Atlantic: Travel and Travel Writing in Modern Times*, edited by Thomas Adam and Nils Roemer. College Station: Texas A&M University Press, 2011.

Adam, Thomas, and Gisela Mettele, eds. *Two Boston Brahmins in Goethe's Germany: The Travel Journals of Anna and George Ticknor*. Plymouth: Lexington Books, 2009.

Adams, Henry. "To Charles Francis Adams, Jr., Dresden. June 7, 1859." In *The Letters of Henry Adams, 1858–1892*. Massachusetts Historical Society, 1982.

Adams, John Quincy. *Memoirs of John Quincy Adams*. Vol. 1. Philadelphia: Lippincott, 1874.

Albers, Kate Palmer, and Jordan Bear. "Photography's Time Zones." In *Before-and-After Photography: Histories and Contexts*, edited by Jordan Bear and Kate Palmer Albers, 1–11. London: Bloomsbury, 2017.

Albers, Patricia C., and William R. James. "Travel Photography: A Methodological Approach." *Annals of Tourism Research* 15, no. 1 (1988): 134–58.

Albrecht, Joachim. "Konzessionierte und connivendo geduldete Juden—von der Gnade einer Aufenthaltsgenehmigung für Juden im Dresden des 18. Jahrhunderts." In *Der alte jüdische Friedhof in Dresden*, edited by HATiKVA e. V. Berlin: Hentrich und Hentrich, 2002.

Allbeson, Tom. *Photography, Reconstruction and the Cultural History of the Postwar European City*. London: Routledge, 2021.

Alternative für Deutschland (AfD). *Manifesto for Germany: The Political Programme of the Alternative for Germany*. Stuttgart: AfD, 2016.

Alternative für Deutschland (AfD) Kreisverband Dresden. *Kommunalwahlprogramm 2024*. Dresden: AfD, 2024. https://afd-dd.de/kommunalwahlprogramm-2024/

Amann, Melanie. *Angst für Deutschland*. München: Dröhmer, 2017.

Andersen, Gerd. "Ein kleiner Papierschnipsel oder Nullpunkt der Räumlichkeit." In Andreas Rosenthal, . . . *angesichts der Güte*, edited by Kunsthaus Kloster Gravenhorst. Wuppertal: J. Abels, 2008.

Andersen, Hans Christian. *Andersen's Works: Pictures of Travel*. Boston: Houghton, Mifflin and Company, 1871.

Arbeitskreis gegen das Vergessen Bibra. *Juden in Bibra, unvergessen: Tage der Begegnung in Bibra vom 17.–20. Mai 2007*. Bibra, 2008.

Arnold, Jörg. *The Allied Air War and Urban Memory: The Legacy of Strategic Bombing in Germany*. Cambridge: Cambridge University Press, 2011.

Ashcroft, G. J. "The Conserved European City as Cultural Symbol: The Meaning of the Text." In *Modern Europe: Place, Culture, and Identity*, edited by Brian J. Graham. New York: Arnold, 1998.

Assmann, Aleida. *Cultural Memory and Western Civilization: Functions, Media, Archives*. New York: Cambridge University Press, 2011 [1999].

Assmann, Jan. *Cultural Memory and Early Civilization: Writing, Remembrance, and Political Imagination*. New York: Cambridge University Press, 2011 [1992].

"Aufruf von Dresdner Autoren." literaturner.de, December 4, 2017. https://literaturner.de/aufruf-von-dresdner-autoren/

Ayhan, Kaya. "The Use of the Past by the Alternative for Germany and the Front National: Heritage Populism, Ostalgia and Jeanne D'Arc." *Journal of Contemporary European Studies* 31, no. 2 (2023): 1–14. https://doi.org/10.1080/14782804.2021.1981835

Backes, Uwe, and Steffen Kailitz. "Ergebnisse." In *Sachsen—eine Hochburg des Rechtsextremismus?*, edited by Uwe Backes and Steffen Kailitz. Göttingen: Vandenhoeck and Ruprecht, 2020.

Baloglu, Seymus, and Ken W. McCleary. "A Model of Destination Image Formation." *Annals of Tourism Research* 26, no. 4 (1999): 868–97.

Barnouw, Dagmar. *The War in the Empty Air: Victims, Perpetrators, and Postwar Germans*. Bloomington: Indiana University Press, 2005.

Barthes, Roland. *Image, Music, Text*. New York: Hill and Wang, 1977.

Barthes, Roland. *Mythologies.* New York: Hill and Wang, 1972.

Batty, Michael, and Paul Longley. *Fractal Cities—A Geometry of Form and Function.* London: Academic Press, 1994.

"Begründung zum Bebauungsplan Nr. 155 Dresden-Altstadt I Nr. 28, Prager Straße/ Nord-West Einkaufszentrum." *Dresdner Amtsblatt* 5 (2006): 6.

Behringer, Wolfgang. "Die großen Städtebücher und ihre Voraussetzungen." In *Das Bild der Stadt in der Neuzeit, 1400–1800,* edited by Wolfgang Behringer and Bernd Roeck. München: C. H. Beck-Verlag, 1999.

Benda-Beckmann, Bas von. *German Historians and the Bombing of German Cities: The Contested Air War.* Amsterdam: Amsterdam University Press, 2015.

Bender, Justus. *Was will die AfD? Eine Partei verändert Deutschland.* München: Pantheon, 2017.

Bergander, Götz. *Dresden im Luftkrieg.* Köln: Böhlau, 1977.

Bergander, Götz. "Vom unattraktiven zum besonders lohnenden Ziel: Dresden in den Luftkriegsplanungen der Alliierten." In *Das rote Leuchten: Dresden und der Bombenkrieg,* edited by Matthias Neutzner, Oliver Reinhard, and Wolfgang Hesse. Dresden: Edition Sächsische Zeitung, 2005.

Bergdolt, Klaus. *Deutsche in Venedig.* Darmstadt: Primus, 2011.

Bergdolt, Klaus. "Dresden und Venedig." *Dresdner Hefte* 40 (1994): 66–74.

Berger, Gabriel. "War die DDR antisemitisch?" In *Bpb Deutschland Archiv,* March 18, 2021. www.bpb.de/328430

Berger-Fiedler, Róża, director. *Herr Schmidt von der Gestapo: filmische Dokumentation einer Beamtenkarriere.* Documentary. Berlin: DEFA, 1987.

Bertolaso, Marco. "'Wir manipulieren nicht, wir zitieren Historiker.'" deutschlandfunk.de, February 13, 2016. https://www.deutschlandfunk.de/die-zahl-der-opfer-von-dresden-1945-wir-manipulieren-nicht.2626.de.html?dram:article_id=345493

Beschreibung der Königlich Sächsischen Residenzstadt Dresden und der umliegenden Gegend. Für Fremde bearbeitet. Dresden: Walther, 1807.

"Beseitigung der Brandruine der Dresdner Synagoge unter Mitwirkung der Technischen Nothilfe Ortsgruppe Dresden." Bundesarchiv in Berlin. Eingangsnummer: B 2037-1; Archivsignatur: 20196. http://www.bundesarchiv.de/benutzungsmedien/filme/view/B2037?back=1

Betz, Hans Georg. "Facets of Nativism: A Heuristic Exploration." *Patterns of Prejudice* 53 (2019): 111–35.

Betz, Hans-Georg, and Fabian Habersack. "Regional Nativism in East Germany: The Case of the AfD." In *The People and the Nation: Populism and Ethno-Territorial Politics in Europe,* edited by Reinhard Heinisch, Emanuele Massetti, and Oscar Mazzoleni. New York: Routledge, 2019. https://doi.org/10.4324/9781351265560

Beyer, Andreas. "Bernardo Bellotto (Canaletto) und die Skyline von Dresden: Zur Bildkarriere einer Stadt." In *Mythos Dresden: Eine kulturhistorische Revue,* edited by Deutsches Hygiene-Museum Dresden. Köln: Böhlau, 2006.

BfV-Pressekonferenz. "BfV-Pressekonferenz vom 12. März 2020 zum Stand der Bekämpfung des Rechtsextremismus." Verfassungsschutz.de, March 12, 2020.

Bianchini, Franco. "Introduction. European Urban Mindscapes: Concepts, Cultural Representations and Policy Applications." In *Urban Mindscapes of Europe,* edited by Godela Weiss-Sussex and Franco Bianchini. Amsterdam: Rodopi, 2006.

Bonarou, Christina. "The Poetics of Travel through Unravelling Visual Representations on Postcards: A Critical Semiotics Analysis." *Journal of Tourism, Heritage & Services Marketing* 7, no. 1 (2021): 44–53. https://doi.org/10.5281/zenodo.4519317

Boog, Horst. "Der strategische Bombenkrieg der Alliierten gegen Deutschland 1939–1945. Ein Überblick." In *Alliierter Bombenkrieg: Das Beispiel Dresden*, edited by Lothar Fritze and Thomas Widera. Göttingen: Vandenhoeck & Ruprecht Unipress, 2005.

Bove, Jens, and Sebastian Lux. "Erlösung durch Sozialismus: Der Bildband *Dresden—Eine Kamera klagt an* von Richard Peter sen." In *1945-Köln und Dresden: Fotografien von Hermann Claasen und Richard Peter sen*, edited by LVR-Landesmuseum Bonn and Deutsche Fotothek in der SLUB Dresden. Bonn: Landschaftsverband Rheinland, 2015.

Braber, Natalie. "The German Language and Reunification 1990: The Effect of Emotion on the Use of Modal Particles in East and West Berlin." PhD diss., St. Andrews University, 2001.

Brajer, Sven. *Am Rande Dresdens: Das völkisch-nationale Spektrum einer 'konservativen Kulturstadt' 1879–1933.* Dresden: Thelem, 2022.

Brenner, Henny. *Das Lied ist aus.* Zürich: Pendo Verlag, 2001.

Breymayer, Ursula. "Der engagierte Dokumentarist: Richard Peter Senior." In *Ende und Anfang: Photographen in Deutschland um 1945*, edited by Klaus Honnef, Ursula Breymayer, and Deutsches Historisches Museum. Berlin: Deutsches Historisches Museum, 1995.

Brockmann, Stephen. *Nuremburg: The Imaginary Capital.* Rochester, NY: Camden House, 2006.

Brox, Enzo, and Tommy Krieger. "Weniger Zuzug nach Dresden: Rechte Proteste verschrecken junge Leute!" *ifo Dresden berichtet* 28, no. 4 (2021): 12–17.

Brubaker, Rogers. "Between Nationalism and Civilizationism: The European Populist Moment in Comparative Perspective." *Ethnic and Racial Studies* 40, no. 8 (2017): 1191–1226.

Brüning, Eberhard. "Saxony Is a Prosperous and Happy Country." In *Traveling Between Worlds: German-American Encounters*, edited by Thomas Adam and Ruth Gross. Arlington: University of Texas Press, 2006.

Buck, Alica. "Reisemagazine im Anthropozän: Merian und die Darstellung der Natur." In *Handbuch Zeitschriftenforschung*, edited by Oliver Scheiding and Sabina Fazli. Bielefeld: transcript, 2022.

Bundesinnenministerium des Innern und für die Heimat. *Verfassungsschutzbericht 2023: Fakten und Tendenzen.* Berlin, 2024.

Bundeszentrale für politische Bildung and Robert-Havemann-Gesellschaft e.V. "Dresden und die Gruppe Wolfspelz." 2019. www.jugendopposition.de/145413

Bundeszentrale für politische Bildung and Robert-Havemann-Gesellschaft e.V. "Jugendorganisationen der DDR: Friedensgebete und Montagsdemonstrationen." 2022. www.jugendopposition.de/145465

Burger, Eberhard. "The Reconstruction of the Frauenkirche in Dresden." In *Revival of Dresden*, edited by Wolfram Jäger and C. A. Brebbia. Ashurst: WIT Press, 2000.

Burgin, Victor. "Art, Common Sense and Photography." *Camerawork* 3 (1976): 86–91.

Büro für Statistik der Juden, Berlin-Halensee. *Zeitschrift für Demographie und Statistik der Juden* 4, no. 9 (1908).

Busse, Beatrix, Ingo Warnke, and Jennifer Smith, eds. *Place-Making in the Declarative City*. Berlin: De Gruyter, 2020.

Busse, Horst, and Udo Krause. *Lebenslänglich für den Gestapokommissar*. Berlin: Staatsverlag der DDR, 1989.

Buzard, James. *The Beaten Track: European Tourism, Literature, and the Ways to "Culture," 1800–1918*. Oxford: Oxford University Press, 1993.

Buzard, James. "The Grand Tour and After (1660–1840)." In *The Cambridge Companion to Travel Writing*, edited by Peter Hulme and Tim Youngs. Cambridge: Cambridge University Press, 2002.

Çakmak, Erdinç, and Laura Gorlero. "The PEGIDA Movement and Social Conflict in Dresden, Germany: An Investigation of the Impacts of Far-Right Populism on Tourism in Europe." In *Tourism and Hospitality in Conflict-Ridden Destinations*, edited by Rami K. Isaac, Erdinç Çakmak, and Richard Butler, 153–67. New York: Routledge, 2019.

Castor, Markus A. "Rocco di Linar und die Mathematica Militaris der Dresdner Fortifikation in italienischer Manier. Städteplanung von der Bild- zur Raumordnung." In *Elbflorenz: Italienische Präsenz in Dresden 16.-19. Jahrhundert*, edited by Barbara Marx. Dresden: Verlag der Kunst, 2000.

Cheshmehzangi, Ali. *Identity of Cities and City of Identities*. Singapore: Springer Nature, 2020.

Chesterfield, Philip Dormer Stanhope, Earl of. *The Letters of Philip Dormer Stanhope, Earl of Chesterfield*. Edited with introduction, notes, and index by John Bradshaw. London: Allen, 1913.

Chong, Dennis, and James N. Druckman. "Framing Theory." *Annual Review of Political Science* 10 (2007): 103–26.

Christmann, Gabriela. *Dresdens Glanz, Stolz der Dresdner: Lokale Kommunikation, Stadtkultur und städtische Identität*. Wiesbaden: Deutscher Universitätsverlag, 2004.

Christmann, Gabriela. "Städtische Identität als kommunikative Konstruktion." Institut für höhere Studien, 2003. https://www.researchgate.net/publication/48667110_Stadtische_Identitat_als_kommunikative_Konstruktion

Claasen, Hermann. *Gesang im Feuerofen*. Düsseldorf: L. Schwann, 1947.

Clough, Patricia. *Helmut Kohl, Ein Porträt der Macht*. Munich: Dtv, 1998.

Colomb, Claire, and Ares Kalandides. "The 'Be Berlin' Campaign: Old Wine in New Bottles or Innovative Form of Participatory Place Branding?" In *Towards Effective Place Brand Management: Branding European Cities and Regions*, edited by Gregory John Ashworth and Mihalis Kavaratzis. Cheltenham: Edward Elgar, 2010.

Cray's Reiseführer: Dresden und die Sächsische Schweiz. Berlin: Berliner Verlagsanstalt, 1890.

Crew, David. *Bodies and Ruins*. Ann Arbor: University of Michigan Press, 2017.

Dagen, Susanne. "Charta 2017—Zu den Vorkommnissen auf der Frankfurter Buchmesse 2017." October 16, 2017. https://www.openpetition.de/petition/online/charta-2017-zu-den-vorkommnissen-auf-der-frankfurter-buchmesse-2017

Dale, Robert. "Visualizing the Red Army's Demobilization: Photography, Reconstructing Community and Creating Post-War Memory." *Journal of War and Culture Studies* 15, no. 2 (2022): 157–82. https://doi.org/10.1080/17526272.2022.2065118

De Bruhl, Marshall. *Firestorm: Allied Airpower and the Destruction of Dresden.* New York: Random House, 2006.

Deckert, Renatus, ed. *Die wüste Stadt: Sieben Dichter über Dresden.* Frankfurt a. M.: Insel, 2005.

Dehn, Stephan. "Die nationalsozialistische Propaganda in Sachsen 1921–1945." PhD diss., Universität Leipzig, 2016. https://core.ac.uk/download/pdf/351712164.pdf

Dehn, Stephan. "Mutschmanns Machtkampf gegen Anton Groß." *Neues Archiv für sächsische Geschichte* 86 (2015): 225–40.

Demshuk, Andrew. *Three Cities after Hitler: Redemptive Reconstruction Across Cold War Borders.* Pittsburgh: University of Pittsburgh Press, 2021.

Dennis, Mike, and Norman LaPorte. *State and Minorities in Communist East Germany.* Oxford: Berghahn, 2011.

Derenthal, Ludger. *Bilder der Trümmer- und Aufbaujahre: Fotografie im sich teilenden Deutschland.* Marburg: Jonas Verlag, 1999.

Die Deutsche Arbeitsfront. *Urlaubsfahrten und Wanderungen 1938.* Stuttgart: N.S. Gemeinschaft "Kraft durch Freude"; Gau Württemberg-Hohenzollern, 1938.

Deutscher Organisationsausschuß des Weltkongresses für Freizeit und Erholung. *Amtlicher Führer zum Weltkongress Freizeit und Erholung: Hamburg 23.-30. Juli 1936.* Hamburg: Deutscher Organisationsausschuß, 1936.

Deutschland—Zeitschrift für Industrie, Handel und Schiffahrt 3, no. 8. Hamburg: Adolf Ernst Schultze Verlag, 1940.

Diamant, Adolf, ed. *Chronik der Juden in Dresden: Von den ersten Juden bis zur Blüte der Gemeinde und deren Ausrottung.* Darmstadt: Agora, 1973.

Diefendorf, Jeffry. "Memories of the Bombing of German Cities in World War II." *German History* 32, no. 4 (2014): 615–32. https://doi.org/10.1093/gerhis/ghu108

Dietrich, Andrea. "Die Entwicklung der Stadt Dresden zu einer Tourismusmetropole von den Anfängen bis zum Vorabend des Ersten Weltkriegs." PhD diss., Hochschule für Verkehrswesen, Leipzig, 1992.

Dietrich, Ewald Christian Victorin. *Der treue Führer in der Böhmisch-Sächsischen Schweiz.* Prag, Leitmeritz, Teplitz: Medau, 1839.

Donath, Matthias. *Architektur in Dresden 1939–1945.* Meißen: Elbland, 2016.

Donavan, Barbara. "Populist Rhetoric and Nativist Alarmism: The AfD in Comparative Perspective." *German Politics and Society* 38, no. 1 (2020): 55–76. https://doi.org/10.3167/gps.2020.380104

Dornhof, Sarah. "Manaf Halbouni's 'Monument' Installation in Dresden (2017)." In *Public Space Democracy: Performative, Visual and Normative Dimensions of Politics in a Global Age,* edited by Nilüfer Göle. London: Routledge, 2022.

Dr. Lahmann's Sanatorium Weisser Hirsch in Weisser Hirsch bei Dresden: Prospekt und Jahresbericht. 29th ed. Dresden: Dr. Lahmann, 1912.

Dresden. Fotografiert von Willy Pritsche und anderen. Mit einem Geleitwort von Ludwig Renn. Dresden: Sachsenverlag Dresden, 1958.

Dresden. Merian 1, no. 12. Hamburg: Hoffmann und Campe, 1949.

Dresden. Merian 20, no. 10. Hamburg: Hoffmann und Campe, 1967.

Dresden. Merian 48, no. 1. Hamburg: Hoffmann und Campe, 1995.

Dresdner Geschichtsverein. *Dresden: die Geschichte der Stadt.* Dresden: Junius, 2005.

Driftmann, Markus. "Mythos Dresden: Symbolische Politik und deutsche Einheit." *Politik und Geschichte* 21, no. 22 (2009). https://www.bpb.de/apuz/31986/mythos-dresden-symbolische-politik-und-deutsche-einheit

Droit, Emmanuel. "Frieden." In *Erinnerungsorte der DDR*, edited by Martin Sabrow. München: Beck, 2009.

Düringer, Janna, and Rainette Lange. "Dresden bleibt Dresden—die Stadt in der Reiseliteratur." In *Dresden. Ethnografische Erkundungen einer Residenzstadt*, edited by Rolf Lindner and Johannes Moser. Leipzig: Leipziger Universitätsverlag, 2006.

Ebbrecht, Tobias. "Bilder, die es nicht geben dürfte." *Filmblatt* 112, no. 44 (2010/2011): 37–54.

Eckart, Hubert. "Brennpunkt Theater—kippt Dresden." *Bühnentechnische Rundschau* 2 (2019). https://www.der-theaterverlag.de/buehnentechnische-rundschau/aktuelles-heft/artikel/brennpunkt-theater-kippt-dresden/

Eckersley, Susannah. "Between Appropriation and Appropriateness: Instrumentalizing Dark Heritage in Populism and Memory?" In *European Memory in Populism*, edited by Chiara De Cesari and Ayhan Kaya. London: Routledge, 2020.

Eisman, April. "Symbolic Erasures and Populist Discontent: The Post-War Rebuilding of Historic Dresden." *Monatshefte* 114, no. 1 (2022): 24–25.

Ellrich, Hartmut. *Dresden 1933–1945: Der historische Reiseführer.* Berlin: Ch. Links Verlag, 2008.

Else Frenkel-Brunswik Institut. "Vernetzung und aktuelle Entwicklungen in der rechten Telegram-Szene Sachsens." *Digital-Report* 2 (2023).

Fache, Thomas. "DDR Antifaschismus und das Gedenken an die November Pogrome 1938." *Medea* 2 (2008): 1–23.

Fehringer, Kathrin. "Workaround am eigenen Leib. Prothetik bei Otto Dix und in der französischen Gegenwartsliteratur." *ilinx—Berliner Beiträge zur Kulturwissenschaft* 4 (2017): 24–40.

Fickus, Paul-Georg. "Richard Peter sen.—Fotografien aus dem zerstörten Dresden." Master's thesis, Universität Köln, 1995.

Field, Henry M. *Summer Pictures: From Copenhagen to Venice.* New York: Sheldon, 1859.

Fischer, Daniel. *Stadtbürgerlicher Eigensinn in der DDR?.* Leipzig: Leipziger Universitätsverlag, 2022.

Fischer, Joachim. "Prager Straße in Dresden: Zur Architektur-Soziologie eines utopischen Stadtensembles." *Ausdruck und Gebrauch* 5 (2004): 4–14.

Fischer, Joachim. "Rekonstruktivismus als soziale Bewegung. Die revolutionäre Rückkehr der okzidentalen Stadt." *Geographische Revue* 14 (2012): 27–42.

Floßmann, Dimitrana, and Hartwig Floßmann. "Bibra (Ein Rückblick auf 300 Jahre jüdisches Leben)." In *Juden in Südthüringen geschützt und gejagt: Eine Sammlung jüdischer Lokalchroniken*, vol. 3, edited by Hans Nothnagel. Suhl: Verlag Buchhaus Suhl, 1999.

Foucault, Michel. *The Archaeology of Knowledge.* New York: Pantheon Books, 1972 [1969].

Fox, Thomas C. "Writing Dresden Across the Generations." In *Victims and Perpetrators: 1933–1945. (Re)Presenting the Past in Post-Unification Culture*, edited by Lauren Cohen-Pfister and Dagmar Wienroder-Skinner. Berlin: De Gruyter, 2006.

Francesconi, Sabrina. "Images and Writing in Tourist Brochures." *Journal of Tourism and Cultural Change* 9, no. 4 (2011): 341–56.

Franklin, Wayne. *James Fenimore Cooper: The Early Years.* New Haven: Yale University Press, 2007.

Frei, Norbert, and Johannes Schmitz. *Journalismus im Dritten Reich.* München: Beck, 1989.

Freud, Sigmund. "Aus einem Brief an Martha Bernays vom 20.12.1883." In *Zukunft seit 1560. Die Anthologie*, edited by Karin Kolb, Gilbert Lupfer, and Martin Roth. Dresden: Staatliche Kunstsammlungen, 2010.

Frisch, Max. *Graf Öderland.* Frankfurt: Suhrkamp, 1963 [1951].

Fröhlich, Anke. "Kunst, Kultur und Bildung: Höfische Festkultur im Augusteischen Dresden." In *Geschichte der Stadt Dresden: Vom Ende des Dreißigjährigen Krieges bis zur Reichsgründung*, edited by Reiner Groß and Uwe John. Stuttgart: Theiss, 2005.

Fuchs, Anne. "Psychotopography and Ethnopoetic Realism in Uwe Tellkamp's 'Der Turm.'" *New German Critique* 116 (2012): 119–32. http://www.jstor.org/stable/23259406

Fuchs, Anne. *After the Dresden Bombing: Pathways of Memory, 1945 to the Present.* London: Palgrave, 2012.

"Für ein gemeinsames Erinnern: Gespräch der *Dresdner Hefte* mit Vertretern der Jüdischen Gemeinde in Dresden." In *Dresdner Hefte* 45, 2nd ed. (2000): 91–96.

Galinat, Felicitas. "Das Bürgerforum: Die Dresdner und das 'Monument': ein Stück in 4 Akten." cybersax.de, 2017. https://www.cybersax.de/stadtgespraech/details/article/das-buergerforum/

Gänshirt-Heinemann, Susanne. "'Fremde' in Dresden." In *Geschichte der Stadt Dresden: Von der Reichsgründung bis zur Gegenwart*, edited by Holger Starke. Stuttgart: Theiss, 2006.

Garsztecki, Stefan, Thomas Laux, and Marian Nebelin, eds. *Brennpunkte der "neuen" Rechten: Globale Entwicklungen und die Lage in Sachsen.* Bielefeld: transcript Verlag, 2023.

Geller, Jay Howard. *Jews in Post-Holocaust Germany, 1945–1953.* Cambridge: Cambridge University Press, 2005.

Gesellschaft für Christlich-Jüdische Zusammenarbeit Dresden e. V. *Juden in Sachsen: Ihr Leben und Leiden.* Leipzig: Evangelische Verlagsanstalt, 1994.

Gesellschaft für Christlich-Jüdische Zusammenarbeit Dresden, Arbeitskreis Gedenkbuch, *Buch der Erinnerung: Juden in Dresden; deportiert, ermordet, verschollen; 1933–1945.* Dresden: Thelem, 2006.

Gesellschaft Historischer Neumarkt e. V., Dresden. *Der Wiederaufbau des Neumarkts: Herz und Seele der Stadt.* Dresden: Michael Imhof Verlag, 2019.

Glasenapp, Jörn. *Die deutsche Nachkriegsfotografie. Eine Mentalitätsgeschichte in Bildern.* Paderborn: Wilhelm Fink, 2008.

Glasenapp, Jörn. "Nach dem Brand: Überlegungen zur deutschen Trümmerfotografie." *Fotogeschichte* 91 (2004): 47–64.

Goebel, Rolf J. "Gesamtkunstwerk Dresden: Official Urban Discourse and Durs Grünbein's Poetic Critique." *German Quarterly* 80, no. 4 (2007): 492–510.

Goethe, Johann Wolfgang. *Autobiography: Truth and Fiction Relating to My Life.* Translated by John Oxenford. Vol. 1. Philadelphia: J. H. Moore, 1902. https://www.gutenberg.org

Goethe, Johann Wolfgang. *Dichtung und Wahrheit: Erster und zweiter Teil.* Leipzig: Tempel Verlag, 1811–1812. https://gutenberg.spiegel.de

Goffman, Erving. *Frame Analysis: An Essay on the Organization of Experience.* Cambridge, MA: Harvard University Press, 1974.

Goldenbogen, Nora. *Die Dresdner Synagoge: Geschichte und Geschichten.* Berlin: Teetz/Hentrich und Hentrich, 2004.

Goldenbogen, Nora. "Nationalsozialistische Judenverfolgung in Dresden seit 1938—ein Überblick." *Dresdner Hefte* 45, 2nd ed. (2000): 76–84.

Goldhammer, Herbert, and Karin Jeschke. *Dresdner Gedenkorte für die Opfer des NS-Regimes.* Dresden: Ddp Goldenbogen, 2002.

Göpffarth, Julian. "Activating the Socialist Past for a Nativist Future: Far-Right Intellectuals and the Prefigurative Power of Multidirectional Nostalgia in Dresden." *Social Movement Studies* 20, no. 1 (2021): 57–74.

Gottschalck, Kaspar Friedrich. *Dresden, seine Umgebungen und die Sächsische Schweiz: ein Taschenbuch für Reisende.* Dresden: H. M. Gottschalck, 1842.

Gräfe, Roland. "Die Entstehung und Entwicklung der Albertstadt." *Dresdner Hefte* 53, 2nd ed. (2012): 22–30.

Grayling, A. C. *Among the Dead Cities.* New York: Walker, 2006.

Grey, Thomas S. "Dresden." In *Wagner in Context,* edited by David Trippett. Cambridge: Cambridge University Press, 2024.

Griffin, Michael. "The Great War Photographs: Constructing Myth and History of Photojournalism." In *Picturing the Past: Media, History and Photography,* edited by Bonnie Brennen and Hanno Hardt. Urbana: University of Illinois Press, 1999.

Groh, Christian. "Was Pforzheim angetan wurde: Erinnerungsorte und Denkmäler zum Luftkrieg." In *Luftkrieg: Erinnerungen in Deutschland und Europa,* edited by Jörg Arnold, Dietmar Süß, and Malte Thießen. Göttingen: Wallstein, 2009.

Groß, Reiner. "Ratsregiment und Stadtverwaltung." In *Geschichte der Stadt Dresden: Vom Ende des Dreißigjährigen Krieges bis zur Reichsgründung,* edited by Reiner Groß and Uwe John. Stuttgart: Theiss, 2005.

Grünbein, Durs. *Porzellan: Poem vom Untergang meiner Stadt.* Frankfurt: Suhrkamp, 2005. Translated by Karen Leeder as *Porcelain: Poem on the Downfall of My City.* New York: Seagull, 2020.

Grünbein, Durs. *Schädelbasislektion.* Frankfurt: Suhrkamp, 2000 [1991].

Gryglewski, Marcus. "Zur Geschichte der nationalsozialistischen Judenverfolgung in Dresden 1933–1945." In *Die Erinnerung hat ein Gesicht. Fotografien und Dokumente zur Nationalsozialistischen Judenverfolgung in Dresden 1933–1945,* edited by Norbert Haase, Stefi Jersch-Wenzel, Hermann Simon, and Marcus Gryglewski. Leipzig: Kiepenheuer, 1998.

Günzel, Klaus. *Romantik in Dresden.* Frankfurt: Insel, 1997.

Güttler, Ludwig, et al. "Ruf aus Dresden." February 12, 1990. https://www.frauenkirche-dresden.de/foerdergesellschaft/wie-alles-begann

Haase, Norbert. "Bücherverbrennung und 'Säuberung' Dresdner Bibliotheken." *Dresdner Hefte* 77 (2004): 52–61.

Hachtmann, Rüdiger. *Tourismusgeschichte.* Göttingen: UTB Vandenhoeck & Ruprecht, 2007.

Häder, Michael, and Sabine Häder. "Die Architekturwahrnehmung prägt in Dresden das Verbundenheitsgefühl mit dem Wohnort: Ergebnisse einer kommunalen Umfrage und der ALLBUS-Befragung." *Informationsdienst Soziale Indikatoren* 63 (2019): 1–5. https://doi.org/10.15464/isi.63.2019.1-5

Hagen, Joshua. "Historic Preservation in Nazi Germany: Practices, Patterns, and Politics." In *Heritage at the Interface: Interpretation and Identity,* edited by Glenn Hooper. Gainesville: University Press of Florida, 2018. https://doi.org/10.2307/j.ctvx06znr.9

Hagen, Joshua. *Preservation, Tourism, Nationalism: The Jewel of the German Past.* New York: Routledge, 2006.

Hahn, Hans-Joachim. "PEGIDA auf der Bühne. Volker Löschs *Das Blaue Wunder* in Dresden." *Monatshefte* 12, no. 2 (2020): 274–94.

Hahn, Walter. *Über den Dächern von Dresden.* Edited by Jens Bove. Leipzig: Lehmstedt 2008.

Hammer-Schenk, Harold. *Synagogen in Deutschland.* Hamburg: Hans Christians Verlag, 1981.

Hariman, Robert, and John Louis Lucaites. *No Captions Needed: Iconic Photographs, Public Culture, and Liberal Democracy.* Chicago: University of Chicago Press, 2007.

Hariman, Robert, and John Louis Lucaites. "Public Identity and Collective Memory in US Iconic Photography: The Image of 'Accidental Napalm.'" *Critical Studies in Media Communication* 20, no. 1 (2003): 35–66.

Hartewig, Karin. *Zurückgekehrt: Die Geschichte der jüdischen Kommunisten in der DDR.* Köln: Böhlau, 2000.

Haugen, Einar. "The Implementation of Corpus Planning Theory and Practice." In *Progress in Language Planning,* edited by Juan Cobarrubias and Joshua A. Fishman. Berlin: Mouton, 1983.

Hauptdirektion des volkseigenen Einzelhandels. *Hotelführer der DDR 1970.* Karl-Marx Stadt: Konsum Verlag, 1970.

Hauser, Arnold. *The Social History of Art.* New York: Routledge, 1999 [1951].

Held, Steffen. "Von der Entrechtung zur Deportation: Juden in Sachsen." In *Sachsen in der NS-Zeit,* edited by Clemens Vollnhals. Leipzig: Kiepenheuer, 2002.

Helfricht, Jürgen. *Die Synagoge zu Dresden.* Taucha: Tauchaer Verlag, 2001.

Herder, Johann Gottfried. "Kunstsammlungen in Dresden." *Adrastea* (1802). http://gutenberg.spiegel.de/buch/adrastea-6371/38

Herf, Jeffrey. *Divided Memory: The Nazi Past in the Two Germanys.* Cambridge, MA: Harvard University Press, 1997.

Hermann, Konstantin. "Der Führerbesuch 1934 und die Treuekundgebung 1944 in Dresden." In *Führerschule, Thingplatz, "Judenhaus": Orte und Gebäude der nationalsozialistischen Diktatur in Sachsen,* edited by Konstantin Hermann. Dresden: Sandstein Verlag, 2014.

Hertel, Christiane. "Dis/Continuities in Dresden's Dance of Death." *Art Bulletin* 82, no. 1 (2000): 83–116.

Herzog, Kurt. *Wir marschierten nach Nürnberg*. Dresden: Kommunalverlag Sachsen, 1938.

Hesse, Wolfgang. "Bild-Geschichte(n): Dresden 1939 bis 1945—die Kriegszeit in Fotografien und Filmen." In *Das rote Leuchten: Dresden und der Bombenkrieg*, edited by Oliver Reinhard, Matthias Neutzner, and Wolfgang Hesse. Dresden: Edition Sächsische Zeitung, 2005.

Hesse, Wolfgang. "Der 'Engel' von Dresden: Trümmerfotografie und visuelles Narrativ der Hoffnung." In *Das Jahrhundert der Bilder 1900 bis 1949*, edited by Gerhard Paul. Göttingen: Vandenhoeck & Ruprecht, 2008.

Hildebrandt, Dieter, director. *Der gelbe Stern. Die Judenverfolgung 1933–1945*. Documentary. Germany, 1980.

Höcke, Björn. "Dresdner Gespräche mit Björn Höcke." YouTube video, posted by compacttv, January 17, 2017. https://www.youtube.com/watch?v=sti51c8abaw&feature=youtu.be&t=6225

Hoffmann, Helmut. *Nachbelichtet*. Dresden: Ddp Goldenbogen, 2001.

Hoffmann, Kay. "Sinfonie des Krieges: Die Deutsche Wochenschau im Zweiten Weltkrieg." In *Geschichte des dokumentarischen Films in Deutschland. Vol. 3 "Drittes Reich" 1933–1945*, edited by Peter Zimmermann and Kay Hoffmann. Stuttgart: Reclam, 2005.

Hübner, Ulrich. "Der Neubau der Augustusbrücke von 1910." In *Dresdner Hefte* 94 (2008): 35–43.

Illustrirter Dresden-Prager-Führer: Malerische Beschreibung von Dresden, der Sächsischen Schweiz mit Teplitz, der Dresden-Prager Eisenbahn und Prag. Leipzig: Weber, 1852.

Irving, David. *The Destruction of Dresden*. London: W. Kimber, 1963.

Irving, Washington. *The Journals of Washington Irving*. Vol. 1, edited by William Trent and George Hellman. Boston: The Bibliophile Society, 1919.

Jaeger, Stephan. *The Second World War in the Twenty-First-Century Museum: From Narrative, Memory, and Experience to Experientiality*. Berlin: De Gruyter, 2020. https://doi.org/10.1515/9783110664416

James, Jason. *Preservation and National Belonging in Eastern Germany: Heritage Fetishism and Redeeming Germanness*. Hampshire: Palgrave Macmillan, 2012.

James, Jason. "Undoing Trauma: Reconstructing the Church of Our Lady in Dresden." *Ethos* 34 (2006): 244–72. https://doi.org/10.1525/eth.2006.34.2.244

Jerzak, Claudia. "Sakralisierte Räume und die Institutionalisierung multiperspektivischer Erzählung." In *Erinnern wozu? Beiträge zur politisch-historischen Bildung*, edited by Uwe Hirschfeld. Berlin: Lit Verlag, 2015.

Jesse, Eckhard, Thomas Schubert, and Tom Thieme. *Politik in Sachsen*. Wiesbaden: Springer Verlag, 2014.

Jessen, Ina. *Ein deutscher Maler: Otto Dix und der Nationalsozialismus*. Berlin: De Gruyter, 2022.

Joachimsthal, Georg. "Einweihung der neuen Synagoge in Dresden." *Der Weg: Zeitschrift für Fragen des Judentums* 5, no. 25 (1950): 7.

Joel, Tony. *The Dresden Firebombing: Memory and the Politics of Commemorating Destruction.* London: Tauris, 2013.

Jüdische Gemeinde Groß-Berlin und der Verband der jüdischen Gemeinden der Deutschen Demokratischen Republik. *Nachrichtenblatt der jüdischen Gemeinde Groß-Berlin und des Verbandes der jüdischen Gemeinden der Deutschen Demokratischen Republik.* Berlin (East) and Dresden: December 1972, December 1987, December 1988.

Kansteiner, Wulf. "Finding Meaning in Memory: A Methodological Critique of Collective Memory Studies." *History and Theory* 41, no. 2 (2002): 179–97.

Kirsch, Ingrid. "Die Israelitische Religionsgemeinschaft zu Dresden während der Zeit der Weimarer Republik." In *Einst und jetzt: Zur Geschichte der Dresdner Synagoge und ihrer Gemeinde,* edited by Jüdische Gemeinde Dresden. Dresden: Ddp Goldenbogen, 2001.

Kirsch, Ingrid. "Das Ringen um die rechtliche Gleichstellung der Dresdner Juden und ihrer Religionsgemeinde von 1830 bis 1871." *Dresdner Hefte* 22 (2000): 19–26.

Kläbe, Johann Gottlob August. *Neuester Dresdner Wegweiser für Fremde und Einheimische.* Dresden: Hilschersche Buchhandlung, 1797.

Kleinert, Hubert. *Die AfD und ihre Mitglieder.* Wiesbaden: Springer, 2018.

Kleist, Heinrich von. "An Wilhelmine von Zenge (Leipzig, 21.05.1801)." *Briefe.* Munich: Hanser Verlag, 1961. http://gutenberg.spiegel.de/buch/briefe-7043/3

Klemm, Heinrich. *Vollständiger illustrirter Führer durch ganz Dresden, seine Umgebung und die Böhmische Schweiz.* Dresden: Klemm, 1858.

Klemperer, Victor. *I Will Bear Witness: 1942–1945.* New York: Random House, 1999.

Koerner, Joseph Leo. *Caspar David Friedrich and the Subject of Landscape.* London: Reaktion Books, 1990.

Kolb, Karin, Gilbert Lupfer, and Martin Roth. *Zukunft seit 1560. Die Anthologie.* Dresden: Staatliche Kunstsammlungen, 2010.

Kolditz, Gerald. "Zur Entwicklung des Antisemitismus in Dresden während des Kaiserreichs." *Dresdner Hefte* 45 (1996): 37–45.

Komitee für die 750-Jahr-Feier der Stadt Dresden. *Thesen und Rahmenplan für die 750-Jahr-Feier der Stadt Dresden.* Dresden: 1955.

König, René. "Die soziale Struktur der Stadt." In *Soziologische Studien zu Gruppe und Gemeinde. René König: Schriften,* edited by Kurt Hammerich. Wiesbaden: Springer, 2006.

Korpela, Kalevi. "Place-Identity as a Product of Environmental Self-Regulation." *Journal of Environmental Psychology* 9 (1989): 241–56.

Koshar, Rudy. *German Travel Cultures.* Oxford: Berg, 2000.

Kropf, Karl. "Urbanism, Politics, and Language: The Role of Urban Morphology." *Urban Morphology* 1 (2011): 157–61.

Kulke, Torsten. "Rekonstruktion im Zeitalter der Moderne—Dresden als Zentrum städtebaulicher und architektonischer Debatten." In *Dresden: Der Wiederaufbau des Neumarkts: Herz und Seele der Stadt,* edited by Gesellschaft Historischer Neumarkt e. V. Dresden: Michael Imhof Verlag, 2019.

Kunz, Manfred. "Chronik: Stadtgeschichte—Militärgeschichte," *Militärhistorisches Museum der Bundeswehr in Dresden 10: Dresden und das Militär* (2006): 6–9.

Kunz, Manfred. "Ein Stück von Sachsens Glanz—das Arsenal in der Dresdner Albertstadt." *Militärhistorisches Museum der Bundeswehr in Dresden 5: Arsenal und Museum* (2003): 5–16.

Künzl, Hannelore. *Islamische Stilelemente im Synagogenbau des 19. und frühen 20. Jahrhunderts.* Frankfurt am Main: P. Lang, 1984.

Lalli, Marco. "Urban Related Identity: Theory, Measurement and Empirical Findings." *Journal of Environmental Psychology* 12 (1992): 285–303.

Lässig, Simone. "Vom Mittelalter in die Moderne? Anfänge der Emanzipation der Juden in Sachsen." *Dresdner Hefte*, 2nd ed. 45 (2000): 9–18.

Lau, Raymond W. K. "Tourist Sights as Semiotic Signs: A Critical Commentary." *Annals of Tourism Research* 32, no. 2 (2011): 711–14.

Lefeber, Julia. "Interview—Monument—Manaf Halbouni." *NDSM*, July 22, 2022. https://www.ndsm.nl/en/story/interview-monument-manaf-halbouni/

Lehmann, Emil. *Ein Halbjahrhundert in der israelitischen Religionsgemeinschaft zu Dresden: Erlebtes und Erlesenes.* Dresden: Salomon, 1890. https://www.diss-duisburg.de/Internetbibliothek/Artikel/Lehmann%20Dresden%20.pdf

Lehmann, Emil. "Der polnische Resident Berend Lehmann, der Stammvater der israelitischen Religionsgemeinde zu Dresden." In *Emil Lehmann Gesammelte Schriften*, 116–53. Berlin: Herman, 1899.

Lehmann, Emil. "Schutz und Förderung jeder redlichen Arbeit." In *Emil Lehmann Gesammelte Schriften.* Berlin: Herman, 1899.

Lehnert, Volkmar. "Symboldispositiv und Affektwirkung: Architektursoziologie der Synagoge in Dresden." MS thesis/Diplomarbeit, Technische Universität Dresden, 2011.

Lerm, Matthias. *Abschied vom alten Dresden: Verluste historischer Bausubstanz nach 1945.* Rostock: Hintsorff Verlag, 2000.

Leuter, Peter. "Gruss aus Dresden: Verlage, Themen, Künstler, Dokumente." *Dresdner Geschichtsbuch* 4 (1998): 195–209.

Lieber, Maria. "Die italienische Präsenz am Hofe August des Starken und seiner Söhne—Erste Überlegungen." In *Elbflorenz: Italienische Präsenz in Dresden 16.-19. Jahrhundert*, edited by Barbara Marx. Dresden: Verlag der Kunst, 2000.

Lindau, W. U. *Neues Gemählde von Dresden.* Dresden: Arnoldische Buchhandlung, 1817.

Löffler, Fritz. *Bernardo Bellotto genannt Canaletto: Dresden im 18. Jahrhundert.* Leipzig: Koehler und Amelang, 1985.

Löffler, Fritz. *Das alte Dresden: Geschichte seiner Bauten.* Dresden: Sachsenverlag, 1955.

Lösch, Volker. "Graf Öderland—Wir sind das Volk." First performed November 28, 2015, Staatsschauspiel Dresden. Directed by Volker Lösch.

Löw, Martina. *Soziologie der Städte.* Frankfurt: Suhrkamp, 2008.

Lowenthal, David. *The Past Is a Foreign Country—Revisited.* Cambridge: Cambridge University Press, 2015.

Lubich, Barbara, director. *Come Together: Dresden und der 13. Februar.* Documentary. Hechtfilm, 2012.

Lucius, Caroline. "Briefwechsel mit Christian Fürchtegott Gellert in Leipzig, 1764." Reprinted in *Dresden in alten und neuen Reisebeschreibungen*, edited by Wolfgang Paul. Düsseldorf: Droste, 1990.

Lühr, Hans-Peter, and Ilse Frischmann. "Das war die absolute Ausgrenzung." *Dresdner Hefte* 35 (1993): 27–33.

Lupfer, Gilbert. "Planungen für das Gauforum Dresden." In *Führerschule, Thingplatz, "Judenhaus": Orte und Gebäude der nationalsozialistischen Diktatur in Sachsen*, edited by Konstantin Hermann. Dresden: Sandstein Verlag, 2014.

Lynch, Kevin. *The Image of the City*. Cambridge, MA: MIT Press, 1960.

MacCannell, Dean. *The Tourist: A New Theory of the Leisure Class*. Berkeley: University of California Press, 1999 [1976].

Magirius, Heinrich. "Die Augustusbrücke." *Dresdner Hefte* 94 (2008): 25–34.

Magirius, Heinrich. "Stadtbild- und Denkmalpflege." In *Geschichte der Stadt Dresden*, vol. 3, edited by Holger Starke. Stuttgart: Theiss, 2005.

Magirius, Heinrich. "Der Wiederaufbau des Dresdner Neumarkts aus der Sicht eines Denkmalpflegers." In *Dresden: Der Wiederaufbau des Neumarkts: Herz und Seele der Stadt*, edited by Gesellschaft Historischer Neumarkt e. V. Dresden: Michael Imhof Verlag, 2019.

Mannheim, Karl. "Die Bedeutung der Konkurrenz im Gebiete des Geistigen." In *Verhandlungen des 6. Deutschen Soziologentages vom 17. bis 19. September 1928 in Zürich: Vorträge und Diskussionen in der Hauptversammlung und in den Sitzungen der Untergruppen*. Tübingen: Mohr Siebeck, 1929. https://nbn-resolving.org/urn:nbn:de:0168-ssoar-188028

Marek, Katja. "Rekonstruktion und Kulturgesellschaft: Stadtbildreparatur in Dresden, Frankfurt am Main und Berlin als Ausdruck der zeitgenössischen Suche nach Identität." PhD diss., Universität Kassel, 2009.

Margalit, Gilad. *Guilt, Suffering, and Memory: Germany Remembers Its Dead of World War II*. Bloomington: Indiana University Press, 2010.

Margalit, Gilad. "Der Luftangriff auf Dresden, seine Bedeutung für die Erinnerungspolitik der DDR und für die Herauskristallisierung einer historischen Kriegserinnerung im Westen." In *Narrative der Shoah. Repräsentationen der Vergangenheit in Historiographie, Kunst und Politik*, edited by Susanne Düwell and Mathias Schmidt. Paderborn: Schöningh, 2002.

Marquard, Odo. "Gesamtkunstwerk und Identitätssystem: Überlegungen im Anschluss an Hegels Schellingkritik." In *Der Hang zum Gesamtkunstwerk*, edited by Harald Szeemann. Frankfurt a. M.: Sauerländer Verlag, 1983.

Marwick, Marion. "Postcards from Malta: Image, Consumption, Context." *Annals of Tourism Research* 28, no. 2 (2001): 417–38.

Marx, Barbara. "Diplomaten, Agenten, Abenteurer im Dienst der Künste: Kunstbeziehungen zwischen Dresden und Venedig." In *Venedig—Dresden: Begegnung zweier Kulturstädte*, edited by Barbara Marx and Andreas Henning, 10–67. Leipzig: Seemann, 2010.

Marx, Barbara. "Vorwort." In *Elbflorenz: Italienische Präsenz in Dresden 16.-19. Jahrhundert*, edited by Barbara Marx. Dresden: Verlag der Kunst, 2000.

Marx, Barbara, and Andreas Henning, eds. *Venedig-Dresden: Begegnung zweier Kunststädte*. Leipzig: Seemann, 2010.

Marx, Harald. "Dresden und die Wiedereröffnung der Gemäldegalerie 1956." In *Geschichte der Stadt Dresden*, vol. 3, edited by Holger Starke. Stuttgart: Theiss, 2006.

Mayer, Susann. "Feuerwehrmann und Kunstliebhaber." In *Jüdisches Leben: Facetten der Geschichte und Gegenwart.* Universitätsjournal-Sonderausgabe, 24. Dresden, 1999.

McKay, Sinclair. *The Fire and the Darkness: The Bombing of Dresden, 1945.* New York: St. Martin's Press, 2020.

Meckenstock, Günter. "Schleiermachers Theorie der Geselligkeit [2006]." In *Protestantismus und Moderne: Studien zu Theologie, Philosophie und Ethik*, edited by Anette Hagan, Michael Pietsch, and Dirk Schmid. Berlin: De Gruyter, 2022. https://doi.org/10.1515/9783110745498-015

Meidner, Ludwig. "Anleitung zum Malen von Großstadtbildern." *Das neue Programm. Kunst und Künstler* 12, no. 5 (1914): 312–14.

Meyer, Beate. "'Der Eichmann von Dresden,' 'Justizielle Bewältigung' von NS-Verbrechen in der DDR am Beispiel des Verfahrens gegen Henry Schmidt." In *Deutsche, Juden, Völkermord. Der Holocaust als Geschichte und Gegenwart*, edited by Jürgen Matthäus and Klaus-Michael Mallmann. Darmstadt: WBG, 2006.

Milligan, Melinda. "Displacement and Identity Discontinuity: The Role of Nostalgia in Establishing New Identity Categories." *Symbolic Interactions* 26, no. 3 (2003): 381–403.

Milton, John. "On the Morning of Christ's Nativity." In *Poems of Mr. John Milton.* London: 1645 [1629].

Ministerium für Inneres und Sport des Landes Sachsen-Anhalt. *Verfassungsschutzbericht 2023.* Magdeburg, 2024.

Mitchell, W. J. T. *Picture Theory.* Chicago: University of Chicago Press, 1995.

Monteath, Peter. "A Day to Remember: East Germany's Day of Remembrance for the Victims of Fascism." *German History* 26, no. 2 (2008): 195–218.

Morgan, Paul. "Towards a Developmental Theory of Place Attachment." *Journal of Environmental Psychology* 30, no. 1 (2010): 11–22.

Moritz, Tino, and Toralf Staud. "Rechtsaußen, mittendrin." In *Unter Sachsen*, edited by Heike Kleffner and Matthias Hausner. Berlin: Ch. Links Verlag, 2017.

Mudde, Cas, and Cristóbal Rovira Kaltwasser. *Populism: A Very Short Introduction.* Oxford: Oxford University Press, 2017.

Müller, Carolin. "From Musical Activism to Musical Citizenship: Dresden's Banda Internationale." PhD diss., Ohio State University, 2020.

Müller, Carolin. "Heritage Mobilisation as Radical Politics in a Left-Wing Social Movement." *Journal of Intercultural Studies* 45, no. 1 (2024): 127–45. https://www.tandfonline.com/doi/full/10.1080/07256868.2023.2268001?src=

Müller, Jan-Werner. *What Is Populism?* Philadelphia: University of Pennsylvania Press, 2016.

Müller, Rolf-Dieter. *Der Bombenkrieg 1939–1945.* Berlin: Links Verlag, 2004.

Müller, Rolf-Dieter. "Die militärische Bedeutung Dresdens im Frühjahr 1945 und die Auswirkungen der alliierten Luftangriffe." In *Die Zerstörung Dresdens 13. bis 15. Februar 1945*, edited by Rolf-Dieter Müller, Nicole Schönherr, and Thomas Widera. Göttingen: Vandenhoeck & Ruprecht Unipress, 2010.

Müller, Rolf-Dieter, Nicole Schönherr, and Thomas Widera. *Die Zerstörung Dresdens 13. bis 15. Februar 1945: Gutachten und Ergebnisse der Dresdner Historikerkommission zur Ermittlung der Opferzahlen.* Göttingen: Vandenhoeck & Ruprecht Unipress, 2010.

Müller, Susanne. *Die Welt des Baedekers: Eine Medienkulturgeschichte des Reiseführers 1830–1945.* Frankfurt: Campus, 2012.

Münkler, Herfried. "Antifaschismus als Gründungsmythos der DDR: Abgrenzungsinstrument nach Westen und Herrschaftsmittel nach innen." In *Der missbrauchte Antifaschismus. DDR-Staatsdoktrin und Lebenslüge der deutschen Linken*, edited by Manfred Agethen et al. Freiburg: Herder, 2002.

Murdock, Caitlin. "Tourist Landscapes and Regional Identities in Saxony, 1878–1938." *Central European History* 40 (2007): 589–621.

Musolff, Andreas. *Metaphor, Nation and the Holocaust: The Concept of Body Politics.* New York: Routledge, 2010.

Nas, Peter J. M., Marlies de Groot, and Michelle Schut. "Introduction: Variety of Symbols." In *Cities Full of Symbols: A Theory of Urban Space and Culture*, edited by Peter Nas. Leiden: Leiden University Press, 2011.

Nas, Peter J. M., and Annemarie Samuels, eds. *Hypercity: The Symbolic Side of Urbanism.* New York: Kegan Paul, 2006.

Neidhardt, Hans Joachim. "Wozu eine Gesellschaft Historischer Neumarkt Dresden e. V." In *Der Wiederaufbau des Neumarkts: Herz und Seele der Stadt*, edited by Gesellschaft Historischer Neumarkt e. V., Dresden. Dresden: Michael Imhof Verlag, 2019.

Neitzel, Sönke. "The City under Attack." In *Firestorm: The Bombing of Dresden, 1945*, edited by Paul Addison and Jeremy A. Crang. Chicago: I. R. Dee, 2006.

Nelson, Thomas, Zoe M. Oxley, and Rosalee A. Clawson. "Toward a Psychology of Framing Effects." *Political Behavior* 19 (1997): 221–46.

Netzwerk Kultur Dresden. "Postplatzkonzert am 23. März: Angst—Prozession der Angsthasen." *netzwerk-kultur-dresden.de*, March 23, 2015. https://netzwerk-kultur-dresden.de/postplatzkonzert-am-23-maerz-angst-prozession-der-angsthasen/

Neue Ansicht von Dresden: Für Reisende von einem Reisenden. Leipzig: Leo, 1799.

Neutzner, Matthias. "Die Bergung, Registratur und Bestattung der Dresdner Luftkriegstoten." Dresden.de, March 17, 2010. https://www.dresden.de/media/pdf/stadtarchiv/Historikerkommission_Dresden1945_Bericht_TP1_V1_0.pdf

Neutzner, Matthias. "Heidefriedhof: Lernen am konfliktbeladenen Ort." *Dresdner Hefte* 127 (2016): 75–85.

Neutzner, Matthias. "Vom Alltäglichen zum Exemplarischen: Dresden als Chiffre für den Luftkrieg der Alliierten." In *Das rote Leuchten: Dresden und der Bombenkrieg*, edited by Oliver Reinhard, Matthias Neutzner, and Wolfgang Hesse. Dresden: Edition Sächsische Zeitung, 2005.

Neutzner, Matthias. "Vom Anklagen zum Erinnern." In *Das rote Leuchten: Dresden und der Bombenkrieg*, edited by Oliver Reinhard, Matthias Neutzner, and Wolfgang Hesse. Dresden: Edition Sächsische Zeitung, 2005.

Nitzschke, Katrin. *Dresden: Literarische Spaziergänge.* Frankfurt a. M.: Insel, 1999.

Nolan, Mary. "Germans as Victims during World War II: Air Wars, Memory Wars." *Central European History* 38, no. 7 (2005): 7–40. https://doi.org/10.1163/1569161053623651

Nora, Pierre. "Between Memory and History: Les Lieux de Mémoire." *Representations* 26 (1989): 7–24. https://www.jstor.org/stable/2928520

Nossack, Hans Erich. *The End: Hamburg 1943.* Chicago: University of Chicago Press, 2004.

Nossack, Hans Erich. *Der Untergang*. Berlin: Suhrkamp, 2021 [1948].

Overy, Richard. *The Air War 1939–1945.* London: Europa, 1980.

Overy, Richard. *The Bombers and the Bombed: Allied Air War Over Europe, 1940–1945.* New York: Penguin, 2014.

Overy, Richard. *The Bombing War: Europe, 1939–1945.* London: Allen Lane, 2013.

Patzelt, Werner J. "Pegida-Demonstranten und Deutschlands Demokratie." *Zeitschrift für Parlamentsfragen* 49, no. 1 (2018): 111–28.

Paul, Jürgen, Thomas Kantschew, and Uwe Kröger. *Der Wiederaufbau der Frauenkirche zu Dresden.* 3rd ed. Dresden: Gesellschaft zur Förderung des Wiederaufbaus der Frauenkirche Dresden e.V., 1997.

Paulsen, Krista E. "Place." In *The Wiley-Blackwell Encyclopedia of Urban and Regional Studies*, edited by Anthony M. Orum and Dennis R. Judd. United Kingdom: Wiley, 2019.

Peschel, Andreas. "Die Entwicklung der Dresdner NSDAP bis 1933." *Dresdner Geschichtsbuch* 18 (2013): 151–70.

Peter, Richard. *Dresden: eine Kamera klagt an.* Dresden: Dresdener Verlagsgesellschaft KG, 1950.

Peter, Richard. "Gute Fotos kosten Zeit und Mühe." *fotografie* 4 (1960): 149–51.

Petzold, Stephan. "Challenging the Politics of German Victimhood: Memory Activism and the Contested Anniversary of the Dresden Bombing since 2005." *German Life and Letters* 73, no. 3 (2020): 441–63.

Piefel, Matthias. *Antisemitismus und völkische Bewegung im Königreich Sachsen 1879–1914.* Göttingen: Vandenhoeck & Ruprecht Unipress, 2004.

Pieper, Christine. "Juden in Sachsen 1933 bis 1945: Ein defizitäres Forschungsfeld." *Medaon* 15 (2014). http://www.medaon.de/pdf/MEDAON_15_Pieper.pdf

Porsch, Lisa Marie, and Marie-Theres Ueberlein. "'Streitbar! Wie frei sind wir mit unseren Meinungen?'—Uwe Tellkamp und Durs Grünbein im Dresdner Kulturpalast." In Cathleen Bochmann, ed., *Bürgerdialoge in Zeiten der Krise.* Wiesbaden: Springer Nature, 2022.

Prager, Brad. *Aesthetic Vision and German Romanticism: Writing Images.* Rochester, NY: Camden House, 2007.

Prager, Brad. "Air War and Allegory." In *Bombs Away! Representing the Air War over Europe and Japan*, edited by William Rasch and Wilfried Wilms. Amsterdam: Amsterdamer Beiträge zur neueren Germanistik, 2006.

Prattes, Vanessa. "'Inzidenz bei 1933': Visuelle Inszenierungs- und Emotionalisierungsstrategien des Opfer- und Widerstandsmythos in der 'Querdenken-Bewegung.'" *Zeitschrift für Kultur- und Kollektivwissenschaft* 9, no. 1 (2023): 155–98. https://doi.org/10.14361/zkkw-2023-090108

Pretes, Michael. "Tourism and Nationalism." *Annals of Tourism Research* 30, no. 1 (2003): 125–42.

Raffelhüschen, Bernd. *SKL Glücksatlas 2023.* München: Penguin, 2023. https://www.skl-gluecksatlas.de/artikel/staedteranking-2023/dresden.html

Rahne, Hermann. "Die 'Festung Dresden' von 1945." *Dresdner Hefte* 41 (1995): 19–31.

Rahne, Hermann. "Zur Geschichte der Dresdner Garnison im Zweiten Weltkrieg 1939 bis 1945." In *Verbrannt bis zur Unkenntlichkeit: Die Zerstörung Dresdens 1945*, edited by Stadtmuseum Dresden. Dresden: DZA Verlag, 1994.

Ramet, Sabrina P. *Social Currents in Eastern Europe: The Sources and Consequences of the Great Transformation*. Durham: Duke University Press, 1995.

Rat der Stadt Dresden. *Das Buch der Stadt Dresden*. Dresden: Industrie- und Verkehrsverlag, 1924–1930.

Rat der Stadt Dresden. *Dresden*. Dresden: Grafischer Großbetrieb Völkerfreundschaft Dresden, 1960s.

Rat der Stadt Dresden. *Dresden, Kleine Städtereihe 14*. Leipzig: Brockhaus, 1965.

Rat der Stadt Dresden. *Du und Deine Stadt: 5 Jahre Aufbauarbeit der Stadtverwaltung Dresden*. Dresden: Dresdner Verlagsgesellschaft, 1950.

Ratcliffe, Eleanor, and Kalevi M. Korpela. "Memory and Place Attachment as Predictors of Imagined Restorative Perceptions of Favourite Places." *Journal of Environmental Psychology* 48 (2016): 120–30.

Referat Fremdenverkehr beim Rat der Stadt Dresden. *Dresden*. Dresden: VEB Landesdruckerei Sachsen, 1961.

Rehberg, Karl-Siegbert, and Matthias Neutzner. "The Dresden Frauenkirche as a Contested Symbol: The Architecture of Remembrance after War." In *War and Cultural Heritage: Biographies of Place*, edited by Marie Louise Stig Sorensen and Dacia Viejo-Rose. Cambridge: Cambridge University Press, 2015.

Reich Committee for Tourist Travel. *Germany: Periodical for Scenery, Travel, and Touring*. Berlin: Reich Committee for Tourist Travel, 1934.

Reichert, Friedrich. "750-Jahr-Feier Dresdens im Juni 1956." *Dresdner Geschichtsbuch 1* (1995): 195–202.

Reichert, Friedrich. *Foto Schaarschuch—Dresden: Bildbericht 1927 bis 1955*. Dresden: Stadtmuseum Dresden, 1996.

Reimann, Siegfried. "Der 'Förderverein Bau der Synagoge Dresden e. V.'—Seine Entstehung und seine Ziele." *Dresdner Hefte* 45, 2nd ed. (2000): 85–90.

Reitzenstein, Bruni. *Mein Dresden: Die zerrissene Stadt*. Aired June 26, 2019, ZDF. https://www.zdf.de/dokumentation/dokumentation-sonstige/mein-dresden-die-zerrissene-stadt-100.html

Reuband, Karl-Heinz, ed. *Dresden im Wandel: Kulturelle Repräsentationen und soziale Transformationen*. Dresden: Thelem, 2022.

Reynié, Dominique. "'Heritage Populism' and France's National Front." *Journal of Democracy* 27, no. 4 (2016): 47–57.

Richter, Otto. *Dresden sonst und jetzt*. Dresden: Edition Sächsische Zeitung, 2007 [1905].

Richter, Ralf. "Die Geschichte der 'Englischen Kolonie' in Dresden." *Dresdner Hefte* 70 (2002): 47–55.

Ristau, Daniel. *Bruch/Stücke: Die Novemberpogrome in Sachsen 1938*. Berlin: Hentrich und Hentrich, 2018.

Rodenberger, Axel. *Der Tod von Dresden*. Dortmund: Landverlag, 1951.

Rodenberger, Axel. *Der Tod von Dresden*. 5th ed. Frankfurt a. M.: Müller-Rodenberger, 1963.

Rogg, Matthias. "Der historische Ort." In *Militärhistorisches Museum Dresden: Aus-*

stellungsführer, edited by Gorch Pieken and Matthias Rogg. Dresden: Sandstein Verlag, 2011.

Rösch, Viktoria, et al. "Kunst und Kultur in der polarisierten Stadt. Dresdner Kultureinrichtungen als Vermittelnde zwischen 'Diversität' und 'Ethnopluralismus'?" *Theoretische Beiträge des Zentrums für Integrationsstudien* (2020). https://nbn-resolving.org/urn:nbn:de:bsz:14-qucosa2-707892

Rosellini, Jay Julian. *The German New Right*. London: Hurst, 2019.

Rosenfeld, Gavriel D. *Munich and Memory: Architecture, Monuments, and the Legacy of the Third Reich*. Berkeley: University of California Press, 2000.

Rosseaux, Ulrich. "Das ambivalente Jubiläum: die 750-Jahr-Feier Dresdens 1956." *Dresdner Hefte* 87 (2006): 50–59.

Rossi, Aldo. *The Architecture of the City*. Cambridge, MA: MIT Press, 1982 [1966].

Roszczynska-Kurasinska, Magdalena, Anna Domaradzka, Anna Wnuk, and Tomasz Oleksy. "Intrinsic Value and Perceived Essentialism of Culture Heritage Sites as Tools for Planning Interventions." *Sustainability* 13 (2021): 5078. https://doi.org/10.3390/su13095078

Rotstein, Siegmund. "Vorwort." In *Lebenslänglich für den Gestapokommissar*, by Horst Busse and Udo Krause. Berlin: Staatsverlag der DDR, 1989.

Rubin, Eli. *Amnesiopolis: Modernity, Space and Memory in East Germany*. Oxford: Oxford University Press, 2016.

Rüegg, Sonja. *Ich hasse nicht die Schweiz, sondern die Verlogenheit: das Schweiz-Bild in Max Frischs Werken "Graf Öderland," "Stiller" und "Achtung, die Schweiz" und ihre zeitgenössische Kritik*. Zürich: Chronos, 1998.

Schaarschuch, Kurt. *Bilddokument Dresden, 1933–1945*. Dresden: Rat der Stadt Dresden, 1945.

Schälike, Valerija. "Die Russisch-Orthodoxe Kirche in Dresden und ihre Gemeinde." *Dresdner Hefte* 74 (2003): 72–77.

Scheer, Regina. "'Stille Helden' in Dresden." In *Die Schuhe der Toten*, edited by Gorch Pieken. Dresden: Sandstein, 2014.

Schenk, Jan. "Verbrannte Orte. Idee, Ziele und Entwicklungen des Citizen-Science-Projekts zu den Bücherverbrennungen 1933." In *Erinnerungskultur digital: Herausforderungen und Chancen für die historische und politische Bildung*, edited by Thomas Bürger and Roland Löffler. Dresden: Sächsische Landeszentrale für Politische Bildung, 2024. https://doi.org/10.25366/2024.90

Schill, Gerhard. "Rassenhaß als Bestandteil imperialistischer Politik." In *Gedenke! Vergiß Nie!: 40. Jahrestag des faschistischen "Kristallnacht"-Pogroms; Eine Dokumentation*, edited by Verband der Jüdischen Gemeinden in der Deutschen Demokratischen Republik. Berlin: Union-Verlag, 1979.

Schivelbusch, Wolfgang. *The Railway Journey*. Oakland: University of California Press, 1986.

Schlegel, August Wilhelm von. "Die Gemälde." In *August Wilhelm von Schlegel's vermischte und kritische Schriften*, edited by Eduard Böcking, Vol. 3. Leipzig: Weidmann'sche Buchhandlung, 1846.

Schmeitzner, Mike. *Der Fall Mutschmann: Sachsens Gauleiter vor Stalins Tribunal*. Markkleeberg: Sax-Verlag, 2011.

Schmeitzner, Mike. "Tödlicher Hass: Antisemitismus und Judenverfolgung in Dresden 1933–1945." *Medaon* 10 (2016): 1–28. http://www.medaon.de/pdf/medaon_19_Schmeitzner.pdf

Schmitz, Walter, ed. *Die Zerstörung Dresdens: Antworten der Künste.* Dresden: Thelem, 2005.

Schnatz, Helmut. *Tieffliieger über Dresden? Legenden und Wirklichkeit.* Köln: Böhlau, 2000.

Schneede, Uwe M. *Otto Dix.* München: Beck, 2019.

Schneider, Haley. "Deliberative Topoi and the Pull of the Future: Bridging Disparate Visions of Dresden Elbe Valley." *Rhetoric Society Quarterly* 49, no. 5 (2019): 495–516.

Schornstein, Leo Jehuda. "Erlebnisbericht aus Dresden." In *Chronik der Juden in Dresden: Von den ersten Juden bis zur Blüte der Gemeinde und deren Ausrottung*, edited by Adolf Diamant. Darmstadt: Agora, 1973.

Schreyer, Thomas, and Ulf Schmidt. *Das blaue Wunder.* Hamburg: Rowohlt Theater Verlag, 2019. First performed January 26, 2019, Staatsschauspiel Dresden. Directed by Volker Lösch.

Schulz, Heinz. "Die Herstellung von militärischem Bedarf in Dresden (1900–1920)." In *Dresdner Geschichtsbuch 11* (2005): 171–92.

Schulz, Heinz. "Der Rüstungsstandort Dresden 1933–1945." In *Sachsen im Bombenkrieg—und nun auch Dresden*, edited by Militärhistorisches Museum Dresden. Dresden: Militärhistorisches Museum Dresden, 2005.

Schumann, Gustav. *Dresden. Der lustige Baedeker.* Vol. 2. Stuttgart: Schwabacher'sche Verlagsbuchhandlung, 1888.

Scott, Clive. *Spoken Image: Photography and Language.* London: Reaktion Books, 1999.

Semmens, Kristin. *Seeing Hitler's Germany: Tourism in the Third Reich.* New York: Palgrave, 2005.

Sen, Arijit, and Lisa Silverman. *Making Place: Space and Embodiment in the City.* Bloomington: Indiana University Press, 2013.

Sennett, Richard. *Flesh and Stone: The Body and the City in Western Civilization.* New York: Norton, 1994.

Seydewitz, Max. *Die unbesiegbare Stadt*, 5th ed. Berlin: Kongress, 1962.

Seydewitz, Max. *Zerstörung und Wiederaufbau von Dresden.* Berlin: Kongress, 1955.

Shoshan, Nitzan. "Spatial Configurations of Right-Wing Populism in Contemporary Germany." *International Journal of Urban and Regional Research* (2019). https://www.ijurr.org/spotlight-on/political-geographies-of-right-wing-populism/spatial-configurations-of-right-wing-populism-in-contemporary-germany/

"Siebtes Pioniertreffen 1982 in Dresden." YouTube, shared by Ernst Steiger, October 5, 2009. https://www.youtube.com/watch?v=rW98LVme-AM

Silverstein, Michael. "'Cultural' Concepts and the Language-Culture Nexus." *Current Anthropology* 45, no. 5 (2004): 621–52.

Sinn, Andrea. "Returning to Stay? Jews in East and West Germany after the Holocaust." *Central European History* 53 (2020): 393–413.

Sparing, Rudolf. "Der Tod von Dresden. Ein Leuchtzeichen des Widerstandes." *Das Reich*, March 4, 1945.

Springer, René. "Presseerklärung: Plünderung unserer Sozialkassen beenden." *AfD*

Bundestag Fraktion. November 15, 2023. https://afdbundestag.de/rene-springer-pluenderung-unserer-sozialkassen-beenden/

Staatsbetrieb Sachsenforst. *Der Nationalpark Sächsische Schweiz als regionaler Wirtschaftsfaktor.* Schriftenreihe des Nationalparks Sächsische Schweiz. Dresden: Staatsbetrieb Sachsenforst, 2010.

Staatsministerium des Inneren und Sächsischer Verfassungsschutz. *Sächsischer Verfassungsbericht 2023.* Dresden, 2024.

Staatsschauspiel Dresden, "Graf Öderland/Wir sind das Volk." YouTube, posted by Staatsschauspiel Dresden, December 11, 2015. https://www.youtube.com/watch?v=tr3_6R5LpIw

Stadtfeuerwehrverband Dresden e.V. *Berufsfeuerwehr Dresden 1868–2018.* Erfurt: Sutton Verlag, 2018.

Stadtleitung Dresden der SED. *Patrioten gegen Barbaren: Aus der Chronik des Kampfes gegen Faschismus und Krieg in Dresden in den Jahren 1933–1945.* Dresden: Stadtleitung Dresden der SED, 1985.

Stangl, Paul. *Risen from Ruins: The Cultural Politics of Rebuilding East Berlin.* Stanford: Stanford University Press, 2018.

Starke, Holger, "Das Judenlager Hellerberg." In *Geschichte der Stadt Dresden,* vol. 3, edited by Holger Starke. Stuttgart: Theiss, 2006.

Starke, Holger. "Vom Werkstättenareal zum Industriegelände." In *Dresdner Geschichtsbuch 5* (1999): 150–98.

Statistisches Amt der Landeshauptstadt Dresden. *Dresden in Zahlen 1937.* Dresden: Statistisches Amt der Landeshauptstadt Dresden, 1939.

Statistisches Amt der Stadt Dresden. *Die Verwaltung der Stadt Dresden 1927.* Dresden: Statistisches Amt, 1929.

Statistisches Amt der Stadt Dresden. *Die Verwaltung der Stadt Dresden 1933.* Dresden: Statistisches Amt, 1935.

Statistisches Reichsamt. *Statistisches Jahrbuch für das Deutsche Reich, 1939–1940.* Berlin: 1940.

Sternberger, Dolf. *Panorama oder Ansichten vom 19. Jahrhundert.* Hamburg: Goverts Verlag, 1938.

Süß, Dietmar. *Death from the Skies: How the British and Germans Survived Bombing in World War II.* New York: Oxford University Press, 2014.

Suttner, Irina, and Gunda Ulbricht. "Henry Schmidt: Leiter des Judendezernats der Dresdner Gestapo." In *Braune Karrieren,* edited by Christine Pieper, Mike Schmeitzner, and Gerhard Naser. Dresden: Sandstein, 2012.

Swensen, Grete, and Karoline Daugstad. "Travels in Imaginary Landscapes: An Analysis of Four Cultural Historic Guidebooks." *Belgeo* 3 (2012). http://journals.openedition.org/belgeo/7219

Tallis, Raymond. *Michelangelo's Finger: An Exploration of Everyday Transcendence.* New Haven, CT: Yale University Press, 2010.

Taylor, Frederick. *Dresden, Tuesday, February 13, 1945.* New York: HarperCollins, 2004.

Taylor, J. Bayard. *Views Afoot.* New York: Wiley and Putnam, 1846. https://www.gutenberg.org.

Tellkamp, Uwe. "Das späte Atlantis: Dresdner Aufzeichnungen." *Sezession* 90 (2019): 42–47.

Tellkamp, Uwe. *The Tower: Tales from a Lost Country.* London: Penguin, 2014.

Tellkamp, Uwe. *Der Turm: Geschichte aus einem versunkenen Land.* Frankfurt: Suhrkamp, 2008.

Ten Dyke, Elizabeth A. *Dresden: Paradoxes of Memory in History.* London: Routledge, 2001.

Thackeray, William Makepeace. *The Newcomes.* 1854. Available at https://www.gutenberg.org

Thießen, Malte. *Eingebrannt ins Gedächnis: Hamburgs Gedenken an Luftkrieg und Kriegsende 1943 bis 2005.* Hamburg: Dölling und Galitz, 2007.

Thüringer Ministerium für Inneres und Kommunales. *Verfassungsschutzbericht 2023 Freistaat Thüringen.* Erfurt, 2024.

Timm, Angelika. "The Burdened Relationship." *Israel Studies* 2, no. 1 (1997): 22–49.

Tompkins, David. "Israel as Friend and Foe: Shaping East German Society through Freund- and Feindbilder." In *Becoming East German: Socialist Structures and Sensibilities after Hitler*, edited by Mary Fulbrock and Andrew I. Port. Oxford: Berghahn, 2013.

Trimborn, Jürgen. "Das 'Wunder von Dresden': Der Wiederaufbau der Frauenkirche: Ein kritischer Blick auf das größte Rekonstruktionsprojekt des Jahrhunderts." *Die Alte Stadt* 97 (1997): 127–49.

Ulbricht, Gunda. "Geschichte der Jüdischen Gemeinde im vergleichenden Überblick zu sächsischer und deutscher Geschichte von 1697 bis 1872." In *Der alte jüdische Friedhof in Dresden*, edited by HATiKVA e. V., 284–88. Berlin: Hentrich und Hentrich, 2002.

Ulbricht, Gunda. "Sie waren es nicht? Bürgerlicher Konsens im Nationalsozialismus." *Dresdner Hefte* 93 (2008): 55–64.

Ullrich, Uwe. *Zur Geschichte der Juden in Dresden.* Dresden: Hille, 2001.

Urry, John, and Jonas Larsen. *The Tourist Gaze 3.0.* London: Sage, 2011.

Urry, John. *The Tourist Gaze: Leisure and Travel in Contemporary Societies.* London: Sage, 1990.

Vees-Gulani, Susanne. "Diagnosing Billy Pilgrim: A Psychiatric Approach to Kurt Vonnegut's *Slaughterhouse-Five*." *Critique: Studies in Contemporary Fiction* 44, no. 2 (2003): 175–84.

Vees-Gulani, Susanne. "From Frankfurt's Goethehaus to Dresden's Frauenkirche: Architecture, German Identity, and Historical Memory after 1945." *The Germanic Review: Literature, Culture, Theory* 80, no. 2 (2005): 143–63.

Vees-Gulani, Susanne. "The Politics of New Beginnings: The Continued Exclusion of the Nazi Past in Dresden's Cityscape." In *Beyond Berlin: Twelve German Cities Confront the Nazi Past*, edited by Gavriel Rosenfeld and Paul B. Jaskot. Ann Arbor: University of Michigan Press, 2008.

Vees-Gulani, Susanne. "The Ruined Picture Postcard: Dresden's Visually Encoded History and the Television Drama *Dresden*." *New German Critique* 38, no. 1 (2011): 85–113. https://doi.org/10.1215/0094033X-2010-024

Vees-Gulani, Susanne. "Symbol of Reconciliation and Far-Right Stronghold? Pegida, AfD and Memory Culture in Dresden." *German Politics and Society* 39, no. 1 (2021): 56–78.

Vees-Gulani, Susanne. *Trauma and Guilt: Literature of Wartime Bombing in Germany.* New York: De Gruyter, 2003.

Verband der Jüdischen Gemeinden in der Deutschen Demokratischen Republik. *Gedenke! Vergiß Nie! 40. Jahrestag des faschistischen "Kristallnacht"-Pogroms; Eine Dokumentation.* Berlin: Union-Verlag, 1979.

Verkehrsamt der Stadt Dresden. *Berlin-Dresden in 1 ½ Stunden.* Dresden: Dr. Güntzsche Stiftung, 1936.

Virchow, Fabian. "PEGIDA: Understanding the Emergence and Essence of Nativist Protest in Dresden." *Journal of Intercultural Studies* 37, no. 6 (2016): 541–55. https://doi.org/10.1080/07256868.2016.1235026

Volk, Sabine. "Conceptualising Europe from the Far Right: The Mobilisation of Intellectual Heritage in Germany." *Journal of European Studies* 52, no. 3–4 (2022): 238–54. https://doi.org/10.1177/00472441221115564

Volk, Sabine. "Explaining PEGIDA's 'strange survival': An Ethnographic Approach to Far-Right Protest Rituals." *Political Research Exchange* 4, no. 1 (2022). https://doi.org/10.1080/2474736X.2022.2136036

Volk, Sabine. "'Wir sind das Volk.' Representative Claim-Making and Populist Style in the PEGIDA Movement's Discourse." *German Politics* 29, no. 4 (2020): 599–616. https://doi.org/10.1080/09644008.2020.1742325

Volk, Sabine, and Manès Weisskircher. "Defending Democracy against the 'Corona Dictatorship'? Far-Right PEGIDA during the COVID-19 Pandemic." *Social Movement Studies* 23, no. 6 (2024). https://doi.org/10.1080/14742837.2023.2171385

Vonnegut, Kurt. *Armageddon in Retrospect.* New York: Putnam, 2008.

Vonnegut, Kurt. *Slaughterhouse-Five.* New York: Delacorte, 1969.

VORHIN—Erinnerungskultur im Zentralwerk. "Folge 3: Tagesmarsch zur Judenabteilung," October 17, 2017. YouTube, posted by Zentralwerk, January 3, 2018. https://www.youtube.com/watch?v=iDl321U5VMc&t=6054s

Vorländer, Hans. "Zerrissene Stadt: Kulturkampf in Dresden." *APuZ: Dresden* (2016). https://www.bpb.de/shop/zeitschriften/apuz/219407/zerrissene-stadt/#footnote-target-5

Vorländer, Hans, Maik Herold, and Steven Schäller. *PEGIDA and New Right-Wing Populism in Germany.* London: Palgrave Macmillan, 2018.

Vüllers, Johannes, and Sebastian Hellmeier. "Does Counter-Mobilization Contain Right-Wing Populist Movements? Evidence from Germany." *European Journal of Political Research* 61 (2022): 21–45. https://doi.org/10.1111/1475-6765.12439

Wagner, Andreas. *Machtergreifung in Sachsen.* Köln: Böhlau, 2004.

Wagner, Kirsten. "Die visuelle Ordnung der Stadt. Das Bild der Stadt bei Kevin Lynch." *H-Soz-Kult,* September 14, 2006. https://www.hsozkult.de/debate/id/fddebate-132142

Wagner, Richard. *Das Kunstwerk der Zukunft.* Leipzig, 1850. https://www.deutschestextarchiv.de/wagner_zukunft_1850

Walter, Franz. "Sachsen—Ein Stammland der Sozialdemokratie?" *Politische Vierteljahresschrift* 32, no. 2 (1991): 207–31. http://www.jstor.org/stable/24196320

Walther, Alexander. "Jewish Anti-Fascism?: 'Kristallnacht' Remembrance in the GDR between Propaganda and Jewish Self-Assertion." In *New Perspectives on Kristallnacht: After 80 Years, the Nazi Pogrom in Global Comparison,* edited by Steven J. Ross, Wolf Gruner, and Lisa Ansell. West Lafayette: Purdue University Press, 2019. https://doi.org/10.2307/j.ctvh9w1k7.16

Wandel et al. "Zur Architektur der Neuen Synagoge in Dresden." *Dresdner Hefte* 45, 2nd ed. (2000): 90–93.

Weber, Christoph D. "'A Blemish on the History of the Twentieth Century'? Legends and Fabrications Surrounding the Mass Cremations in the Wake of the Dresden Air Raids, February 1945." *Oxford German Studies* 47, no. 4 (2018): 486–504.

Weber, Gregor J. M. "Die Galerie als Kunstwerk: Die Hängung italienischer Gemälde in der Dresdener Galerie 1754." In *Elbflorenz: Italienische Präsenz in Dresden 16.-19. Jahrhundert*, edited by Barbara Marx. Dresden: Verlag der Kunst, 2000.

Weidauer, Walter. *Inferno Dresden: Über Lügen und Legenden um die Aktion "Donnerschlag,"* 1965, 4th ed. Berlin (East): Dietz, 1982.

Weil, Francesca. *Uns geht es scheinbar wie dem Führer . . . Zur späten sächsischen Kriegsgesellschaft (1943–1945).* Göttingen: Vandenhoeck & Ruprecht Unipress, 2020.

Weil, Francesca, Uwe Hirschfeld, Jonas Kühne, and Fruzsina Müller. "Editorial." *Totalitarismus und Demokratie* 18 (2021): 147–52. https://doi.org/10.13109/tode.2021.18.2.147

Weisskircher, Manès. "The Strength of Far-Right AfD in Eastern Germany: The East-West Divide and the Multiple Causes behind 'Populism.'" *Political Quarterly* 91, no. 3 (2020): 614–22.

Wenzkat, Ingrid. "Fritz Löffler: Das alte Dresden." In *Geschichte der Stadt Dresden*, vol. 3, edited by Holger Starke. Stuttgart: Thesis, 2005.

Widera, Thomas. "Gefangene Erinnerung: Die politische Instrumentalisierung der Bombardierung Dresdens." In *Alliierter Bombenkrieg. Das Beispiel Dresden*, edited by Thomas Widera and Lothar Fritze. Göttingen: Vandenhoeck & Ruprecht Unipress, 2005.

Wilke, Karin. "Staatsbürgerkunde im Staatstheater." karinwilke.de, January 25, 2019. http://karinwilke.de/staatstheater-hetzt-mit-steuermitteln-gegen-die-afd/

Williams, Daniel R. "'Beyond the Commodity Metaphor,' Revisited." In *Place Attachment: Advances in Theory, Methods and Applications*, edited by Lynne C. Manzo and Patrick Devine-Wright. London: Routledge, 2014.

Wittenbecher, Günter, director. *Als die Synagogen brannten—Pogromnacht 1938.* DDR RF, 1988. Available at Deutsches Rundfunkarchiv. https://www.dra.de/de/

Wnuk, Anna, Tomasz Oleksy, and Maria Lewicka. "Attached to Place, Threatened by Newcomers? The Threat to a Place's Cultural Continuity as a Mediator Between Place Attachment and Attitudes Towards War Refugees." *Journal of Environmental Psychology* 92 (2023). https://doi.org/10.1016/j.jenvp.2023.102182

Wodak, Ruth. *The Politics of Fear: What Right-Wing Populist Discourses Mean.* London: Sage, 2015.

Wolf, Paul. "Historische Stadtform und künftige Gestaltung der Stadt Dresden." *Deutsche Bauzeitung* 42, no. 72 (1938): B1137–B1143.

Wotte, Herbert, Wolfgang Göthel, and Siegfried Hoyer. *Brockhaus Stadtführer Dresden.* Leipzig: Brockhaus, 1968.

Wotte, Herbert, Wolfgang Göthel, and Siegfried Hoyer. *Brockhaus-Stadtführer Dresden.* Leipzig: Brockhaus, 1975.

Yoder, Jennifer A. "'Revenge of the East'? The AfD's Appeal in Eastern Germany and Mainstream Parties' Responses." *German Politics and Society* 38, no. 2 (2020): 35–58. https://doi.org/10.3167/gps.2020.380202

Zehring, Maximilia, and Eseme Domahidi. "German Corona Protest Mobilizers on Telegram and Their Relations to the Far Right: A Network and Topic Analysis." *Social Media and Society* 9, no. 1 (2023). https://doi.org/10.1177/2056305123115 5106

Zeitgenossen e. V. and Jüdische Gemeinde Dresden. "Die neue Synagoge ist für mich. . . ." Dresden, 2011. http://zeitgenossen-dresden.de/die-neue-synagoge-ist -fur-mich/

Ziegner, Sylvia. "Der Bildband *Dresden—eine Kamera klagt an* von Richard Peter senior. Teil der Erinnerungskultur Dresden." PhD diss., Marburg an der Lahn, 2012.

Ziegner, Sylvia, and Jens Bove. "Beruf Arbeiterfotograf: Zum Werk und zur Rezeption von Richard Peter sen." In *Die Eroberung der beobachtenden Maschinen: Zur Arbeiterfotografie der Weimarer Republik*, edited by Wolfgang Hesse. Leipzig: Leipziger Universitätsverlag, 2012.

Zuschlag, Christoph. "Die Dresdner Ausstellung 'Entartete Kunst' 1933 bis 1937." In *Geschichte der Stadt Dresden*, vol. 3, edited by Holger Starke. Stuttgart: Thiessen, 2006.

Zuschlag, Christoph. "Die Dresdner Ausstellung 'Entartete Kunst' 1933–1937." *Dresdner Hefte* 22, no. 77 (2008): 17–25.

Index

Note: Page entries in italics refer to illustrations or tables.

Ackermann, Marion, 247–48
Adam, Thomas, 73–74
Adams, Henry, 70
Adams, John Quincy, 71, 74
"Aktion Sühnezeichen" (Action Reconciliation), 179
Albers, Kate Palmer, 100
Albertstadt, 19
Allbeson, Tom, 99, 103
"Als die Synagogen brannten—Pogromnacht 1938" (When the Synagogues Were Burning—Pogrom Night 1938), 156
Das alte Dresden: Geschichte seiner Bauten (Löffler), 124–25
Alter Annenfriedhof, 171
Alternative for Germany (AfD)
  creation of, 223–24, 234
  criticism of *Monument*, 252
  Dagen and, 263
  growth of, 226
  and integration of far-right ideas into Dresden bombing narrative, 235, 236–41
  and Lösch's protest plays, 254, 256–58, 259, 260, 261
  platform of, 224, 226–27, 234, 243
  public reaction to protesters opposing, 259
  radicalization of, 225
  support for, 12, 221, 224, 225–26, 327n26
Altmarkt
  AfD's Dresden bombing commemoration rhetoric at, 237–39
  bombing memorials at, 239–41
  cremation of bodies on, 163, *164*, 238–39
  increased size of, 175–76
  Jeremias on reconstruction of, 133
Altstadtgesundung (old town recuperation), 150, 175
American travelers and visitors, 70–72
Andersen, Hans Christian, 65–66
". . . Angesichts der Güte" (. . . Facing Kindness) (Rosenthal), 272–75
antisemitism. *See* Jewish persecution
Antonov, Aleksei, 285n59
Apfel, Holger, 323n82
Apocalyptic Landscapes (Meidner), 31–32
"Appeal [Call] from Dresden" (Ruf aus Dresden), 198–99
art collection, under August I and August II, 55–56
Asche, Sigfried, 133
Assisi, Yadegar, 2–4
Assmann, Aleida, 29
Assmann, Jan, 29
atomic bomb, 41, 42, 44–45, 172
August II (Friedrich August I, August the Strong), 53, 54, 55
August III (Friedrich August II), 53, 54, 55–56
Augustus Bridge, *84*, 289n15

Bachmann, Lutz, 228, 229, 249
Bähr, George, 141
Banda Internationale, 248
Barnouw, Dagmar, 288n119
Barthes, Roland, 18, 26–27, 29
Bastei, *69*, 70
Bear, Jordan, 100
Begegnung mit dem Judentum, 181–82
behavioral symbolism, 53, 54–57
Bellmann bookstore, 87
Bellotto, Bernardo (Canaletto). *See* Canaletto (Bernardo Bellotto)
Bergander, Götz, 277n2
Berlin Wall, 116, 132, 194
Beyer, Marcel, 264, 280n23
Bianchini, Franco, 62
Bilddokument Dresden: 1933–1945 (Schaarschuch), 97–103, 106
"Bilder aus der Heimat" series, 92–93
Das Blaue Wunder (The Blue Wonder), 254, 256–62
Boog, Horst, 277n2
book burnings, 87–88
Book of the City of Dresden, 85–86
Brandt, Willy, 161
Brenner, Henny, 155–56, 159
Brockhaus Stadtführer/Atlas (Brockhaus City Guide/Atlas), 120–21, 122–23
Brockmann, Stephen, 280n22
Buck, Wilhelm, 146–47
Burgin, Victor, 286n80
Burning City (Meidner), *31*

Canaletto (Bernardo Bellotto), 58–59
  Dresden from the Right Bank of the Elbe Below the Augustus Bridge, 2–4, *3*, 57–58
  The Ruins of the Old Kreuzkirche, 58, *59*
Canaletto View, 2, 4, 58
capitalism, and National Socialist fascism, 139, 160
Carolabrücke, 80, 174, *175*
catastrophic urban views, expressionistic, 31–35. See also *View from the Rathausturm toward the South* (Peter)
Charta 2017, 263–64
Cheshmehzangi, Ali, 4
Chesterfield, Lord, 60
Chiaveri, Gaetano, 54
Chicago Daily Tribune, 24, 25
Christian Democrats (CDU), 223, 225
Christian iconography, 33–34
Christians, and Holocaust remembrance, 181–82
Christian symbolism, and calls for Frauenkirche reconstruction, 198–200, 201
Christmann, Gabriela B., 5–6, 78
Chrupalla, Tino, 237
Churchill, Winston, 41, 44
Claasen, Hermann, 33
Clemens, Johannes, 154, 213
Clive, Scott, 34
Cold War, 28, 41, 44, 160, 182, 194, 285n59
comparative photography, 96, 97–107, 138. *See also* war photography
contested spaces, 245–54
Cooper, James Fenimore, 72
coproducing, 32–33
corpus planning, 193
Coulognes, Henri, 280n23
counter-demonstrations, 249–50, 253
Covid-19 pandemic, 223, 228, 317n8
culture
  clashes of definitions of, 271
  and contested spaces in historic center, 245–50
  dynamic understanding of, 271
  and far-right rhetoric, 243–45
  and military significance of Dresden, 23–24, 25
  rejection of new ideas concerning definition of, 252–53
  and rise and politics of Dresden bombing narrative, 29

Dagen, Susanne, 263–64
Dale, Robert, 36
da Tola, Benedikt, 52
da Tola, Gabriel, 52
Day of Remembrance for the Victims of Fascism, 160, 163, 165, 169–70
De Bruhl, Marshall, 277n2
de-drawing, 273, 275
Dehrenthal, Ludger, 101
Demshuk, Andrew, 150, 320n46
"Deportation of the last Dresden Jews to

the camp at Hellerberg on 23rd/24th November 1942," 157–59
deportations of Jews, 151, 157–59
Destruction of Dresden, The (Irving), 44–45
Deutsche Reform (German Reform), 143
Deutschland—Zeitschrift fur Industrie, Handel und Schiffahrt (Germany—Magazine for Industry, Trade, and Shipping), 91, *92*
Diettrich, Fritz, 129
di Linar, Rocco, 51
discursive symbolism, 53, 57–58
Dix, Otto, 144–47
"Dolchstoßlegende" (Stab-In-the-Back Myth), 145
Dornhof, Sarah, 250
Dresden. *See also* Dresden, history of; Dresden, postwar narratives on; Dresden bombing; Dresden bombing narrative; post-reunification rebuilding projects
  AfD's affinity for, 235
  character and distinction of, 5, 6, 7
  exceptionality of, 46
  far right groups' engagement with destiny of, 234–35
  happiness of residents, 6–7
  history as garrison town, 18–19
  Jewish life in, before 1933, 141–47
  as militarily significant target, 15–16, 18–21, 23–24, 25, 45, 277n2
  official tour of, organized by GDR, 27–28
  panoramas of, 67–68
  as peace symbol, 42
  and place identity, 5–6
  rebuilding and marketing as socialist city, 108–27, 137
  reconstruction of, 40, 97–98
  as right-wing stronghold, 241
  role in National Socialism, 147–51
  750th anniversary of, 111–13
  visual representations and identity of, 8
  war photography in, 286n82
  as war production site, 19–20
Dresden (Sachsenverlag coffee-table book), 115–16, *117*
Dresden, history of, 49–50
  Dresden as artistic, intellectual, and societal stage, 62–70
  Dresden's construction as city with high imageability and symbolic and performative function, 50–59
  Dresden's development as cultural icon, 50
  Dresden's rise as travel destination and deepening urban mindscape, 59–62
  foreign visitors, 70–76, 89–90
  marketing of Dresden for leisure travel, 76–85
  preservation and marketing of Dresden's image and heritage from 1914 to 1945, 85–94
Dresden, postwar narratives on, 95–96
  photo books of destruction, 97–107, 138
  rebuilding and marketing as socialist city and travel icon, 108–27, 137, 174–75
  and reconstruction, 97–98, 116–27
  West German travel magazines, 127–38
Dresden bombing. *See also* Dresden bombing narrative; *View from the Rathausturm toward the South* (Peter)
  casualties of, 44–45, 281n3
  commemoration of, and rise of far right, 231–35
  commemoration of Jewish persecution and, 163–71, 178, 181, 182–83
  framed as historical event, 116
  Frauenkirche as *lieu de mémoire* for, 188–91
  impact of, 1, 15–17, 20, 23–24
  literary representations of, 280n23
  memorialization of, 49, 221
  Nazi propaganda concerning, 7
  neo-Nazi commemoration of, 209
  news reports on, 22–25
  preparations for, 314n126
  scholarship on, 1–2, 277n2
  as series of multiple bombardments, 20–21
  as Western operation, 285n59
Dresden bombing narrative, 15–18
  and Dresden's military significance, 18–21

Dresden bombing narrative (*continued*)
  framed with Peter's photograph, 17, 18, 37–44
  and Holocaust remembrance, 162, 163–71, 178, 181, 182–83, 207–8
  integration of far-right ideas into, 235–41
  literature on, 44–46
  Nazi era as blind spot in, 222
  and Peter's *View from the Rathausturm toward the South*, 30
  precursors facilitating pictorial and verbal, 49–50
  rise and politics of, 21–29
  and understanding and presenting history in Dresden, 208
  witness reports cementing victim narrative, 46–47
Dresden castle, 52
Dresden: Eine Kamera klagt an (Peter), 36, 103–7, 138, 300n23, 300n26
Dresden Fire Department, 152
Dresden für alle (Dresden for All), 248
"Dresden: Germany's Wonderful City of Culture," *86*
Dresden sonst und jetzt (Richter), 78–80, *79*
"Dresden's Painters," 101–3
Dresden Synagogue. *See* New Synagogue; Postwar Synagogue (1950); Semper Synagogue
Dresdner Arbeitskreis Begegnung mit dem Judentum (Dresden Working Group Encountering Judaism), 179
Dresdner Volkszeitung, 87–88
Driftmann, Markus, 198
Dr. Lahmann's Sanatorium, 74, *75*
Du und Deine Stadt: 5 Jahre Aufbauarbeit der Stadtverwaltung Dresden (You and Your City: 5 Years of Construction by the Dresden City Government), 108–11
dynamic art, 252–53

East Germany. *See* German Democratic Republic (GDR)
education, 74–75
Ehrenhain (Grove of Honor), 168–69. *See also* Heidefriedhof Memorial Park
"Einladung an einen Freund" (Raschke), 129
"Elbflorenz," 52
Engert, Rolf, 130–31
engraving techniques, 67
"Entartete Kunst" (Degenerate Art) show, 88, 149
Eschwege, Helmut, 280n20
etching techniques, 67
exclusive moral representation, 223

far right. *See also* Alternative for Germany (AfD); neo-Nazis; Pegida (Patriotic Europeans against the Islamization of the Occident)
  confrontation of, 243–44, 245–54
  Dagen's defense of, 263–64
  Dresden memory culture and, 231–35
  and Dresden's narrative of loss and victimhood, 244–45
  impact on tourism, 244
  integration of ideas into Dresden bombing narrative, 235–41
  and Lösch's protest plays, 254–62
  platform and objectives of, 243
  rise of, 221–22, 223–30
  support for, 221, 224, 225–26, 243, 327n26
fascism
  Day of Remembrance for the Victims of Fascism, 160, 163, 165, 169–70
  and defining future of Dresden, 108
  Dresden as victim of, 39
  Dresden bombing and Jewish persecution as acts of, 139, 140, 141, 165, 166, 168, 181
  Memorial for the Victims of Fascism, 168, *170*
  as outcome of capitalism, 139, 160
  and persecution of Jews during Nazi era, 173, 177–78, 210
Field, Henry M., 71
Fingerzeig (pointing finger), 34
Fischer, Daniel, 298n2
Fischer-Gravelius, Gottfried, 130
Florence, 50, 52, 54
Foer, Jonathan Safran, 280n23
fortification system, 51, 53
Foucault, Michel, 319n25
framing theory, 17
Frauenkirche
  before and after bombing, *98*, 100

as antiwar memorial, 187–93
as attractor and amplifier in peace and reconciliation discourse, 201–7
citizen initiative calling for reconstruction of, 195, 198–200
commemoration events at, 317n7
comparative photography of, 103
consecration of rebuilt, 202–4
and construction of Dresden, 54
far-right view on reconstruction of, 236
and Holocaust remembrance, 165
Jeremias on preservation of ruins of, 133
as material fix point for identity, 185
as memorial, 176
as *meta-lieu de mémoire*, 200
Monument installation at, 250–52
post-reunification modifications in public rhetoric regarding, 194
post-reunification symbolism of, 186, 195–98
public response to reconstruction of synagogue versus, 208, 209–10
reconstruction and symbolic meaning of, 183, 195–98
reconstruction of, as sacred journey, 193–200
restoration of, during National Socialist era, 149
as static symbol, 251–52
as uniting Dresden's architectural past and loss, 186
and Young/Thalmann Pioneers gathering, 189–91
Free German Youth (FDJ), 194
Freie Sachsen (Free Saxons), 226, 229
Freud, Sigmund, 74–75
Freyer, Thomas, 256
Friedrich, Caspar David, 66–67
Friedrich August I (August II, August the Strong), 53, 54, 55
Friedrich August II (August III), 53, 54, 55–56
Frisch, Max, 255
Frischmann, Ilse, 148, 308n40
Fritz, Stephan, 317n10
Füllers, Johannes, 249

Gansel, Jürgen, 323n82
Gau Forum, 150, 151
Gauland, Alexander, 257
Gau Württemberg-Hohenzollern, 89
GDR Association of People of Jewish Faith, 178
Gedenke! Vergiss nie! (Remember! Never Forget!), 178
"Gedicht über Dresden" (Grünbein), 268
"Der gelbe Stern" (The Yellow Star), 156, 311n81
"Die Gemälde" (Schlegel and Schlegel), 63–64
German Democratic Republic (GDR). *See also* Peaceful Revolution
architecture of, 206–7
desired symbolism for Frauenkirche, 188–89
Dresden bombing rhetoric in, 27
and Holocaust remembrance, 160–64
Monday protests against, 189, 222, 227
official tour of Dresden organized by, 27–28
peace activists' criticism of, 192–93
position concerning Dresden bombing, 40, 41
prosecution of war criminals in, 179–80, 181
and recoding of "peace" trope, 194–98
relationship to Judaism and Jewish citizens, 173–74
and remembrance of National Socialist era, 8–9
scholarship on urban history regarding, 9
and societal language planning, 193–94
Germany: Periodical for Scenery, Travel, and Touring, 89–90
Gesamtkunstwerk, 56, 67
Gesang im Feuerofen (Claasen), 33
Goebbels, Joseph, 148, 151, 283n29
Goethe, Johann Wolfgang, 60–61
Goffman, Erving, 17. *See also* Framing Theory
Göpffarth, Julian, 229
Gottschalck, Friedrich, 67
Graf Öderland (Frisch), 254, 255
Graf Öderland–Wir sind das Volk (Count Öderland–We Are the People), 254–56, 258

Grayling, A. C., 277n2
"Grieving Girl in a Sea of Tears," 169
Griffin, Michael, 286n78
Grillparzer, Franz, 66
Großer Garten, 150
Grote, Ludwig, 131
Grünbein, Durs, 136–37, 230, 264–65, 268–71, 280n23
Die Grünen (The Greens), 226
Guderian, Heinz, 20
guidebooks. *See* travel guides

Hager, Kurt, 170
Hahn, Walter, 238–39, 286n82, 331n88
  View from the Rathausturm (Hahn), *36*, 37
Halbouni, Manaf, 250–52
Hannusch, Heidrun, 217
Hanuschek, Sven, 280n23
happiness, of Dresden residents, 6–7
Hariman, Robert, 29, 33
Härtling, Peter, 133, 135
Haugen, Einar, 193
"healthy city" idea, 175
Heidefriedhof Memorial Park, 168, *170*, 232
  memorial stone at, 116
Hellerberg, 157–59, 179
Hellmeier, Sebastian, 249
Herder, Johann Gottfried, 63
heritage populism, 222, 325n2
Hertel, Christiane, 169
Hilbert, Dirk, 239
Hildebrandt, Dieter, 156. *See also* "Der gelbe Stern" (The Yellow Star)
Hirsch, Ernst, 157
Hitler, Adolf, 148–49, 151
Höcke, Björn, 224, 234–36, 257, 258
Hoffmann, Helmut, 154, 214, 330n69
Hofkirche, 54, 121
Höhne, Erich, 157, 286n82
Holocaust, 152, 160–83, 185, 207–8, 210, 216–17, 232–33, 323n82. *See also* Jewish persecution
Honecker, Erich, 127, 164, 189–90
Hotel Stadt Rom, 206
Höxter, Aron, 213, 214, 215
Höxter, Margot, 214
human chain, 231–32, 329n68
hypercity, 57, 94

iconic photograph, 29, 36
iconic symbolism, 53
ideal city, 52, 289n7
identity
  discursive symbolism and strengthening of Dresden's, 57–58
  Dresden's postwar, 103
  Frauenkirche as material fix point for, 185
  Frauenkirche's reconstruction and post-reunification, 193–94
  German culture and, 243
  in Grünbein's *Porzellan*, 269–70
  and imageability, 51
  intertwining of city and, 57, 280n22
  place-bound, 100–101
  place identity, 5–6
  reorientation of Dresden citizens,' 108
  urban identity, 4, 7
  and visual representations of Dresden, 8
imageability, 50–51, 53–54
image banks, 62
Image of the City, The (Lynch), 50–51
imagetext, 35
industrial development, 78–80, 83, 86, 91
Inferno Dresden (Weidauer), 40–41
Institut fur Staatspolitik (Institute for State Politics, IfS), 268, 336n58
Interessengemeinschaft 13. Februar, 231–32
Interhotels, 302n64
International Federation of Resistance Fighters (FIR), 168
Irving, David, 44–45, 46, 288n119
Irving, Washington, 71–72
Israel, 174
Italy, as influence on Dresden's construction, 50, 52, 54–55

Jeremias, Brigitte, 133
Jewish life, in Dresden before 1933, 141–47
Jewish persecution, 139–41. *See also* Holocaust
  deportations of Jews, 151, 157–59
  memory of, in Socialist Dresden, 148, 160–83, 185, 207–8, 216–17
  November Pogroms, 151–59, 161–62, 165, 178, 181–82, 208, 210–17

remembrance of, and rise of far right, 232–33
in Saxony, 140, 143–44
"Juden in Sachsen: Ihr Leben und Leiden" (Jews in Saxony: Their Life and Suffering) exhibition, 182
"Judenlager Hellerberg," 157–59, 179

Kaltwasser, Cristóbal Rovira, 330n72
Kapp-Putsch (1920), 145
Kästner, Ida, 280n23
Kempowski, Walter, 280n23
Kirby, Gustavus Town, 90
Kirchner, Hans Ludwig, 144
Kläbe, Johann Gottlieb August, 63
Kleine Städtereihe (Short City Guides), 120, 121–22
Kleist, Heinrich von, 64–65
Klemm, Heinrich, 68, 293n70
Klemperer, Eva, 311n85
Klemperer, Victor, 159, 311n85
Koerner, Joseph Leo, 34
Kohl, Helmut, 195–98, 199, 203
Köhler, Horst, 203–4
König, René, 4
Koshar, Rudy, 298n140
Kraft durch Freude (Strength through Joy) organization, 89, 90
Krah, Maximilian, 326n23
Kreis, Wilhelm, 150
Kreuzkirche (Church of the Holy Cross), 58, *59*, 181–82
Kristallnacht, 165, 168
Kulturpalast, 176
"Kulturschande," 135–36

landmarks, rebuilt, 201–4. *See also* Frauenkirche; Zwinger
Lang, Will, 27–28, 105
language planning, 193–95
Lappe, Herbert, 214
leftist politics, 244, 262–63
Lehmann, Emil, 143
Leippe, Heinrich, 128
Leipzig-Dresden railway connection, 73–74
Lethem, Jonathan, 280n23
Leupold, Hans, 213, 323n90
Libermann, Kurt, 99
Life magazine, 27–28
Lindau, W. U., 65
Die Linke (The Left), 226
Löffler, Fritz, 124–25, 132, 303n80
Lösch, Volker, 254–62
Löw, Martina, 5
Löwenkopf, Leon, 173–74
Lowenthal, David, 203
Lucaites, John Louis, 29, 33
Lucius, Caroline, 58
Ludendorff, Erich, 145
Lynch, Kevin, 50–51

MacCannell, Dean, 60, 201
Mannheim, Karl, 252
Margalit, Gilad, 27, 28
Maria Josepha, 55
Marquard, Odo, 56
Marx, Barbara, 52
material symbolism, 53–54
Mauro, Alessandro, 55
McKay, Sinclair, 277n2
meaning, and imageability, 51
medicine, natural, 74, 75–76
Meidner, Ludwig, 31–32, 144
Memorial for the Victims of Fascism, 168, *170*
memory discourse, 46–47, 182
Merian, Matthäus, the Elder, 289n15
Merian magazine, 128–33, 134–37, 198
Merkel, Angela, 243, 259
Meyer, Beate, 180
Meyer, Julius, 171–72
Military History Museum of the German Armed Forces, 9–10
Milton, John, 33
Miracle of Bern, 321n47
Mitchell, W. J. T., 18, 35
Monday demonstrations (Pegida), 246, 248–49
Monday protests, 189, 222, 227
Monument (Halbouni), 250–52
Moritz, Prince, 51, 52
Mozart Fountain, *131*
Mudde, Cass, 330n72
Mulisch, Harry, 280n23
Müller, Achatz von, 204
Müller, Carolin, 244
Müller, Jan-Werner, 223
Müller, Rolf-Dieter, 277n2
Murdock, Caitlin, 293n71

Mutschmann, Martin, 148, 150–51
mythologies, creation of modern, 26–27, 29

Nachrichtenblatt des Verbandes der Jüdischen Gemeinden in der Deutschen Demokratischen Republik, 181
Nadler, Hans, 135–36
Nas, Peter J. M., 52, 53, 54
National Democratic Party of Germany (NPD), 223–24
National Socialism. *See also* Nazi Party (Nationalsozialistische Deutsche Arbeiterpartei, NSDAP)
 memory of Jewish persecution and, 160–83, 207–8, 216–17
 and November Pogroms, 151–59
 remembrance of era, 8–9
 Saxony and Dresden's roles in, 147–51
 and tourism, 87–93, 297n127
naturalization, and creation of modern myth, 26
natural medicine, 74, 75–76
nature, 66–67, 68–70
Nazi Party (Nationalsozialistische Deutsche Arbeiterpartei, NSDAP). *See also* National Socialism; neo-Nazis
 definition of victims of, 160
 as not real Dresdeners, 216
 and rise and politics of Dresden bombing narrative, 7, 21–22, 28
 Saxony and Dresden as early supporters of, 147–48
Neidhardt, Hans Joachim, 204–5
Neitzel, Sönke, 21
neo-Nazis, 209, 231, 232. *See also* far right
Neuer Annenfriedhof, 171
Neues Deutschland, 163, *164*
Neugebauer, Alfred, 210, 212, 213, 214, 215, 216–17. *See also* Star of David, from Semper Synagogue
Neugestaltungsstädte, 149
Neumarkt, reconstruction of, 205–6
Neutzner, Matthias, 25, 283n22
"Never again February 13," 165, *166*
"Never again Inferno Dresden," 165
"Never Again Kristallnacht," 165, *167*
Newcomes, The (Thackeray), 70
New Jewish Cemetery, 162, 171
New Synagogue, 171–73, 207–20
Nikolaikirche, 188
Nolde, Emil, 144
Nossack, Hans Erich, 33
nostalgia, 31, 229, 243, 258, 267
Novalis, 64
November Pogroms, 151–59, 161–62, 165, 178, 181–82, 208, 210–17

Orosz, Helma, 232
Overy, Richard, 277n2, 285n59

Pabel, Hilmar, 43–44
panoramic view, 77–78, 97–98, 295n106
Patzelt, Werner J., 331n90
Paul, Jean, 71–72, 133
"peace," recoding of trope of, 194–98
Peaceful Revolution, 188, 196, 204, 222, 227, 256, 317n8
peace movement, 179, 188–93, 201–7
Pegida (Patriotic Europeans against the Islamization of the Occident)
 as anti-refugee, 258
 demise of, 228–29
 and Dresden as "city of resistance," 241
 growth of, 228
 and Lösch's protest plays, 255–56, 259
 platform of, 227–28, 243
 and "Prozession der Angsthasen" (Scaredy-Bunny Procession), 248–49
 public reaction to protesters opposing, 259
 rise of, 226
 support for, 221
Permoser, Balthasar, 53
personality, of cities, 5, 6, 7
Peter, Richard. See also *View from the Rathausturm toward the South* (Peter)
 Dresden: Eine Kamera klagt an, 36, 103–7, 138, 300n23, 300n26
 images of Prager Straße, 133–34
 rubble photography of, 103, 286n82
photo books, of Dresden's destruction, 97–107, 138
photography, comparative, 96, 97–107, 138

Piek, Wilhelm, 163–64
Pinkert, Alexander, 143
place identity, 5–6
pointing, 34, 38–39
Polish Jews, expulsion of, 151
Pöppelmann, Daniel, 53–54
Porzellan: Poem vom Untergang meiner Stadt (Grünbein), 268, 269–70
postcards, 83, *84*, 119, 168
post-reunification rebuilding projects, 185–87
  debates over, 207–20
  Frauenkirche as attractor in peace discourse, 201–7
  Frauenkirche memorial in 1980s, 187–93
  Frauenkirche's reconstruction as sacred journey, 193–200
  as sacred, 252
Postwar Synagogue (1950), 171–73
Prager, Brad, 34
Prager Straße, 133–34, 144, 150, 175–76, 206
Prager Straße (Dix), 144–47
"Prozession der Angsthasen" (Scaredy-Bunny Procession), 248–49
Prussia, military presence in Dresden, 19

Querdenker movement, 228, 244, 257, 317n8

Raschke, Martin, 129, 304n92
rebuilt landmarks, 201–4. *See also* Frauenkirche; Zwinger
reconciliation
  and construction of New Synagogue, 209, 219–20
  and Frauenkirche reconstruction, 12, 186, 195, 197–98, 200, 201–7, 209
redemptive reconstruction, 320n46
Reformverein, 143–44
refugees, 22, 24, 223–24, 230, 234, 235–36, 258–59, 283n24
Das Reich, 22–24
Reich Committee for Tourism, 89
Reich's Theater Festival, 89
Reimann, Siegfried, 208
Renn, Ludwig, 116
repoussoir, 32, 33
Reynié, Dominique, 325n2
Ricchino, Francesco, 52
Richter, Otto, 85, 174
  Dresden sonst und jetzt, 78–80, *79*
Ristau, Daniel, 311n81
Rodenberger, Axel, 41–43
Romantic movement, 34
Roosevelt, Theodore, 75–76
Rosenlöcher, Thomas, 125
Rosenthal, Andreas, 272–75
Rossi, Aldo, 186
Rudolf-Friedrichs-Brücke (Carolabrücke), 80, 174, *175*
Rudolph, Wilhelm, 286n82
Rüegg, Sonja, 255

Sachsenverlag, 115–16
Sächsische Schweiz (Saxon Switzerland), 66, 68–70
Sächsische Zeitung, 167, 168, 170, 265, 314n121, 314n133
"Save the Neumarkt" initiative, 205–6
Saxon State Theater, 246, 247, 254–62
Saxony
  Dresden as court residence and capital, 51
  and Dresden's history as garrison town, 18–19
  Jewish population of, 143
  political characteristics of, 223, 224–25, 229–30
  remembrance in, 8
  role in National Socialism, 147–51
Schaarschuch, Kurt, 97–103, 106, 299n4
Schelling, Friedrich, 64
Schill, Gerhard, 127, *177*, 178, 191
Schivelbusch, Wolfgang, 295n106
Schlegel, August Wilhelm, 63–64
Schlegel, Caroline, 63–64
Schlegel, Friedrich, 63–64
Schmidt, Henry, 158, 179–80, 181
Schmidt, Ulf, 256
Schmöller, Heinz, 249
Schnatz, Helmut, 284n39
Schneider, Hans, 152
Scholz, Olaf, 243
Schornstein, Leo Jehuda, 152–53
Schreitmüller, August, 30, 32, 37, 44, 104–5
"Schuhe der Toten: Dresden und die Shoah" exhibition, 217

Schulz, Wilfried, 247
Schulze, Ingo, 280n23
Semmens, Kristin, 297n127
Semper, Gottfried, 93, 142–43, 156, 167–68, 178, 307n12
Semper Art Gallery, 112–13, *114*
Semper Opera Building, 125–27, 137, 246, *247*, 307n12
Semper Synagogue, *142*, *154*. *See also* New Synagogue; Star of David, from Semper Synagogue
  design and construction of, 141–43
  destruction of, 140, 141, 151, 152–56
  Dresden bombing narrative and destruction of, 162, 168
  location of, 174
  materials on destruction of, 210–17
  memorialization of destruction of, 209
  monument at site of, 176–78
  responsibility for destruction of, 210
  Star of David from, 172, 187, 210–17
  in *Wochenschau* newsreel, 93
Sennett, Richard, 57
Seven Years' War (1756–63), 58
Seydewitz, Max, 37–40
sgraffiti, 52
Slaughterhouse-Five (Vonnegut), 45
Social Democratic Party of Germany (SPD), 144
Socialist Unity Party of Germany (Sozialistische Einheitspartei Deutschlands, SED), 96, 123, 125, 162–63, 174, 189–91, 194
societal language planning, 193–95
Society Historic Neumarkt, 205–6
Sophienkirche, 123
Sparing, Rudolf, 23–24, 46
Stadt-Rundschau, 119
Stangl, Paul, 123
Star of David, from Semper Synagogue, 172, 187, 210–17
status planning, 193
steamships, 76
Stein, Dorothea, 133
Steinmeier, Frank-Walter, 237
Sternberger, Dolf, 295n106
structure, and imageability, 51
Summer Olympics (Berlin, 1936), 90
Süß, Dietmar, 277n2
Syrian war, 250–52
Taylor, Bayard, 73
Taylor, Frederick, 277n2
Technische Nothilfe, 156
Tellkamp, Uwe, 263–68, 269, 271, 280n23
terror bombing, 22, 277n2
Thackeray, William Makepeace, 70, 293n76
Theater and Culture Week of the Reich (Reichstheaterwoche), 148
Theaterplatz, 246, *247*
Thrandorff, Karl Friedrich Eusebius, 56
Ticknor, Anne, 72, 74
Ticknor, George, 72, 74
Der Tod von Dresden (Rodenberger), 41–43
tourism
  and confrontation of far right, 246
  and Dresden as artistic, intellectual, and societal stage, 62–63, 65–70
  Dresden's cultural worth and success in, 272
  Dresden's rise as travel destination, 59–61
  Dresden visitor numbers by year, *81*, 298n140
  far right's impact on, 244
  foreign visitors, 70–76, 89–90
  hotels in Dresden, 302n64
  marketing of Dresden for leisure travel, 76–85
  and post-reunification rebuilding projects, 207
  postwar marketing of Dresden as socialist city and travel icon, 108–27, 137
  preservation and marketing of Dresden's image and heritage from 1914 to 1945, 85–94
  value in visitor sites, 201–2
  West German travel magazines, 127–38
tourist brochures, 119–23, 297n127. *See also* travel guides
touristic gaze, 85
train travel, 76–78, 82–83
travel guides, 62–63, 65, 67–70, 77–78, 119–23, 293n71, 303n68
travel magazines, West German, 127–38
Der Turm: Geschichte aus einem versunkenen Land (Tellkamp), 263, 265–67

Ulbricht, Walter, 123, *124*
Die unbesiegbare Stadt (Seydewitz), 37–40
Urban, Jörg, 238
urban cultural heritage sites, value in, 201–2
urban history, scholarship on, 9
urban identity, 4, 7
urban mindscape, 60–62
Urry, John, 85, 119, 201, 202

Venice, 54–55
Vereinigung der Verfolgten des Naziregimes (Association of Victims of the Nazi Regime/Federation of Antifascists, VVN), 164–65, 313n110
Verein zur Förderung Dresdens und des Fremdenverkehrs (Society for the Promotion of Dresden and Tourism), 80–83
View from the Rathausturm onto the Inner City Cleared from Rubble (Pabel), 43–44
View from the Rathausturm toward the South (Peter), *16*
  framed with Dresden bombing narrative, 17, 18, 37–44
  as iconic photograph, 29–35
  objective of, 35–36
  and postwar representation of Dresden bombing, 96
  reproduction of, 36–37
  and Rosenthal's ". . . Angesichts der Güte," 272–75
  shooting of, 15
Virchow, Fabian, 229
visitor sites, value in, 201–2
Volk, Sabine, 226, 229–30
von Loen, Johann Michael, 53
Vonnegut, Kurt, 45–46, 280n23
Vorländer, Hans, 245, 253

Wagner, Herbert, 209
Wagner, Otto, 171
Wagner, Richard, 56, 148
"Wailing Shall Be in All Streets" (Vonnegut), 45–46
Walser, Martin, 280n23
war criminals, prosecution of, 179–80, 181
war photography, 286n78, 286n82. *See also* comparative photography
Washington Post, 24, 25
Weber, Gregor J. M., 55–56
Weidauer, Walter, 40–41, 125, 165, 166, 303n80
Weil, Francesca, 309n60
Weißer Hirsch, 265–68
West German travel magazines, 127–38
Wettiner Platz, 87
White Rose resistance group, 232
white rose symbol, 231–33
Wittenbecher, Günter, 156
Wochenschau newsreel, 92–93
Wodak, Ruth, 330n72
Wolf, Albert, 213
Wolf, Paul, 150
Wonneberger, Christoph, 188, 317n8
World's Recreation Congress, 90
World War I, 19, 85, 145
Die Wunde Dresden (The Dresden Wound), 254
Würzburg, 20–21
Wüstefeld, Michael, 125
Wutbürger (enraged citizens), 257, 325n4

Young/Thalmann Pioneers, 189–91, *192*

"Zaubertrick" (Grünbein), 136–37
Zeiss-Ikon company, 157–59
Zeitgenossen (Contemporaries), 219
Zero Hour, 95
Zimmering, Max, 169
Zwinger
  Adams on, 71
  and dust jacket for *Die unbesiegbare Stadt*, 39
  as example of material symbolism in evoking meaning, 53–54
  featured on *Merian* magazine, 132
  Härtling on, 133
  reconstruction of, 112–13, *114*, 121, 122
  in Schaarschuch's comparative photographs, 100